The Highlands makes a compelling case for land-use planning and resource management strategies that could help ensure a sustainable future for the region—strategies that could in turn be applied to other landscapes threatened by urbanization across the country. The Highlands are a valuable resource. And now, so is *The Highlands*.

RICHARD G. LATHROP Jr. is a professor in the department of ecology, evolution, and natural resources and director of the Center for Remote Sensing and Spatial Analysis at Rutgers University. He has been actively involved in Highlands environmental policy and research for many years.

The Highlands

The Highlands

CRITICAL RESOURCES, TREASURED LANDSCAPES

Edited by Richard G. Lathrop Jr.

Rivergate Books
an Imprint of
Rutgers University Press
New Brunswick, New Jersey, and London

Library of Congress Cataloging-in-Publication Data

The Highlands : critical resources, treasured landscapes / edited by Richard G. Lathrop Jr.
   p. cm.
  Includes bibliographical references and index.
  ISBN 978-0-8135-5133-3 (hardcover : alk. paper) — ISBN 978-0-8135-5134-0 (pbk. : alk. paper)
   1. Natural history—Highlands (N.Y. : Region) 2. Natural history—New Jersey—New Jersey Highlands. I. Lathrop, Richard G. (Richard Gilbert) II. Title.

  QH104.5.H55H55 2011
  508.749—dc22

                           2011004709
A British Cataloging-in-Publication record for this book is available from the British Library.

Visit our Web site: http://rutgerspress.rutgers.edu

Manufactured in the United States of America

Contents

Illustrations and Tables

Black and White

Color Plates

Color plates appear between pages 202 and 203.

Tables

Preface

Richard G. Lathrop Jr.

Always intrigued by the blank spaces on any map, I was first attracted to the Highlands by their wild character, as an antidote to suburban life in the sprawling Philadelphia–New York City–Hartford megalopolis. Repeated forays into the Highlands revealed a much richer, more complex, and more interesting landscape than I had first imagined. As I delved a little deeper, I soon realized that what appears to be untrammeled forest today was vastly different one hundred and two hundred years ago, and that human and natural history in the Highlands are incredibly tangled and interwoven. A classic example of this is Sparta Mountain in the northwest Highlands of New Jersey, once the site of the Edison Iron Works. Early in American colonial history, the discovery of iron-bearing rock formations spawned the development of a widespread iron-mining industry with both surface and deep-shaft mines all across the Highlands region. Iron furnaces and forges were built to process the ore. Villages and farms were settled to shelter and feed the miners and furnace workers. The neighboring forests were chopped down and turned into charcoal to fuel the furnaces. By the mid-1800s, the Highlands were largely denuded of forest. As recounted in chapter 11, during the last decade of the nineteenth century the Edison Iron Works comprised a huge ore-processing facility and on-site housing for hundreds of employees, all surrounded by an extensive network of open-pit and deep-shaft mines. In less than ten years, the whole enterprise went bust, the buildings were dismantled, and site was abandoned.

It is hard to fathom, glancing around Sparta Mountain today, that a little more than one hundred years ago this place hosted a massive industrial and housing complex. Grasses, shrubs, and trees are well established, and second-growth forest has reclaimed the land. Closer examination reveals several concrete footings and other building foundations scattered among the undergrowth of the returning forest. Erosion has softened the edges of the abandoned pits, filling in the bottoms with tumbled boulders. The many stages of natural succession—from initial establishment of lichens and mosses on the bare rocks, followed by colonization of forbs and ferns in the crevices deep enough to hold pockets of soil—are evident. Where water has not collected into pools of unknown depth, grasses and shrubs have invaded the hollows and pit floors. If the area were not surrounded by a rusting cyclone fence (ostensibly put up to protect the public from stumbling over the edge of a quarried cliff but today riddled with gaps making for easy trespass), one might be forgiven if one somehow mistook these for natural geological formations. Only subtle differences in the forest structure and composition reveal where a cleared field or homesite may have been one hundred years prior. Here at Sparta Mountain, as elsewhere across the Highlands, the forests and wetlands have regrown to the point that the land's wild character has gained the upper hand.

I am struck by the incredible resilience of the Highlands ecosystem as well as the host of connections between the Highlands proper and the broader mid-Atlantic and southern New England region. As with any number of places across the region, given the chance, natural vegetation communities will reclaim once-ravaged industrial wastelands, and functioning ecological systems will reassert their primacy. Forests will grow and mature, wildlife will return, and clean, clear waters will flow from the hills. The Highlands' history provides hope that forests and watersheds abused by misguided land-use practices today might be protected and restored to provide vital open space and ecosystem services to the broader region's many human residents.

With this in mind, I set about to bring together a number of leading experts on the Highlands to provide readers with a more thorough understanding and appreciation of the Highlands region, its environment, and its cultural and natural history. So, as Abraham Lincoln once said in his famous 1858 House Divided speech, "If we could first know where we are, and whither we are tending, we could better judge what to do, and how to do it."

This book would not have possible without the generous contributions of all the coauthors for which it has been a labor of love. My sincere thanks to Mike Siegel of Rutgers Geography Department, and John Bognar of Rutgers Walton Center for Remote Sensing & Spatial Analysis, for their help in creating and/or formatting all the maps, graphics, and photos, as well as to Dwight Hiscano for contributing his wonderful photograph that graces the front cover. I want to thank Rutgers Press editors Marlie Wasserman, Peter Mickulas, Suzanne Kellam, and Doreen Valentine as well as copy editors Patti Bowers and Will Hively for shepherding me through the long process of getting this book ready for print. Finally I would like to gratefully acknowledge the constructive input provided by several anonymous reviewers.

Funding for the publication of this book was provided through a grant by the Northeastern Area State and Private Forestry unit of the U.S. Department of Agriculture Forest Service, Newtown Square, Pennsylvania. Additional financial support was provided by the Walton Center for Remote Sensing & Spatial Analysis, School of Environmental & Biological Sciences, Rutgers University.

The Highlands

Introduction

Richard G. Lathrop Jr.

Thirty miles north of New York City, the broad Hudson River constricts into a narrow gorge overshadowed by rugged rocky ridges rising up to nearly fourteen hundred feet. In 1609, Henry Hudson and the crew of the *Half Moon* were the first Europeans to visit and describe this dramatic landscape, known today as the Highlands (fig. I.1). In his journal Robert Juet (1609), Hudson's first mate, described the narrows of the Hudson: "The Montaynes looke as if some Metall or Minerall were in them. For the Trees that grow on them were all blasted, and some of them barren with few or no Trees on them." More than three hundred years later, in 1914, William Thompson Howell described the Highlands as "a sort of wilderness oasis, in the desert of cultivated country which surrounds them. They are only a pocket-edition wilderness, a few hundred square miles in area, but in a remarkable degree they have preserved their characteristics for three hundred years, during all the time they have been inhabited to some extent." Perusal of modern-day satellite imagery reveals the Highlands as a dense green rampart smack dab up against the gray rectangular grid of the New York City metro region (see plate 1). Nearly one hundred years later, Howell's comments on the Highlands as a "wilderness oasis" still hold, but why were they true then and why now?

Adjacent to some of the most densely populated areas in the United States and undergoing increasing pressure from sprawling development, the Highlands region presents a compelling case study in how humans in concert with environmental forces have shaped and continue to shape a landscape. Equally compelling are the myriad efforts that have been undertaken through watershed protection, open-space preservation, and bioregional conservation planning to conserve the essential elements of that landscape. Simultaneously there has been a push to forge a broader regional multistate identity that spans more parochial interests. A 1992 report by the U.S. Forest Service concluded that the Highlands represent "a landscape of national significance," helping to bring it to wider attention. Spurred by additional Forest Service studies and the concerted efforts of conservation organizations and state government, the U.S. Congress passed the Highlands Conservation Act in 2004

Figure I.1. The *Half Moon* at the Highlands. While relations with native Lenni Lenape Indians were reasonably amicable on the way upriver, Hudson and the crew of the *Half Moon* had a violent encounter with a local band on their way back downriver. Designer: Thomas Moran; Engraver: Robert Hinshelwood. From William Cullen Bryant and Sydney Howard Gay, *A Popular History of the United States*, vol. 1. (New York: Charles Scribner's Sons, 1881). Credit: Picture Collection, New York Public Library, Astor, Lenox, and Tilden Foundations.

and President George W. Bush signed this landmark legislation into law. This act set the stage for a unique experiment in multistate land use and for conservation planning and management that is ongoing.

So where exactly are the Highlands? Our view is more expansive than William Howell's, encompassing a four-state region that extends from Pennsylvania, in the south, northeast up through New Jersey, New York, and into Connecticut (see plate 2). The Highlands come under many different local names. The epicenter of the Highlands region, where rock-ribbed ridges rise dramatically from the Hudson River, has been known since the colonial days as the Hudson Highlands. Crossing the Hudson River, the ridges and forests of the Highlands continue north into the northwest corner of Connecticut, where they take the name of the Taconics, Housatonic Highlands, or the Litchfield Hills before blending seamlessly with the Berkshires of Massachusetts. It is here that the Highlands reach their greatest elevation of more than twenty-three hundred feet above sea level. Back the other direction into New Jersey, the Highlands go under a number of local names: Ramapo Mountains, Sparta Mountain, Musconetcong Mountain. Across the Delaware River into Pennsylvania, the Highlands narrow and take on the names of South Mountain, the Reading Prong, and the Furnace Hills, referring to a series of ridges rising up to nearly fourteen hundred feet in height that extend to the banks of the Susquehanna River.

Physiographically, the Highlands are generally defined by the extent of their underlying Precambrian crystalline bedrock and its upland terrain. Based on these primary factors, the Commission for Environmental Cooperation (1997) has mapped the boundaries of the Highlands ecoregion as encompassing nearly 1.85 million acres. Administratively, the federal Highlands Conservation Act in 2004 takes a more expansive view by including the entirety of the area of any municipality that falls partly within the Highlands ecoregion, thereby extending the boundary well beyond the ecoregion proper and encompassing nearly 3.5 million acres (see plate 1). For a number of administrative and political reasons, the federal Highlands region was extended farther south into Pennsylvania beyond the extent of the Highlands ecoregion. Inexplicably, portions of New York State, especially up along the Connecticut border, that would appear to fall within the Highlands ecoregion were excluded from the federally defined region.

For the purposes of this book, the official federal Highlands Conservation Act boundary will be used to define the Highlands region. In some instances, due to their use of information that is available only at a county level, authors may take an even more expansive view to include the entire county area of any county that intersects the Highlands Conservation Act boundary. In Pennsylvania this includes Berks, Bucks, Chester, Dauphin, Lancaster, Lebanon, Lehigh, Montgomery, Northampton, and York counties. In New Jersey, the Highlands region includes Bergen, Hunterdon, Morris, Passaic, Somerset, Sussex, and Warren counties. In New York, the Highlands cover portions of Beacon, Dutchess, Orange, Putnam, Rockland, and Westchester counties. In Connecticut, only Fairfield and Litchfield counties are considered within the Highlands region. While the primary focus of the book will be on the core of the Highlands in the states of New Jersey and New York, the Pennsylvania and Connecticut portions of the Highlands are also included.

Given the great importance of the Highlands and the increasing attention they are receiving both within and outside the mid-Atlantic and southern New England region, it is surprising that up to this point there have been so few books that explore the depth and breadth of the Highlands. The objective of this book is to fill that gap, to provide readers with a more thorough understanding and appreciation of the Highlands region, its environment, and its rich cultural and natural history. The contributors to this book are leading researchers and specialists, all of whom have had a long and personal interest in the Highlands. The book was written at a level that should be accessible to students, teachers, policymakers, and interested laypersons—anyone who is interested in learning more about the Highlands. Our goal is to present the scientific, cultural, and natural history behind sound land-use planning and environmental management.

Chapters 1 through 5 delve into what controls the essential characteristics of the Highlands landscape: its bedrock geology, its glacial and surficial geology, its soils and water. In chapter 1, Alec Gates and David Valentino trace how the many transformations that the Highlands underwent through deep geological time have led to the incredibly complex bedrock geology of today. In chapter 2, Scott Stanford illuminates the central role that continental glaciation had in further modifying the terrain and the distinction between the glacially sculpted northern Highlands versus the unglaciated southern Highlands. In chapter 3, John Tedrow and Richard Shaw dig into the soils of the New York–New Jersey Highlands and the role that the underlying bedrock and glacial drift have in determining the suitability of the land for various human uses. One key landscape feature that sets the Highlands apart from surrounding regions is the abundance of natural lakes, large reservoirs, and coldwater streams that serve as a source of drinking water, habitat, and recreation. To many, water is the defining issue of the Highlands. Otto Zapecza, Don Rice, and Vincent dePaul, in chapter 4, provide an overview of the region's complex surface and groundwater hydrology. In chapter 5, Dan Van Abs discusses the role and history of the Highlands as a critical water supply for its residents as well for millions of people outside the region. Depending on how you calculate it, today the Highlands provide drinking water to upward of 15 million people.

Chapters 6 through 10 focus on the ecology of the Highlands. In chapter 6, Emily Southgate provides a long-term perspective on the natural history of the Highlands forests and the influence that people—from Native Americans to all others through the early twentieth century—have had on the structure and composition of the forest. William Schuster discusses the structure and function of Highlands forests and investigates the dynamic processes that shape forest ecosystems today in chapter 7. An array of wetland habitats, while only a comparatively small component of the Highlands environment, is critical to the region's biodiversity and integrity and is the focus of chapter 8, by Joan Ehrenfeld. Although adjacent to some of the United States' most densely populated areas, the Highlands provide a range of important habitats that support a wealth of biological diversity. Gerry Moore and Steven Glenn, in chapter 9, focus on plant life, with special attention to threatened, endangered, and rare plant species, while in chapter 10 Elizabeth Johnson discusses biodiversity and important wildlife habitats of the region.

The preceding chapters place special emphasis on issues that are important to the Highlands and are universally affecting open lands adjacent to growing metropolitan regions, such as the effects of changing land use, habitat fragmentation, invasive plants/animals, pollution, and climate change. Because humans have had and will continue to have a critical role in shaping the Highlands landscape, the human cultural history of the region cannot be ignored. Ted Kury and Peter Wacker, in chapter 11, discuss the impact that iron mining had on the Highlands and on subsequent transportation and industrial development. In chapter 12, Richard Lathrop deals with the history of farming and agricultural land use as well as the more recent transformation from a rural to more suburban landscape. In chapter 13, Daniel Chazin explores the history of hiking and outdoor recreation in the Highlands and the important role this area plays in providing open space and outdoor recreation to the mid-Atlantic and southern New England region's growing human population. In chapter 14, Robert Pirani, Tom Gilbert, and Corey Piasecki discuss the history of land-use planning and policy in the Highlands and the development of the Highlands' regional identity. Finally, in chapter 15, Richard Lathrop, Mary Tyrrell, and Myrna Hall examine the implications of future land-use change and possible alternative futures for the Highlands.

It is our hope that this book will help to promote understanding of the Highlands as a coherent region with a unique identity, to explain the significance of its resources as critical to the mid-Atlantic and southern New England states and beyond, and to underline why this landscape is treasured by so many.

References

Commission for Environmental Cooperation. 1997. "Ecological Regions of North America: Toward a Common Perspective." Commission for Environmental Cooperation, Montreal, Quebec, Canada. ftp://ftp.epa.gov/wed/ecoregions/na/CEC_NAeco.pdf.

Howell, W. T. 1914. *The Highlands of the Hudson.* Self-published scrapbook in New York Public Library Photographic Archives.

Juet, R. 1609. *Juet's Journal of Hudson's 1609 Voyage.* Transcribed by Brea Barthel, 2006, from the 1625 edition of *Purchas His Pilgrimes.* Albany, NY: New Netherland Museum. http://www.halfmoonreplica.org/Juets-journal.pdf.

Part I

Geological Setting

One of the most aesthetically appealing aspects of the Highlands is the rocks: big, bold, substantial rocks—from the occasional sheer rock cliff with a skirt of tumbled talus at its base to the stray glacial "erratic" boulder the size of a small house. As we learn in chapter 1, the Highlands are composed of billion-year-old bedrock that formed the roots of the ancient Grenville Mountains. Over the eons, the Highlands rose and fell only to rise again, and the bedrock subsequently folded and transformed under the tremendous pressures of colliding continental plates. The native bedrock metamorphosed into various forms of gneiss, a crystalline rock that is highly resistant to weathering and erosion. The shearing forces of the colliding plates also faulted and fractured the bedrock, creating conduits for mineral-rich fluids that cooled to form veins rich in iron. These deposits of iron served as the impetus for much of the early industrial development of the Highlands, playing a vital role in the rise of the United States as an industrial powerhouse in the nineteenth century.

Tens of thousands of years earlier, during what is known as the Wisconsin (or Wisconsinan) glacial episode, a continental-scale ice sheet bulldozed southward across the Highlands, stopping in New Jersey. The resulting terminal moraine forms a boundary separating the northern glaciated and the southern unglaciated Highlands. Chapter 2 recounts how, north of the moraine, glaciers sculpted the landscape, gouging valleys while scraping ridgetops bare. In the glacially gouged low spots, water pooled to form lakes and ponds. The moving ice and meltwater transported, sifted, and deposited sand and gravel in beds tens of feet thick in some Highlands valleys. The resulting valley-fill aquifers serve as a big sponge, holding millions of gallons of potable water (a vital resource, as we learn later in part II, for Highlands residents).

Along with geology and topography, a location's soils are a major determinant of possible human use of the land. Chapter 3 discusses the many factors that determine a location's soil, attributes of the soil, and how these characteristics vary across the Highlands landscape. On the glacially scoured uplands, the soils are often shallow and rocky; generally unsuitable for agriculture, such areas remain or have returned to forest. In low spots on the landscape, fine-grained clays have been deposited, forming an impervious layer that impedes the downward infiltration of water. Under these conditions, the higher water tables and waterlogged soils promote wetlands vegetation. South of the moraine, the valleys are broader, and the soils, often formed from calcareous limestone, are deeper and mellower, making for rich farmland.

The diversity of the Highlands forest and wetland ecosystems that are the subject of part III is a reflection of the interplay between the bedrock geology, topography, glacial history, and soils.

1

Bedrock Geology of the Highlands

Alexander E. Gates and David W. Valentino

Introduction

The rocks of the Highlands physiographic province represent some of the most striking and fascinating geologic relationships ever assembled in one place. Great variations in the geology of an area such as this are the products of global-scale movements of the earth's surface, which is broken into what are known as tectonic plates. Over the earth's long history, these plates have come together and drifted apart in several different episodes, which are part of much bigger supercontinental plate tectonic cycles. At one time, all the continents of the earth came together to form a single massive supercontinent surrounded by a single massive ocean. The colliding landmasses buckled and overrode each other to produce lofty mountain ranges. The assembled tectonic plates later drifted apart, and new ocean basins filled the resulting voids between them. The Highlands province underwent not one but two supercontinental cycles, the older Rodinian cycle and the younger Pangean cycle (Gates et al. 2006). These cycles of opening and closing of major ocean basins, of continental drifting and colliding, are recorded in the dramatic geologic relations and rock units of the Highlands. There are not many places on earth that can boast this much activity and diversity.

The Highlands physiographic province is essentially interchangeable with what is known in geological science circles as the Reading Prong geologic province (Drake 1984), which is one of a chain of crystalline rock provinces that form the spine of the Appalachian Mountains from northern Vermont to Alabama (fig. 1.1). The Reading Prong or Highlands province extends from Reading, Pennsylvania, through western Connecticut and forms the link between the crystalline Blue Ridge Mountains to the south and the Green Mountains–Berkshires to the north (Bartholomew and Lewis 1988; Drake 1984; Rankin, Drake, and Ratcliffe 1993). These rocks are the oldest in the Appalachians, dating from about 1.3 to 1.0 billion years old in what is known as the Proterozoic age (sometimes referred to as the Precambrian age) (Mose 1982; Volkert 2004). They once formed the roots or base of the most expansive

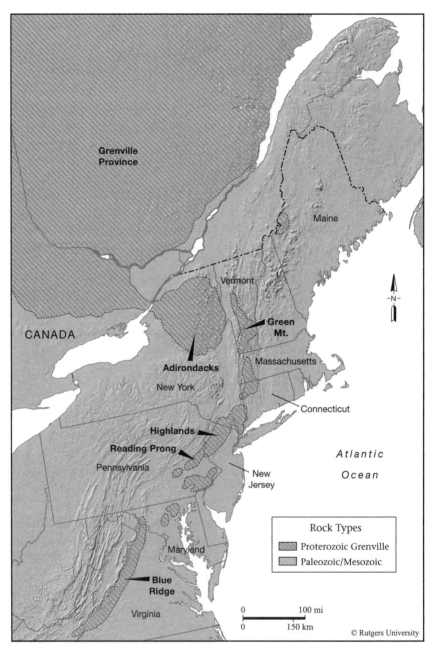

Figure 1.1. General map of the northeastern United States and eastern Canada showing the distribution of Proterozoic-age Grenvillian basement rocks and the Highlands. © Rutgers University.

mountain system ever in the history of the earth. This system, the Grenville mountain belt, was a major feature of the supercontinent Rodinia, which existed from about 1.0 billion to 750 million years ago (Ma) (Dalziel, Salada, and Gahagan 1994; Gates et al. 2004; Gates et al. 2006). Through subsequent continent collisions, uplift, erosion, and removal of a more than 25 km thickness of rock, the base of these former lofty mountains is now exposed at the surface as the Highlands. Looking at the geology of the Highlands today is like looking at the roots of the Himalayas with the mountains removed.

The Highlands bedrock of Grenville origin is composed of tough, coarse crystalline rock that is mainly grayish in color and somewhat banded. The rocks are termed crystalline because as they formed, individual minerals grew into large crystals that were tightly knitted together. More than 90 percent of these crystalline rocks were formed through metamorphism at extremely high temperatures and pressures and are classified as gneiss, which is a banded metamorphic rock (Drake 1984). Whether starting as igneous underground bodies of magma (plutons) or mixed rocks of sedimentary origin, these original rocks were recrystallized through the great heat and pressure of the mountain-building process. The remaining 10 percent or less of the crystalline rocks are igneous rocks that intruded the gneiss as bodies of magma and were not overtly affected by later metamorphism.

In terms of geological time, the Proterozoic-age rocks that form the base of the Highlands are significantly older than the more recently deposited Paleozoic- and Mesozoic-age rocks of the surrounding region (Drake 1984; Rankin, Drake, and Ratcliffe 1993). Compared to these softer sedimentary rocks, the crystalline bedrock of the Highlands is very resistant to weathering and erosion. This contrast in resistance is the reason for the great relief along the edges of the Highlands. Along most of its length, from the southern end in Pennsylvania northward to the Hudson River in New York, the Highlands province is cut off sharply to the southeast by the extensive Ramapo Fault system and bounded by the Mesozoic-age sedimentary and igneous rocks of the Newark basin (Gates and Costa 1998) (fig. 1.2). Paleozoic-age sedimentary rocks of the Valley and Ridge province bound the Highlands to the northwest, and those of the Taconic sequence wrap around the northwestern and southeastern sides of the Reading Prong section in Pennsylvania (Ratcliffe et al. 1972; Lash and Drake 1984; Drake et al. 1989). Along this northwestern margin, the rocks of the Highlands are complexly interspersed with those of the Valley and Ridge (Drake 1984). The interfingering of the weaker Valley and Ridge rocks along with the presence of faults and fracture zones that break up the crystalline rocks, allowing them to be more quickly eroded, helped to create the interior valleys of the Highlands. These low valleys interspersed with the crystalline rock ridges give the Highlands region its rugged topography of today.

From a geological perspective, the Highlands are subdivided into eastern,

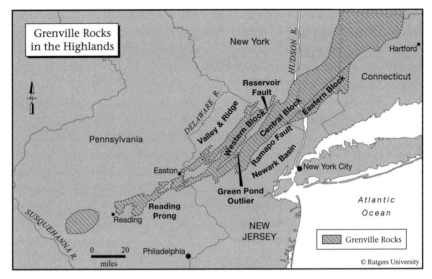

Figure 1.2. General geologic map of the Highlands from Connecticut to Pennsylvania. The slash-marked area represents Proterozoic rocks of Grenville origin. Modified from Gundersen 2004. © Rutgers University.

central, and western blocks (fig. 1.2) by major faults and differences in rock types (Gates and Costa 1998). Many of the rock units cross these faults, and their relations are still areas of geological science debate. The eastern Highlands block lies east of the northeast-striking Ramapo Fault and extends east across the Hudson River, across southern New York, and into Connecticut (Drake 1984). The central block is bounded to the west by the Reservoir Fault and the Paleozoic sedimentary rocks of the Green Pond outlier and extends northward across New York to northwestern Connecticut. The western block extends from the New York–New Jersey border to the Reading area of Pennsylvania and is most complexly interspersed with the Valley and Ridge rocks. Historical geologic mapping of the Highlands has left the rock units with numerous local names (named by location), or else they are named simply by their rock type (Spencer 1904; Bayley 1910). Most of these classifications are not descriptive or instructive because they are not adopted region-wide, and therefore numerous correlations are required to make sense of their relations. The detailed separations of rocks in previous mappings are very complicated and difficult to follow. In this chapter, the rock units are described based on their large-scale distribution and interrelations (stratigraphy). The rocks of the Highlands can be generally grouped by their plate tectonic origin. The crystalline rocks contain detailed evidence of the Rodinian supercontinent plate tectonic cycle from about 1.3 billion to 900 Ma. The sedimentary cover sequence contains evidence of the Pangean supercontinent plate tectonic cycle from about 500 to 250 Ma. Figure 1.3 outlines the major geological events

Rodinian Cycle – Formation of Rodinian Supercontinent

FEATURE	EVENT	ROCKS	GEOLOGICAL AGE	DATES
Volcanic island arc forms	Ocean basin between proto-S. & N. America begins to close	Volcanic & Sedimentary (now gneiss)	Mid-protozeroic	1300–1100 Ma
Grenville Mountains form	First deformation: Grenville Orogeny collision of S. & N. American plates	Granite and pegmatite gneiss	Mid-protozeroic	1060–1020 Ma
Lateral shifting of land	Second deformation: Strike-slip faults, escape tectonics	Diorite, granite, and magnetite	Mid-protozeroic	1008–980 Ma
Chestnut Hill rift basins	Rodinian break-up begins	Sandstone, volcanics, and hematite	Late-protozeroic	740–570 Ma
Passive margin deposits	Iapetus Ocean forms	Hardyston Kittitany formations	Cambrian-Ordovician	540–460 Ma

Pangean Cycle – Formation of Pangean Supercontinent

FEATURE	EVENT	ROCKS	GEOLOGICAL AGE	DATES
Deep basin on Iapetus Margin	Iapetus Ocean begins to close	Martinsburg Shales form	Ordovician	460–440 Ma
Taconic Mountains: Highlands thrust atop Martinsburg	Taconian Orogeny: collision of island arc & N. America	Thrust faults and folding	Mid-Ordovician	440–420 Ma
Large river system	Erosian of Taconian Mountains	Green Pond-Shawangunk conglomerates	Silurian	420–400 Ma
Acadian Mountains form & erode	Acadian Orogeny: collision of Baltica & N. America	Catskill/Bellvale sands & conglomerates	Devonian	400–360 Ma
Alleghanian Mountains form	Alleghanian Orogeny: collision of Africa & N. America	Folding of sediments, Thrust faulting	Carboniferous	300–250 Ma
Rift basins on Atlantic Margin	Opening of Atlantic Ocean, Break-up of Pangea	Newark Basin, Red Beds, & volcanics	Mesozoic	225–200 Ma

Figure 1.3. Significant geological features and events along with characteristic bedrock types and formations during the Rodinian and Pangean cycles.

that have shaped Highlands geology along with the associated features and rock types as well as the geological age and approximate dates when these events occurred.

Rodinian Supercontinent Cycle

The Rodinian cycle began about 1.3 to 1.2 billion years ago with the building of a volcanic island arc in a manner similar to the building of Japan or the Aleutian Islands of today (Drake 1984; Gates et al. 2001, 2006; Gundersen 2004) (fig. 1.3). The magma rising from chambers beneath the Rodinian island arc cooled and crystallized into various forms of intrusive igneous granite (Drake 1984; Drake, Aleinikoff, and Volkert 1991; Volkert and Drake 1999; Volkert et al. 2000; Volkert 2004). These granitic rocks cover a comparatively small area, approximately 1,300 km2, extending from eastern Pennsylvania up through New Jersey. Of greater importance are the extensive volcanic lava flows interlayered with fragments of volcanic material (volcaniclastics) that were deposited in the nearby ocean as aprons of marine sediments surrounding the island arcs. At the same time, on the opposite side of the ocean basin from the volcanic island arc, the ancient continent of Amazonia (proto–South America) was undergoing erosion, with the resulting sediments transported and deposited in the ocean basin margin forming beds of shale, sandstone, and limestone (referred to as passive margin sediments).

The next stage of the Rodinian cycle saw a massive collision between the volcanic island arc (part of the proto–North American plate) and the proto–South American plate about 1,060–1,020 Ma (Dalziel, Salada, and Gahagan 1994) (fig. 1.3). This continental collision is called the Grenville orogeny and is envisioned to be an event similar to the one that built the Himalayan Mountains (Windley 1986). An orogeny is a mountain-building event that involves the collision of two tectonic plates. The Grenville orogeny produced the first deformation event subjecting the volcanic and sedimentary rocks to intense heating and pressure, creating the metamorphic gneiss we see commonly across the Highlands today (Young and Cuthbertson 1994).

The volcanic rocks recrystallized into strongly black- and white-gray-banded metavolcanic gneisses. The dark-colored bands (termed mafic) were formed from the extruded basalt lava flows and contain medium-size crystalline grains rich in iron and magnesium. The light-colored bands of gneiss were formed from the volcaniclastic materials and are composed of medium- to coarse-size grains of the minerals quartz and plagioclase, broadly classified as quartzofeldspathic gneiss. Banding ranges from 5 cm to 2 m in thickness with varying amounts of dark and light rock types. The passive margin sedimentary shale, sandstone, and limestone deposits were metamorphosed into belts of rock up to 2 km wide containing various forms of metasedimentary gneiss (Gundersen 2004). Gneiss derived from shale is most easily recognized in the field by its well-defined black and white banding and an abundance of the mineral biotite, which shines in sunlight. Within the shale-derived gneiss are layers of rock rich in the minerals graphite, pyrite, and garnet. Graphite was mined at several locations across the Highlands. The metamorphosed sandstone (metasandstone) is a gray gneiss that is interlayered with metamorphosed shale in bands from 2 to 20 cm thick.

One of the more notable deposits of metasedimentary rocks is the significant body of marble (metamorphosed limestone) and related calcareous rocks in the western block of the Highlands known as the Franklin marble. It extends from the Big Island area of New York to the Chestnut Hill area of Pennsylvania, with the largest amounts in New Jersey (Drake 1984). These metamorphosed limestones locally contain fossils of stromatolite mounds that formed in shallow saline waters and were often associated with mats of cyanobacteria (blue-green algae). The stromatolites formed by gradually accreting calcium carbonate (limestone) and growing vertically over time to form the mound-like structures. In addition to the significant exposures of marble, the Franklin-Sterling area of New Jersey is well known for zinc mineralization and was the site of a major zinc-mining operation.

The intense heating and deformation that formed the current gneisses also produced huge folds in the bedrock. The shape of the folding consistently indicates that the rock units were forced northwestward during the collision. The folded rocks were sheared to such an extent that they folded back over themselves, piling up to form flat-lying sheets in what are known as nappes. Named for huge flat-lying folds in the Alps, nappes transport and thicken the earth's crust to produce mountains in zones of continental collisions such as the Himalayas and Alps. In the Highlands, the nappe-thickened crust was in the range of 80 km thick. A geologic map for the Hudson Highlands region of southern New York (fig. 1.4) illustrates the convoluted layering and folding. Evidence of this folding process is visible in the rocks themselves, in folds of the gneiss layers that are 5 to 20 cm thick and generally flat-lying (recumbent). The folds are nearly hairpin shaped and commonly asymmetric, with one side shorter than the other and the lower side flattened out (fig. 1.5a).

Subsequent to the Rodinian collision, magma with a composition of diorite (medium gray) and granite (light colored) intruded the area in the form of sheets that range in thickness from 5 to 200 m and are up to 10 km long (for example, the Sterling Forest granite sheets and Lake Tiorati metadiorite in fig. 1.4). Local melting of the Highland gneisses also produced magma now seen as the migmatites, granites, and the pegmatite dikes that occur throughout the area. As the granite/diorite intruded, fragments of the surrounding gneiss bedrock were often plucked away and incorporated into the granitic matrix (known as xenoliths).

A second deformation event occurred as the result of lateral shifting of the tectonic plates (i.e., horizontal or strike-slip movement of the plates

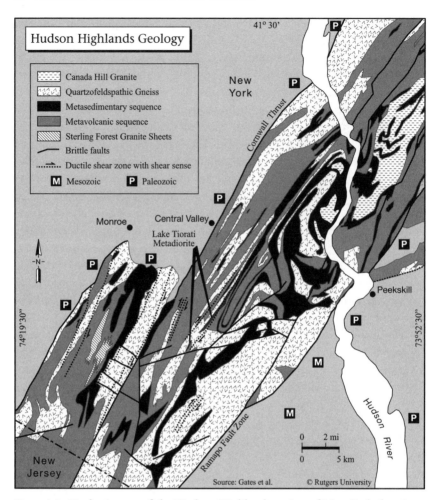

Figure 1.4. Geologic map of the Hudson Highlands region of New York showing the distribution of rock sequences, defined by related assemblages of rock types. Modified from Gates et al. 2006. © Rutgers University.

grating against each other, rather than a vertical dip-slip movement). Within the Highlands this took the form of northeast–southwest trending strike-slip faulting similar to the San Andreas faulting in California during a period of rapid uplift and erosion at approximately 1,008 Ma to 980 Ma (fig. 1.3) (Gates et al. 2004). These faults include the Ramapo Fault and the Reservoir Fault, among others. An east-west-striking lateral shear system appears to have formed synchronously in the Adirondacks of northern New York. This conjugate system may have formed crossing fault zones that were simultaneously active, analogous to the fault zones observed in the Himalayan mountain-building process (Gates et al. 2004). In sharp contrast to the early part of the Rodinian collision, the layering from this fault activity is nearly

a

b

Figure 1.5. (a) Outcrop of the metasedimentary gneiss with recumbent folds associated with the first deformation phase. (b) Upright open fold in quartzofeldspathic gneiss associated with the second deformation phase. Photos by Alec Gates.

vertical. These faults are also associated with the intrusion of several types of magma. In the late stages of the faulting, large cracks opened in the fault zones and fluids flushed through them, leaving large deposits of magnetite (iron ore) that were later mined.

A 35 km wide zone of ductile faults (i.e., where the rock deformed plastically without fracturing versus a brittle fault where fracturing occurs) formed
during this event and overprinted all previous features to varying degrees.
Individual faults range from 0.5 to 2 km in thickness, although the boundaries
are diffuse and difficult to determine in some areas. The ductile fault zones
are marked by stretched rock that has recrystallized into a fine-grained texture
and is oriented in linear patterns (called mylonites), indicating that all movement was lateral or strike-slip. Outcrop-scale gentle to open upright folds also
occur adjacent to the fault zones locally (fig. 1.5b). These folds plunge gently
from due north to north-northeast. The folds occur within 150 m of the shear
zone boundary and result from essentially wrinkling of the gneiss adjacent
to the faults.

Subsequent to the strike-slip faulting event, the supercontinent of Rodinia
underwent a tectonically quiet period to close out the Proterozoic age. At
least 200 million years passed before the breakup of Rodinia began (fig. 1.3).
In the Highlands, this event is marked by faulting and the opening of small
isolated interior rift basins. These basins were nonmarine and contained both
river and lake sediments and volcanic rocks known as the Chestnut Hill Formation (Drake 1984; Gates and Volkert 2004). There is some uncertainty as
to when this event took place. There are two distinct periods of activity in
the breakup of Rodinia in the Appalachians, one about 740 Ma and the other
about 570 Ma. The Chestnut Hill Formation could be from either one.

Pangean Cycle

While the Rodinian cycle formed the basic backbone of the Highlands, the
Pangean cycle that followed took that basic structure and moved it around,
adding to it here and there, subtracting elsewhere. Most notably, a veneer of
sedimentary rocks of Paleozoic age was superimposed on the Proterozoic-
age crystalline gneisses and granites, and segments of the Highlands were
picked up and thrust overtop younger Paleozoic-age rocks of the adjacent
Ridge and Valley province. The relationships among these Paleozoic rocks
are complex in both the type of units and the nature of the contact with one
another and with the underlying crystalline rocks. Between the faulting and
the severe erosion that took place during the early Paleozoic time, virtually
any of the Paleozoic sedimentary rock units, from the base of the sequence
(i.e., the oldest Paleozoic rocks of Cambrian age) through the Green Pond–
Shawangunk formations (the youngest of Silurian-Devonian age), may be in
contact with the crystalline rocks of the Highlands. The sedimentary rocks
are the same as those found in the Valley and Ridge geologic province to
the west of the Highlands (Drake et al. 1989; Hatcher 1989; Rankin, Drake,
and Ratcliffe 1993). The contact between the two provinces is gradual, with
interfingering of strips of sedimentary versus crystalline rock units until one

province gives way to the other. The strips of sedimentary rocks, most commonly either limestone or shale, both of which easily weathered, have eroded to form the floors of the Highlands' steep-walled interior valleys.

The breakup of Rodinia, which began in the late Proterozoic, continued into the early Paleozoic and set the stage for the subsequent plate drifting, what is known as a passive margin phase. It was at this time that the Iapetus Ocean developed off the current east coast of what would be North America (fig. 1.3). The Highlands province was submerged in the Iapetus Ocean and was subsequently covered by these passive margin deposits. The base of the Paleozoic sedimentary sequence, formed during the Cambrian age, is the Hardyston Formation (called the Poughquag Formation in New York), which is a series of sandstone-to-conglomerate rocks deposited in a shallow freshwater-to-marine environment. Overlying the Hardyston is the Kittatinny Group of limestone and dolomite units (known as the Wappinger Group in New York) deposited in a calm water, tropical, shallow marine environment. This plate-drifting phase was short-lived because, by the early to middle Ordovician age, the building of the Pangean supercontinent began with a series of continental collisions. It was during these subsequent continent collisions that the Iapetus Ocean closed (Hatcher 1989).

The first shift in the tectonics of the Highlands region began with the deposition of the Martinsburg Formation (Hudson River shales) (Drake 1984; Drake et al. 1989) (fig. 1.3). The shallow-water passive margin was replaced by a deep basin through active downward warping of the Highland crust. The cause of this radical change was the approach of a volcanic island arc that caused the current east coast of North America (called Laurentia for that time period) to be warped downward through heavy loading. The collision of the island arc with Laurentia occurred about 450 Ma, forming the Taconian orogeny. It thrust the Highlands province upward and westward over the shales of the Martinsburg Formation.

The Taconian orogeny produced an extensive mountain chain that stretched all along the eastern seaboard of Laurentia (fig. 1.3). Large rivers drained the eroded sediments from these mountains westward into a shallow sea. The erosion removed much of the sedimentary cover rocks, exposing the underlying crystalline rocks, and the rivers deposited new sediments onto both the crystalline and sedimentary cover rocks. The Green Pond Formation and its equivalent Shawangunk Formation were derived from the Silurian continental sediments eroded from the Taconian mountains that blanketed the area (Drake et al. 1989; Faill 1997). The Shawangunk is so resistant to weathering that it forms prominent ridges from New York to Alabama (Hatcher 1989). Likewise, the Green Pond Outlier, a highly resistant quartzite conglomerate rock of a purplish matrix with white pebbles, sits atop the crystalline bedrock forming a ridge that bisects the western Hudson and New Jersey Highlands (Drake 1984) (fig. 1.2).

The next event was the Acadian orogeny, in which Baltica (northwestern Europe) collided with Laurentia to the north of the Highlands (fig. 1.3). This late Silurian to Devonian (400 to 360 Ma) event does not appear to have deformed the Highlands, but sedimentation shed from the mountains to the northeast blanketed the area. These sediments include the entire Catskill sequence but also the Bellvale and Schunemunk formations. Similar to the Green Pond Outlier, these rocks are highly resistant to weathering and now form the mountain ridges of the same name in the Highlands.

The late Carboniferous Alleghanian orogeny imposed the main regional deformation on the Valley and Ridge sedimentary rocks (fig. 1.3) (Hatcher 1989; Faill 1997). This 250–300 Ma event produced a classic foreland fold and thrust belt across the Appalachians to the west of the Highlands province. The large fold system in the Green Pond Outlier of the Highlands was formed during this event. All major northeast faults were reactivated and experienced extensive amounts of movement. A disconnected keel of crystalline rock within the Martinsburg Formation along the northwestern margin of the Hudson Highlands was broken into a string of crystalline rock fragments (Gates 1996). These erosion-resistant fragments now form a chain of hills up to 2 km long and 150 m higher than the general elevation of the plain formed by the less resistant shales.

The sedimentary rocks of the Valley and Ridge province were deformed several times through the Paleozoic during each of the Taconian, Acadian, and Alleghanian orogenies (Hatcher 1989). The Highlands province was also deformed during these events, but it acted as a rigid block. This block was transported westward and faulted over the sedimentary rocks of the Valley and Ridge province (Herman et al. 1996). This type of overthrust faulting and emplacement on younger rocks is quite common in other mountain regions of the world (Wolfe 1977). There is debate as to how much of the Highlands is transported on faults and lying on the sedimentary rocks and how much is rooted in crystalline rocks beneath.

The final major deformation was the Mesozoic faulting during the formation of the Newark rift basin (Gates and Costa 1998) (fig. 1.3). The Ramapo Fault system was reactivated as a normal fault (i.e., where the earth's crust is being stretched) during this event and experienced thousands of meters of movement. Many northeast-trending faults were also reactivated as normal, and a group of west-northwest faults was also formed late in the event. These faults appear to be responsible for the current seismic activity in the New York metropolitan area. Pervasive fracture systems formed in conjunction with this deformation event. These fracture zones are the main conduits for groundwater in the Highlands because the crystalline rocks are impervious to the movement of water as compared to most sedimentary rocks, in which water can more easily percolate between the sedimentary grains.

Mineral Deposits in the Highlands

The complex geological history of the Highlands was accompanied by the deposition of many different types of minerals, some of which became commercially important (Bayley 1910; Gundersen 2004). The titanic forces involved in the Grenville continental collision resulted in extensive strike-slip faulting. Later, fluids containing magnetite (iron oxide) and related minerals infiltrated and were deposited in the strike-slip shear zones. It has been proposed that the iron that formed these deposits originated from underlying volcanic rocks that were part of the volcanic island arc formed during the Rodinian cycle (Gundersen 2004). These iron deposits occur along the regional layering of the gneisses, often forming slanting to near vertical seams. The magnetite associated with late stages of strike-slip faulting can cut across the gneissic layering. Thicknesses of the mineralized veins range from 2 m to 15 m. Hematite, an iron oxide mineral similar to magnetite but red in color and more oxidized, is also found in the Highlands. It is associated with the deposition of the Chestnut Hill Formation in the rift basins formed during the breakup of the Rodinian supercontinent.

These mineral deposits were important to the subsequent industrial development of the Highlands. Along the northwest border of the Highlands in northwestern of New Jersey, the Franklin–Sterling Hill area was home to a major zinc mine that closed in 1986 after nearly 140 years of operation. The Hudson Highlands in New York contained the only active uranium mine east of the Mississippi River. From 1730 through the Civil War, the magnetite deposits of the four-state Highlands region were the source of premium iron in the United States. In New Jersey alone it is estimated that there were 440 active magnetite mines during the eighteenth and nineteenth centuries. The now abandoned mines constitute a public safety hazard and are an impediment to subsequent development because of open or water-filled shafts as well as surface subsidence and sinkholes formed by the collapse of shafts and tunnels (Shea 1977). Polluted runoff from mining wastes (tailing piles) that still remain can also be a contributing factor to the degradation of water supplies in some localities (Gilchrist et al. 2009). Although the iron mining essentially ended in the early twentieth century, the crystalline bedrock of the Highlands is still rich in magnetite ore. Active mining for other minerals is also defunct, but quarrying of the crystalline gneiss as crushed stone for construction material is still commercially active in many places across the Highlands.

Summary and Conclusions

The Highlands Province exists because of its bedrock geology, which is about as complex as any on earth. There were basically two supercontinental plate tectonic cycles that produced this geology. The Rodinian supercontinent cycle formed the crystalline rocks that make up the Highlands, and the Pangean supercontinent cycle elevated them to their current prominence. The Rodinian cycle involved the closure of an ocean basin between the protocontinents of North America and South America about 1.2–1.0 billion years ago. The North American side was characterized by a volcanic chain of islands along the coast, whereas the South American side was quiet and similar to the Atlantic coast of today. When the two collided in the Grenville orogeny about 1,050 Ma, they produced what was probably the largest mountain range ever on earth. It was as high as the Himalayas and stretched from Scandinavia to Texas. The rocks exposed today formed the roots of those Grenville Mountains.

The rock layers were folded on top of themselves (as nappes), thickening the earth's crust to form the mountains. The once sedimentary and volcanic rocks were pressurized and heated to the point of melting, and they metamorphosed into the gneiss that characterizes the Highlands today. The layering of the rocks from this event is nearly horizontal. Magma intruded along the folds to form large plutons of igneous rocks. As a second part of this continental collision, a 35 km wide lateral strike-slip fault system formed similar in size to the San Andreas Fault in California. This event appears to have lasted from about 1,008 to 980 Ma. This shear system appears to have been synchronously active with faults in the Adirondacks of New York, forming a broad zone of crossing strike-slip faults similar to that in the Himalayas today.

A long period of erosion and tectonic inactivity followed the collision before Rodinia began to break apart. The rift basins containing the Chestnut Hill Formation of New Jersey and Pennsylvania mark the beginning of this event. About 500 Ma the Iapetus Ocean formed off the east coast of proto–North America (Laurentia), which was in the tropics at the time. This ocean was short lived, however; it began to close by 450 Ma with the Taconian orogeny, followed by the 390 Ma Acadian orogeny and the 250 Ma Alleghanian or Appalachian orogeny. These collisional events helped to build the new supercontinent of Pangea. They also added new pieces of land to the east coast and built a new mountain range where the old one had been. The rocks of the Highlands region were elevated to the height of a new mountain range by moving it upward along large faults. This uplift still persists in the height of the Highlands. The faults created zones of weakness in the crystalline rocks and helped to intersperse the bands of sedimentary rocks that exist in the western Highlands.

The last tectonic event came in the breakup of Pangea. Africa pulled away from North America to form the Atlantic Ocean. Rift basins again formed along the margin including the large Newark-Gettysburg basins, which bound the Highlands to the southeast. Several other faults within the Highlands were reactivated during this event. Weathering and erosion reduced the elevation of the Highlands to its current level over the past 200 million years. Exceptional amounts of erosion occurred during glacial advances, which will be discussed in more depth in the next chapter. Erosion has been preferential in the faulted zones and the interspersed weaker sedimentary rocks. There has been some continuing earthquake activity in the Highlands, but it is minor compared to that around more active fault zones such as the Pacific Rim. The faults and fracture systems related to faulting in the Highlands control much of the groundwater flow in the region. Rather than percolating through the rock matrix, groundwater moves through the fractures in the bedrock. As will be seen in chapter 4, fracture systems are notoriously poor purifiers of groundwater, so the quality of the Highlands water supply is easily compromised.

References

Bartholomew, M. J., and S. E. Lewis. 1988. "Peregrination of Middle Proterozoic Massifs and Terranes within the Appalachian Orogen, Eastern U.S.A." *Trabajos de Geologia* 17:155–165.

Bayley, W. S. 1910. "Iron Mines and Mining in New Jersey." Geological Survey of New Jersey Final Report Series VII. Trenton, NJ: MacCrellish and Quigley.

Dalziel, I.W.D., L.H.D. Salada, and L. M. Gahagan. 1994. "Paleozoic Laurentian-Gondwana Interaction and the Origin of the Appalachian-Andean Mountain System." *Geological Society of America Bulletin* 106:243–252.

Drake, A. A., Jr. 1984. "The Reading Prong of New Jersey and Eastern Pennsylvania: An Appraisal of Rock Relations and Chemistry of a Major Proterozoic Terrane in the Appalachians." In *The Grenville Event in the Appalachians and Related Topics,* ed. M. J. Bartholomew, 75–109. Geological Society of America Special Paper 194.

Drake, A. A., Jr., J. N. Aleinikoff, and R. A. Volkert. 1991. "The Byram Intrusive Suite of the Reading Prong—Age and Tectonic Environment." In *Contributions to New Jersey Geology,* ed. A. A. Drake Jr., D1–D14. U.S. Geological Survey Bulletin 1952.

Drake, A. A., Jr., A. K. Sinha, J. Laird, and R. E. Guy. 1989. "The Taconic Orogen." In *The Appalachian-Ouachita Orogen in the United States,* ed. R. D. Hatcher Jr., W. A. Thomas, and G. W. Viele, 101–176. The Geology of North America, vol. F-2. Boulder, CO: Geological Society of America.

Faill, R. T. 1997. "A Geologic History of the North-Central Appalachians, Part 2: The Appalachian Basin from Silurian through Carboniferous." *American Journal of Science* 297:726–761.

Gates, A. E. 1996. "Megaboudins and Lateral Extension along the Leading Edge of a Crystalline Thrust Sheet, Hudson Highlands, New York, USA." *Journal of Structural Geology* 18:1205–1216.

Gates, A. E., and R. E. Costa. 1998. "Multiple Reactivations of Rigid Basement Block Margins: Examples in the Northern Reading Prong, USA." In *Basement Tectonics 12: Central North America and Other Regions,* ed. M. C. Gilbert and J. P. Hogan, 123–153. Dordrecht: Kluwer Academic Publishers.

Gates, A. E., D. W. Valentino, J. R. Chiarenzelli, G. S. Solar, and M. A. Hamilton. 2004. "Exhumed Himalayan-Type Syntaxis in the Grenville Orogen, Northeastern Laurentia." *Journal of Geodynamics* 37:337–359.

Gates, A. E., D. W. Valentino, M. L. Gorring, J. R. Chiarenzelli, and M. A. Hamilton. 2001. "Bedrock Geology, Geochemistry and Geochronology of the Grenville Province in the Western Hudson Highlands, New York." In *Geology of the Lower Hudson Valley: New York State Geol. Assoc. Guidebook*, ed. A. E. Gates, 177–204.

Gates, A. E., D. W. Valentino, M. L. Gorring, E. R. Thern, and J. R. Chiarenzelli. 2006. "Rodinian Collisional and Escape Tectonics in the Hudson Highlands, New York." In *Excursions in Geology and History: Field Trips in the Middle Atlantic States*, ed. F. J. Pazzaglia, 65–82. Geological Society of America Field Guide 8.

Gates, A. E., and R. A. Volkert. 2004. "Vestiges of an Iapetan Rift Basin in the New Jersey Highlands: Implications for the Neoproterozoic Laurentian Margin." *Journal of Geodynamics* 28:387–409.

Gilchrist, S., A. E. Gates, Z. Szabo, and P. Lamothe. 2009. "Impact of AMD on Water Quality in Critical Watershed in the Hudson River Drainage Basin: Phillips Mine, Hudson Highlands, New York." *Environmental Geology* 57:97–409.

Gundersen, L.C.S. 2004. "Tectonics and Metallogenesis of Proterozoic Rocks of the Reading Prong." *Journal of Geodynamics* 37:361–379.

Hatcher, R. D., Jr. 1989. "Tectonic Synthesis of the U.S. Appalachians." In *The Appalachian-Ouachita Orogen in the United States*, ed. R. D. Hatcher Jr., W. A. Thomas, and G. W. Viele, 511–535. The Geology of North America, vol. F-2. Boulder, CO: Geological Society of America.

Herman, G. C., D. H. Monteverde, R. W. Schlishe, and D. M. Pitcher. 1996. "Foreland Crustal Structure of the New York Recess, Northeastern United States." *Geological Society of America Bulletin* 109:955–977.

Lash, G. G., and A. A. Drake Jr. 1984. "The Richmond and Greenwich Slices of the Hamburg Klippe in Eastern Pennsylvania: Stratigraphy, Sedimentology, Structure and Plate Tectonic Implications." U.S. Geological Survey Professional Paper 1312.

Mose, D. G. 1982. "1,300-Million-Year-Old Rocks in the Appalachians." *Geological Society of America Bulletin* 93:391–399.

Rankin, D. W., A. A. Drake Jr., and N. M. Ratcliffe. 1993. "Proterozoic North American (Laurentian) Rocks of the Appalachian Orogen." In *Precambrian Conterminous U.S.*, ed. J. C. Reed et al., 378–403. The Geology of North America, vol. C-2. Boulder, CO: Geological Society of America.

Ratcliffe, N. M., R. L. Armstrong, B. H. Chai, and R. G. Senechal. 1972. "K-Ar and Rb-Sr Geochronology of the Canopus Pluton, Hudson Highlands, New York." *Geological Society of America Bulletin* 83:523–530.

Shea, T. K. 1977. *Abandoned Magnetite Iron Mines of New Jersey*. Trenton, NJ: Department of Labor and Industry.

Spencer, A. C., 1904. "Genesis of the Magnetite Deposits in Sussex County, New Jersey." *Mining Magazine* 10:377–381.

Volkert, R. A. 2004. "Mesoproterozoic Rocks of the New Jersey Highlands, North-Central Appalachians: Petrogenesis and Tectonic History." In *Proterozoic Tectonic Evolution of the Grenville Orogen in North America*, ed. R. P. Tollo, L. Corriveau,

J. McLelland, and M. J. Bartholomew, 459–475. Geological Society of America Memoir 197.

Volkert, R. A., and A. A. Drake Jr. 1999. "Geochemistry and Stratigraphic Relations of Middle Proterozoic Rocks of the New Jersey Highlands." U.S. Geological Survey Professional Paper 1565-C.

Volkert, R. A., M. D. Feigenson, L. C. Patino, J. S. Delaney, and A. A. Drake Jr. 2000. "Sr and Nd Isotopic Compositions, Age and Petrogenesis of a-Type Granitoids of the Vernon Supersuite, New Jersey Highlands, USA." *Lithos* 50, no. 4: 325–347.

Windley, B. 1986. "Comparative Tectonics of the Western Grenville and the Western Himalaya." In *The Grenville Province*, ed. J. M. Moore, A. Davidson, and A. J. Baer, 341–348. Geological Association of Canada Special Paper 31.

Wolfe, P. E. 1977. *The Geology and Landscapes of New Jersey*. New York: Crane and Russak.

Young, D. A., and J. Cuthbertson. 1994. "A New Ferrosilite and Fe-Pigeonite Occurrence in the Reading Prong, New Jersey, USA." *Lithos* 31:163–176.

2

Glaciation and Landscape History

Scott D. Stanford

The landforms of the Highlands owe much to the tectonic events described in chapter 1 but are of much more recent origin. The ancient gneisses that formed in the roots of the Grenville mountain range more than a billion years ago and the younger sedimentary rocks that were faulted and folded along with the gneisses during the several periods of Appalachian mountain building between 450 and 250 million years ago (Ma) are the foundation materials for the modern Highlands landscape. The repeated northwest–southeast tightening and loosening of the tectonic vise that formed the Grenville Mountains, then the Iapetus Ocean, then the Appalachian Mountains, and finally the Atlantic Ocean created a bedrock substructure with a northeast–southwest grain. This grain, etched by weathering, river erosion, and glaciers, defines the Highlands today as a physiographic region and is the distant inheritance of its tectonic origins.

As described in chapter 1, the last major tectonic event recorded in rocks of the Highlands region is rifting that began to break up the Pangea continent about 240 Ma. By about 200 Ma continued rifting began to form the Atlantic Ocean basin to the east of the Highlands. The Atlantic has widened continuously ever since. Rivers draining to the Atlantic have eroded many vertical miles of rock from the Appalachians, including the Highlands, during this period and have deposited the resulting sediment in the Atlantic to form the continental shelf and coastal plain. This erosion continuously erased and reshaped Highlands landforms to such an extent that the history of the landscape we see today can be traced back only to about 10 Ma. During this time, Highlands topography was shaped by the interactions of sea level, climate, and glaciation. River erosion was the primary agent of landscape development from 10 to 2 Ma. Since 2 Ma, repeated episodes of glaciation and boreal climate produced the final elements of the landscape we see today. This chapter will describe these events and their effects on the Highlands landscape, from oldest to youngest, and then briefly discuss how they affect water resources.

Preglacial Rivers and Sea Level

The Highlands began to emerge as a distinct topographic feature starting at about 10 Ma. For a long period before 10 Ma, perhaps between about 70 and 30 Ma, the area that is now the Highlands was submerged under the Atlantic Ocean. As part of the continental shelf, marine sediments equivalent to those that today underlie the coastal plain were deposited and covered the Highlands (Stanford, Ashley, and Brenner 2001). Global sea level lowered when Antarctic glaciers began to grow at about 30 Ma, causing a shift from continental shelf to coastal settings in the Highlands area. By 10 Ma renewed growth of Antarctic ice, and perhaps of small glaciers in Arctic regions, led to a further lowering of sea level and the subsequent emergence of the Highlands as a landscape of broad, shallow valleys and low uplands. The covering of marine and coastal deposits eroded away. The river network on this low-relief landscape was unlike that of today. Several rivers flowed southeasterly in a transverse direction across the grain of the Highlands ("former rivers" on fig. 2.1), which had been masked by the covering of coastal sediment. Although no sediments from these rivers are preserved in the Highlands today, their existence is indicated by aligned ridgetop gaps between Andover and Ledgewood, New Jersey; Oxford and Glen Gardner, New Jersey; and Allentown and Spinnerstown, Pennsylvania. These gaps, which are known as wind gaps because they do not contain through-flowing rivers today, align with wind or water gaps through Kittatinny Mountain and Blue Mountain to the northwest. The aligned gaps lead southward to the Beacon Hill Gravel, which is a river-plain deposit preserved as erosional remnants on the highest hills in the coastal plain, and to the Bryn Mawr Formation, which is an equivalent deposit in the Pennsylvania Piedmont. The Beacon Hill contains chert and quartzite pebbles eroded from rocks of the Highlands and from the Valley and Ridge province northwest of the Highlands, indicating southerly river flow. North of the late Wisconsinan glacial limit (fig 2.1), glacial erosion has deeply scoured the landscape, and preglacial drainage cannot be reconstructed with any confidence. It is possible that the Ramapo valley in New York marks the route of a preglacial transverse stream like those to the south.

Remnants of the low-relief landscape drained by the rivers are preserved on the plateau-like summits of Schooleys Mountain and Scotts Mountain in New Jersey, and smaller areas around Fredericksville and Seisholtzville, Pennsylvania, and Fairmount, New Jersey. These summit plateaus, with gentle relief of about 150 feet, are known as peneplains ("almost plains"). Schooleys Mountain is a famous example of this late-nineteenth-century concept (Davis and Wood 1889; Salisbury 1898), which fell into disfavor in the latter half of the twentieth century but has been revived with new data on sea level,

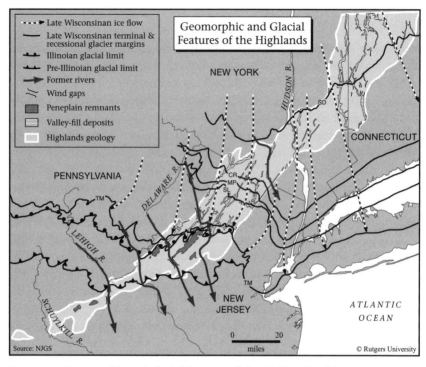

Figure 2.1. Geomorphic and glacial features of the Highlands. Abbreviations on late Wisconsinan glacier margins are TM = terminal moraine, SL = Silver Lake moraine, MP = Mud Pond moraine, CR = Cherry Ridge moraine, SD = Shenandoah moraine. Glacial limits and valley-fill deposits are based on Braun (1996b), Cadwell (1989), Connally and Sirkin (1986), Stanford, Witte, and Harper (1990), Stanford (1993), Stone, Stanford, and Witte (2002), Stone et al. (2005), and Witte (1997b). *Source*: NJGS. © Rutgers University.

tectonics, climate, and stratigraphy (the vertical sequences of rock layers or strata) (Stanford, Ashley, and Brenner 2001).

With the continued decline of sea level after 10 Ma, possibly to below modern sea level at times, rivers deepened valleys by eroding their channels into bedrock. Soft rock such as shale and soluble rock such as limestone, dolomite, and marble erode more rapidly than hard, insoluble rock such as granite, gneiss, and quartzite. Rivers flowing on outcrops of soft rock will deepen and extend their valleys faster than those flowing on hard rock. Hard-rock rivers will be diverted gradually into the deepened soft-rock valleys as the two intersect. This diversion process is known as "stream capture." Soft rocks in the Highlands crop out in northeast–southwest trending belts, along the tectonic grain, and streams on these belts captured the older southeast-flowing streams that crossed belts of hard rock. By about 3 Ma, a series of such stream captures had created the trellis-like drainage network of today. The Delaware

River, previously only one of the several transverse streams, became the master stream of the southern Highlands because, unlike streams to the north, it crosses only a narrow belt of resistant gneiss (Witte 1997a). Soft-rock tributaries to the Delaware, such as the Pequest, Lehigh, Pohatcong, and Musconetcong, captured the former transverse streams north and south of the Delaware. Farther west, the Schuylkill River at Reading, Pennsylvania, passes around the west end of the gneiss outcrop, avoiding hard rock altogether. In the northern Highlands, the Hudson and Housatonic rivers probably became master streams in a manner similar to the Delaware, although glacial erosion has obscured preglacial drainage patterns in this area. By 3 Ma, when a period of high sea level halted incision for a time, the general form of the modern Highlands was in place.

Pre-Illinoian Glaciation

Large glaciers began to grow in the Northern Hemisphere at around 2.5 Ma. The largest of these northern glaciers is the Laurentide ice sheet, which has grown about ten times in the past 2 Ma from centers in northern Quebec and west of Hudson Bay to cover most of Canada and much of the northern United States. At its maximum extent, the Laurentide was the largest glacier on earth, and the Highlands span its southernmost limit. Only the largest of the many advances had sufficient ice volume to overtop the Catskill plateau and Adirondack Mountains to reach the Highlands. There is evidence in the Highlands for at least three such advances: the pre-Illinoian, Illinoian, and late Wisconsinan glaciations.

The earliest glaciation, known as the pre-Illinoian, extended the farthest south and covered all the Highlands north of the Allentown, Pennsylvania, area (fig. 2.1). Sediments deposited by this glacier include till, which is a mixture of sand, silt, clay, gravel, and boulders laid down directly from glacial ice, and a few sand and gravel deposits laid down by meltwater in lakes and river plains. The sediments are deeply weathered and eroded and are sparsely preserved in the belt between the pre-Illinoian and Illinoian glacial limits. Here the deposits occur on flat uplands and divides where they have been protected from stream and hillslope erosion. Pre-Illinoian till is most widespread on broad, flat divides in limestone valleys (for example, the Pohatcong, Musconetcong, and Long valleys in New Jersey, and the Lehigh and Saucon valleys in Pennsylvania), where most surface water drains downward through solution channels in the limestone bedrock and does not erode surface material by flowing overland.

The topographic position of the deposits, although lowered in places by solution collapse of the underlying limestone, indicates that streams have deepened their valleys by as much as two hundred feet into the underlying bedrock since the pre-Illinoian glaciation. Such incision requires time and, along with the intense weathering, indicates great age. Although there is no way to directly date these deposits, reversed magnetic polarity of some of the pre-Illinoian sediments and fossil pollen associated with them indicate that the deposits are more than eight hundred thousand years old (Sasowsky 1994; Stanford, Ashley, and Brenner 2001). The oldest Laurentide glacial deposits are in the Missouri River valley in Nebraska, Iowa, Missouri, and Kansas, where they are dated by interbedded volcanic ash from Yellowstone eruptions to around 2 Ma. The pre-Illinoian glaciation here may be just as old.

Details of this glaciation are difficult to reconstruct because the deposits are so eroded, but the few surviving meltwater sediments record both glacial river plains and lakes in valleys, as in later glaciations, although valleys were somewhat wider and shallower than they are today. Lakes were ponded in the Lehigh, Little Lehigh, and Saucon valleys near Allentown, Pennsylvania, and in the Cooks Creek valley near Riegelsville, Pennsylvania, all of which drained toward and so were dammed by the pre-Illinoian margin (Braun 1996a). The Pohatcong, Musconetcong, and Long valleys in New Jersey likely contained river plains because they slope away from ice margins.

The pre-Illinoian glaciation was followed by another period of stream downcutting between 2 Ma and about 200,000 years ago, this time in response to renewed lowering of sea level due to growth of northern ice sheets. This downcutting or incision created narrow inner valleys one hundred to two hundred feet deep set within the older, broader valleys. This inner-valley topography is still characteristic of the southern Highlands. During this period, chiefly between 800,000 and 200,000 years ago, there were about eight major Laurentide glaciations. Some of these may have advanced into the Highlands, although any deposits from these advances have been eroded or are indistinguishable because of intense weathering from the pre-Illinoian deposits. It is possible that none of these advances had sufficient volume to overtop the Catskills and Adirondacks.

Illinoian Glaciation

The next Laurentide glaciation with sufficient volume to advance into the Highlands is known as the Illinoian advance, which covered the Highlands north of a line from Morristown, New Jersey, to Easton, Pennsylvania (fig. 2.1). There are no direct means of dating this advance, but the Illinoian deposits are much less weathered and eroded than those of pre-Illinoian age yet noticeably more weathered than deposits of the younger late Wisconsinan glaciation. The degree of weathering and the age of related glacial and marine deposits in Long Island and coastal New England indicate that the Illinoian glacier most likely reached its maximum position about 150,000 years ago.

Illinoian deposits are exposed in a five-mile-wide belt south of the late Wisconsinan limit; they also occur beneath late Wisconsinan deposits in the

Pequest, Musconetcong, and Rockaway valleys just north of the late Wisconsinan limit. Illinoian till also occurs in the cores of some drumlins (streamlined hills of glacial sediment formed under a glacier) beneath late Wisconsinan till, throughout the northern Highlands. In the outcrop belt, Illinoian till blankets gentle to moderate slopes but is eroded from steep slopes. In valleys, meltwater sediments form small river plains and glacial-lake deltas in modern valley bottoms, and till forms small moraines (ridges of till laid down along the glacier margin) in the Lamington, Long, and Pohatcong valleys in New Jersey. This pattern of landforms differs from that of pre-Illinoian terrain, where deposits are present only on the flattest surfaces on uplands and are absent from valley bottoms.

In the outcrop belt, Illinoian meltwater deposits record the presence of glacial lakes in the Rockaway, Lamington, and Pequest valleys, which drained toward, and so were dammed by, the glacier. There were glacial river plains in the Musconetcong, Delaware, Pohatcong, and Long valleys, which drained away from the glacier. North of the late Wisconsinan limit there were surely similar complexes of lakes and river plains in valleys through the northern Highlands, but sedimentary evidence for them was eroded away during the late Wisconsinan glaciation.

After the Illinoian glacier retreated, there was an interglacial warm period like that of today, with a peak around 125,000 years ago, followed by a return to a colder and occasionally boreal climate starting around 110,000 years ago. This colder period marked the initiation and growth of the Wisconsinan stage of the Laurentide ice sheet. The Wisconsinan glacier did not attain sufficient volume to overtop the Catskills and Adirondacks until about 25,000 radiocarbon years ago (ka), when it reached its maximum size during a period known as the late Wisconsinan.

Late Wisconsinan Glaciation

The late Wisconsinan glacier covered the Highlands north of a line between Denville and Belvidere, New Jersey. Unlike the earlier glaciations, the age of the late Wisconsinan is known from radiocarbon dates of organic material recovered from sediments beneath late Wisconsinan deposits on Long Island, from sediments deposited in proglacial lakes that extended in front of the glacier limits in New Jersey, and from postglacial sediments atop late Wisconsinan deposits north of the glacial limit in New Jersey, Pennsylvania, New York, and Connecticut (Harmon 1968; Sirkin and Stuckenrath 1980; Cotter et al. 1986; Stone and Borns 1986; Muller and Calkin 1993; Stanford 2000; Stone, Stanford, and Witte 2002; Stone et al. 2005). These dates indicate that ice arrived at its limit at about 21 ka. It had retreated from the New Jersey Highlands by about 18 ka and from the Connecticut Highlands by about 15.5 ka. Unlike pre-Illinoian and Illinoian deposits and landforms, late Wisconsinan deposits are only slightly weathered and eroded. Apart from regrowth of forest, development of floodplains along main streams, and human activity, the landscape left by the late Wisconsinan glacier is largely unaltered.

Ice Advance and Bedrock Erosion

The late Wisconsinan glacier advanced southerly to southeasterly across the Highlands from the Kittatinny, Wallkill, and mid-Hudson valleys (fig. 2.1). Ice flow is recorded by striations, drumlins, erratic dispersal, and erosional forms on bedrock. This ice was part of a large glacier lobe flowing down the Hudson-Champlain lowland. During advance it eroded almost all earlier glacial deposits and weathered rock material, and it exposed and sculpted the underlying bedrock. Today, between 20 and 30 percent of the surface of the northern Highlands is glacially exposed bedrock outcrop. On hard rocks such as gneiss and quartzite, glacial erosion created smooth, sloping ledges on north and northwest slopes that faced advancing ice, and cliffs on lee slopes that faced south and southeast. As glaciers move across bedrock obstacles, basal ice experiences increased pressure on the up-ice side of the obstacle. The increased pressure melts ice at the base of the glacier, producing a film of water that in turn causes sliding and abrasion. The abrasion produces smooth, sloping ledges on the bedrock surface. Water from the basal melting migrates through fractures in the bedrock to the lee side of the obstacle, where ice is moving away from the rock and pressure is low. Here the water refreezes, cracking the rock along fractures and locking it onto the base of the glacier. The moving glacier then transports the blocks away, creating cliffs. This process is known as quarrying or plucking. Abrasion and plucking are responsible for the distinctive ledge-and-cliff landforms of ridges and hills in the northern Highlands. These ledge-and-cliff forms occur at all scales, from small outcrops no larger than a car to entire mountain ridges.

Soft rocks such as shale, weathered marble, and weathered limestone in valley bottoms did not offer resistance to ice flow and were instead scoured by ice or by meltwater flowing under pressure beneath the glacier to form overdeepened troughs. Most of these overdeepenings were filled with meltwater deposits during glacial retreat and are not visible as landforms today, although many small overdeepened rock basins on uplands are the sites of natural wetlands and ponds, such as Terrace Pond, West Pond, and Surprise Lake on Bearfort Mountain in New Jersey. These ponds occupy scourings in shaley rock layered between harder quartzite beds. Another example is Cedar Pond in Sterling Forest, New York, which occupies a scouring in soft, weathered micaceous gneiss bordered by ridges formed on harder granitic gneiss.

Glacial Deposits

There are two main types of glacial sediment: till, a nonlayered mix of sand, silt, clay, gravel, and boulders laid down directly by glacial ice; and meltwater deposits, which are layered and sorted sand, gravel, silt, and clay laid down by meltwater in lakes and river plains. During the late Wisconsinan advance through the Highlands, till was deposited in ramps along the lower parts of hillslopes that faced advancing ice, and in drumlins. It is as much as one hundred feet thick in ramps and two hundred feet thick in drumlins. The ramps were formed as sediment in the ice was released and emplaced by the same pressure-melting mechanism that produced abraded ledges higher on the same slopes. The grain size and color of till as well as the rock types the till contains reflect the local bedrock or the bedrock within several miles upglacier from the site of till deposition. Gneiss bedrock produces a yellowish to light gray sandy to silty-sandy till with many boulders (fig. 2.2a). Shale, limestone, and marble yield a grayish brown silty to sandy-silty till. This till occurs chiefly along the northwest edge of the Highlands in New Jersey and western New York, where material eroded from the Kittatinny-Wallkill and mid-Hudson valleys was deposited by the glacier (Denny 1938; Stanford 1993), and in marble-floored valleys in Connecticut and eastern New York (Stone et al. 2005). There are also a few small deposits of reddish silty till derived from red shale in the belt of Paleozoic sedimentary rock in Union and Berkshire valleys in New Jersey.

At its maximum position, the glacier margin stabilized and deposited the terminal moraine, a linear belt of till forming a complex of ridges and basins. The terminal moraine averages about 2 miles wide and 100 to 150 feet thick. The volume of sediment in the moraine indicates that the glacier margin stood at the terminal position for at least several hundred years. In part, this stability reflects topographic pinning of the ice margin in deep, east–west trending segments of the Rockaway, Musconetcong, and Pequest valleys, where ice was several hundred feet thicker than on uplands (Stanford 1993).

At the moraine, and as the ice margin retreated northward from it, meltwater draining from the glacier deposited sand, gravel, silt, and clay in glacial lakes and river plains. Lakes formed in valleys that drained toward the glacier (and so were dammed by it) and in valleys that were dammed by previously deposited glacial sediment. Examples of ice-dammed valleys include the Wallkill and its tributaries in the northwest Highlands in New Jersey and western New York; the lower Rockaway and south tributaries to the Pequannock River in New Jersey; Fishkill Creek and Swamp River in New York; and the Still, Hollenbeck, and Blackberry rivers and Valley Brook in Connecticut. Several modern lakes, held in by sediment dams left from the larger ice-dammed lakes, survive in these settings, including Green Pond and Budd Lake in New Jersey and Whaley Lake in New York. Examples of sediment-dammed valleys include the upper Pequest, upper Musconetcong, and upper Rockaway in New Jersey, all dammed by the terminal moraine; the Ramapo, Croton, and Tenmile river valleys in New York; and the Housatonic in Connecticut, all of which were sequentially dammed by earlier lake deposits. The Hudson valley itself was occupied by a large sediment-dammed lake held in by the terminal moraine at the narrows between Staten Island and Brooklyn. A number of modern natural lakes remain in sediment-dammed basins, including Lake Hopatcong in New Jersey, which is dammed by the terminal moraine, and Greenwood Lake on the New York–New Jersey line, which is dammed by drumlins.

River plains formed in valleys that drained away from the glacier and were not sediment dammed, and so were not ponded. Examples include the Delaware, lower Musconetcong, Wanaque, and northerly tributaries of the Pequannock in New Jersey, and the Canopus and Peekskill Hollow valleys in New York. In many ponded valleys, lakes either filled completely with sediment or lowered and drained as their dams were eroded, and river plains were then deposited on top of the lake sediments.

Three types of deposits were laid down in lakes: lacustrine fans, deltas, and lake-bottom deposits. Lacustrine fans are sand and gravel deposits (fig. 2.2b) laid down on the bottom of a lake at the mouths of subglacial tunnel channels, which are pipelike conduits that drain meltwater from a glacier. Water in these conduits is typically a fast-flowing, sediment-rich slurry under high pressure that slows abruptly when exiting the tunnel, depositing gently inclined beds ranging from cobble-and-boulder gravel to fine sand in knolls and fans along the glacier margin. Where the ice margin stabilizes for a period of several years, the fan deposit may build upward to the lake surface, where the deposit then grows out into the lake as a delta. Deltas are also deposited where meltwater streams from bordering uplands enter lakes. Deltas typically consist of inclined beds of sand marking the prograding delta front, overlain by thin horizontal beds of gravel laid down by streams draining across the top of the delta. Their flat tops mark the former lake level. Lake-bottom deposits are laid down on a lake floor in quiet water away from a glacier margin. They consist of thinly layered silt, fine sand, and clay that settle out from turbid lake water. Because they fill the lowest parts of a valley, lake-bottom deposits are generally overlain by postglacial floodplain and wetland sediments. The total thickness of lake sediments averages fifty to one hundred feet but can be as much as three hundred feet.

Glacial river-plain deposits are laid down in networks of shallow channels known as braidplains and range from sand and pebbly sand to boulder gravel. Silt and clay are kept suspended in flowing water and are flushed down-valley into lakes or out to sea. The glacial river deposits form terraces and plains with surfaces ten to forty feet above modern streams and are generally less than fifty feet thick.

The elevation and location of lake and river deposits allow reconstruction of the sequence of lake levels and spillways and the geometry of ice margins needed to maintain or drain lakes (Stanford 1993; Witte 1997b; Stone, Stanford, and Witte 2002; Stone et al. 2005). Ice margins during retreat are also marked by three recessional moraines on uplands in the western New Jersey

a

b

Figure 2.2. (a) Till near Mount Arlington, N.J. Boulder-rich, sandy till like this is typical of that produced by glacial erosion of gneiss bedrock in the Highlands. (b) Lacustrine fan deposits near Buttzville, N.J. Beds of sand and gravel like these were laid down where subglacial meltwater discharged into glacial lakes. Lacustrine fan gravels are important aquifers in the Highlands. Photos by S. Stanford.

Highlands known as the Silver Lake, Mud Pond, and Cherry Ridge moraines (Stanford 1993) and by a recessional position along the northern edge of the Highlands in New York known as the Shenandoah Moraine (Connally and Sirkin 1986) (fig. 2.1). These moraines are much smaller than the terminal moraine and represent much less time, but like the terminal moraine, they mark alignments of deep east–west trending valleys where thicker ice slowed

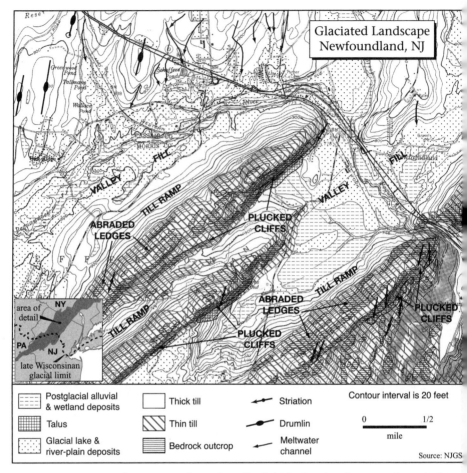

Figure 2.3. Map of area around Newfoundland, N.J., showing features of a typical glaciated landscape in the northern Highlands. Base map from U.S. Geological Survey Newfoundland, New Jersey, 7.5-minute quadrangle. Geology from Stanford (1991).

ice-margin retreat. The Silver Lake, Mud Pond, and Cherry Ridge moraines correspond to the deep, east–west valleys of the Pequannock River, West Brook, and Hewitt Brook, respectively, in New Jersey, and the Shenandoah Moraine is situated along the prominent east–west trending escarpment marking the Highlands boundary on the south side of the Fishkill Creek valley in New York.

The combination of valley-fill deposits, till ramps, drumlins, and ledge-and-cliff outcrops creates a distinctive landform mosaic characteristic of the northern Highlands, north of the late Wisconsinan glaciation limit (fig. 2.3). The sharp alternation of sand and gravel plains in valleys, till ramps mantling valley-side slopes, rough bedrock-outcrop uplands, and wetlands and ponds in former lake bottoms and scoured rock basins provided the landscape platform for the agricultural and settlement patterns, water resources, and ecologic habitats that we see today, which are discussed in later chapters of this book.

Periglacial Features

South of the late Wisconsinan glaciation limit, a different set of processes related to periglacial climate (severe freezing in areas bordering glaciers), rather than direct glacial action, led to a different set of landform details and surficial materials (fig. 2.4). During the late Wisconsinan and Illinoian glaciations, and probably during earlier glaciations that did not reach the Highlands,

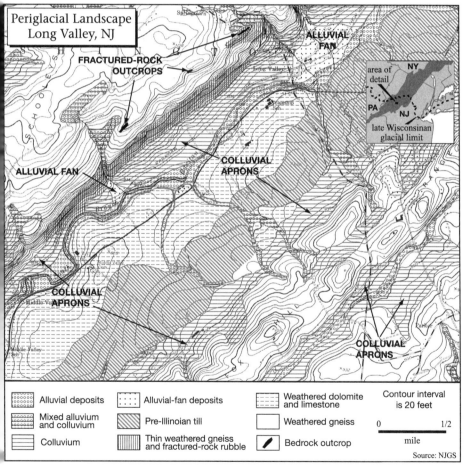

Figure 2.4. Map of area around Long Valley, N.J., showing features of a typical periglacial landscape in the southern Highlands. Base map from U.S. Geological Survey Hackettstown, New Jersey, 7.5-minute quadrangle. Geology from Stone, Stanford, and Witte (2002).

conditions for a distance of more than a hundred miles south of the ice sheets were similar to those of boreal and tundra areas today. Permafrost (permanently frozen ground) was intermittently present, and deciduous forest was replaced by mixed conifer forest and grassland or tundra grassland with little tree cover. During thaws, permafrost impeded drainage, creating waterlogged soils and increasing runoff. Waterlogging, increased runoff, reduced tree cover, and more frequent freezes and thaws all led to increased downhill movement of soil and rock compared to such movement under temperate conditions. The eroded debris collected at the foot of hillslopes in aprons of rocky sediment known as colluvium. These colluvial aprons are ubiquitous along the base of steep slopes throughout the southern Highlands and are as much as seventy feet thick.

Debris that eroded from slopes also entered mountain streams. Where these streams emptied into valleys, they deposited gravelly alluvial fans, another common feature of the southern Highlands. Sand and gravel deposited by meltwater draining from the glacier as it stood at the late Wisconsinan terminal moraine (and also such deposits from the earlier Illinoian terminus) formed narrow braidplains in the Delaware and Musconetcong valleys.

As discussed in chapter 3, most of the surface in the southern Highlands is mantled by deeply weathered rock material, consisting of rocky, clayey sand atop gneiss and clayey silt atop limestone and dolomite, so exposed outcrops are limited to a few ridgetops and steep slopes. These outcrops were fractured by repeated freezing and thawing to create rock rubble. The widely scattered small, rubbly outcrops characteristic of the southern Highlands contrast markedly with the extensive ledges and cliffs indicative of glacial erosion in the northern Highlands.

Postglacial Features

Hillslopes stabilized both in the southern Highlands and in the newly deglaciated northern Highlands after permafrost melted and full forest vegetation became reestablished. Pollen preserved in postglacial lakes and bogs indicates that reforestation by pine and spruce occurred between 14 and 12 ka (Harmon 1968; Cotter et al. 1986; Peteet et al. 1993; Maenza-Gmelch 1997; Russell and Stanford 2000; also see chapter 6 in this volume). Postglacial landscape change has been minor compared to glacial and periglacial effects. With the return of forest cover, peat began to accumulate in wetlands. Numerous glacially scoured bedrock basins on uplands, some ice-block basins within glacial deposits in the northern Highlands, and one basin dammed by colluvium on Musconetcong Mountain in the southern Highlands gradually filled with peat, which is as much as forty feet thick in places (Waksman et al. 1943), to become marshes and swamps. Some basins that have not filled remain as ponds.

In valleys, streams reestablished courses on drained lake bottoms or braid-plains in the northern Highlands or on colluvial aprons and alluvial fans in the southern Highlands. These streams, free from heavy glacial and perigla-cial sediment loads, eroded into glacial and colluvial deposits to create flood-plains. Where streams eroded through thick deposits, they formed narrow ra-vines, such as Sparta Glen, which was eroded through a till ramp near Sparta, New Jersey. Smaller gullies and scarps were eroded by groundwater seepage and runoff on the lower parts of till ramps and colluvial aprons. In wider parts of drained lake basins, the former lake floors were too low-lying to be eroded and instead became marshes, swamps, or broad floodplains. Examples include the Great Swamp near Pawling, New York, and Great Meadows in the Pequest valley, New Jersey. Layers of peat and alluvial silt, sand, and clay in these lowlands are generally less than twenty feet thick.

A final postglacial detail is the talus deposits that accumulated as rockfall at the foot of plucked cliffs in the northern Highlands. Small talus deposits are common at the foot of gneiss cliffs. Larger deposits occur at the foot of cliffs in quartzite, which forms taller vertical faces than gneiss. Good examples of quartzite talus occur below plucked cliffs on the southeast sides of Green Pond Mountain, Kanouse Mountain, and Copperas Mountain near New-foundland, New Jersey (fig. 2.3).

Glacial Deposits and Water Resources

Valley-fill deposits (fig. 2.1) are the most productive groundwater aquifers (un-derground layers of water-bearing bedrock or sediments) in the Highlands, as will be discussed later in chapter 4. Coarse sand and gravel are four to six orders of magnitude more permeable than fractured gneiss, and five to ten times as porous, and so have the capacity to supply much more water than an equal volume of rock. Valley-fill aquifers occur where meltwater deposits are generally greater than one hundred feet thick. Sand and gravel in lacustrine fans, deltas, and, less commonly, river plains are the aquifers; silt, clay, and fine sand lake-bottom deposits are confining or semiconfining beds that im-pede the downward flow of water.

The vast majority of valley-fill aquifers in the Highlands are glacial-lake deposits because river-plain deposits, while permeable, are generally less than fifty feet thick. Within lacustrine valley fills, lake-bottom sediments are five to seven orders of magnitude less permeable than sand and gravel, so the distribution of lake-bottom sediments within the valley fill is an important control on recharge and groundwater flow. Till is generally absent within val-ley fills, although it may be present beneath the valley fill as a discontinuous layer on bedrock. An important exception to this rule is in valley fills along the terminal moraine in New Jersey, where till of the moraine was emplaced atop late Wisconsinan and earlier Illinoian-age lake sediments, and then buried by

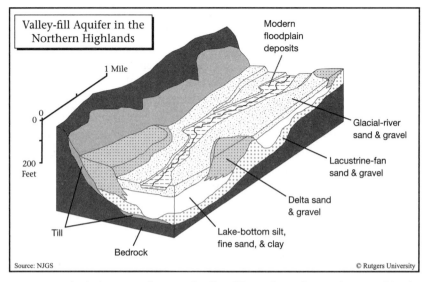

Figure 2.5. Block diagram of a typical valley-fill aquifer in the northern Highlands. Sand and gravel deposits are aquifers where sufficiently thick and saturated. Lake-bottom deposits are confining or semiconfining beds.

additional lake sediments and river-plain deposits during glacial retreat (Stanford 2006). Permeability of the silty sand till of the Highlands is intermediate between sand and gravel and lake-bottom deposits, and it generally acts as a semiconfining material. Sandy, boulder-rich till may be nearly as permeable as sand and gravel.

Figure 2.5 shows a typical valley fill north of the terminal moraine. In this case, the lake deposits are overlain by a river-plain sand and gravel laid down after the lake drained, a circumstance that was common in sediment-dammed lakes. In valleys where lakes did not drain or fill with sediment, the river-plain deposit is absent. Lacustrine fans, deposited sequentially at the mouths of subglacial tunnel channels at the bottom of the lake on the bedrock floor, form an irregular lower sand and gravel. At stable ice margins, the fans build up to the lake surface and then grow out into the lake as deltas. Deltas are also deposited against the valley side by meltwater draining from adjacent uplands. Lake-bottom sediment fills in the low areas in front of the deltas, burying the lacustrine fans. After the lake lowers or drains, river-plain sand and gravel are deposited on the former lake floor, covering the lake-bottom sediment. Finally, postglacial streams etch floodplains into the river-plain deposits. These events create a two-aquifer system: a lower, lacustrine-fan aquifer, confined in places by the lake-bottom sediments; and an upper, unconfined aquifer, consisting of the river-plain deposits and deltas. Where the confining unit is absent (for example, at former ice margins and along the valley walls where fans are in contact with deltas), surface water can recharge the lower aquifer.

Where the surficial sediments are too thin to be aquifers, they contribute to the hydrologic system by storing and conveying water, recharging bedrock aquifers and streams. Till in the northern Highlands and, to a lesser degree, colluvium in the southern Highlands, is ten to twenty times more porous than gneiss and quartzite bedrock (Melvin et al. 1992). They generally occupy footslopes and upland valleys and so are favorably situated to capture and store runoff from upslope bedrock outcrop terrain, releasing it gradually to valley-bottom streams through seepage and springs on the lower parts of slopes. Sand and gravel valley-fill deposits serve the same reservoir function in lowland valleys (Wandle and Randall 1994). Glacial and periglacial deposits thus provide both an archive of natural history and a living water resource.

References

Braun, D. D. 1996a. "Surficial Geology of the Allentown East 7.5' Quadrangle, Lehigh, Northampton, and Bucks Counties, Pennsylvania." Harrisburg: Pennsylvania Geological Survey, Open-File Report 96-43, scale 1:24,000.

———. 1996b. "Surficial Geology of the Allentown 30 × 60-Minute Quadrangle." Harrisburg: Pennsylvania Geological Survey, Open-File Report 96-48, scale 1:100,000.

Cadwell, D. H. 1989. "Surficial Geologic Map of New York, Lower Hudson Sheet." Albany: New York State Museum, Map and Chart Series 40, scale 1:250,000.

Connally, G. G., and L. A. Sirkin. 1986. "Woodfordian Ice Margins, Recessional Events, and Pollen Stratigraphy of the Mid-Hudson Valley." In *The Wisconsinan Stage of the First Geological District*, Eastern New York, ed. D. H. Cadwell, 50–72. Albany: New York State Museum, Bulletin 455.

Cotter, J.F.P., J. C. Ridge, E. B. Evenson, W. D. Sevon, L. Sirkin, and R. Stuckenrath. 1986. "The Wisconsinan History of the Great Valley, Pennsylvania and New Jersey, and the Age of the 'Terminal Moraine.'" In *The Wisconsinan Stage of the First Geological District*, Eastern New York, ed. D. H. Cadwell, 22–49. Albany: New York State Museum, Bulletin 455.

Davis, W. M., and J. W. Wood Jr. 1889. "The Geographic Development of Northern New Jersey." *Proceedings of the Boston Society of Natural History* 24:365–423.

Denny, C. S. 1938. "Glacial Geology of the Black Rock Forest." Cornwall-on-the-Hudson, NY: The Black Rock Forest, Bulletin 8.

Harmon, K. P. 1968. "Late Pleistocene Forest Succession in Northern New Jersey." PhD diss., Rutgers University.

Maenza-Gmelch, T. E. 1997. "Vegetation, Climate, and Fire during the Late-Glacial-Holocene Transition at Spruce Pond, Hudson Highlands, Southeastern New York, USA." *Journal of Quaternary Science* 12:15–24.

Melvin, R. L., B. D. Stone, J. R. Stone, and N. J. Trask. 1992. "Hydrogeology of Thick Till Deposits in Connecticut." Hartford, CT: U.S. Geological Survey, Open-File Report 92-43.

Muller, E. H., and P. E. Calkin. 1993. "Timing of Pleistocene Glacial Events in New York State." *Canadian Journal of Earth Science* 30:1829–1845.

Peteet, D. M., R. A. Daniels, L. E. Heusser, J. S. Vogel, J. R. Southon, and D. E. Nelson. 1993. "Late-Glacial Pollen, Macrofossils and Fish Remains in Northeastern U.S.A.—the Younger Dryas Oscillation." *Quaternary Science Reviews* 12:597–612.

Russell, E.W.B., and S. D. Stanford. 2000. "Late-Glacial Environmental Changes South of the Wisconsinan Terminal Moraine in the Eastern United States." *Quaternary Research* 53:105–113.

Salisbury, R. D. 1898. "The Physical Geography of New Jersey." Trenton: New Jersey Geological Survey, Final Report, vol. 8.

Sasowsky, I. D. 1994. "Paleomagnetism of Glacial Sediments from Three Locations in Eastern Pennsylvania." In *Late Wisconsinan to Pre-Illinoian (G?) Glacial and Periglacial Events in Eastern Pennsylvania: Guidebook, 57th Field Conference of the Friends of the Pleistocene, Northeastern Section*, ed. D. D. Braun, 21–23. Bloomsburg, PA: U.S. Geological Survey, Open-File Report 94-434.

Sirkin, L. A., and R. Stuckenrath. 1980. "The Portwashingtonian Warm Interval in the Northern Atlantic Coastal Plain." *Geological Society of America Bulletin* 91:332–336.

Stanford, S. D. 1991. "Surficial Geologic Map of the Newfoundland Quadrangle, Passaic, Morris, and Sussex Counties, New Jersey." Trenton: New Jersey Geological Survey, Geologic Map Series 91-3, scale 1:24,000.

———. 1993. "Late Wisconsinan Glacial Geology of the New Jersey Highlands." *Northeastern Geology* 15:210–223.

———. 2000. "Overview of the Glacial Geology of New Jersey." In *Glacial Geology of New Jersey: Guidebook for the 17th Annual Meeting of the Geological Association of New Jersey*, ed. D. P. Harper and F. R. Goldstein, II.1–II.24. Trenton: Geological Association of New Jersey.

———. 2006. "Glacial Aquifers of the New Jersey Highlands." In *Environmental Geology of the Highlands: Field Guide and Proceedings for the 23rd Annual Meeting of the Geological Association of New Jersey*, ed. S. Macaoay and W. Montgomery, 80–98. Trenton: Geological Association of New Jersey.

Stanford, S. D., G. M. Ashley, and G. J. Brenner. 2001. "Late Cenozoic Fluvial Stratigraphy of the New Jersey Piedmont: A Record of Glacioeustasy, Planation, and Incision on a Low-Relief Passive Margin." *Journal of Geology* 109:265–276.

Stanford, S. D., R. W. Witte, and D. P. Harper. 1990. *Hydrogeologic Character and Thickness of the Glacial Sediment of New Jersey*. Trenton: New Jersey Geological Survey, Open-File Map 3, scale 1:100,000.

Stone, B. D., and H. W. Borns. 1986. "Pleistocene Glacial and Interglacial Stratigraphy of New England, Long Island, and Adjacent Georges Bank and Gulf of Maine." *Quaternary Science Reviews* 5:39–53.

Stone, B. D., S. D. Stanford, and R. W. Witte. 2002. "Surficial Geologic Map of Northern New Jersey." U.S. Geological Survey, Miscellaneous Investigations Series Map I-2540-C, scale 1:100,000.

Stone, J. R., J. P. Schafer, E. H. London, M. L. DiGiacomo-Cohen, R. S. Lewis, and W. B. Thompson. 2005. "Quaternary Geologic Map of Connecticut and Long

Island Sound Basin." U.S. Geological Survey, Scientific Investigations Series Map 2784, scale 1:150,000.

Waksman, S. A., H. Schulhoff, C. A. Hickman, T. C. Cordon, and S. C. Stevens. 1943. "The Peats of New Jersey and Their Utilization." Trenton: New Jersey Department of Conservation and Development, Bulletin 55, Part B.

Wandle, S. W., Jr., and A. D. Randall. 1994. "Effects of Surficial Geology, Lakes and Swamps, and Annual Water Availability on Low Flows of Streams in Central New England, and Their Use in Low-Flow Estimation." Marlborough, MA: U.S. Geological Survey, Water Resources Investigations 93-4092.

Witte, R. W. 1997a. "Late History of the Culvers Gap River: A Study of Stream Capture in the Valley and Ridge, Great Valley, and Highlands Physiographic Provinces, Northern New Jersey." In *Pliocene-Quaternary Geology of Northern New Jersey, Guidebook for the 60th Annual Reunion of the Northeastern Friends of the Pleistocene,* ed. S. D. Stanford and R. W. Witte, 3.1–3.16. Trenton: New Jersey Geological Survey.

———. 1997b. "Late Wisconsinan Glacial History of the Upper Part of Kittatinny Valley, Sussex and Warren Counties, New Jersey." *Northeastern Geology and Environmental Sciences* 19:155–169.

In addition to the publications cited in the text and listed below, detailed (1:24,000 scale) surficial geologic maps are available for most of the Pennsylvania, New Jersey, and Connecticut Highlands. These maps show the extent of glacial and periglacial deposits, weathered-rock material, bedrock outcrop, and the stratigraphy of valley fills, and most have discussions of local glacial history. They can be obtained from the Pennsylvania Geological Survey (http://www.dcnr.state.pa.us/topogeo/gismaps/geomaps.aspx), the New Jersey Geological Survey (http://www.njgeology.org/pricelst/geolmapquad.htm), and, for Connecticut, the U.S. Geological Survey (http://www.usgs.gov/pubprod/) or the Connecticut Department of Environmental Protection (http://www.ct.gov/dep/cwp/view.asp?a=2688&q=322396&depNav_GID=1511). The maps can also be searched using the National Geologic Map Database (http://ngmdb.usgs.gov/).

3

Major Soils of the Highlands

John C. F. Tedrow and Richard K. Shaw

Introduction

The term "soil" has somewhat different connotations within various disciplines. Soil is generally considered to be the uppermost portion of the earth's crust. The gardener or agriculturalist generally considers soil to be the six- to twelve-inch layer of earth in which plants grow. Some investigators consider the term "soil" to reflect certain geologic materials and use such terms as glacial soil, windblown soil, bedrock soil, sandstone soil, limestone soil, and so on to reflect the parent material from which the soil is derived. Engineers generally use the term "soil" as mineral (e.g., sand, clay) or organic material resting on bedrock and focus on soil-binding properties such as texture and compaction among many others as related to construction.

A vertical cut through the soil will generally show various layers (a.k.a. horizons) that have their own distinguishing properties, such as color, texture, moisture levels, fabric, mineral composition, and organic matter content. Collectively the soil layers make up the soil profile. The terms "surface," "subsoil," and "substratum" or "parent material" are used to denote the A, B, and C horizons, respectively. The substratum, or C horizon, is that portion of the soil profile that is little affected by soil-forming processes. Soil profiles are generally depicted as having a depth of about three to four feet, but in other situations the depth may be only a few inches. In other locations the profiles may have depths of many feet.

Soil scientists (pedologists) consider the soil to be a function of the interaction of five factors: parent material, climate, biotic processes, topography, and time. Simonson (1959) expanded the soil-forming processes to include additions, losses, translocations, and transformations. To some extent, these processes take place in all soils, but the influence of the five soil-forming factors affects their balance, resulting in a distinctive set of horizons and related soil properties for a given set of conditions.

With admitted weaknesses in any soil classification system, soil maps constitute one of the best single-source methods of dividing the landscape into component natural types. However, soil maps should be used in concert with information concerning geology and vegetation. While climate, geologic, vegetation, and pedologic conditions are generally similar across the four-state Highlands region of Pennsylvania, New Jersey, New York, and Connecticut, local conditions are important in the characterization and mapping of soils. This chapter discusses some of the key factors determining suitability, limitations, and soil characteristics of the major soil types of the Highlands region in relation to various land uses. A brief history of some of the more important soil names that have been used in the region as well as the currently used soil series is included.

Parent Material of the Highlands Soils

Parent material on which Highlands soils were formed is largely determined by the underlying bedrock, the overlying glacially deposited material, and, in rarer cases, deposits of organic matter. As described in chapter 1, the Highlands physiographic province (sometimes referred to as the Reading Prong) consists of a series of crystalline intrusive and metamorphic bedrock ridges interfingered with valleys underlain by softer sedimentary shale, limestone, or marble bedrock. The four-state federal Highlands Conservation Act area extends out of the Highlands proper to include portions of the limestone valleys to the west and the Triassic lowlands to the east, areas with quite different topography, parent material, and, consequently, soils.

Glacial features of the Highlands are very important in dictating the nature of the soil, particularly with respect to texture, mineral composition, drainage, acidity, age of the deposits, and related properties. Salisbury (1902) was one of the first to give details concerning character of the glacial drift in the Highlands of New Jersey and correlate the nature of the resulting till with the bedrock from which it was formed. As described in chapter 2, there were three major glacial epochs in the Highlands in New Jersey and Pennsylvania, whereas farther north in New York and Connecticut only the more recent Wisconsinan epoch is represented. This chronology is relevant in depicting soil formation, especially that in the Highlands. The more recent Wisconsin-age glaciers extended south into the northern half of the Highlands of New Jersey (see fig. 2.1). Thus, all of New York and Connecticut Highlands are north of the Wisconsinan terminal moraine, all of the Pennsylvania Highlands are south, and the New Jersey Highlands are roughly bisected. South of the terminal moraine, drift from earlier glacial epochs (i.e., Illinoian and pre-Illinoian) can be locally important as parent soil material (Salisbury 1902).

Bedrock and glacial drift undergo weathering-induced chemical changes. North of the terminal moraine, the time since the retreat of the Wisconsinan glaciation has been determined based on the depth of leaching of carbonate-bearing gravel (MacClintock 1940, 1954). Krebs and Tedrow (1957) found that the carbonate-bearing till north of the moraine was generally leached to depths of about thirty-six inches. Mineral alteration in the variously aged tills is generally reflected in the B and C horizons of the soils in that the older deposits have brighter colors than is the case with the younger ones. The southern boundary of the Wisconsin-age glacial deposits marks one of the most distinctive natural soil boundaries in the Highlands in that land to the south is not only leached of carbonate rock to considerable depths but there is also a general "browning effect" of the soil matrix. Cook recognized the deep-seated weathering present in the early till when he stated that "between Lebanon and Hampton remarkable examples of the change of rock to earth are to be seen. The decayed gneiss or granite that had once been solid rock is now so soft it can be dug with a shovel. Between Annandale and High Bridge, the steam excavator takes it out as readily as it would earth from a sand bank" (1874, 12).

Soils of the Highlands

George H. Cook (1874) published a soils map of New Jersey in 1874, the first of its kind in America. His map of the New Jersey portion of the Highlands describes soil varieties largely as perceived at the present. Since Cook's time there have been a number of soil surveys conducted throughout the state. Additional work was conducted in the New Jersey Highlands by Quakenbush (1955) and Tedrow (1986) and in New York by Cline (1955) and Cline and Marshall (1977). A significant number of soil names that were used during the early years have been discontinued; other names have been added or redefined.

The Soil Conservation Service, now reconstituted as the Natural Resources Conservation Service (NRCS) of the U.S. Department of Agriculture (USDA), is the lead federal agency responsible for classifying and mapping soils nationwide. The NRCS county soil surveys, more recently superseded by the soil survey geographic digital database, provide detailed information about the soils of the four-state Highlands region. These surveys are mapped to the soil series (the finest level of classification) in the USDA Soil Taxonomy (Soil Survey Staff 1999). At a coarser level of classification, similar soil series are grouped into soil orders. Soil series refer to a group of soils with a similar sequence of horizons formed in the same parent material under comparable climate and vegetation. Along with two or more phase terms (surface texture, slope class, stoniness, etc.), the series essentially serves as the main mapping unit of soil in USDA soil surveys. The more narrow definition of a soil series, along with the natural variation in soil properties, has sometimes led to differences in the correlation of similar soils in adjoining surveys along state or even county borders. Currently there are more than nineteen thousand soil series in use in the United States and nearly four hundred in the Highlands physiographic province. The underlying parent material is used as the basis of organizing the following discussion of soils found across the four state Highlands region.

Soils in Wisconsinan Glacial Till

The earliest USDA soil surveys used the Gloucester series to refer to soils formed in late Wisconsinan granitic and gneissic till throughout the Northeast. These surveys in New Jersey also used Gloucester for those soils formed in the older, or pre-Wisconsinan, till deposits in the Highlands. In general, the soil was described as having a brown loam or sandy loam surface and a brownish yellow similarly textured subsoil. Some stony and gravelly types or phases were mapped, and both the Sussex area (Jennings 1914) and Bergen area (Lee, Tine, and Gillett 1925) surveys discuss the "compact" subsoil present in some areas. In USDA surveys, the series is no longer mapped in New Jersey but is used for sandy-skeletal (greater than 35 percent rock fragments in a sandy matrix) till soils in New York and New England. Tedrow (1986) retains the name Gloucester for soils formed in crystalline till over red sedimentary bedrock east of the Ramapo Fault.

In the current soil maps, a formidable discrepancy appears between New Jersey and New York in the Highlands area. Since the 1960s New Jersey surveys have all used the Rockaway series, characterized by a more advanced stage of development than the equivalent soil in those states to the north (fig. 3.1; table 3.1). A slight to moderate accumulation of translocated clay in

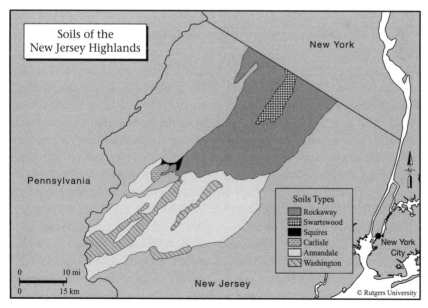

Figure 3.1. Map of major soils in the New Jersey portion of the Highlands region as mapped by Tedrow (1986). © Rutgers University.

Table 3.1. Soils of the Highlands of New Jersey

Map number	Map name	USDA surveys 1970–present	Soils and land
1	Rockaway	Rockaway, Rock outcrop	Deep, well-drained, acid soil formed on stony, crystalline upland till.
2	Swartswood	Rockaway, Hollis, Chatfield	Deep, well-drained, strongly acid soil formed on stony upland till.
3	Squires	Wassaic	Deep, well-drained, limestone soil formed mainly in undulating valleys.
4	Carlisle	Timakwa, Adrian, Carlisle, Catden	Deep, poorly drained muck and peat on flat, water-saturated depressions and basins, some places underlain by marl.
5	Annandale	Annandale, Califon, Gladstone, Parker	Deep, well-drained, acid soil formed on gravelly to stony uplands of early, highly weathered, crystalline till.
6	Washington	Washington	Deep, well-drained, moderately acid soil formed on undulating valleys of early weathered limestone till.

Note: Map names for New Jersey derived from Quakenbush (1955) and Tedrow (1986). Dominant soil series as defined by the USDA Natural Resource Conservation Service soils maps.

the subsoil, defined as an argillic horizon, places it in the Ultisol order in the USDA soil taxonomy. The Rockaway series is also described as containing a dense, firm, water- and root-restrictive horizon formed in the lower subsoil, known as a "fragipan." However, even the earliest surveyors noted that some soils lacked a fragipan (or, more simply, a pan), and the separation of those areas with and without this condition on a soil map was difficult. Soils without a fragipan are listed as inclusions in most Rockaway map units. The thickness of the fragipan layer can also vary, with a "thin pan" phase recognized in recent updates of some county surveys in New Jersey.

Rockaway soils are sandy loam or loam textured, with prominent coarse fragments, from boulder to gravel size, ranging up to about 40 percent throughout the profile. Soil acidity values are very strongly acid to strongly acid (pH from 4.5 to 5.5) throughout. The slow permeability of the fragipan induces lateral movement of water and generally renders the soil unsuited for septic systems. Some of the nonstony phases of Rockaway are considered prime farmland in New Jersey; the stone and boulder content is the main limitation for field crop production. Rockaway soils can be either well drained or moderately well drained. In New Jersey, the former generally denotes a high water table that remains below forty inches during the growing season; in the latter it can reach an eighteen-inch depth. For fragipan soils, however, a perched water table condition, above the pan, is common in late winter and early spring and following extended rainfall. Geographically associated with Rockaway soils on the lower landscape positions are the somewhat poorly drained Hibernia soils, which can have a high water table between six and eighteen inches from the surface during the growing season.

A close equivalent to Rockaway, used in New York and Connecticut surveys, is the Paxton series, formed in dense basal till. Unlike the fragipan, the dense layer of basal till is considered an inherited substratum condition rather than the result of soil-forming processes. The lack of a measurable clay increase in the subsoil places the Paxton soils in the less developed Inceptisol order. Apart from the subsoil, Paxton soils generally have physical, chemical, and mineralogical properties similar to those of Rockaway. The ratings and interpretations for the two soils are similar, with a water- and root-restrictive layer at a comparable depth serving as a limitation for many types of development. Surveys in these two states also acknowledge a deep till soil without the firm substratum, the Charlton series. In some areas of New York, Paxton and Charlton are mapped together as a complex, essentially inseparable in the same landscape. Without the restrictive layer, Charlton is a much more suitable soil for most types of agricultural use and urban development. It is considered to be among the most productive soils for New England dairy farms.

Each of the three deep till soils described earlier has its own associated wetter or off-drainage series. The poorly drained Ridgebury (where the high water table can rise to within six inches of the surface during the growing season) and very poorly drained Whitman (with water at or ponded above the surface for a significant period during the growing season) series are mapped in New Jersey, even though they are more similar to and are usually mapped with Paxton. Woodbridge is the moderately well-drained affiliate in dense basal till. Sutton (moderately well drained) and Leicester (poorly drained) are the wetter associates of Charlton, with the noncompacted or "friable" substratum. Ridgebury, Whitman, and Leicester are all hydric soils, associated with wetland vegetative communities, described in chapter 8. In general, the wetter soils in the late Wisconsinan till areas often display slightly finer textures than the well drained, due to the redeposition and accumulation of eroded silt and clay in lower areas. The Alden series is also used for very poorly drained areas in the Highlands. The parent material is described as a silty "depositional mantle" over till, and the soil typically has a silt loam surface over a silty clay loam subsoil.

The Netcong series, exclusive to New Jersey, is mapped on the terminal moraine of the late Wisconsinan glaciation. It is generally similar in chemical and mineralogical properties to Rockaway, with comparable soil textures and a slightly greater amount of coarse fragments (up to 50 percent). However, it lacks the fully formed argillic horizon (clay subsoil) and firm fragipan. A nonstony phase of Netcong is considered prime farmland in New Jersey.

Connecticut surveys also contain four other associated till soils: Montauk, with a sandy substratum, and Broadbrook, with a silty mantle, are dense substratum soils; Canton, with a loamy mantle over a sandy substratum, and Gloucester, a sandy-skeletal soil, are friable substratum soils. The excessively coarse substratum provides poor filtration and limits the use of septic systems on the latter two soils.

All three states use similar soil series in those areas where the till is shallow to bedrock. Chatfield soils are moderately deep (twenty to forty inches) to bedrock, and Hollis soils are shallow (ten to twenty inches). The more recent surveys in New Jersey include these series as major components, usually together in a complex; others use a Rockaway-Rock outcrop map unit. With the associated bedrock outcrops, Chatfield and Hollis soils present a formidable obstruction to agriculture, home building, and most kinds of development in general. In New Jersey, current land use in the various Chatfield-Hollis-Rock outcrop map units is greater than 75 percent woodland. Almost 70 percent of the total area in Rockaway soils is also in woodland, with less than 5 percent in agriculture. Less than half of the area in Netcong soils is woodland, with more than one-third in urban development.

The Wisconsin-age till soils in the limestone valleys of the Connecticut and eastern New York Highlands include Nellis (well drained) and Amenia (moderately well drained), both with carbonates in the upper forty inches, and Stockbridge (well drained) and Georgia (moderately well drained), with carbonates deeper than forty inches. Most land in these soils is cleared and put in silage corn, hay, and pasture. Wassaic (New Jersey) and Galway (New Jersey and New York) are both moderately deep to bedrock till soils. At the eastern edge of the Highlands in New York and Connecticut are the Wethersfield soils, formed in till from the Triassic-age sedimentary rocks, which are generally too stony for intensive agriculture.

Soils in Glacial Meltwater Deposits

Glacial meltwater (glaciofluvial) deposits in the valleys occupy a much smaller portion of the total area in the Highlands than the till and are generally characterized by gentler slopes and fewer surface stones and boulders. The Merrimac series was used in the earliest surveys for soils formed on glacial meltwater stream deposits in the region, including the Bernardsville (Patrick 1923) and Bergen (Lee, Tine, and Gillett 1925) soil survey areas within the New Jersey Highlands. Loam, sandy loam, and loamy sand surface textures were differentiated, usually with a sandy loam subsoil and a stratified substratum of sand and gravel. The series is still in use in New York and New England.

The Budd series was used in New Jersey from the 1940s to differentiate the somewhat more pedologically developed outwash soils in the state from those in the rest of New England, in a manner similar to Rockaway. The USDA replaced it with the name Riverhead in 1970. Riverhead soils are well drained with a sandy loam or loam surface, sandy loam subsoil, and a coarser-textured (sand and gravel) substratum. Reaction ranges from extremely acid to moderately acid (pH 3.5 to 6.0). Horseneck (moderately well drained), Pompton (somewhat poorly drained), and Preakness (poorly and very poorly drained) are the off-drained associates in New Jersey.

Sandy-skeletal Hinckley soils are found on coarser-textured deposits on glacial terraces, outwash plains, and deltas. Otisville is a similar soil but was originally established for sedimentary rather than crystalline rock parent material. Both soil series are used in the Highlands region in New Jersey for generally similar conditions. Other New York and Connecticut soils in meltwater deposits vary in particle-size distribution through the soil profile. The Haven series has a thick (up to thirty-six inches) loam or silt loam cap over sandy or sandy- skeletal material. Knickerbocker has a thinner (up to twenty inches) sandy loam mantle over a sandy substratum, similar to Merrimac but with fewer rock fragments. Windsor, with sandy textures throughout the profile, is the state soil of Connecticut, preferred for the production of shade tobacco.

The excessively coarse substratum of these glaciofluvial soils leaves them generally unsuited for septic systems because rapid permeability in the substratum poses a high risk for groundwater pollution. Riverhead soils are prime farmland in New Jersey, but their good drainage and ease of excavation make them well suited for urban development as well (Eby 1976). More than half of the land use for Riverhead soils in New Jersey is urban development, with a small area remaining in agriculture (about 12 percent). Hinckley and Otisville soils, prone to droughtiness, have a similar proportion of area in agriculture, with about 40 percent remaining in woodland. Other important agricultural soils formed in meltwater deposits include Hazen (with an argillic horizon) in New Jersey and Copake (without the argillic) in Connecticut and New York. Hero is an associated moderately well-drained soil. These are all characterized by a loamy solum (surface and subsoil combined) with an excessively coarse substratum.

Soils in Former Glacial Lake Basins

Portions of some Highland valleys were once occupied by glacial meltwater lakes during the late Wisconsinan glaciation. Many of the soils in the former lake basins are characterized by various thicknesses of organic materials, which tend to accumulate because of the slow decomposition of vegetative matter when saturated with water (Waksman et al. 1943). The early USDA surveys described these very poorly drained organic soils as muck. The

Belvidere area soil survey (Patrick 1920) cited the agricultural importance of the organic soils when drained; celery, lettuce, and onions were the principal crops. Three classes of thickness of organic material were differentiated: typical (greater than twenty-four inches), intermediate (ten to twenty-four inches), and shallow (less than ten inches). Farmland value increased with thickness. Since 1950 the organic soils in New Jersey have been mapped to the series level. The Histosol soil order includes those soils with greater than sixteen inches of organic soil material in the top thirty-two inches of the profile. Organic soil material has at least 20 to 30 percent (depending on the clay content) of organic matter by weight.

Three soil series, all Histosols, have been commonly used: Carlisle for those soils with greater than fifty-one inches of organic material; and Palms and Adrian with sixteen to fifty-one inches of organic over loamy and sandy mineral material, respectively. More recently these three, originally established in Michigan, have been replaced by the local equivalents Catden, Natchaug, and Timakwa. As described in chapter 8, these organic soils, all very poorly drained, are generally associated with wetland vegetation communities under natural conditions.

Organic materials in these soils can vary in degree of decomposition from peat (the least decomposed stage with recognizable plant residues, in the USDA classification) to mucky peat to muck (the most decomposed with few recognizable plant residues). Organic soils in the Highlands region are dominated by highly decomposed muck (or sapric materials). The soil pH is generally very strongly acid to slightly acid (pH 5.0 to 6.5). The organic soils when drained are easily cultivated, making them well suited to growing certain types of vegetables and, in more recent years, commercial sod. But subsidence, decomposition, and wind erosion, all resulting from drainage, have served to lower the soil surface over time.

Most (about 70 percent) of the total Histosol area in the New Jersey Highlands is the thick Catden/Carlisle type, and only a small portion (around 6 percent) of this area is cultivated. The Timakwa/Adrian type, with a sandy substratum, comprises about one-quarter of the total area, with almost 20 percent in agriculture (fig. 3.1; table 3.1). Part of the area of the central New Jersey Highlands known as Great Meadows, in cultivation since about 1880, now extensive sod farms, fits the latter type. The "Black Dirt Region," about sixteen thousand acres in southern Orange County, New York, noted for its yellow globe onions, is predominantly a very deep phase of Catden/Carlisle, with more than ninety-six inches of organic material present in some areas (Olsson 1981).

The Wallkill series first appeared in New Jersey in the Sussex area soil survey (Jennings 1914) and remains in use today. It refers to very poorly drained soils formed in alluvium (stream deposits) overlying organic soil material, found primarily in the Wallkill valley in New York and New Jersey. Due to the thickness (sixteen to forty inches) of the overlying mineral material, the Wallkill soil classifies as an Entisol, or soil of recent origin, rather than a Histosol, Almost 25 percent of Wallkill soils in New Jersey are in cultivation.

The Whippany (somewhat poorly drained) and Parsippany (poorly drained) series are used for soils formed in silty and clayey sediments (generally exceeding a clay content of 35 percent) associated with glacial lake deposits. Originally established for the Triassic lowland area, these series are now used in the New Jersey Highlands areas as well. These are among the finest-textured soils in the state. Their slow permeability, high water table, and low relief make these soils poorly suited for urban development.

Soils in Pre-Wisconsinan Till or Other Parent Material

The early surveys used the Gloucester series to denote soils formed in both late Wisconsinan and older pre-Wisconsinan till in the Highlands. The Chester series referred to soils derived from the weathering in place of the gneissic bedrock. The typical Chester profile was described as a light brown or grayish brown loam with a yellow clay loam subsoil of friable consistence. The series was established in Pennsylvania for soils weathered from micaceous schist, a metamorphic rock formed from mica-rich sandstone. Eventually, owing to differences in rock type and the presence of both glacial and colluvial (resulting from downslope movement) materials in the New Jersey Highlands, the Annandale series replaced Chester there (fig. 3.1; table 3.1). Like Rockaway, the Annandale series has a fragipan in the lower subsoil. But the differences between the soils, due to the advanced age of the latter, are striking. Annandale soils have a thicker subsoil and zone of translocated clay, with a solum thickness that can reach close to sixty inches, often with a saprolitic (soft, weathered bedrock) substratum below. Subsoil textures of clay loam and sandy clay loam textures are common, and the continual accumulation of clay can eventually work to degrade the fragipan (Ciolkosz et al. 1989). The clay mineral suite features abundant kaolinite and some hydroxyl-interlayered vermiculite as well as some gibbsite at depth (Tedrow 1986). Annandale is usually described as one of the more highly weathered soils in New Jersey, and its classification in the Red-Yellow Podzolic great soil group in the former USDA system associated it more closely with the soils of the southeastern United States (Krebs and Tedrow 1958).

Califon (moderately well or somewhat poorly drained) and Cokesbury (poorly drained) are the wetter associates of Annandale. The latter is a hydric soil that often develops wetland plant communities. Parent materials for all three soils include old gneissic till and residuum as well as some colluvium. The Gladstone series was adopted in New Jersey in 1969 for those soils formed in residual and colluvial materials without a fragipan, replacing the Edneyville series. In other respects it is similar to Annandale. The Parker series is used for younger residual soils on the less stable, rockier landscapes. It lacks the argillic horizon, has textures of loam and sandy loam with a high coarse-fragment content throughout the profile (greater than 35 percent), and is somewhat excessively drained (a seasonal high water table rarely above sixty inches from the surface). In current USDA soil surveys, Gladstone, Parker, Califon, and Cokesbury are also the primary soils of the Reading Prong in Pennsylvania. The Edgemont series is also used for soils formed on the more quartzitic rocks.

Nonstony areas of Annandale, Gladstone, and Califon soils are prime farmland in New Jersey. From 25 to 30 percent of the land in Annandale soils, about 20 percent in Gladstone, and about 15 percent in Califon soils are used for agriculture, with slightly less than 50 percent of each remaining in woodland. In contrast, almost 70 percent of Parker soils are in woodland, with less than 10 percent in agriculture.

Soils derived from limestone, in particular, have long been valued for their agricultural productivity. Washington soils, formed in pre-Wisconsin-age till and colluvium that is dominated by limestone gravel, are among the best agricultural soils in northern New Jersey (Tedrow 1986) (fig. 3.1; table 3.1). Bartley is the moderately well-drained associate. The nature of the parent rock, specifically the proportion of limestone to siliceous rock such as shale or sandstone, affects soil properties and serves as one criterion for separating the residual soils. In the formation of these soils, the limestone dissolves, and the siliceous "impurities" remain. In general, the higher the percentage of limestone in the rock, the higher the clay content and the redder the color (due to higher hematite content) of the resulting soils (Ciolkosz et al. 1995). In the Pennsylvania Highlands and surrounding valleys, the residual soils from siliceous limestone include Duffield, Murrill (colluvium along the edge of the valley), and Clarksburg (moderately well drained). These are yellow soils with up to 35 percent clay. The Oley Valley, nestled between the arms of the Reading Prong in Berks County, is dominated by Duffield soils. The valley's soils are rich, well drained, and easily worked, making for prime agricultural land that is intensively farmed to this day (see plate 3) (Pennsylvania Department of Conservation and Natural Resources 2002).

Adjacent to the eastern edge of the Highlands in New Jersey and Pennsylvania is the Piedmont physiographic region, which is underlain by Triassic (Newark) Basin with red sedimentary and associated igneous rocks. Soils in the former, where the persistent color is inherited from the parent rock, generally show little in the way of horizon differentiation. These soils are acidic, nutrient poor, and susceptible to erosion, and they can be droughty, but are still widely used for agriculture. These residual soils are generally differentiated by rock type and depth to bedrock. Important agricultural soils on red shale include the moderately deep (to bedrock) Penn and the moderately well-drained Readington. Arendtsville (formed on more acidic materials) and Pattenburg (high in rock fragments) are important agricultural soils on conglomerate. Soils derived from the dark-colored (mafic) igneous rocks have better chemical and physical properties for crop growth, although steep slopes and stoniness can limit agricultural value. Neshaminy (well-drained) and Mount Lucas (moderately well-drained and somewhat poorly drained) soils are the main agricultural soils. Associated poorly drained soils are To-whee in the upland flats and depressions and Bowmansville on flood plains formed in recent alluvial deposits.

Conclusions

While many soil properties such as depth of the parent material, moisture conditions, organic components, and soil profile morphology tend to change within short distances, there are some general patterns across the Highlands. Soils formed from the crystalline bedrock or the corresponding glacial drift are generally poorly suited for agriculture owing to their acid nature, steep slopes, shallow depth to bedrock, and rocky character. Similarly, these soils may provide impediments to urban development by inhibiting septic percolation as well as increasing engineering and construction costs. Interfingered in some of the main interior valleys as well as the neighboring valleys outside the Highlands proper are richer, deeper soils derived from limestone and other sedimentary rocks that are eminently suited for agriculture. The gentler terrain and deeper soils make these Highland valleys more suitable for urban development as well. Nevertheless, even in the valleys, the character of the soils must still be considered in land-use decisions. Soils formed on glacial meltwater deposits are often unsuited for septic systems because the rapid permeability through the excessively coarse substratum poses a high risk for groundwater pollution. The slow permeability and high water table of wetland soils generally make them unsuitable for urban development. As will be seen in the chapters 6 and 12, the character of the soils and terrain was an important determinant of later European settlement patterns and consequent agricultural and development history.

References

Ciolkosz, E. J., R. C. Cronce, W. D. Sevon, and W. J. Waltman. 1995. "Genesis of Pennsylvania's Limestone Soils." University Park: Pennsylvania State University Agronomy Series No. 135.

Ciolkosz, E. J., W. J. Waltman, T. W. Simpson, and R. R. Dobos. 1989. "Distribution and Genesis of Soils of the Northeastern United States." *Geomorphology* 2:285–302.

Cline, M. G. 1955. "Soil and Soil Associations of New York." Cornell Extension Bulletin 930.

Cline, M. G., and R. L. Marshall. 1977. "General Soils Map of New York State." Ithaca, NY: Cornell University.

Cook, G. H. 1874. "The Soils of New Jersey—Their Origin and Distribution. First Annual Report of the N.J. State Board of Agriculture." Legislature document paper 30:11–54.

Eby, C. E. 1976. "Soil Survey of Morris County, New Jersey." Washington, DC: U.S. Government Printing Office.

Jennings, H. 1914. "Field Operations of 1911. Soil Survey of the Sussex Area, New Jersey." Washington, DC: U.S. Government Printing Office, USDA Bureau of Soils.

Krebs, R. D., and J.C.F. Tedrow. 1957. "Genesis of Three Soils Derived from Wisconsin Till in New Jersey." *Soil Science* 83:207–218.

———. 1958. "Genesis of Red-Yellow Podzolic and Related Soils in New Jersey." *Soil Science* 85:28–37.

Lee, L. L., J. E. Tine, and R. L. Gillett. 1925. "Soil Survey of the Bergen Area, New Jersey." U.S. Government Printing Office, USDA Bureau of Chemistry and Soils.

MacClintock, P. 1940. "Weathering of the Jerseyan Till." *Geological Society America Bulletin* 51:103–116.

———. 1954. "Leaching of Wisconsin Glacial Gravels in Eastern North America." *Geological Society of America Bulletin* 65:369–384.

Olsson, K. S. 1981. "Soil Survey of Orange County, New York." Washington, DC: U.S. Government Printing Office, USDA Soil Conservation Service.

Patrick, A. L. 1920. "Field Operations of 1917: Soil Survey of the Belvidere Area, New Jersey." Washington, DC: U.S. Government Printing Office, USDA Bureau of Soils.

———. 1923. "Field Operations of 1919: Soil Survey of the Bernardsville Area, New Jersey." Washington, DC: U.S. Government Printing. Office, USDA Bureau of Soils.

Pennsylvania Department of Conservation and Natural Resources. 2002. "Land Resources: Manatawny Creek." Pennsylvania Rivers Registry Number 41. http://www.dcnr.state.pa.us/brc/rivers/riversconservation/registry/manland.pdf.

Quakenbush, G. A. 1955. "Our New Jersey Land." New Jersey Agricultural Experiment Station Bulletin 775.

Salisbury, R. D. 1902. "The Glacial Geology of New Jersey." Final Report of the State Geologist, vol. V. Trenton, New Jersey.

Simonson, R. W. 1959. "Outline of a Generalized Theory of Soil Genesis." *Soil Science Society of America Proceedings* 23:152–156.

Soil Survey Staff. 1999. "Soil Taxonomy: A Basic System of Soil Classification for Making and Interpreting Soil Surveys." 2nd ed. Natural Resources Conservation Service. U.S. Department of Agriculture Handbook 436.

Tedrow, J.C.F. 1986. *Soils of New Jersey*. Malabar, FL: Kreiger Publishing.

Waksman, S. A., H. Schulhoff, C. A. Hickman, T. C. Cordon, and S. C. Stevens. 1943. "The Peats of New Jersey and Their Utilization." Trenton: New Jersey Department Conservation and Development Bulletin 56b.

Part II

Water and Watersheds

Clean and abundant water is a resource that we often take for granted in the humid northeastern United States. Turn on the tap, and as long as drinkable water flows out, that is the end of story for many of us. However, as the two chapters in this next section make abundantly clear, the backstory behind water is much more complex and much more interesting. Indeed, many consider water as *the* critical resource in the present-day Highlands; many of the fights over land (as we see in chapter 14 of this book) are in reality fights over water. While iron may have been the key Highlands commodity in the nineteenth century, water has become the key commodity of the twentieth century and will likely remain so in the twenty-first century.

Chapter 4 discusses the importance of the hydrological cycle in determining the quality and quality of both the surface and groundwater in the Highlands. The region's abundant precipitation either infiltrates the surface to become groundwater or runs off across the surface to a neighboring stream. Whereas water can infiltrate between the grains of porous sedimentary rocks, water has a hard time infiltrating through the tightly knit crystalline matrix of the gneiss bedrock so characteristic of the Highlands. Instead of moving through the rock matrix (and consequently being filtered in transit), water moves through the open conduits formed by the many fractures. As a result, these so-called fractured rock aquifers do not store large amounts of water, and the groundwater that is there can be easily compromised. Where they occur, valley-fill aquifers are sources of large amounts of readily available water, but this groundwater is also easily polluted. One of the most important twists about the Highlands is that most of the surface water supplies stored in the region's many reservoirs are exported beyond the Highlands proper to serve the citizens of the broader mid-Atlantic and southern New England metropolitan region. Residents living within the Highlands rely primarily on groundwater pumped from wells.

The connection between human alteration of the landscape (through development and agriculture) and the consequent degradation of the region's water quality is a critical issue. As discussed in chapter 5, the mid-1800s brought increasing recognition that water-borne disease constituted a major public health challenge and that protecting watersheds protected public health. Metropolitan governments outside the Highlands looked to the Highlands as the ideal nearby location to acquire watershed land and to situate reservoirs. A complex system of reservoirs and interconnections to move water around has evolved over the past century and a half. While the Highlands produce millions of gallons of water per day, water supplies have been highly taxed during periods of prolonged drought, leading to shortages and severe water use restrictions. More recently, the concept of water rights has expanded to ensure sufficient releases of water to sustain downstream aquatic ecosystems. With the increasing competition for the remaining open lands, there are fewer prospects of building new reservoirs, thus engendering a greater emphasis on management and protection of existing supplies. The best strategy in the long term is to preserve the integrity of the Highlands watersheds and aquifer recharge zones by minimizing development and keeping these areas as protected open space. By harnessing the natural filtration capacity of the region's forests and wetlands, we can minimize expensive investments in water filtration and treatment facilities.

4

Groundwater and Surface Water Hydrology

Otto S. Zapecza, Donald E. Rice, and Vincent T. dePaul

Introduction

Highlands water has long been recognized as a critical resource necessary to meet long-term public water-supply needs. As early as the nineteenth century, prior to the construction of major reservoirs, water-supply reports began documenting the region's potential as an important source of water for the developing urban centers in northeastern New Jersey and New York City (Vermeule 1894; La Forge 1905). These studies urged conservation, noting the natural advantages of the region as a collecting ground owing to its many natural storage basins, abundant rainfall, and elevation, which allowed for economical delivery of water by gravity flow to the growing population centers immediately to the east.

The Highlands Coalition has estimated that the Highlands region of Pennsylvania, New Jersey, New York, and Connecticut provides and protects water for more than 15 million people. Large population centers in New York City and New Jersey alone are dependent on much of the water supply provided by Highlands sources. As discussed in greater detail in chapter 5, major reservoir systems within the New Jersey, New York, and Connecticut Highlands supply more than 640 million gallons of water per day (mgd). Almost 90 percent of this surface water is exported from the Highlands to supply the adjacent major metropolitan areas. Groundwater is the primary source of water supply for businesses and residents within the Highlands region. Highlands aquifers supply more than 280 mgd of groundwater for public, domestic, irrigation, commercial, and industrial uses.

The Highlands natural landscapes and undisturbed forests protect water quality in aquifers and streams; however, Highlands watersheds and the water they protect are considered to be at risk based on indicators such as increasing impervious surface, urban runoff, population growth, land-use change, and hydrologic modification of streams. An understanding of the region's groundwater and surface hydrology, the science behind the resource, provides a basis for making informed water-supply planning and management decisions, which can ensure a sustainable supply of clean water for human needs while maintaining the region's stream habitat and ecological health.

The Groundwater System

Groundwater is the primary source of water used within the Highlands region. The characteristics of Highlands aquifers and the function of the groundwater flow system are directly related to the underlying geology and soils that control the infiltration, storage, movement, availability, and chemistry of water. The geologic nature and prevalent soil types of the Highlands region are presented in chapters 1 through 3.

Highlands Aquifers

Highlands aquifers are classified in two categories: bedrock and glacial valley fill. Bedrock aquifers include those composed of crystalline metamorphic rock and those composed of sedimentary limestone, sandstone, and shale. Groundwater flow in bedrock aquifers is through a complex series of interconnected fractures, joints, solution openings, and bedding planes. Low storage capacity and well yields typify these aquifers owing to the smaller volume of interconnected openings in consolidated bedrock when compared to the porous sand and gravel of valley-fill aquifers. Carbonate aquifers composed of limestone or dolomite with larger solution openings can provide substantially higher well yields than other bedrock aquifers, particularly where overlain by the more permeable sand and gravel of glacial valley-fill deposits. Glacial valley-fill aquifers are composed mainly of permeable sand and gravel deposits, and like carbonate aquifers they are typified by higher well yields. The distribution of bedrock and glacial valley-fill aquifers in the Highlands region is shown in plate 4.

Crystalline rock aquifers are composed of crystalline metamorphosed sedimentary and igneous rocks of Precambrian age and are exposed over more than 50 percent of the region. Rock types consist primarily of coarse-grained gneiss, schist, and granite of various mineral composition. Fine-grained metamorphic slates such as phyllite are common in New York State. Crystalline rocks are typically more resistant to erosion than other rock types and form the upland regions. Crystalline rocks generally provide the high elevations and relief typical of Highlands topography. Production wells in crystalline rock aquifers commonly yield ten to one hundred gallons of water per minute.

Carbonate rock aquifers are composed predominantly of Paleozoic-age limestones and dolomites and are exposed over 18 percent of the region. These rock types are less resistant to erosion and are subject to dissolution and therefore found on the valley floors interspersed between more resistant crystalline and clastic (sedimentary) rocks that form the valley walls. Production wells in carbonate rock aquifers typically yield one hundred to five hundred gallons per minute and may locally yield more than one thousand gallons per minute where large solution openings are present.

Clastic rock aquifers are composed of Paleozoic-age sedimentary sandstone, shale, conglomerates, and quartzite and are exposed over about 6 percent of the region. These rock types locally overlie carbonates in some valleys. The more erosion-resistant clastic rocks form predominant northeast-to-southwest-trending ridges known locally in New Jersey and New York as Green Pond, Bearfort, Kanouse, and Bellvale mountains. Clastic rock aquifers yield quantities of water similar to those of crystalline rock aquifers.

Newark Basin aquifers of Mesozoic age are composed mainly of sandstone and shale formations of the Newark Supergroup. These aquifers are exposed over about 25 percent of the region. Other Newark Basin rock types present include conglomerates, basalt, and diabase. Newark Basin aquifers are exposed over approximately 10 percent of the area within the Highlands Conservation Act boundary in Connecticut, New York, and New Jersey, but they make up almost 48 percent of the Highlands region in Pennsylvania. Locally these aquifers go by the name of the Gettysburg Basin in Pennsylvania and the Hartford Basin in Connecticut. Production wells in Newark Basin aquifers commonly yield fifty to two hundred gallons of water per minute.

Glacial valley-fill aquifers, a by-product of the Wisconsinan glaciation, are composed primarily of unconsolidated sand and gravel (see fig. 2.5). These aquifers form narrow belt-like deposits of small areal extent in New Jersey, New York, and Connecticut. Glacial valley-fill aquifers comprise channels up to three hundred feet thick in parts of the Highlands and can store and transmit substantial quantities of water. Valley-fill aquifers commonly yield five hundred to one thousand gallons of water per minute to individual wells and may locally exceed two thousand gallons per minute.

Groundwater Flow—Recharge and Discharge

Precipitation is the primary source of water in Highlands aquifers. Groundwater moves along flow paths of varying length, depth, and travel time from areas of recharge to areas of discharge in the groundwater system. Aquifer recharge can be highly variable because it is determined by local precipitation and seasonal evapotranspiration rates, influenced by topographic relief, and based on the capacity of the land surface to accept infiltrating water. Permeability, or the degree to which aquifers in the Highlands have the ability to store and transmit water, is based on the amount and connectivity of openings in the underlying bedrock or sediment.

Highlands bedrock aquifers (fig. 4.1) are recharged from precipitation that infiltrates downward through the overlying soil and into fractures, joints, solution openings, or bedding plane partings in the underlying bedrock. Groundwater in bedrock aquifers naturally flows in a circuitous route through these

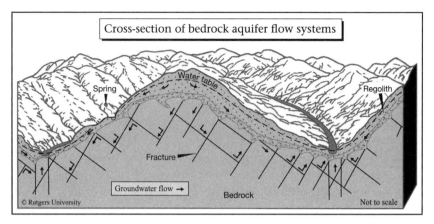

Figure 4.1. Cross-section of bedrock aquifer flow systems. © Rutgers University.

rock openings from upland recharge areas to discharge areas at lower altitudes such as springs, streams, and wetlands. Well yields are dependent on the degree of interconnectivity of these openings, the thickness and permeability of the regolith (an unconsolidated overlying layer composed of soil, weathered bedrock, or alluvium), and the amount of water available in storage.

Highlands glacial valley-fill aquifers (fig. 4.2) receive much of their recharge from precipitation that falls on the surrounding uplands that are underlain by till or bedrock, both of which are less permeable than the valley-fill deposits. Some recharge is by infiltration of precipitation that falls directly on the valley floor, and some is by inflow from the adjacent bedrock. The low permeability and steep slopes of the adjacent mountains restrict the infiltration of precipitation, so most of the precipitation that falls on the mountains flows overland to their base and infiltrates into the highly permeable glacial sediments near the valley wall (Voronin and Rice 1996). The sources of recharge to the aquifer system are also the sources of water reaching supply wells. The withdrawal of water from a well causes drawdown in the aquifer thereby causing water to flow from the aquifer to the well. In some situations the sole source of water to a shallow supply well may be the precipitation that infiltrates over the contributing recharge area directly in the vicinity of the wellhead (fig. 4.2a). If a well located near a stream is pumped at a sufficiently high rate, the natural hydraulic gradient (aquifer discharging to stream) can be reversed with the resulting drawdown inducing leakage from the stream downward to the aquifer and then to the well (fig. 4.2b). If water is withdrawn from a deep well open to the valley-fill aquifer and confined from the surface by a lower-permeability clay layer, the area contributing recharge to the well will tend to be spread over a wide area and may not include the location of the wellhead itself or may not induce leakage from an overlying stream (fig. 4.2c). Wells withdrawing water from a carbonate rock aquifer that

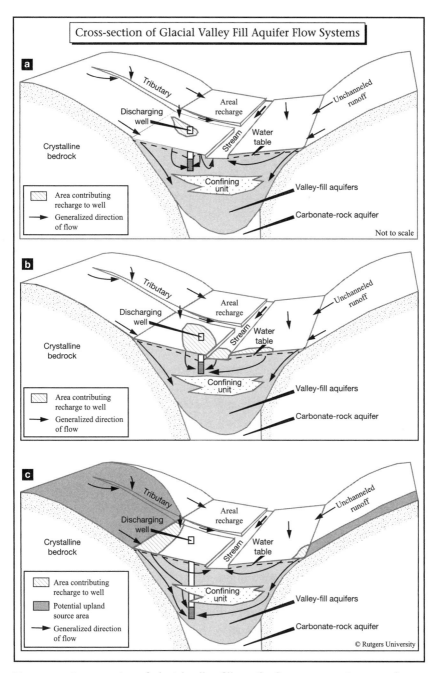

Figure 4.2. Cross-section of glacial valley-fill aquifer flow systems. Sources of water to wells: (a) area contributing recharge to a shallow well; (b) area contributing recharge to a shallow well that induces infiltration of surface water; (c) areas contributing recharge to a deep well and potential upland source areas of runoff. © Rutgers University.

underlies a valley-fill aquifer can draw significant quantities of water from the overlying valley-fill aquifer (Nicholson and Watt 1998).

Groundwater Withdrawals

The areal distribution of groundwater withdrawals from major water-supply wells in the Highlands region is shown on the map in plate 5. These wells include more than twenty-five hundred high-capacity wells that withdraw more than 213 mgd for municipal, industrial, and commercial supply, irrigation, and mining uses that report water withdrawal data to federal, state, or local agencies. Plate 5 provides information on the general location of the wells, the annual volume of withdrawal per well circa 2000, and the aquifer that each well draws water from. Areas of note include those with large-volume withdrawals, typically from glacial aquifers in New Jersey and from carbonate aquifers in Pennsylvania. Also of note is the widespread consistency of low yields from wells in crystalline rock aquifers.

Figure 4.3 provides a breakdown of reported groundwater withdrawals, circa 2000, for high-capacity wells within the Highlands region by aquifer and by state. Estimates of self-supplied domestic well withdrawals and total withdrawals for all categories are provided. All numbers are in millions of gallons per day.

Glacial valley-fill aquifers are the most productive aquifers in the Highlands region. Seventy-four million gallons per day are withdrawn from glacial aquifers in New Jersey, New York, and Connecticut, with more than 47 mgd withdrawn from these aquifers in New Jersey alone. Carbonate rock aquifers provide almost 71 mgd across the region; they are most productive in Pennsylvania, where they have the greatest areal extent, yielding 51 mgd. More than half of Pennsylvania's carbonate aquifer withdrawals are based on quarry dewatering practices that account for about 27.5 mgd. Much of this water is discharged to local streams. Crystalline rock aquifers have the greatest areal extent in the Highlands region but are significantly lower yielding, providing just less than 24 million gallons total. Clastic rock aquifers, because of their very limited extent and low yields, account for less than 5 mgd. Newark Basin aquifers provide almost 19 mgd in the Pennsylvania Highlands, where they have a large areal extent. More than 16 mgd are withdrawn from Newark Basin aquifers in the New York Highlands, mostly from a relatively small area in and around Rockland County (plate 5).

Self-supplied domestic well withdrawals are rarely measured or reported but are a significant source of potable water (drinking water) because of the rural nature of the Highlands region. Per capita use coefficients that generally range from 60 to 85 gallons per day per person can be used to estimate self-supplied withdrawals based on the percentage of self-supplied population in each municipality provided by U.S. census data. Using this method, self-supplied domestic withdrawals are estimated to be almost 68 mgd. Figure 4.3

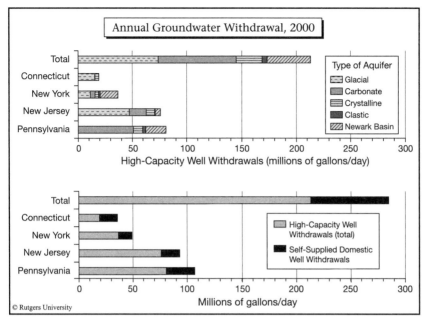

Figure 4.3. Groundwater withdrawals by aquifer and by state, 2000. © Rutgers University.

provides estimated totals for each state. The distribution of estimated self-supplied domestic withdrawals is shown by municipality on the map in plate 6. Areas with the largest self-supplied domestic withdrawals occur in Vernon Township in Sussex County and West Milford Township in Passaic County, New Jersey; East Fishkill in Dutchess County, New York; and Danbury in Fairfield County, Connecticut. Municipalities with low domestic water use are either rural with low population, such as northwestern Litchfield County in Connecticut, or are predominantly served by public supply sources, such as eastern Morris County, New Jersey.

Surface Water Systems

Highlands surface water bodies, including streams, rivers, lakes, and reservoirs, are a crucial source of water for human and ecological needs. More than 750 mgd are withdrawn from Highlands surface water sources, primarily reservoirs that are spread across the four-state region. Most reservoir usage within the Pennsylvania Highlands is by Highlands residents within that state. However, almost 90 percent of the 640 mgd of water withdrawn from reservoirs in the New Jersey, New York, and the Connecticut Highlands is transferred to hundreds of communities outside the Highlands region. Highlands streams, rivers, and lakes also provide critical habitats for fish, plants, and wildlife; offer abundant recreational opportunities; and contribute to the scenic and aesthetic qualities of the region. An in-depth view of surface water supplies and major reservoir systems of the Highlands is presented in chapter 5.

Principal River Basins

The rivers and streams within the Highlands are contained within twelve major river basins (see plate 7). In Pennsylvania these basins include the Susquehanna, Schuylkill, Brandywine, Lehigh, and Delaware. Major tributaries in the Susquehanna River basin are the Conestoga River and the Conewago, Pequea, Octoraro, and Chickies creeks. In New Jersey the principal basins include the Upper Delaware, Raritan, Passaic, and Wallkill. The Upper Delaware basin has three major Highlands streams that discharge to the Delaware River: the Pequest River, the Musconetcong River, and Pohatcong Creek. Highlands rivers in the Raritan basin include the Lamington River, North Branch Raritan River, and South Branch Raritan River. The major Highlands rivers of the Passaic basin are the Pompton, Rockaway, Whippany, Pequannock, and Ramapo rivers. Originating in New Jersey, the Wallkill River drains northward into New York State and into the Hudson River. The principal river basins in the New York Highlands also include the northern part of the Passaic basin drained by the Ramapo River, a major tributary to the Passaic, and the Fishkill and Croton basins, both with rivers draining southwestward into the Hudson River. Principal basins in the Connecticut Highlands include the Housatonic and Farmington, both with rivers that drain into Long Island Sound.

Headwater Streams

Three major rivers, the Susquehanna, Delaware, and Hudson, transect the Highlands, flowing southward through the region for as much as thirty miles on the way to the Atlantic Ocean. The environmental importance of the Highlands surface water systems, however, is the network of headwater streams that profoundly influence the downstream quality of larger streams, rivers, lakes, and reservoirs. A headwater stream is a small stream that has no more than one stream flowing into it, and such streams are the origins of larger rivers. The Highlands are the headwaters area of large river systems such as the Passaic, Raritan, and Wallkill in New Jersey and New York.

Headwater streams provide critical ecological services such as sediment, nutrient, and flood control, wildlife habitat, and high-quality water supply to downstream higher-order streams. Headwater streams with vegetated buffers help to reduce sediment delivery to larger streams, thereby reducing siltation, dredging costs, and flood frequency. These buffered areas also reduce delivery of excess nutrients and other contaminants, which improves recreational opportunities and reduces water-treatment costs, human-health risks, and degradation of downstream waters. Headwater streams and their adjacent vegetation provide areas for wildlife habitat and add protection and essential food materials for downstream segments while increasing ecosystem diversity. Headwater streams generally begin in steeper terrain and have small basin areas very sensitive to land-use change. They are sentinels of the Highlands surface water system.

Streamflow Monitoring

Streamflow commonly is measured at a gaging station—a structure located on the banks of a stream. A continuous-record gaging station records stream stage data at regular intervals throughout the day (Wahl, Thomas, and Hirsch 1995). The data, usually collected at fifteen-minute intervals, are used to compute daily mean-flow values. The rates of flow are expressed in cubic feet per second (cfs) and define the quantity and variability of streamflow passing the station. One "cfs" is equal to a volume of water one foot high and one foot wide flowing a distance of one foot in one second, the equivalent of 7.48 gallons of water flowing each second. Streamflow records integrate the effects of climate, topography, geology, land use, and human activities within a watershed and show the distribution and magnitude of stream discharge in time.

Most modern gaging stations provide streamflow-discharge data on a real-time basis through satellite, radio, and telephone telemetry. When flooding occurs, stream gages are indispensable as tools for flood forecasting and warning along rivers and streams. Time-critical streamflow data are also used for up-to-date observations of drought conditions for the optimum management of water supplies and provide information on current stage and flow conditions for fisherman, canoeists, kayakers, boaters, and other recreational users.

Historical streamflow records compiled over many decades provide the long-term statistics needed by engineers, water managers, and planners. High-flow statistics are used to design bridges, dams, and flood-control structures, and low-flow statistics are used for allocating surface water withdrawals, estimating groundwater availability in watersheds, and for setting waste-load allocation limits. The statistics are also a critical part of studies of total maximum daily loads. As of 2009, there were sixty-two continuous streamflow-gaging stations in the Highlands region operated and maintained by the U.S. Geological Survey (USGS) in cooperation with other federal, state, and local agencies (plate 7). Many of these stations have been operating since the 1920s or 1930s. Real-time and historical streamflow data for both active and discontinued gaging stations are stored in the USGS National Water Information System, which is available at http://waterdata.usgs.gov/nwis/sw/.

Climatic Factors—Streamflow Variability

The constant movement of water through a watershed, also known as the hydrologic cycle (fig. 4.4), is driven by the precipitation that falls on the land surface. About half of the precipitation that the Highlands receives is lost to the atmosphere through evapotranspiration. The remainder of the precipitation either infiltrates into the ground and recharges groundwater or runs off the land surface to surface water sources during storms or snowmelt. The groundwater in turn discharges to streams, which is known as stream baseflow, and over the long term generally equals the amount of water infiltration or recharge into the ground. Stream baseflow is responsible for maintaining flow in streams even during prolonged dry periods and comprises the predominant amount of water in most Highlands streams. Precipitation and seasonal climatic conditions control the natural variability of streamflow.

Seasonal Variability

The amount of precipitation the Highlands receives varies geographically based mainly on topography, and generally averages forty-one to fifty-eight inches per year across the region (see plate 8). The areas of highest elevation generally receive the most precipitation. Precipitation in the Highlands does not exhibit a significant seasonal pattern and is distributed fairly uniformly throughout the year. However, streamflow does vary seasonally. The seasonal pattern of streamflow for relatively unregulated rivers in the Highlands is exemplified in the bar graph of average monthly discharge recorded at a stream gage on the South Branch of the Raritan River near High Bridge in Hunterdon County, New Jersey, shown in figure 4.5. During December through February, precipitation can be either rain or snow, and streamflow rates differ accordingly. During March and April the saturated condition of the soil,

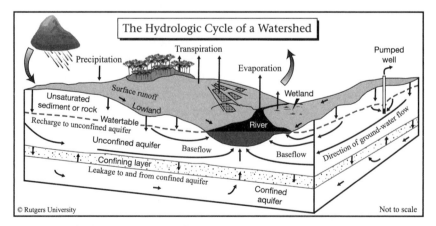

Figure 4.4. The hydrologic cycle of a watershed. © Rutgers University.

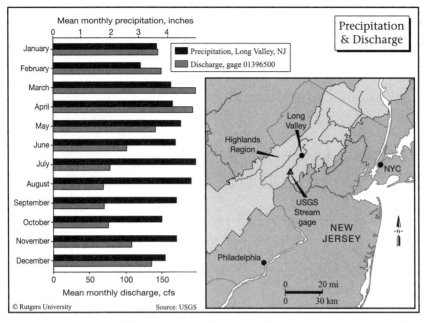

Figure 4.5. Mean monthly precipitation for Long Valley, N.J., and mean monthly discharge for USGS gaging station 01396500 (South Branch Raritan River near High Bridge, N.J.). *Source:* USGS. © Rutgers University.

greatly reduced evapotranspiration, and snowmelt may cause high rates of runoff. The May through October period is usually marked by low rates of streamflow because of increased evapotranspiration and the increased absorptive capacity of soils. Although local flooding is more common in the spring, extremely high flows and floods can result from large thunderstorms and hurricanes during the summer and early fall. During the fall, stream runoff typically increases in response to the decrease in evapotranspiration after the first killing frost.

Annual Variability

On a year-to-year basis over the past century, precipitation in the Highlands has varied as much as ten to fifteen inches from annual averages. The annual variability in precipitation significantly affects annual totals of stream discharge specifically in very wet or prolonged dry periods, as shown in figure 4.6. These variations in turn affect the quantity and quality of water available downstream. Long-term streamflow records throughout the Highlands show that during the drought of record (1961–1966) total annual stream discharge averaged 40 to 70 percent less than long-term averages. During unusually wet years, such as 1952, 1975, 1984, and 1996, total annual stream discharge was 70 to 90 percent greater than long-term averages. Floods and droughts

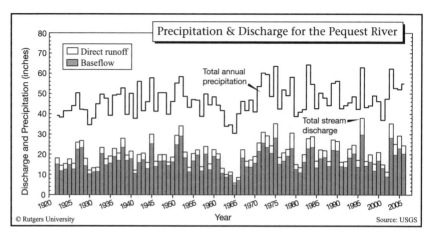

Figure 4.6. Relation of total annual precipitation to total annual stream discharge, baseflow, and direct runoff for the Pequest River in Pequest, Warren County, N.J. *Source*: USGS. © Rutgers University.

affect the quality of surface water. During floods, large quantities of pollutants are washed into streams, but because of the large volume and velocity of the water, the pollutants are diluted and move quickly downstream. During droughts, however, streamflows may not be sufficient to dilute effluents from industries, sewage treatment plants, and contaminants that may be in the groundwater that is discharging to streams.

An important factor when considering streamflow variability and trends in the Highlands region is the substantial upward trend in precipitation for much of the mid-Atlantic area as well as most of the eastern United States (Lins 2005). Average annual precipitation values from the Office of the New Jersey State Climatologist for northern New Jersey Climate Division 1, which includes all of the New Jersey Highlands, show that during the period 1971–2000 annual precipitation averaged about 5 inches more than during the 1895–1970 period, whereas the 2001–2007 period averaged about 7 inches more than the 1895–1970 period (i.e., 1895–1970: 44.6 inches; 1971–2000: 49.8 inches; 2001–2007: 51.8 inches). Average annual temperatures for Northern New Jersey Climate Division 1 show a warming trend of 2 degrees Fahrenheit for the 2001–2007 period in comparison to average annual temperatures for the 1895–1970 period (i.e., 1895–1970: 50.6°F; 1971–2000: 50.9°F; 2001–2007: 52.6°F).

Total annual streamflow for a period of eighty-four years (1922–2006), recorded at a gaging station on the Pequest River in Pequest, Warren County, New Jersey, is shown in figure 4.6 and is compared to local annual precipitation for the period. The steplike increase in streamflow after 1970 shown in figure 4.6 mimics the increase in precipitation over the period. The direct relationship of annual precipitation to annual stream discharge for the Pequest River is similar to that which occurs over most of the Highlands region. About half the precipitation that falls on the watershed leaves the watershed as stream discharge. Most of the remainder that does not discharge as streamflow leaves the basin as evapotranspiration. Of particular importance are the two components of streamflow. Baseflow, the groundwater component of streamflow, makes up about 83 percent of total stream discharge, and direct overland runoff of precipitation makes up the remaining 17 percent. Also of note is that there is only a slight variation in the percentage of these two components over the entire period. Although baseflow and runoff percentages remain fairly consistent within the same watershed, baseflow and runoff percentages vary from watershed to watershed and are important indicators of dependable groundwater and surface water yields, changing hydrologic conditions, and watersheds in transition.

Watersheds in Transition

The forested ridges, wetlands, and valleys within the Highlands provide crucial ecological services by economically purifying, protecting, and storing large quantities of water. Highlands undisturbed landscapes promote healthy in-stream habitats and aid in the prevention of costly downstream flooding and soil erosion. Conversely, human activities such as land-use change, forest fragmentation, population growth, and urbanization are major factors in changing hydrologic and environmental conditions within watersheds. These changes can affect the quality, quantity, and distribution of water recharging an aquifer or running overland to streams. An increase in impervious surfaces such as parking lots, buildings, and roads decreases the amount of land through which precipitation can infiltrate and recharge an aquifer. Water that cannot infiltrate into the ground increases the amount of runoff, potentially increasing the rate of soil erosion, flood frequency, and surface water contamination. The loss of recharge water also changes the timing of streamflow. Less water flows to streams during dry periods as baseflow, whereas more water flows to streams during wet periods as immediate runoff. These changes in the hydrology of a watershed are accompanied by ecological and hydrological impacts: increased flooding during high-intensity rainstorms, decreased water-supply storage during droughts, degraded water quality, and ensuing ecosystem stresses.

As human activities alter the hydrology of Highlands watersheds, changes in groundwater levels, streamflow characteristics, biotic integrity, and stream health are key indicators of changing watershed conditions. Long-term systematic measurements of groundwater levels and streamflow conditions, including water quality and ecosystem analysis, provide the essential data needed to evaluate changes in the resource over time, forecast trends, and monitor the effectiveness of water management and protection strategies. Examples of monitored changes and potential trends are provided in the following sections.

Groundwater Level Trends

Groundwater systems are dynamic and adjust continually to short-term and long-term changes in climate, groundwater withdrawal, and land use. Water-level measurements from observation wells are the principal source of information about hydrologic stresses acting on aquifers and how these stresses affect groundwater recharge, storage, and discharge.

Chart A in figure 4.7 shows four groundwater-level hydrographs (a graph showing changes in water level or discharge over a period of time) from selected monitoring wells in Morris County, New Jersey, with long-term continuous daily records. These hydrographs show typical fluctuations of water levels within the various aquifers of the New Jersey Highlands over a period beginning in the early 1990s through 2008. Water levels typically are highest in winter and early spring as a result of reduced evapotranspiration, low temperatures, snowmelt, and spring rains that recharge the aquifers. Groundwater levels typically start to decline as summer begins and continue to decline through late fall. Groundwater withdrawals are highest in summer when water is used for irrigation and recreation, and when evaporation and transpiration rates are highest. Water levels typically are lowest in late fall and rise again during winter, completing the cycle. Of note are the aquifers' responses to periods of prolonged drought such as during mid-1994 to late 1995, mid-1998 to mid-1999, and mid-2001 through 2002. Water levels fell approximately five to twenty feet on average during these periods. Shallow wells that draw water from levels just below the water table could experience problems with water yield or go dry during prolonged periods of drought.

Chart B of figure 4.7 shows a water-level hydrograph from a well in East Hanover Township, Morris County, New Jersey. This well is screened in the glacial valley-fill aquifer within the Whippany River Basin. The hydrograph shows the effect of long-term withdrawals on aquifer water levels from 1966 through 2008. The declining water levels are a result of groundwater withdrawals from the aquifer exceeding the natural recharge rate of the aquifer. The sharp rise in water levels beginning in 2003 is attributed to reduced withdrawals from the aquifer and use of alternative surface-water sources.

Stream Baseflow

The availability and sustainability of Highlands water resources are dependent on stream baseflow (that part of a stream's discharge that is attributable to groundwater rather than surface runoff) (fig. 4.4). The amount of base-

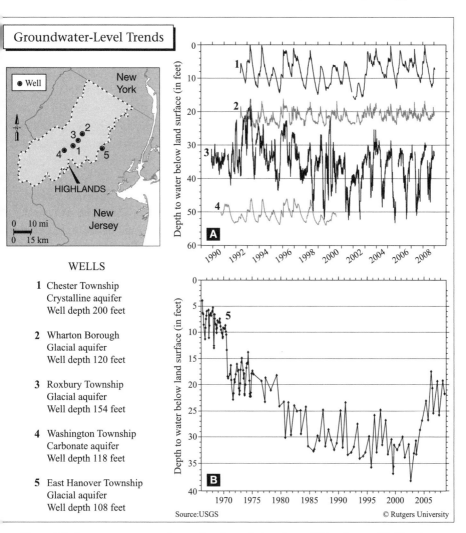

Groundwater-Level Trends

WELLS

1 Chester Township
Crystalline aquifer
Well depth 200 feet

2 Wharton Borough
Glacial aquifer
Well depth 120 feet

3 Roxbury Township
Glacial aquifer
Well depth 154 feet

4 Washington Township
Carbonate aquifer
Well depth 118 feet

5 East Hanover Township
Glacial aquifer
Well depth 108 feet

Source:USGS   © Rutgers University

Figure 4.7. Long-term groundwater-level trends in selected New Jersey Highlands aquifers. *Source*: USGS. © Rutgers University.

flow provided to streams within Highlands watersheds is an indicator of the water-yielding capacity of the aquifer or aquifers that provide the baseflow and the ability of the stream to sustain flow. Under natural conditions, the amount of streamflow composed of baseflow is controlled by the amount of precipitation recharging the groundwater system, the infiltration capacity of the soil, and the ability of underlying aquifers to store and transmit water. The amount of total streamflow that is composed of baseflow versus the amount that is composed of runoff can be modified by land-use changes that reduce recharge and increase surface runoff. These changes can include new buildings, paving, soil compaction, and other development activities. With-drawal of water from wells or ponds and leakage to sewers can also reduce the amount of groundwater available for discharge to streams. Maintaining stream baseflow is crucial to maintaining stream temperatures, stream qual-ity, habitat, and aquatic life.

Plate 9 shows the regional distribution in baseflow characteristics of subwatersheds within the Highlands region circa 2000. The percentage of streamflow composed of baseflow, also known as the baseflow index, was cal-culated for 333 subwatersheds in the region using computer simulation rain-fall-runoff models. The models incorporate detailed climatic, topographic, geologic, land cover, and soils data and are calibrated to long-term stream gage data. The models were developed by the USGS to support a regional update of conditions and resources within the Highlands by the U.S. Forest Service (2002 and 2010).

Model results indicate that, on average, baseflow comprises 68 percent of streamflow over the Highlands region. The proportion of baseflow in a stream is strongly dependent on the geology, soils, and degree of develop-ment in the watershed. In rocky areas with little or no sediment cover and (or) with soils of low permeability, the groundwater contribution to stream-flow is small because groundwater storage capacity is minimal and infil-tration and groundwater recharge is low, or both. In areas with thick gla-cial deposits and (or) carbonate rocks with solution channels that can store large amounts of groundwater, the groundwater contribution to streamflow is large. The map in plate 9 shows that baseflow accounts for more than 80 percent of total streamflow in many of the watersheds along the western boundary of the New Jersey and New York Highlands, where many water-sheds are underlain by a high percentage of carbonate and glacial aquifers (plate 4), and in areas of Pennsylvania where carbonate aquifers are present. Wide areas of the Pennsylvania Highlands are underlain by Newark Basin aquifers composed of lower-permeability shales, sandstones, and igneous rocks. These rock types in conjunction with moderate to high degrees of development in the area yield baseflow percentages less than 60 percent. In the Connecticut Highlands, watersheds that contribute the lowest baseflow percentage to streams are dominated by low-permeability crystalline rocks and glacial till or by large areas of open surface water. Conversely, those wa-tersheds dominated by coarse-grained stratified glacial deposits, primarily in the valleys of larger rivers and streams, contribute the highest percent-age of baseflow to streams. Areas where baseflow accounts for less than 50 percent of streamflow occur in some of the most urbanized areas of the Highlands region, some with documented large groundwater withdrawals, including the Harrisburg metropolitan area in Pennsylvania; eastern Morris County, New Jersey; Rockland County, New York; and the Danbury area of Connecticut.

Changes in Watershed Hydrology

The implications of continued patterns of land-use change, urban development, rapid population growth, and forest fragmentation are major environmental concerns for the future of the Highlands and its resources, as discussed in chapter 15. To assess the effects of potential urbanization on Highlands watersheds, the USGS evaluated potential changes in streamflow and evapotranspiration that might be caused by increasing the existing (as of 1995) impervious surface cover to the amount that would be present based on a maximum build-out model developed by Rutgers University (U.S. Forest Service 2002). Computer-simulated differences between 1995 conditions and maximum build-out are shown in figure 4.8. The data points represent the degree to which baseflow, runoff, total streamflow, and evapotranspiration would change, in inches per year, in relation to the percent increase of impervious surface in each of 182 subwatersheds in the New York and New Jersey Highlands. Trend lines show the relationship of increasing impervious surface to each water budget component. As the percentage of impervious

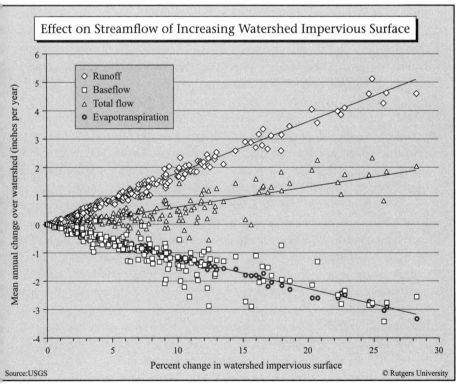

Figure 4.8. The effect of increasing watershed impervious surface on streamflow. *Source*: USGS. © Rutgers University.

surface in a watershed increases, runoff increases, baseflow decreases, total streamflow increases, and evapotranspiration decreases. The linear trend of the relation implies that changes in the components of streamflow are fairly proportional to changes in impervious surface. To bring this into perspective, average mean annual streamflow for these subwatersheds is about 25 in/yr, average baseflow is about 18.5 in/yr, and average runoff is about 6.75 in/yr. The trend line of increasing runoff suggests a potential 50 percent or more increase in stream runoff and a potential 10 percent or more decrease in stream baseflow in watersheds projected to have a greater than 15 percent increase in impervious cover over conditions in 1995. Evapotranspiration decreases in response to increased impervious cover because of the increase in surface runoff, less infiltration and lower soil moisture available for root system uptake, and the overall decrease in land area available for vegetative cover.

Biotic Integrity and Stream Health

Changing hydrologic and environmental conditions in watersheds are also measured by the status of aquatic communities such as benthic macroinvertebrates, fish, and algae. They are often used as biological indicators of stream health because of their ability to discriminate, in a predictable way, human influences on the environment while providing an effective means of gaging long-term trends in surface-water quality and in stream habitat, as related to changing flow conditions.

From their headwaters to major river confluences, Highlands streams provide an intricate array of habitats that support a highly diverse complex of aquatic organisms. Aquatic communities depend on these diverse physical habitats to supply the necessary living conditions for survival and reproduction, including clean water, current velocity, substrate complexity, dissolved oxygen, and temperature. Development of the landscape represents one of the most significant direct impacts to the structure and function of aquatic ecosystems in the Highlands. Losses of riparian and wetland areas along stream corridors, increases in sediment loads, higher water temperatures, losses of substrate complexity, increases in runoff volume, and increases in contaminants as a result of development have been found to substantially alter the environmental condition of streams and lakes, resulting in a measurable loss of biotic integrity (Kennen and Ayers 2002). Studies by the U.S. Geological Survey's National Water-Quality Assessment program indicate that urban and suburban development, particularly when it replaces forest and wetlands, results in changes to the natural flow of streams, degradation to aquatic habitats, a reduction in biological diversity, and a shift toward less desirable invasive species that are more tolerant of disturbance (Ayers, Kennen, and Stackelberg 2000; Fisher et al. 2004).

The environmental importance of aquatic communities is recognized by the Clean Water Act, which requires states to restore and maintain the quality and biotic integrity of surface water bodies. This requirement, which is administered by the U.S. Environmental Protection Agency, has been integral in the development of statewide biologically based water-quality monitoring programs. As an example of the importance and application of these programs, results and analysis of stream biomonitoring in New Jersey are outlined below with an evaluation of aquatic community status and stream health in the Highlands.

The New Jersey Department of Environmental Protection's Ambient Biomonitoring Network (AMNET) is a statewide network of sampling sites designed to monitor the condition of benthic macroinvertebrate communities in New Jersey streams. Benthic macroinvertebrates are primarily bottom-dwelling fauna, without spinal columns, that can be seen with the naked eye. They include insects, worms, mollusks, and crustaceans, and they play an integral role in the aquatic food web. The AMNET sampling network incorporates more than 800 sites, of which 136 are currently within the New Jersey Highlands. The ecological condition of each site is assessed based on the composition of the macroinvertebrate community and the pollution tolerance levels of individual taxa. Levels of impairment (i.e., nonimpaired, moderately impaired, or severely impaired) are assigned based on the presence, diversity, and relative abundance of species collected at each sampling location. Nonimpaired sites have diverse, well-balanced macroinvertebrate communities and include the presence of pollution-sensitive species such as mayfly and stone fly nymphs, caddis fly larvae, and aquatic beetles. Impairment may be indicated by the absence of these sensitive species and by the presence of more pollution-tolerant species such as midges, aquatic sow bugs, leeches, other segmented worms, and blackfly larvae. Moderately impaired sites show alterations of the community from a pristine state with a reduction in species richness and a reduction in sensitive species. An invertebrate community that is dominated by a few pollution-tolerant species characterizes severe impairment. Three rounds of AMNET sampling have been completed. The initial round of sampling was conducted from 1992 through 1996, with a second and third round completed in 2002 and 2007, respectively.

AMNET macroinvertebrate sampling sites and levels of community impairment in relation to an urban land-use coverage for 2002 are shown in figure 4.9 (second round of sampling). The map clearly shows the strong association of urbanization with negative impacts on aquatic community health. Comparatively healthy aquatic populations are associated with Highlands waters. Streams within the Upper Delaware drainage basin as well as south of the Wisconsin terminal moraine in the Highlands were least likely to exhibit an impaired macroinvertebrate community, whereas moderate to severely impaired communities predominated in highly urbanized areas east of the Highlands in the Piedmont and Coastal Plain. This is consistent with a statistical analysis by Kennen (1998) that used data from the first round of

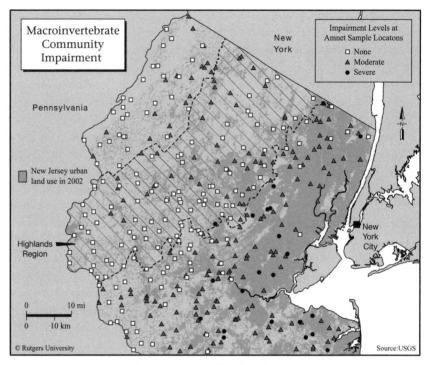

Figure 4.9. New Jersey urban land use and levels of macroinvertebrate community impairment at AMNET sampling locations. *Source:* USGS. © Rutgers University.

AMNET sampling to show the relation of benthic macroinvertebrate community impairment and watershed characteristics. The study shows that the primary factors related to degradation of benthic communities are the percentage of urban land use within the associated watershed as well as the amount of upstream wastewater discharges. Conversely, the total amount of forested land within a drainage basin, essential in maintaining a healthy stream habitat, is the best predictor of an unimpaired community. Furthermore, hydrologic factors such as reduced baseflow and increases in peak discharge commonly associated with urbanization and increasing impervious surface can substantially alter stream habitat. In an evaluation of disturbance thresholds of fish, macroinvertebrates, and algae, Kennen and Ayers (2002) calculate that moderate to severe impairment is detectable in New Jersey streams when the amount of impervious surface cover in the drainage basin reaches approximately 18 percent.

Of the AMNET sites sampled within the New Jersey Highlands, the percentage of sites that showed no impairment was 62, 66, and 57, respectively, for each of the three rounds of sampling. The percentage of sites that exhibited some degree of impairment was 38, 34, and 44, respectively, for each of the three rounds, indicating a shift to degrading conditions in some Highlands streams. Highlands waterways that have impaired communities at more than one sampling site include the Whippany River, the Rockaway River, the Wallkill River, the Musconetcong River, the upper reaches of the Pequannock River, and Pohatcong Creek. Of the non-Highlands sites sampled during the second round, 72 percent showed some degree of impairment, whereas 28 percent were nonimpaired.

Fish, much better known than their macroinvertebrate food supply, occupy the top of the aquatic food chain and are ideal indicators of changes in watershed hydrology because of their sensitivity to a wide variety of stresses associated with water quantity, quality, and habitat. A substantial measure of aquatic ecosystem health in the Highlands region is the ability of its streams to provide the high water-quality and habitat standards necessary for the survival and successful reproduction of trout. An extensive network of cold-water trout fisheries throughout the Highlands makes Highlands streams one of the most popular fishing destinations in the mid-Atlantic region as well as one of the Highlands' most valuable recreational resources. Trout inhabit only the cleanest waters, optimally characterized by a 1:1 ratio of deepwater pools and shallow-water riffles; silt-free rocky substrate; clear, cold oxygenated water with stable flow and temperature regimes (less than 65°F); and well-vegetated, stable banks with abundant in-stream cover (Hudy et al. 2008). For these reasons, state regulators commonly classify and regulate streams according to their suitability to support trout.

In New Jersey, freshwater streams are classified as trout production (natural reproduction occurring), trout maintenance (ability to support trout year round but no reproduction documented), and nontrout (habitat and/or water quality are not conducive to the presence of trout or trout-associated species) under the state's surface water-quality standards. Criteria for certain parameters including temperature, dissolved oxygen, and suspended solids are more stringent for trout waters than for nontrout waters. Trout-production waters are also awarded Category 1 status, one of the state's highest levels of protection. Category 1 designation mandates an antidegradation policy for protection from measurable changes in water quality to maintain the aesthetic value and ecological integrity of these exceptional streams. Approximately 75 percent of all trout-production waters in the state are located within the Highlands. In addition, twenty-nine of thirty-six northern New Jersey streams that have the special designation of wild trout streams are located within the Highlands. Streams designated as wild trout streams are not stocked with hatchery-reared trout, in order to eliminate potential negative effects of hatchery trout on the self-sustaining inhabitants, and have special fishing regulations regarding open season, keeper size, and catch limits to maintain desirable levels of wild trout populations. Other Highlands states have similar wild trout stream designations and management policies. Seven of Connecticut's twenty-eight wild trout management areas are found in the Highlands.

Pennsylvania is host to nearly five hundred streams and rivers designated as class A wild trout waters, of which thirty-two occur in the Highlands.

Although the Highlands continue to provide optimal stream habitat and water-quality conditions for trout production and maintenance, concerns exist about the widespread decline of native species. The eastern brook trout (*Salvelinus fontinalis*), often considered the most valuable indicator species, is the only trout species native to the region and is designated the state fish in Pennsylvania, New Jersey, and New York. In fact, recent genetic research shows that some streams within the New Jersey Highlands contain wild brook trout that are descendants of native species that first appeared following the last glacial recession, more than ten thousand years ago. The two other species of trout common to Highlands streams include the brown trout and rainbow trout, which were introduced to East Coast streams from Europe and the Pacific West Coast, respectively, in the late 1800s. The presence of native brook trout populations often signals the most pristine of conditions because they require the coldest water temperatures of the three species (preferred water temperature is 53–56°F), and they are often found in the environmentally sensitive headwater section of streams.

A comprehensive study of the distribution, status, and threats to brook trout within the eastern United States by Hudy and others (2008) documents the substantial decline of eastern brook trout populations. Brook trout have completely vanished from more than 20 percent of their historic eastern range from Maine to Georgia. In New Jersey, it was estimated that brook trout persist in less than half their original range. Declines in brook trout populations are attributed to urban land use and associated human activities that have a major influence on water quality and aquatic life. According to the study, the most significant factors considered by state fisheries experts to have affected New Jersey's native brook trout have been sedimentation, urbanization, dam inundation, stream fragmentation, high water temperature, and nonnative fish species. Dense road networks contribute to declines in water quality from sedimentation and storm water runoff. Artificial barriers such as dams and road culverts degrade natural habitats, isolate fish populations, and prevent migration to suitable spawning grounds. The destruction of forest canopy and riparian vegetation, which play a critical role in shading the water surface and maintaining cold summer water temperatures, is another contributing factor. The introduction and spread of nonnative competing fish species and the resultant interbreeding, displacement from habitats, and spread of disease has been the largest biological threat to brook trout.

Sustaining the Resource

Sustainable use of the region's water resources requires balancing the use of the resource to meet the competing needs of homes, cities, farms, and industries as requirements to leave water in streams and rivers for environmental and recreational uses expand. Under natural conditions, Highlands aquifers, streams, and watersheds maintain equilibrium and are sustained by a balancing act between precipitation and the interaction of groundwater and surface waters. Human influence on land and water alters this equilibrium and the natural hydrologic regime. A change in one part of the system, whether caused by natural climate variation, withdrawal of groundwater and surface water, or land-use change, results in a balancing response in another part of the system. Measures that mitigate or reduce the effects of human activities and land-use change on watershed hydrology, such as maintaining natural streamflow variability, retaining intact wetlands systems, and reducing sediment loads and impervious surfaces, can provide water-supply managers with regulatory tools to protect and maintain an adequate supply of clean water for human use while simultaneously preserving the biotic integrity of aquatic ecosystems.

To assess the long-term viability of the resource, it is necessary to consider the technical aspects, such as the quantity and quality of water in circulation, as well as the desire of the community to accept or limit economic, social, and environmental impacts. Perhaps the greatest challenge to maintaining a sustainable future for the region's water resources is the development of water-supply management plans, policies, and regulations that balance the many water needs of humans with the water needs of their environment. High-quality hydrologic data and sound hydrologic analysis provide a foundation upon which these plans and policies can be developed.

Acknowledgments

The authors thank Curtis Schreffler and Tammy Zimmerman of the U.S. Geological Survey's Pennsylvania Water Science Center for providing the hydrologic data for the Pennsylvania Highlands used in this chapter, and Elizabeth Ahearn and David Bjerklie of the U.S. Geological Survey's Connecticut Water Science Center for providing the hydrologic data for the Connecticut Highlands used in this chapter.

References

Ayers, M. A., J. G. Kennen, and P. E. Stackelberg. 2000. "Water Quality in the Long Island–New Jersey Coastal Drainages, New York and New Jersey, 1996–98." U.S. Geological Survey Circular 1201.

Fischer, J. M., K. Riva-Murray, E. R. Hickman, D. C. Chichester, R. A. Brightbill, K. M. Romanok, and M. D. Bilger. 2004. "Water Quality in the Delaware River Basin Pennsylvania, New Jersey, New York and Delaware, 1998–2001." U.S. Geological Survey Circular 1227.

Hudy, M., T. M. Thieling, N. Gillespie, and E. P. Smith. 2008. "Distribution, Status, and Land Use Characteristics of Subwatersheds within the Native Range of Brook Trout in the Eastern United States." *North American Journal of Fisheries Management* 28, no. 4: 1069–1085.

Kennen, J. G. 1998. "Relation of Benthic Macroinvertebrate Community Impairment to Basin Characteristics in New Jersey Streams." U.S. Geological Survey Fact Sheet FS-057-98.

Kennen, J. G., and M. A. Ayers. 2002. "Relation of Environmental Characteristics to the Composition of Aquatic Assemblages along a Gradient of Urban Land Use in New Jersey, 1996–98." U.S. Geological Survey Water Resources Investigation Report 02–4069.

La Forge, L. 1905. "Water Resources of the Central and Southwestern Highlands of New Jersey: Contributions to the Hydrology of the United States, 1904." U.S. Geological Survey Water Supply Paper 110, 141–155.

Lins, H. 2005. "Streamflow Trends in the United States." U.S. Geological Survey Fact Sheet 2005–3017.

Nicholson, R. S., and M. K. Watt. 1998. "Simulation of Groundwater Flow Patterns and Areas Contributing Recharge to Streams and Water Supply Wells in a Valley Fill and Carbonate Rock Aquifer System, Southwestern Morris County, New Jersey, 1998." U.S. Geological Survey Water Resources Investigation Report 97–4216.

United States Forest Service. 2002. "New York–New Jersey Highlands Regional Study: 2002 Update." U.S. Department of Agriculture, Forest Service, Northeastern Area State and Private Forestry, NA-TP-02–03.

United States Forest Service. 2010. "Highlands Regional Study: Connecticut and Pennsylvania 2010 Update." U.S. Department of Agriculture, Forest Service, Northeastern Area State and Private Forestry, NA-TP-01–11.

Vermeule, C. C. 1894. *Report on Water Supply, Water Power, the Flow of Streams and Attendant Phenomena*, vol. 3. Trenton, NJ: Geological Survey of New Jersey.

Voronin, L. M., and D. E. Rice. 1996. "Hydrogeology and Simulation of Groundwater Flow, Picatinny Arsenal and Vicinity, Morris County, New Jersey." U.S. Geological Survey Water Resources Investigation Report 96–4061.

Wahl, K. L., W. O. Thomas, and R. M. Hirsch. 1995. "The Stream-Gaging Program of the U.S. Geological Survey." U.S. Geological Survey Circular 1123.

In addition to the publications cited in the text and listed above, several websites were consulted:

Connecticut's Trout Management Program. Inland Fisheries Division, Connecticut Department of Environmental Protection. http://www.ct.gov/dep/lib/dep/fishing/freshwater/troutbroc.pdf.

Highlands Coalition. http://www.highlandscoalition.org/.

New Jersey Department of Environmental Protection. Ambient Biomonitoring Network, http://www.state.nj.us/dep/wms/bfbm/amnet.html.

New Jersey Department of Environmental Protection. NJDEP Surface Water Quality Standards of New Jersey (Edition 200812), (1:2,400): digital GIS data downloaded from http://www.state.nj.us/dep/gis/digidownload/zips/statewide/swqs.zip.

New Jersey Department of Environmental Protection. Surface Water Quality Standards for New Jersey (updated June 2008), N.J.A.C 7:9B, http://www.state.nj.us/dep/wms/bwqsa/swqsdocs.html.

New Jersey Division of Fish and Wildlife. "Freshwater Fishing" issue of the *Fish and Wildlife Digest*, http://www.state.nj.us/dep/fgw/digfsh09.htm#pdf.

New Jersey Division of Fish and Wildlife. "Genetic Diversity of Wild Brook Trout Populations in New Jersey: Conservation and Management Implications." http://www.njfishandwildlife.com/bkt_genetics.htm.

Office of the New Jersey State Climatologist. Monthly Climate Tables, Northern New Jersey Monthly Precipitation 1895–2008, http://climate.rutgers.edu/stateclim/

Pennsylvania Fish & Boat Commission. "Class A Wild Trout Waters." http://www.fish.state.pa.us/classa.pdf.

United States Forest Service. "Northeastern Area: The Highlands of Connecticut, New Jersey, New York, and Pennsylvania," http://www.na.fs.fed.us/highlands/.

5

Water Supply Resources

Daniel J. Van Abs

Introduction

The Highlands region is an area of both prolific and limited water-supply resources. Surface water supplies are quite abundant, primarily from reservoirs created through the damming of Highlands valleys to capture high stream flows. These supplies are predominantly used in areas outside the Highlands—primarily in New York City, the northeastern and east-central parts of New Jersey, and urban regions of western and central Connecticut.

As discussed in chapter 4, groundwater supplies from Highlands aquifers are more limited, particularly in the hard bedrock geologic formations typical of the Highlands ridges where there is minimal storage and movement of water. Most wells in these dense crystalline rock formations are able to supply only the needs of individual residences and other low-volume uses.

Only in the limestone valleys and glacial valley-fill aquifers can groundwater resources be considered prolific, but even here the contribution to regional supplies is constrained. These aquifers are located mostly in the valley areas of the Highlands, which cover only a small portion of the region. Wells in these aquifers can and do support public water-supply systems and industry but cannot provide yields equal to those of the reservoir systems.

During the 1800s the larger Highlands towns generally grew along rivers where waterpower was available from rivers and ample groundwater supplies were available from the underlying aquifers. The combination of favorable geology, topography, and low population within the Highlands region provided an opportunity in the late 1800s and early 1900s for major cities outside the Highlands to purchase inexpensive land, create reservoirs, and export potable (suitable for drinking) surface water from the region. Owing to the unavailability of surplus surface water supply, more recent suburban and exurban population growth across the Highlands region has been forced to rely on groundwater as a source of water. As a result of this land use and water resource history, most of the surface water supply goes to meet needs outside the region, while most groundwater use supports needs within the region. This chapter provides an overview of these various surface water and groundwater resources and their development pattern, and discusses how the Highlands region came to be a major exporter of water supplies.

Surface Water Supplies

Surface water supplies vary significantly from one state to another in the Highlands but in each case depend on the flow of river water into reservoirs that capture high flows and store the water until needed. This reservoir storage provides a buffer against the periodic droughts that affect the area.

Connecticut has reservoirs that provide significant supplies, primarily for the Hartford and Waterbury areas. New York City's Croton watershed reservoirs supply approximately 10 percent of its total needs. New Jersey has many Highlands reservoirs, upon which depend most of the northeastern and central urban areas that are the most densely populated portions of the state. Pennsylvania, conversely, derives almost no direct water supply from reservoirs within the Highlands, although Highlands streams do help support downstream reservoirs and water-supply intakes.

In each case, the "safe yield" of a surface water system is the amount of water, generally in millions of gallons per day, that a reservoir or group of reservoirs can provide during a hypothetical repetition of the worst known drought, called the "drought of record," while releasing sufficient water to protect downstream water uses (both human and ecological). Therefore, safe yields are dependent upon a combination of the reservoir storage capacity and incoming water during droughts, with a large reservoir in a large watershed providing greater safe yield than a small reservoir on a small watershed. As we saw in chapter 4, the hydrologic system of the Highlands includes both groundwater and surface water components that support safe yields. Groundwater flows to streams and rivers comprise much of the surface water flows to reservoirs during severe droughts. Surface water runoff during major storms augments those flows and can be critical to maintaining surface water storage.

The existing surface water reservoirs of the Highlands were nearly all developed by urban areas seeking clean and plentiful water from more rural areas after their local supplies proved inadequate, polluted, or both. Most of these urban communities are located outside the Highlands, although a few small reservoirs provide water to communities within the Highlands region. However, the historic spread of rural settlements, mining, forest cutting, and agriculture throughout most of the northeastern United States meant that these rural areas were not unused. Reservoirs were sited in valleys, which were also the locations of much of the best agricultural lands, town sites, and mill sites. The story of each large reservoir system, from the oldest New York City projects to the most recent New Jersey examples, involves extensive land acquisition and the use of eminent domain by more wealthy cities to acquire reservoir sites in agricultural or forested rural watersheds, even to the extent of removing entire villages and hamlets. Each reservoir now faces a new generation of issues as suburban and exurban development encroaches upon the watersheds of tributary streams to these formerly "distant" reservoirs.

Early in the history of urban settlement in colonial America and the United States, most towns and cities relied for water supply on streams and rivers within or bordering the cities, or on shallow, hand-dug wells within the urban area. Sanitation practices typically ranged from limited to nonexistent because the technology for even primary sewage treatment had not developed and the technology for moving sewage and storm water away from the developed areas was primitive. These limitations applied to both human sewage and the effluent from commercial enterprises within municipal limits, such as tanneries and slaughterhouses.

Inevitably, local water-supply resources were contaminated (NJDWSC 1925; CAPI 1972), often causing epidemics from waterborne diseases such as cholera that threatened urban populations. Only with the advent of drinking-water treatment technology could the contaminated supplies be made safer. Sand filtration systems were slowly adopted in the late nineteenth century by municipalities (U.S. EPA 2000), and the first municipal use of chlorination in this country did not occur until 1908 in Jersey City, New Jersey (Christman 1998). Both approaches achieved major reductions in epidemic disease from drinking water. However, these treatment technologies could not address all pollution problems. The combination of pollution and the growing water needs of cities for both human and industrial use caused the cities to look elsewhere for their water supplies.

New York City's Croton System

Early in its history, the Dutch colony of New Amsterdam and its English successor, which became New York City, depended on in-town water supplies. Shortly after the American Revolution, these supplies included wells operated by the Manhattan Company (as part of its charter that allowed banking operations, the primary focus of its founders). Later supplies were developed from surface waters in upper Manhattan Island, but these quickly became insufficient.

The growing water-supply needs of New York City and the limitations of nearby groundwater and surface water supplies led the city in 1842 to develop the Croton watershed in Westchester County as a surface water supply, the oldest such surface water supply system in the Highlands region. Initially based on a single reservoir, Croton Lake, the Croton system now is composed of ten reservoirs and three controlled lakes on a series of streams that all drain to the New Croton Reservoir (see plate 10). These reservoirs range from less than 1 billion to more than 19 billion gallons in storage capacity and in total represent nearly 90 billion gallons of storage with a composite drainage area of approximately 373 square miles. From the New Croton Reservoir, water is piped to the city and also is used in Westchester County, where much of the reservoir system lies. Two additional reservoirs in the same watershed (West Branch and Boyds Corner) were originally built as part of the Croton system upstream of the Croton Falls Reservoir but now are part of the Catskill/Delaware reservoir system and used as settling basins for water from Roundout Reservoir in the Catskills.

The development of this water supply depended on one of the earliest examples of condemnation of rural private property in the United States through eminent domain for the creation of urban water supplies. Although payments were made to landowners for their property, the use of eminent domain fomented legal challenges and abiding distrust that complicated later efforts to protect the quality of the water supply. This process of public taking of remote watershed properties continued both in the New York City watersheds and in many other areas, including New Jersey as late as the 1960s for the Raritan River reservoir systems.

Eventually, the Croton system proved inadequate to the growing city's needs and was supplemented since the early 1900s by the Catskill/Delaware ("West of Hudson") reservoir system. This system is northwest of the Highlands region and feeds through tunnels to Kensico Reservoir in Westchester County, which is located south of the Croton watershed and outside the Highlands region. One interesting result of the sequential development of the New York City reservoir systems is that various parts of the city are preferentially supplied by the Croton system or the Catskill/Delaware system, rather than all of them receiving a mixed supply. In the case of a drought that affects one water supply system more than the other, the city must pump water between the systems to ensure that no part of its service areas is without sufficient supply.

The Croton system of multiple reservoirs feeding to a common intake point maximizes system yields, currently supplying approximately 10 percent of the total system demand and up to 30 percent during droughts (U.S. DOJ 1998). The Croton system safe yield is approximately 240 million gallons per day (mgd) (USFS 2002). While the percentage of supply seems small, it is worth noting that two of the Croton reservoirs are larger than all but two of New Jersey's reservoirs (Round Valley and Wanaque), that the Croton system as a whole is larger than any single New Jersey reservoir system, and that the total New York City system (Croton and Catskill/Delaware) serves a population greater than that of New Jersey. Therefore, the Croton system is large when seen as a single system, and is small relative only to New York City's total needs, including 1 million residents in the reservoir watersheds outside the city.

The Croton watershed is a mixture of publicly owned and private lands.

The existence of private developed and agricultural lands within the watershed has created concerns about the quality of water collected by the reservoirs. For example, intensified eutrophication (excessive growth of plant life such as algae and floating plants) has occurred in several of the reservoirs due to excessive nutrients arriving from their upstream watersheds. A new filtration plant is being constructed for the Croton system to improve the quality of delivered water (U.S. DOJ 1998). This system is intended to address concerns regarding microbial contamination, taste, odor, and the creation of disinfection by-products. Completion of construction is expected in 2011.

New York City's water needs have been significantly reduced during recent decades as a result of water conservation measures and changing water-use patterns. One measure of water-use efficiency is the gallons of water used per resident, or per capita use, which includes residential, commercial, industrial, and institutional use within the service area. Per capita use in New York City itself has declined in recent decades from nearly 200 gallons per day to approximately 135 gallons per day, and total use has declined from nearly 1,500 mgd to the current 1,000 mgd. This decline in per capita use matches the experience in other urban water systems in the region as indoor water use becomes more efficient, as water-using industries either become more efficient or discontinue operations, and as system maintenance reduces leakage in distribution and service lines. Even so, the Croton system remains a critical part of the New York City system of three independent but linked reservoir systems, as shown by its ability to provide up to 30 percent of water supplies used during droughts.

Passaic River Reservoir Systems

The urban areas of northeastern New Jersey, and particularly Newark and Jersey City, faced supply limitations and degrading water quality in their early water-supply sources similar to but somewhat later than those of New York City. In each case, the cities determined that the most effective and safest water supplies would consist of reservoirs in the less developed parts of northern New Jersey. Newark created five reservoirs in the Pequannock River watershed in the late 1800s (NJDWSC 1925) that now provide a safe yield of 49 mgd (NJDEP 1992). Four of these are upstream of and provide flow to the Charlottesburg Reservoir, from which water is taken for treatment.

Jersey City built two reservoirs in the Rockaway River watershed (Split Rock and Boonton) in the early 1900s that now provide a safe yield of nearly 57 mgd (NJDEP 1992). Because the watershed included a number of industrialized mill towns, Jersey City also constructed a wastewater treatment plant serving these upstream municipalities. This project eliminated most wastewater discharges upstream of the larger (Boonton) reservoir by routing the sewage to below the reservoir (an important objective, given the minimal treatment technology in use at the time) but also had the effect of reducing streamflows to the reservoir by removing water from the upstream watershed.

The North Jersey District Water Supply Commission (NJDWSC) was formed by the legislature in 1916 to develop the Wanaque Reservoir (now the second-largest reservoir in New Jersey) to provide supplies to Newark, members of the Passaic Valley Water Commission, and other municipalities (NJDWSC 1925). Two pumping stations, one of which is actually downstream of the Highlands region, and a second reservoir, the Monksville, were built for the NJDWSC system later in the century to augment supplies. Total safe yield for the NJDWSC system is currently calculated at 173 mgd (NJDEP 1992).

In addition to these larger systems, some small reservoirs exist. Within the Highlands region itself, Boonton Town has a small reservoir providing 1.5 mgd of safe yield, while Butler has a somewhat larger reservoir providing 6 mgd of safe yield. The Southeast Morris County Municipal Utilities Authority operates one small reservoir (Clyde Potts) in Morris County to augment its groundwater supplies, supplying both Highlands and non-Highlands municipalities. Plate 10 shows all Highlands reservoirs and their watersheds in New Jersey, including the Passaic River basin systems. The larger reservoirs range from 11 to 66 billion gallons in storage and represent nearly 128 billion gallons of storage capacity with a safe yield of 455 mgd (NJDEP 1992; NJDEP 1996). The relative use of Highlands water supplies by municipalities in New Jersey is shown in figure 5.1.

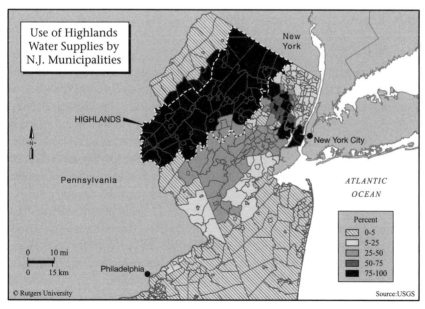

Figure 5.1. Use of Highlands water supplies by New Jersey municipalities.
Source: USGS. © Rutgers University.

Downstream Passaic River Water-Supply Systems

The cities of Paterson, Clifton, and Passaic formed the Passaic Valley Water Commission (PVWC) in 1927, absorbing operations of private water companies that had been providing water to these cities beginning in 1857 using water-supply intakes on the Passaic River in the Paterson area. The primary intake is located at Little Falls, with a backup intake upstream in Wayne. PVWC is also a customer of the North Jersey District Water Supply Commission on behalf of the PVWC members. As such, PVWC relies both directly and indirectly on Highlands water supplies, including the mandatory releases from the Highlands Reservoirs that provide critical flows to the Little Falls intake during droughts. The Little Falls intake is downstream of extensive urban, suburban, and rural areas within both New Jersey and New York State. During severe droughts, it is estimated that the vast majority of river flow (in excess of 90 percent) is treated effluent from upstream municipalities. For this reason, the ability of PVWC to draw from the NJDWSC facilities during drought periods is critical, as is the 2004 upgrade of the PVWC treatment facility.

The Wanaque South Pumping Station was built through a public-private partnership (NJDWSC and United Water–New Jersey, respectively) to provide water for two purposes. The pumping station, which is located downstream of the Highlands but depends on Highlands rivers for much of its flows, can provide water to the Wanaque Reservoir but can also pump directly to reservoirs owned by United Water–New Jersey in the Hackensack watershed (east of the Highlands region) to augment their supplies.

Raritan River Reservoir System

Round Valley and Spruce Run reservoirs (the largest and third-largest New Jersey reservoirs, respectively; see plate 10) were constructed in the 1960s by the State of New Jersey, in one of the few instances where the state took a direct role in constructing new water supplies. (Another was the transformation of the Delaware & Raritan Canal, a former barge canal, into a water supply for central New Jersey.) Both reservoirs were built in agricultural areas acquired by the state through eminent domain. In 1981 the two reservoirs and the canal were transferred to a new state agency, the New Jersey Water Supply Authority (State of New Jersey 1981), which operates the three facilities as an integrated supply of untreated water to water purveyors (both municipal and investor-owned) that supply portions of the counties of Hunterdon, Middlesex, Somerset, and Union. The two reservoirs rely heavily on streamflows from the Highlands region. Spruce Run Reservoir is an on-line reservoir, receiving all its water from tributary streams. Round Valley Reservoir, conversely, is an off-line reservoir that receives almost no water from its tiny watershed. Instead, it is filled almost entirely through pumping from the

South Branch of the Raritan River. Releases from both reservoirs are used to maintain streamflow at downstream locations where water purveyors withdraw water using river intakes. Neither reservoir is used directly for water supply, but together they provide the basis for approximately 176 mgd of the Raritan system's total 241 mgd of safe yield (Shallcross 2005). The tributary watersheds for both reservoirs are predominantly in private ownership, although the lands directly abutting the reservoirs are mostly public. As with the New York City Croton system, the Raritan basin system has been the subject of extensive source water protection and watershed management efforts related primarily to nutrients, turbidity, pathogens (disease-causing organisms), and sedimentation.

Downstream Raritan River Water-Supply Systems

The largest downstream water-supply system and the major customer for the Spruce Run and Round Valley reservoirs is a division of the New Jersey American Water Company (the former Elizabethtown Water Company). Its intake is located on the Raritan River in Bridgewater, New Jersey, well downstream of the Highlands, but the water supply there during droughts is heavily dependent on Highlands flows including releases from the two reservoirs (Shallcross 2005). This division of the New Jersey American Water Company in turn can transfer treated water to bulk customers in the Passaic River basin through pipelines that connect with another division of the same company and with the city of Newark (NJDEP 1992). Water quality at the intake is affected by significant amounts of upstream agriculture, suburban land uses, and wastewater treatment plant discharges but is generally significantly better than at the lower Passaic River basin intakes owing to the lower effluent densities from those upstream activities.

Surface Water Supplies in New Jersey's Delaware and Wallkill Watersheds

New Jersey has no major Highlands reservoirs for potable water in either the Wallkill River or Delaware River watersheds. However, the flow of Highlands water to the Delaware River is important to New Jersey as a major basis for diversions through the Delaware & Raritan Canal, as established through the good-faith agreement among Delaware River basin states and New York City. The Wallkill River in New Jersey drains northeast to the Hudson River and supports local water uses in New York State but does not contribute to the New York City system.

Two minor reservoirs have been constructed by the Hackettstown Utility Authority as alternate supplies for the Hackettstown area in Warren County (within the Highlands). The town of Newton in Sussex County (located just to the west of the Highlands) has one small reservoir, Morris Lake, within the region (NJDEP 1992). Some of these (particularly those of the Hackettstown system) may be discontinued because of their small size and the difficulty of managing them as water supplies.

A nonpotable supply, the Merrill Creek Reservoir, is located in the Delaware River basin portion of the New Jersey Highlands. Merrill Creek is a pumped-storage reservoir that derives its water from the Delaware River during high flow periods and releases that water during drought periods to compensate for evaporative water losses due to downstream electrical power generating facilities on the Delaware, so that water supplies for Philadelphia and other downstream users are not compromised. The reservoir, which is owned by a private consortium of electrical utilities, does not rely on Highlands water supplies.

Surface Water Supplies in Connecticut

Municipalities of western Connecticut make extensive use of Highlands reservoirs or streams for their potable water supply (see plate 10). The Metropolitan District Commission (MDC) provides potable water to the Hartford area drawn from two surface water supplies in the Highlands area of Connecticut: the 9.5-billion-gallon Nepaug Reservoir and the 30.3-billion-gallon Barkhamsted Reservoir. Both are on the Nepaug River, a branch of the Farmington River. The reservoirs provide a safe yield of approximately 55 mgd to approximately four hundred thousand residents. A third reservoir, known as Lake McDonough or the Compensating Reservoir, was constructed at the same time as Nepaug Reservoir to provide flows to downstream manufacturing plants whose owners had opposed a potential loss of water rights through the proposed construction of Nepaug Reservoir in the early twentieth century (Alderman 2001). MDC also owns the West Branch Reservoir along the west branch of the Farmington River, which is just downstream of Colebrook River Lake, a flood control reservoir operated by the U.S. Army Corps of Engineers. Built in the 1930s and 1960s, respectively, both are relatively small impoundments in area, although the Colebrook River Lake occupies four miles of a narrow valley and stores more than 16 billion gallons. The MDC owns approximately thirty thousand acres of forested lands to protect its reservoirs. As with the creation of many other Highlands reservoirs, providing urban water supplies resulted in the displacement of rural land uses and residents (Murphy 2006; Alderman 2001), including limited condemnation of lands.

The city of Waterbury receives water from two Highlands watershed reservoirs developed since the 1920s. The Shepaug and Cairns reservoirs are located in the Shepaug watershed, while three smaller reservoirs (Pitch, Morris, and Wigwam) are in the West Branch watershed, totaling 27.5 mgd in safe yield. While several of these reservoirs are actually located outside the Highlands region, at least some of the tributary streamflows are from the Highlands. Other, smaller systems in Connecticut also rely on Highlands streams, including the Torrington Water Company, an investor-owned utility that provides water to approximately eight thousand customers in the city of Torrington area by diverting an average of about 4 mgd for municipal supply from North Pond, Whist Pond, and Reuben Hart Reservoir in the Housatonic River watershed.

Collecting information on public water supply systems in Connecticut is complicated by the provisions of its recent Freedom of Information Act, which prohibit the state of Connecticut from providing or publishing a wide variety of information regarding water supplies, including facility and reservoir names, locations, safe yields, and so on (Connecticut Statutes 2008). While the state does engage in water-supply planning, nearly all the information is used internally for regulatory and planning purposes and cannot be provided without extensive redaction (S. Messer personal communication, June 12, 2008).

Surface Water Supplies in Pennsylvania

Much of Pennsylvania's section of the Highlands is relatively narrow and is not used extensively for direct surface water supplies. As in the Delaware River and Wallkill River watersheds in New Jersey, though, the flow of Highlands streams to downstream, non-Highlands intakes is important. The Highlands reservoirs of Pennsylvania are shown in plate 10.

Green Lane Reservoir, an 814-acre reservoir on Perkiomen Creek (within the Schuylkill River watershed) in Montgomery County, is owned by Aqua Pennsylvania (formerly Philadelphia Suburban Water Company) and used as a water-supply source for 140,000 people (PA DEP 2008; U.S. EPA 2003). While the reservoir itself is in the Piedmont physiographic province, an area of sedimentary rock to the south of the Highlands, some headwater areas of Perkiomen Creek are located within the Highlands region in Lehigh County (PA DEP 2008). The reservoir was categorized as "hypereutrophic" in the late 1990s, reflecting very high growth rates of plants caused by both point- and nonpoint-source nutrient loadings from rural land uses and suburban development upstream. A water-quality management plan was developed for nutrient reductions in the reservoir (U.S. EPA 2003).

Also in the Schuylkill River basin, Lake Ontelaunee is a smaller reservoir, approximately 1,100 acres in surface area with 3.6 billion gallons of storage. It was completed in 1926 to supplement water supplies for the city of Reading, Pennsylvania, providing roughly 15 mgd, but it is currently troubled by excessive nutrient and sediment loads (Youker 2007). The water-quality management plan developed for phosphorus and sediment (U.S. EPA 2004) identified cropland and transitional land uses (i.e., development activities) as the major sources of the nutrient phosphorus, with less than 5 percent from point sources such as wastewater treatment plants. Sediment is from similar sources, plus rural roads.

Highlands Groundwater Supplies

Water supplies for Highlands communities are primarily from local aquifers. In more developed areas, publicly owned or investor-owned systems provide supplies to customers using water from public community water-supply wells. These systems tend to rely on the more prolific aquifers of the Highlands, as discussed in chapter 4, including carbonate rock and glacial valley-fill (or buried valley) aquifers. Well yields can vary significantly depending on aquifer type, thickness, and transmissivity (the ability of water to move through an aquifer). Public community water-supply systems in the Highlands that use groundwater never approach the size and yields of the larger reservoir systems but often are comparable to the smaller reservoir systems. For example, some of the larger Highlands public community water-supply systems in New Jersey have water allocations of more than 9 mgd, though most are on the order of 2 to 5 mgd. The ability of these aquifers to sustain such yields has been questioned recently through regional and statewide water-supply analyses, as discussed in the next section.

In less developed areas, individual homes and businesses use on-site wells as private water supplies. On-site wells are the norm in Highlands geologic areas that have limited groundwater storage capacity, such as Precambrian crystalline bedrock formations that typically have limited fractures and storage capacity. The very limited capacity of such aquifers has prevented significant development historically, and only with improved well-drilling technology and the increased price of housing (making cost-effective the substantial investment in a deep domestic well) have barriers to development of some areas such as ridgelines been removed or reduced. Many domestic wells in the poorest aquifers rely on the well borehole for storage, with deep pumps lifting the water from wells that can be more than eight hundred feet deep. Such well depth is necessary to capture enough flow from bedrock.

Assessing Water Availability

There is no perfect method for determining how much groundwater and surface water can be made available for human use, but all regulatory systems depend on knowing how much water can be allocated to any one user and to all uses in aggregate. Assessment methods have been changing significantly over the last thirty years, with the advance of scientific knowledge in the fields of hydrogeology, hydrology, and surface water ecosystems, and with enormous improvements in computing technology.

Previously, groundwater allocations were based on pumping tests that determined whether a new supply would impair neighboring groundwater wells in terms of quantity or quality. The impacts of these new supplies on streamflow, wetlands, or the broader aquifer system were not considered.

The use of regional aquifer models beginning in the 1980s began to address regional impacts, while more recently regulatory authorities have begun to include ecological and streamflow impacts as considerations.

Surface water systems, conversely, have long been assessed using watershed-based analysis of "safe yield," as described earlier. Continuation of historic streamflow patterns into a reservoir was assumed, and mandatory release flows (also known as passing flows) were generally set at a given low flow to provide at least minimal downstream flows for pollution dilution and protection of aquatic life.

Because the Highlands region includes many reservoirs, one major concern is the potential impact of upstream groundwater use on the yields of existing surface water supplies. Two issues have been identified. First, there are situations in which water is withdrawn from aquifers upstream of reservoirs, used for residential and commercial purposes, and then discharged below the reservoir as treated wastewater effluent. This process bypasses the reservoir and can remove significant flow from reservoir tributaries, reducing the system's safe yield. This movement of water out of a watershed is called a depletive use. For example, the U.S. Environmental Protection Agency in the 1980s placed a 12-mgd limit on the capacity of the wastewater system that derives essentially all its flows from groundwater supplies upstream of the Jersey City water supply system in the Rockaway River watershed of New Jersey but discharges below the lower (Boonton) reservoir. Although the wastewater system protects the reservoir's water quality, the routing of wastewater below the reservoir can reduce the reservoir's safe yields. The increased development of upstream communities is resulting in wastewater flows very close to the maximum allowed.

Even where water is used and replaced in the watershed upstream of a reservoir or water-supply intake, some flow will be lost to consumptive (evaporative) uses such as agricultural and lawn irrigation and to domestic uses and manufacturing. For this reason, surface water safe yields are sensitive to upstream flow losses due to human water use. Water-quality concerns also arise from such upstream water uses, because of the development they support and the wastewater effluent they may generate. This issue is a major driving concern behind New York City's watershed protection efforts in both the Croton and Catskill/Delaware systems.

Second, beginning in the 1980s, stresses on regional aquifers such as declining aquifer water levels became apparent in the mid-Atlantic states. Agencies began developing regional aquifer models, especially for southeastern Pennsylvania and several New Jersey coastal and glacial aquifers (NJDEP 1996), that predicted the aggregate impacts of well pumping on both the aquifer and the streamflow for major streams. The strong link between groundwater and surface water identified in these models led to a rethinking of surface water safe yields in which the importance of maintaining streamflow patterns was acknowledged, and a rethinking of potential impacts on stream ecosystems. The 1996 New Jersey Statewide Water Supply Plan established planning thresholds for groundwater use to protect both aquifers and surface water supplies. The thresholds were based on estimates of groundwater recharge using baseflow separation techniques, which distinguish streamflows caused by runoff related to precipitation events from the baseflow caused by the movement of groundwater into the streams. The planning threshold for use of water from coastal aquifers and inland aquifers were set at 10 and 20 percent of recharge, respectively (NJDEP 1996), based on empirical evaluation of current conditions. These thresholds were not applied to regulatory purposes but rather served as indicators of locations where further aquifer research would be necessary to set regulatory controls. More sophisticated estimates of groundwater recharge have been developed using a method of the New Jersey Geological Survey (Charles et al. 1993) that allows for estimation of recharge based on the land use and land cover within an area, such as a watershed.

New Jersey agencies have advanced methods to provide more specific planning and regulatory thresholds for groundwater availability. The purpose is to protect streamflows for downstream reservoirs, other human uses, and aquatic ecosystems. The emphasis on ecosystem protection is a critical new facet of water resources management, based on recent research in the field (Richter et al. 2006; Henriksen et al. 2006).

Both the New Jersey Highlands Regional Master Plan and the updated New Jersey Water Supply Plan (NJDEP 2011) further refine this approach using statistical analyses. Both define the groundwater available for both human use and sustaining stream ecosystems as a portion of streamflows typically available in moderate droughts. The primary focus is the difference between two low-flow metrics for drainage basins—the median streamflow for September, which is usually the month with the lowest median flows, and the MA7CD10 (or 7Q10), which is the lowest seven-day flow with a statistical return period of ten years. The low-flow margin is defined as the MA7CD10 subtracted from the median September flow. The "total water availability" for human use is defined as a percentage of this amount. The New Jersey Highlands Council uses thresholds of 5 to 20 percent based on the goals of the New Jersey Highlands Act, with the lowest threshold being used for the protection of high-quality coldwater fisheries and other sensitive aquatic ecosystems. The New Jersey Department of Environmental Protection (NJDEP) uses 25 percent as the threshold for its statewide analyses but incorporates the New Jersey Highlands Council results for the Highlands region. The remaining flows are allocated to maintaining streamflows.

Net water availability is calculated by comparing the total water availability to the consumptive and depletive water uses within the target watershed during September for run-of-the-river surface water withdrawals, and during the summer months for groundwater withdrawals. The distinction in time frame acknowledges that groundwater withdrawals have a delayed and attenuated affect on streamflows, while the impacts of surface water withdrawals are instantaneous. As noted above, consumptive water uses are those that return some of the used water to the same watershed, with the remainder lost to evaporative or transpiration uses, such as irrigation. Depletive water uses are those that remove the water entirely from the watershed, through the transfer of raw, treated, or used water to another watershed or the coastal waters. In both cases, withdrawals from reservoirs are not included because reservoirs draw from storage and are required to provide releases to maintain downstream ecosystems and water uses. The major distinction between the two methods, other than the percentages used, is the way in which the results are applied. NJDEP uses its method to drive planning and research, and to identify situations where applicants for water allocation permits must provide more detailed information on local and watershed impacts. The New Jersey Highlands Council uses its approach to establish sustainable development levels and requires conformance with the results through its independent legislative authority. However, in both cases, NJDEP review of proposed water allocations ensures that localized effects on other water uses, that is, wetlands and other water supply users, are avoided. The low-flow margin method addresses part, but not all, of the water availability issues and is primarily focused on watershed-level impacts.

Another related development in water availability assessments derives from recognition that stream systems require not just some minimal flow to maintain their natural habitat quality but rather an entire range of flows within the historic flow pattern. This approach has been used in some large river systems around the nation (Richter et al. 2006), primarily for reducing the downstream environmental impacts of reservoirs and their water releases. It involves a comparison of various flow statistics (e.g., frequency, magnitude, and duration of high and low flows) from a preimpact base period to an actual or proposed scenario where flows have been affected by human use, reservoir storage, reservoir release protocols, and so on, to determine whether the resulting flows are so significantly different as to constitute a threat to the aquatic ecosystem. The U.S. Fish & Wildlife Service uses a simplified version of this concept for review of hydropower licenses and other impoundments in New England (Lang 1999; Desimone et al. 2002), but the approach has not been used for regulatory purposes in the Highlands region at this time.

One effort to employ this new approach is being pursued in Connecticut. A Connecticut Superior Court decision required that Waterbury release an average of 8.5 mgd to the Shepaug River during summer months, rather than the 1.5 mgd release requirement that dated back to 1921 (Chamberlain 2000), which would have reduced the safe yield of the combined reservoir system. Although this decision was mostly reversed by the Connecticut Supreme Court (Dellapenna 2002), it and similar cases, along with a Connecticut Department of Environmental Protection report (CTDEP 2000), led to the passage of a 2005 Connecticut statute requiring that the Connecticut Department of Environmental Protection devise a new regulatory system for required reservoir releases based on natural seasonal flow patterns.

New Jersey is also developing an "ecological flow goals" approach to address this issue, but the system requires extensive data sets for application to a specific stream (Henriksen et al. 2006). Both the New Jersey Department of Environmental Protection and the New Jersey Highlands Council used case studies of the ecological flow goals approach to develop their water availability thresholds (NJDEP 2009). An operational example of ecological flows is in the Delaware reservoir system of New York City, where the city is cooperating with the four states of the Delaware River basin to improve trout production downstream of its Delaware system reservoirs. The evaluation of flow patterns will continue to develop as a technique for protecting aquatic systems, providing more sophisticated limits and controls on the impacts of both groundwater and surface water withdrawals.

Source Water Protection

Many of the major reservoirs in the Highlands region were created because cities no longer had access to nearby unpolluted water supplies. The Highlands region was at that time considered remote and relatively clean. The region is no longer remote, and recent studies indicate that surface water quality is declining where suburban and exurban development has increased (NJDEP 1998). Groundwater supplies are also sensitive to contamination from overlying land uses, despite the imposition of protective regulations. A variety of federal and state legislative responses exist. The federal Safe Drinking Water Act acknowledged this concern by requiring development of a Source Water Assessment Report for every public water-supply system, both surface water and groundwater (42 USC 300j-13(a)). These reports identify the potential for future contamination of both surface water and groundwater supplies for all public water-supply systems based on the existence of potential pollutant sources and the potential that any contamination could actually reach the drinking water source. The New Jersey Highlands Act (2004) also was predicated in large part on a concern that future development could compromise water supplies. Numerous water-quality management plans, titled "Total Maximum Daily Loads" under the federal Clean Water Act, have been developed to reduce pollutant loads to reservoirs (NJDEP 2008; U.S. EPA 2003; U.S. EPA 2004). Finally, one of the largest source water protection programs in the world has been created and implemented by New York City, primarily to avoid the need to construct a multibillion-dollar water filtration facility for the Catskill/Delaware systems but also to address eutrophication (overenrichment of nutrients leading to noxious algal blooms) and other pollutant issues in the Croton system within the Highlands. Similar but much smaller programs exist in other states, such as the Raritan basin initiative.

Water Supplies for Growth

Growing internal and external demands for water will increase stresses on Highlands resources. Highlands water needs in the northern and central New Jersey area are projected to increase (NJDEP 2008). There is some potential for water-supply development outside the Highlands region in areas that depend in part on streamflows from the Highlands, and some potential for increased safe yields from Highlands reservoirs through improved operating protocols. However, there are no viable sites for new reservoirs in the New Jersey Highlands (NJDEP 1996). New York City has already maximized its use of the Croton watershed; therefore, any additional demands will be met by its other resources. Pennsylvania is unlikely to build additional Highlands reservoirs, owing in large part to the lack of viable sites in an increasingly suburban area, while suburban growth in the Hartford and Waterbury areas of Connecticut could place strains on their Highlands reservoirs. In addition, growth within the Highlands region continues and will increase the pressure on Highlands groundwater supplies to meet those needs (USFS 2002). The mid-Atlantic Highlands region, which for nearly 170 years has supported significant growth, will not be a major source of additional water for growth but rather will support significant growth only through more efficient use of existing supplies.

Summary

When major cities of the mid-Atlantic area faced shortages of clean water, or of any water at all, their viability and future growth depended upon the development of reservoirs in the Highlands region. New York City, Newark, Jersey City, Hartford, and Waterbury along with other cities in Pennsylvania, New Jersey, New York, and Connecticut used the advantageous topography and relatively limited development densities in the Highlands to create reservoirs large and small, directing water from the Highlands to areas that for the most part are outside the region. The Highlands are important for regional water supplies because valleys of the right size made large reservoirs feasible. The result has been a dichotomy in water access within the Highlands, with most Highlands communities relying on local groundwater and small reservoirs for their supplies and most Highlands reservoir supplies being exported. A major exception is the Croton system of New York City, where the city is required by New York statutes to provide water to communities in the reservoir watersheds. The development of the reservoirs in all four states was often facilitated by state legislation or regulation providing exclusive water rights, power of condemnation, bonding authority, and other means by which the purchase of land (from both willing and unwilling landowners) and construction of facilities were eased.

These Highlands reservoirs averted or resolved major water crises where cities faced high disease rates from polluted supplies, or where water simply was not available during drought periods. A great deal of economic growth hinged on the creation of these water supplies. However, because much of the Highlands region is composed of hard rock formations, groundwater supplies for local communities and development tend to be more limited, and therefore local development is concentrated where communities could rely on the better aquifers (generally glacial deposits or carbonate rock) or on supplies from outside the region. For both reservoirs and aquifers, however, the limits of Highlands water resources are being reached, and new growth is forced to rely more on efficient and effective use of existing facilities.

As noted in chapter 6, the Highlands region has not always been the forested area now seen in the four states. Forests have regrown from periods when charcoal production for iron mining and then agriculture resulted in a near denuding of the landscape. The earliest of the reservoirs were constructed as forest regeneration was beginning and have benefited from the resulting high water quality. More recently, a new land use—suburban development—has infringed on the water-supply watersheds as population growth and dispersal from the cities result in the conversion of forests to communities. Where agriculture still exists, recent decades have seen the introduction of more chemically oriented agriculture, offset by a later emphasis on improved farming techniques. The pollutant loadings resulting from both development and agriculture, combined with more stringent quality standards for drinking water, are driving a new emphasis on source water protection to extend the life, quality, and benefits of existing Highlands water supplies.

The combination of a limited potential for new supplies, the allocation of most supplies to urban areas rather than Highlands region communities, and a need for pollutant load reductions from Highlands communities to safeguard both their own supplies and those of outside urban areas creates a potential for significant conflicts over supplies, land use controls, and responsibilities for pollutant controls, as currently seen in the New Jersey Highlands. The coming decades will be fundamentally different from the period of 1840 through 1990, when nearly all Highlands reservoirs were constructed. The focus will be on management and protection rather than construction.

References

Alderman, L. 2001. "Nepaug Statistics." http://www.burlingtonct.us/visitors/documents/NepaugStatistics.pdf.

Center for the Analysis of Public Issues (CAPI). 1972. "Pollution Control on the Passaic River." Princeton, NJ: CAPI.

Chamberlain, F. 2000. "More Water for Shepaug River." *New York Times*, March 26, 2000. http://query.nytimes.com/gst/fullpage.html?res=9B07E2DF173DF935A15750 C0A9669C8B63.

Charles, E. G., C. Behroozi, J. Schooley, and J. L. Hoffman. 1993. "A Method for Evaluating Ground-Water-Recharge Areas in New Jersey." New Jersey Geological Survey, Geological Survey Report 32. Trenton, NJ: New Jersey Department of Environmental Protection.

Christman, K. 1998. "The History of Chlorine." *WaterWorld*, September, Available at the Water Quality & Health Council website, http://www.waterandhealth .org/drinkingwater/history.html.

Connecticut Department of Environmental Protection (CTDEP). 2000. "Report to the General Assembly on State Water Allocation Policies Pursuant to Public Act 98–224." http://ct.gov/dep/cwp/view.asp?a=2720&q=325642&depNav_GID=1654.

Connecticut Statutes. 2008. Freedom of Information Act, Sec. 1–210. (Formerly Sec. 1–19). Access to public records. Exempt records. (b)(19)(ix). Available at http:// search.cga.state.ct.us/dtsearch_pub_statutes.html.

Dellapenna, J. W. 2002. "Middle Atlantic Regional Report—Waterbury's 'Water War.'" American Bar Association, *Water Resources Committee Newsletter 5*, no. 5 (August). http://www.abanet.org/environ/committees/waterresources/news letter/aug02/dellapenna.shtml.

Desimone, L. A., D. A. Walter, J. R. Eggleston, and M. T. Nimiroski. 2002. "Simulation of Ground-Water Flow and Evaluation of Water-Management Alternatives in the Upper Charles River Basin, Eastern Massachusetts." U.S. Geological Survey, Water Resources Investigation Report 02–4234. Northborough, MA.

Henriksen, J. A., J. Heasley, J. G. Kennen, and S. Nieswand. 2006. "User's Manual for the Hydroecological Integrity Assessment Process Software (Including the New Jersey Assessment Tools)." Fort Collins, CO: U.S. Geological Survey. Available at http://www.fort.usgs.gov/products/publications/21598/21598.pdf.

Lang, V. 1999. "Questions and Answers on the New England Flow Policy." Concord, NH: U.S. Fish and Wildlife Service.

Murphy, K. 2006. "A Valley Flooded to Slake the Capital Region's Thirst." *Hog River Journal*, Winter 2006. http://www.hogriver.org/issues/v04n01/flooded.pdf.

New Jersey Department of Environmental Protection (NJDEP). 1992. "New Jersey Statewide Water Supply Plan, Task 2 Report: Water Supply Baseline Data Development and Analyses." Trenton: NJDEP.

——. 1996. "Water for the 21st Century: Statewide Water Supply Plan." Trenton: NJDEP.

——. 1998. "1996 Water Quality Inventory Report." Trenton: NJDEP.

——. 2007. "Minutes of the Water Supply Advisory Council." Trenton: NJDEP.

——. 2008. "Adoption of Amendments to the Northeast, Upper Raritan, Sussex County and Upper Delaware Water Quality Management Plan to Establish Total Maximum Daily Loads in the Non-tidal Passaic River Basin and Pompton Lake/ Ramapo River Addressing Phosphorus Impairments and to Establish Watershed Criteria." New Jersey Register, 40 N.J.R. 2574(b).

——. 2011. "New Jersey Statewide Water Supply Plan," (draft), ch. 5. Trenton: NJDEP.

North Jersey District Water Supply Commission (NJDWSC). 1925. "Report for the Period May 5, 1916 to June 30, 1925." Newark: NJDWSC.

Richter, B. D., A. T. Warner, J. L. Meyer, and K. Lutz. 2006. "A Collaborative and Adaptive Process for Developing Environmental Flow Recommendations." *River Research and Applications* 22:297–318.

Shallcross, A. 2005. "Raritan Basin Water Supply System: Safe Yield Evaluation and Operation Model." Clinton: New Jersey Water Supply Authority.

State of New Jersey. 1981. New Jersey Water Supply Authority Act, N.J.S.A. 58:1B-1 et seq. Available at www.njleg.state.nj.us/.

United States Department of Justice (USDOJ). 1998. "New York City Agrees to Filter Croton Drinking Water System." Press release, May 20, 1998. http://www.usdoj.gov/opa/pr/1998/May/226enr.htm.html.

United States Environmental Protection Agency (USEPA). 2000. "The History of Drinking Water Treatment." EPA-816-F-00–006. Washington, DC: U.S. EPA. Available at http://www.epa.gov/safewater/consumer/pdf/hist.pdf.

———. 2003. "Total Maximum Daily Load of Nutrients for Green Lane Reservoir, Montgomery County, PA." Available at http://www.epa.gov/reg3wapd/tmdl/pa_tmdl/GreenLane/GreenLaneReport.pdf.

———. 2004. "Total Maximum Daily Load for Nutrients and Suspended Sediment, Lake Ontelaunee, Berks and Lehigh County, Pennsylvania." Available at http://www.epa.gov/reg3wapd/tmdl/pa_tmdl/LakeOntelauneeTMDL/LakeontelauneeReport_A_B.pdf.

United States Forest Service (USFS). 2002. "New York–New Jersey Highlands Regional Study: 2002 Update." U.S. Department of Agriculture, Forest Service, Northeastern Area State and Private Forestry, NA-TP-02–03.

Youker, Darrin. 2007. "Protecting Lake Ontelaunee: Thirst for Improvement." *Reading Eagle*, August 25, 2007.

In addition to the publications cited in the text and listed above, several websites were consulted:

Aqua American. "Company Profile for Southeastern Pennsylvania." http://www.aquaamerica.com.

City of Reading, Pennsylvania. "About the Reading Area Water Authority." http://www.readingpa.gov/rawa_about_rawa.asp.

Colebrook, Town of. "Colebrook History at a Glance." http://freepages.history.rootsweb.ancestry.com/~coltsfoot/postcard/colebrook.html.

Delaware River Basin Commission. "Ground Water Protected Area Regulations, Southeastern Pennsylvania"; "Water Resources Plan for the Delaware River Basin"; and "Proposed Rulemaking to Implement a Flexible Flow Management Program for the New York City Delaware Basin Reservoirs." http://www.state.nj.us/drbc.htm.

Earth Science Resource Education Center. "New York City Water Supply." http://www.eserc.stonybrook.edu/cen514/info/NYC/WaterSupply.html.

Metropolitan District Commission. www.themdc.com.

New Jersey Highlands Council. "Technical Report Addenda"; "Water Resources

Technical Report, Volume II—Water Use and Availability"; "Utility Capacity Technical Report"; "Regional Master Plan"; and "Highlands Regional Build Out Technical Report." http://www.highlands.state.nj.us/njhighlands/.

New Jersey Water Supply Authority (NJWSA). "Surface Water Quality and Pollutant Loadings: A Technical Report for the Raritan Basin Watershed Management Project"; and "Watershed Protection Programs Unit." http://www.raritanbasin .org/.

New York City Department of Environmental Protection. "Why New York City Needs a Filtered Croton Supply"; "2006 Long-Term Watershed Protection Program"; "NYC Watersheds"; and "The Croton Water Filtration Project" [includes Minutes of the Croton Facility Monitoring Committee of February 19, 2009]. http://www.nyc.gov/html/dep/html/home/home.shtml.

North Jersey District Water Supply Commission. http://www.njdwsc.com/njdw/ about.htm.

Passaic Valley Water Commission. www.pvwc.com/about/history.htm.

Pennsylvania Department of Environmental Protection (PA DEP). "Watershed Restoration Action Strategy: Subbasin 03E, Perkiomen Creek Watershed." http:// www.dep.state.pa.us/dep/deputate/watermgt/WC/subjects/WSNoteBks/ WRAS-03E.htm.

Rivers Alliance of Connecticut. "Stream Flow Regulation Progress." http://www .riversalliance.org/news&articles.cfm#flow.

Southeast Museum. "The Croton Water System." http://www.southeastmuseum .org/html/croton_reservoir.html.

United States Army Corps of Engineers. Annual Water Data Reports, "Housatonic River Basin: 01205600 West Branch Naugatuck River at Torrington, CT." http:// ct.water.usgs.gov/annual.data/WY1996/adj.01205600.txt.

Upper Perkiomen Watershed Coalition. "Facts about the Upper Perkiomen Watershed"; and "Upper Perkiomen Creek Watershed Conservation Plan." www.upwc watershed.org/facts.htm.

Waterbury Bureau of Water. "2007 Water Quality Report." http://www.water buryct.org/filestorage/458/662/666/CCRWTBY.water-quality-report-2007 .pdf.

Part III

Biodiversity

Forests are central to the character of the Highlands landscape. As high-lighted throughout this section, natural ecosystems are dynamic, continually responding to varying environmental conditions or discrete disturbances; change is a constant. Chapter 6 discusses how the Highlands' forests were heavily exploited in the eighteenth and nineteenth centuries as a home-grown energy source in the form of charcoal to power the iron industry or as fuelwood to heat homes. Most of the region was repeatedly cut over so there is little or no original "virgin" forest to be found. As recounted in chapter 7, when given a reprieve from the wholesale cutting in the late 1800s, these forests quickly regenerated to again cover the Highlands in a thick mantle of upland forest dominated by a mixture of broad-leaved deciduous trees. Chapter 8 explores the region's wetlands and explains how swamps, bogs, and herbaceous marshes add to the landscape's habitat and biotic diversity.

As noted in chapters 9 and 10, the Highlands are home to a rich diversity of plant and animal life, but very few endemic species are unique to the Highlands. In fact, the Highlands forest is quite similar in structure and com-position to forests across the entire sweep of the Appalachians from Georgia to Maine. What makes the Highlands forests different and of special value is their proximity to the teeming human population centers of the Hartford to New York City to Philadelphia region. These renewed forests and wetlands are increasingly valued for the "ecosystem services" they provide, such as their ability to serve as natural water and air filtration systems or their role in storing carbon. Not to be forgotten or belittled—from a selfish human point of view—the Highlands forests, the wetlands, and the resident plant and wildlife provide aesthetic values enhancing the quality of life for the human residents as well. While demonstrating great resiliency in the past, the Highlands forests, wetlands, and native biota are under assault from a host of new forces: habitat conversion, imbalances in wildlife popula-tions, invasive plants, exotic pests, point/nonpoint-source water pollution, atmospheric pollutant deposition, and global climate change. The challenge moving into the future is how to protect the Highlands from the dangers of habitat loss, fragmentation, and homogenization and thus sustain a vital functioning regional ecosystem.

6

Forest History of the Highlands

Emily W. B. (Russell) Southgate

Why Study Forest History?

European settlers who began exploring the Highlands more than three hundred years ago found seemingly limitless forests, ripe for exploitation. Over the next century and a half, they cleared forests to make farms and harvested trees to provide fuel and building materials. From their perspective, they were converting a wilderness into productive land (Cronon 1983). From another perspective, however, the destruction that they visited on these forests was unprecedented in extent, severity, and duration as compared with any disturbances in the preceding eight thousand years, if ever, and the destruction happened at an astonishing rate. Highly destructive fires raged on cutover lands. The discovery of more easily cultivated land farther west, improved transportation, cheaper fuels than charcoal and wood, and more extensive unlogged forests led to abandonment of many of these destructive activities by 1900, and to the recovery of forests in the late nineteenth and early twentieth centuries. As a result, extensive but young forests characterize much of the Highlands in the early twenty-first century. In this chapter, I will discuss the long history of the forests before European settlers arrived and the forest conditions and processes that have changed since they arrived. This perspective will provide a backdrop for considering the distribution of forest types and other vegetation today, which are a consequence not only of climate, physiography, and soils but also of past human actions.

Historical studies show how vegetation has responded to changes in climate and disturbance regimes. Understanding these responses gives us critical insight into ecological processes and greatly improves our ability to address the potential impacts of current and predicted future changes in the environment (Russell 1997; Foster and Aber 2004). Have the activities of the last few centuries altered substrates, seed sources, and other conditions such that reconstruction of precolonial forest composition is unlikely? Do the patterns of forests today reflect those of the past, or are they changed in significant ways?

Are there disturbance factors, such as fire, that characterized precolonial forests but are absent today and need to be restored? Deciphering which features of forests have been robust in the face of disturbances and which have not will help foresters and land managers make better decisions about future forest management.

Classical ecology posited a "climax" vegetation type that was in equilibrium with climate (Clements 1936). While this concept has been greatly modified over the last century, paleoecological research does indeed support the notion that, given sufficient response time, vegetation is in equilibrium with climate (Webb 1986; Parshall and Foster 2002; Webb, Shuman, and Williams 2004; Patterson 2005). However, in contrast to the Clementsian idea of plant communities acting as coherent units, paleoecological evidence strongly supports the individualistic theories of plant community organization, with each species responding to slightly different climate signals (Gleason 1926; Grimm and Jacobson 2004). In addition, on a local scale, species respond to more local changes such as erosion or disease at a more rapid rate, which confounds simplistic predictions about species responses to climate (Davis and Shaw 2001; Webb, Shuman, and Williams 2004). Historical studies allow us to evaluate the responses of forest vegetation to major disturbance events such as deforestation and forest recovery or loss of major species due to disease, and the importance of chronic disturbance events such as fire. These drivers of change act on different spatial and temporal scales and leave legacies that last for differing times.

History can be used to establish analogues, or sets of conditions, that management seeks to create or maintain. In North America, this analogue is often taken to be the conditions that existed before European settlers arrived on the continent, regarded as the "natural" vegetation. However, the question of what is "natural" is not a simple one (Willis and Birks 2006) and relies on a historical perspective. For example, the extent of Native American impact on the pre-Columbian forest vegetation of the Highlands may confound the interpretation of the vegetation as in equilibrium with nonhuman drivers. In addition, climate has changed as the Northern Hemisphere has recovered from the Little Ice Age cooling of 1450–1850, so conditions in 2000 are naturally warmer than they were in 1700, even without anthropogenic (human-caused) climate warming.

In this chapter, I will address several specific questions as well as other more general issues. First, what is the evidence that the forest vegetation of the Highlands region has been in dynamic equilibrium with climate over the last several millennia? Second, how have the driving forces that determine forest extent and composition changed over the last several centuries? Third, what have been the consequences of human disturbances of the forests over these centuries?

How to Study Forest History

There are three major kinds of evidence that ecologists use to establish the history of a forest or any other kind of vegetation: sedimentary, documentary, and field (Russell 1997). Integrating these three, which provide clues about the past on different temporal and spatial scales, gives a composite picture that can be compared with the present and with anticipated changes in the future.

Sedimentary Evidence

Living organisms leave evidence of their existence in the sediments that are preserved in lakes, bogs, and other wetlands. These accumulate over time. A vertical core through them is like a time machine, which a paleoecologist can read from bottom to top to establish the sequence of ecosystems that have produced them. Radiometric dating methods (i.e., measurement of the relative proportion of certain chemical isotopes such as carbon-14 that are lost through time by radioactive decay) can give independent dates of these sediments, though the temporal precision and accuracy is only on the order of fifty to one hundred years. Pollen provides an especially long-lived and distinctive record to establish changes in vegetation and flora in a region (i.e., within an area of 10 to 100 km of a core site). While individual species can sometimes be discriminated, information allowing discrimination to the genus and family level is more common. Many pollen studies from the Highlands, especially north of the Wisconsinan terminal moraine, have provided a detailed and consistent record of changing vegetation over the last fifteen thousand or so years since the Wisconsinan glacier retreated.

The data from these cores are presented in multitaxa diagrams, with the oldest sediment represented at the bottom of the diagram. The relative contributions of the different kinds of pollen can be followed up the core. Because different kinds of plants produce different amounts of pollen, which is carried different distances from the plant, these diagrams do not give a simple one-to-one representation of the vegetation that produced the pollen. In addition, some taxonomic units (taxa), such as oak (*Quercus*), can be identified only to genus, and some, such as the grasses (Poaceae) or sedges (Cyperaceae), only to family. Interpretation of many diagrams and comparison with modern pollen-rain and vegetation, however, has allowed pollen analysts to interpret the pollen record with considerable accuracy in terms of the kind of vegetation that produced it. Other particles in the sediment, such as charcoal, spores, or diatoms, and other sedimentary features expand the interpretation of the pollen record.

Documentary Evidence

Wherever literate people live, they make records. Even illiterate people make some records in drawings. In the Highlands, the documentary record starts in the eighteenth century, with descriptions of the landscape and, most usefully, land surveys. In the eighteenth century, surveyors often recorded the corners of properties by noting a tree or trees at the corner. Summaries of the trees from a region give a fairly unbiased sample of the forest composition at the time of the survey (Russell 1997). Other useful documents include maps, census figures, qualitative forest descriptions, and other ecological and forestry studies in the nineteenth and twentieth centuries as well as other records of disturbance events and commercial activities such as processing iron ore. Even more recent evidence since the mid-twentieth century includes a variety of remotely sensed data such as aerial and satellite photographs.

Field Evidence

The final kind of evidence is field evidence, traces of past activities that still exist on the landscape of today. This may be stone walls in a well-established forest indicating that it was once cleared; numerous multiple-trunked trees indicating that the trees originated as stump sprouts; or even-aged stands of early successional species. These may confirm and expand evidence found in written documents, photographs, or maps.

Using all these kinds of evidence together, we can build a composite picture of changes that have led to the forest composition and extent of today and can infer the causes of these changes. We can also look for evidence of responses to changing driving forces in the past to infer potential responses to predicted changes in driving forces in the future, such as changed climate or disturbance regimes.

The Broad Sweep: Twenty Thousand to Five Hundred Years Ago

The glaciated landscape north of the Wisconsinan terminal moraine includes numerous depressions that have collected sediment since the retreat of the glacier. South of the moraine there are fewer such depressions, but some have yielded good sedimentary records of at least part of the postglacial period. As the glacier began to retreat in the north, south of the moraine there was tundra with sedges (Cyperaceae), grasses (Poaceae) and other herbaceous taxa, and scattered stands of spruce (*Picea*), pine (*Pinus*), and a little fir (*Abies*) (Harmon 1968; Watts 1979; Jackson et al. 1997; Russell and Stanford 2000). This vegetation did not resemble any that is found today, most likely because the

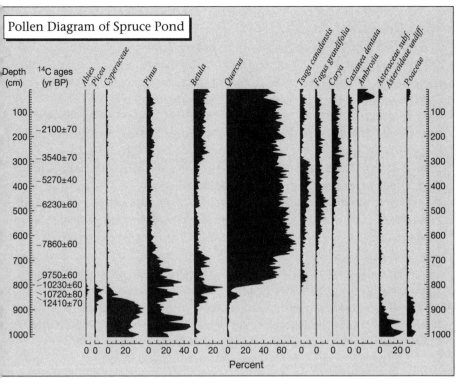

Figure 6.1. Pollen diagram from Spruce Pond, N.Y. Data taken from the North American Pollen Database (www.ncdc.noaa.gov/paleo/pollen.html), plotted using PSIMPOLL. Data contributor, T. Maenza-Gmelch.

climate did not resemble any climate today because it was heavily influenced by the continental glacier present just to the north.

A pollen diagram from Spruce Pond in the New York Highlands gives a detailed record of vegetation change north of the Wisconsinan terminal moraine from about 15,000 years ago to the present (fig. 6.1; Maenza-Gmelch 1997c, 1997a). As the glacier retreated, first tundra, then spruce and pine forest developed as trees spread from southern refugia. This same pattern was time-transgressive as the glacier uncovered land. Generally, pine, sedges, and grasses, usually with some spruce and fir, appeared first, forming an open tundra. This was followed by more spruce and less of the herbaceous species as the forest closed, and then by increasing pine and birch (*Betula*) as the spruce dwindled, responding to a warmer and perhaps drier climate. Several millennia into this expansion of forest, there was a sudden return of very cold conditions, about 12,500 years ago, referred to as the Younger Dryas. Spruce replaced the less cold-tolerant pine, and sedges indicate the redevelopment of tundra (Gaudreau and Webb 1985; Watts 1979; Peteet 2000). This was followed by a sudden warming beginning the Holocene period (starting approximately 12,000 years ago), characterized by warmer climate. Oaks, along with various amounts of other deciduous taxa, replaced the pines as the climate warmed (Maenza-Gmelch 1997c, 1997a). The same general pattern of forest change also occurred south of the Wisconsinan glacial moraine, in New Jersey and Pennsylvania in the Highlands and north to Connecticut.

In general, once oak had become established, there was an increase in hemlock (*Tsuga canadensis*), then beech (*Fagus grandifolia*), followed by hickory (*Carya*), and finally chestnut (*Castanea dentata*). This pattern was first observed by Deevey in 1939 in Connecticut lake sediments and is evident in many pollen studies of northeastern North America.

Unfortunately there is little or no record of the changing populations of herbaceous and shrub species within the forest, because wind-pollinated taxa, especially trees, dominate the pollen record. Even the seed record is very limited because few seeds fall into the sedimentary basins and are buried quickly enough to be preserved. The record of the herbaceous species comes more from the more northern species that have survived in areas south of the main parts of their ranges, often in disjunct populations, indicating that they were present when the climate was colder and, because they were in a favorable microclimate, have been able to survive until today.

All the recent studies that have compared other sedimentary indicators of climate to the modern climatic ranges of species indicate that climate is a controlling and sufficient explanation for the vegetation patterns of the past (Webb, Shuman, and Williams 2004), at a millennial temporal scale and a coarse spatial scale. Local factors such as seed dispersal and topography influenced changes at finer temporal and spatial scales.

Evidence for factors other than climate, soils, and topography controlling the patterns of vegetation prior to European settlement are of necessity circumstantial, although in some areas small watershed basins may give evidence of local vegetation. There is evidence of fire, however, in charcoal that is preserved in sediment. Charcoal is a common component of sediment throughout the Holocene, found at low levels, which indicates a low incidence, though not absence, of fire. Just before European settlement, charcoal in sediments is generally low but present, indicating some low yet consistent presence of fire in the oak-dominated forests. Recent studies suggest that charcoal in sediments is a good indicator of fires in the vicinity of the depositional basin (Gillson and Willis 2008). An excellent example of the local nature of this record is found in the two cores from Spruce and Sutherland ponds in southern New York, 22 km apart (Maenza-Gmelch 1997c, 1997b). Both record the history of the forests from before the establishment of oak forests. Both have a charcoal influx to the sediment estimated to be about 500 mm^2/cm^2 of sediment surface per year for much of the last ten thousand years. In Sutherland Pond, however, from about six thousand to four thousand years ago when hickory appears in the record, there was a significant increase in the charcoal influx to a maximum of about 2,500 mm^2/cm^2 of sediment surface per year. This major deviation allows us to compare the response of the vegetation producing the pollen with this increase of charcoal, representing a greater amount of fire in the local landscape, with the pollen-producing vegetation in a similar area without the increase. Beech and hemlock had been established near both ponds before this time, and although the amount of beech declined at Spruce Pond, it did not at Sutherland. The amount of oak appears to have decreased slightly during the period of increased fire, whereas hemlock increased. Hickory appeared just before this period and stayed at the same level throughout.

The role of fire in the establishment of the oak forest is equivocal. Major studies using other climatic proxies indicate that climate is a sufficient driver for the establishment of oak-dominated forest. Sediment cores that include charcoal find constant presence of charcoal in the sediment, indicating fire in the environment, but the major increase in fire indicated by charcoal at Sutherland Pond between 5,500 and 4,000 years ago is not accompanied by a change in the importance of oak, nor is the decrease in fire associated with a decline in oak. Conversely, and counterintuitively, at Sutherland Pond the influx of hemlock, a species that fire eliminates, mirrors the increase and decrease in charcoal. At nearby Spruce Pond, with about half as much charcoal in the sediment and no increase in the mid-Holocene, oak also constituted about 70 percent of the pollen throughout the Holocene. Historical studies of fire importance in other North American forest systems find that some indicators of climate, especially proxies for drought, are strongly correlated with more fire (Carcaillet et al. 2001; Whitlock and Bartlein 2004). In reviewing both published and unpublished pollen and charcoal data, Patterson (2005) found the relationship between fire and oak to be ambiguous, in agreement with previous work by Clark and Royall (1996). The data support the hypothesis that the major factor determining the dominance of oak in forests in the precolonial forests was climate; where the climate was cooler to the north, hemlock and other northern hardwoods, such as beech and sugar maple, were more important. Fire would have been less important in these forests both because the climate was cooler and because they do not carry fire as readily.

However, there is evidence that a nonclimatic factor may have had a massive impact on one species, eastern hemlock. There was a precipitate decline in hemlock throughout northeastern North America 4,800 years ago (Allison, Moeller, and David 1986). Most studies have concluded that because other species were not affected, a specific pest rather than climate caused the decline. One recent study questions this conclusion, however, finding evidence in numerous cores of a significant drought at the time of the hemlock decline (Foster et al. 2006). It is also possible that the dramatic decline in hemlock may have been exacerbated by a dry climate at the same time as a pest outbreak.

Regardless of the cause of the decline, it took a very long time for hemlock to recover, and it never did reach its predecline levels (Leduc 2003). We have no way of knowing whether this loss affected other species of plants or animals, but it seems likely that species that depended on the hemlock would also have been seriously affected by its loss and would either have recovered slowly or not at all. In the Highlands, this decline in hemlock is apparent in pollen studies (for example, see fig. 6.1), although hemlock never constituted more than about 15 to 20 percent of the forest trees. That climate may also have been a factor in its decline may be seen in the synchronous minimum of beech pollen in Connecticut lake sediment (Gaudreau and Webb 1985).

Another species of interest in terms of its postglacial migration is chestnut. Although this species was common in 1800 wherever oaks were important, it did not become a significant part of the forests of the Highlands until three thousand to four thousand years ago, long after oak had reached its maximum level (Leduc 2003). It never was as important as oak in the forests overall, although it appears to have been a significant species in some locales. It is insect-pollinated and produces its pollen after the trees leaf out, so it is generally underrepresented in the pollen record. Even so, it constituted up to 15 percent of the pollen at some sites.

Two less-clearly defined periods in the last millennium are the Medieval Warm Period, about AD 900–1300, and the Little Ice Age, about AD 1450–1850. A recent study of the pollen record in the lower Hudson valley, just southeast of the Highlands, indicates that there may have been a warmer, dryer period from about AD 800 to 1300 corresponding to the Medieval Warm Period. Neither of these periods is very well distinguished in the pollen studies from the Highlands area.

During the Holocene, human populations also most likely exerted an influence on the forest vegetation, although their influence was generally local and indirect. For example, it is very likely that they played a role in the elimination of the megafauna that characterized the land soon after the glacier melted, but we have little to no evidence that the loss of this megafauna had an impact on the vegetation in a region, although that certainly seems likely. Similarly, an increased fire frequency caused by ignitions started by Native Americans would have affected the forest vegetation, but only those forests that were susceptible to fire would have burned, and there is, again, little evidence for this in the sedimentary record.

There is some written evidence of the use of fire by the Native American populations (Day 1953; Russell 1983). Descriptions of crown fires most likely did not refer to the oak-dominated forests that characterized most of the Highlands. I have found no written descriptions of surface fires in the early days of European settlement, although it is quite likely that at least local surface fires would have escaped from agricultural-clearing fires or campfires under dry, windy conditions on occasion. These fires would have been localized to Native American settlements or camps and trails, and would most likely not have burned extensive tracts, given the rugged topography and frequent streams in the Highlands.

Although there is also little evidence in the pollen record of the Highlands for precolonial agriculture, it is most likely that the Native Americans did have localized influences in river and stream valleys where they cleared their fields. Estimates are that their populations in the Highlands area were small and fairly stable for many millennia before about 3000 BP, well below the carrying capacity of the land. Uplands were particularly lightly settled and were most likely used only for hunting and collecting wild plants and nuts (Fagan 1995). Over the next one thousand years, communities were developing horticulture, especially of local native crops such as goosefoot (*Chenopodium*), and in the first millennium AD they added maize to their crops (Fagan 1995). These horticultural and agricultural activities left little evidence in the pollen record in the Highlands, indicating that only local areas were cleared (Leduc 2003). Impacts of increasing population on the forest would have been indirect, for example, a decrease in deer browsing caused by increased hunting.

Conditions at the Time of European Contact

This climatic and migrational history set the stage for the massive changes that have occurred in the last three hundred years under the influence of European settlers. Because these settlers were literate, we have documentary as well as sedimentary records of forest composition and extent at this time.

A large increase in the amount of ragweed (*Ambrosia*), a native genus, in the pollen record signals the beginning of major land clearance by European settlers. The date of this event differs across the Highlands but is generally in the mid- to late eighteenth century. Just before this event, oak was the dominant genus on the landscape. There was little pollen of nontree species, indicating a heavily forested landscape, which had remained like this for thousands of years. For the several hundred years before the ragweed increase, the amount of beech in the forests had been declining, perhaps in response to Little Ice Age cooling or drying of the climate (Russell et al. 1993). The amount of spruce had increased, confirming a trend toward cooler climate, but it still constituted a very small proportion of the pollen and, by extrapolation, of the forest vegetation, even in Connecticut (Gaudreau and Webb 1985; Leduc 2003). Some cores have a small increase of herbaceous pollen in the few hundred years just before the major rise in ragweed, most likely indicating the beginning of maize agriculture by Native Americans (Russell and Davis 2001).

A frustrating aspect of pollen data is the inability to distinguish the species of oaks. Since various species of oaks flourish in a variety of climates, it is difficult to distinguish any but a very gross climatic or other environmental signal from oak pollen alone. It is also true that because all oaks produce large amounts of pollen, oak is overrepresented in the pollen rain at the expense of insect-pollinated taxa such as maple and chestnut. However, historical records allow us to distinguish oak species on the landscape as it was being surveyed in the eighteenth century, and to find the insect-pollinated taxa with the same likelihood as wind-pollinated ones. These surveys unequivocally distinguish white oak (*Quercus alba*) as the dominant oak species in the southern part of the Highlands area, where oaks constituted 60 percent or more of the stems mentioned in land surveys (Loeb 1981; Whitney 1994; Cogbill, Burk, and Motzkin 2000, fig. 6.2). Following white oak were a variety of other oak species, especially red oak (*Q. rubra*) and black oak (*Q. velutina*), hickory, and chestnut. Surveys in Connecticut reflect a transition to a more northern forest. In surveys of three townships in Litchfield County, Connecticut, the climatically controlled transition to a more northern forest of hemlock and beech is evident (fig. 6.2) (Winer 1955). The data included in Winer unfortunately do not indicate the species of oaks. Surveys from south of the Wisconsinan terminal moraine in New Jersey and Pennsylvania are very similar to those from the north, which indicates that climate rather than soil development was controlling the major pattern of forest composition because climate does not change across the moraine but soil development does, as discussed in chapter 3. Hickory (*Carya*), a very fire-sensitive genus (Huddle and Pallardy 1995) was second to oak in the southern sites, which suggests that fires were not widespread before European settlement.

Both written descriptions and pollen attest to the existence of Native American agricultural fields. For example, a description of New Netherlands, which included New York and New Jersey, in 1649 mentioned "Maize lands, flats and valleys, which have few or no trees" as well as "all sorts of timber standing . . . without order as in other wildernesses" (Anon. 1649). This is consistent with the slight increase in the pollen of herbaceous plants in the few centuries before the major increase in *Ambrosia* that signals clearing by the colonists (Russell and Davis 2001).

An analysis of tree distributions according to elevation in an area just to the west of the Highlands in New York, in the Shawangunk Mountains, indicates that using these surveys we can define forest communities along an elevation gradient. Of 149 eighteenth-century witness trees, which could be located by whether they grew above or below 200 m, 18 of the 20 chestnut oaks (*Quercus prinus*) were above 200 m, along with all 15 of the chestnuts. Conversely, all 4 beeches, all 5 maples (*Acer* spp.), and all 6 basswoods (*Tilia americana*) grew below 200 m. White, red, and black oak and hickory were evenly distributed above and below 200m. Other variety is indicated by a description of well-timbered land as having "all oak and sometimes hicrey [*sic*], never chestnut (Gardiner 1746–1753). Chestnut was dominant in one "Barren Lott," comprising 40 percent of the witness trees (Russell 1981). There were

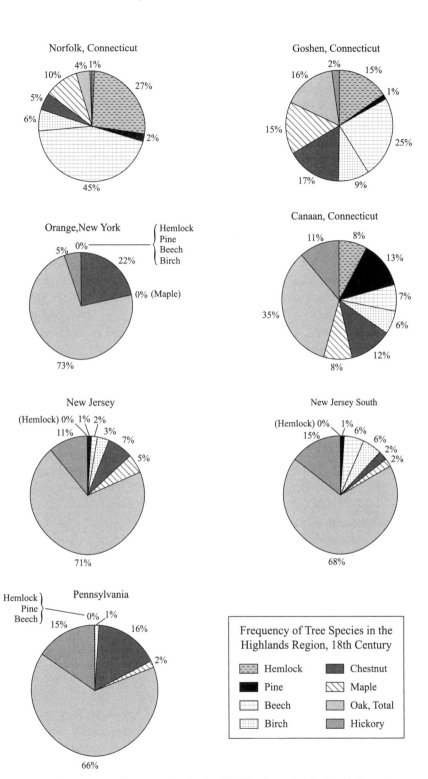

Figure 6.2. Frequency of tree species in the Highlands region in the eighteenth century.

also descriptions of "shrubby white oak" at higher elevations (ibid.). Wetland forests were rarely described. In a New Jersey survey, a stand of shagbark hickories was described in a large "dry swamp" (ibid.). There were, however, fairly large swamps and meadows in this region, as seen by modern topography and some references (Reading 1715).

Changes from 1750 to 1900

Colonists viewed the trees as both impediments and valuable resources. Although much clearing may have involved girdling trees and eventually burning them, very early there was a significant trade in timber, with shipments, mostly oak and hickory, from Manhattan to Europe as early as 1626 (O'Callaghan 1853, I:37–38). Tree bark was also a valuable commodity used for tanning, and it was shipped abroad (Leaming and Spicer 1881). Farmers both used and sold potash, a high-potassium fertilizer, derived from burning trees that they had cleared from their fields (Schmidt 1973; Miller 1980).

Early colonists did not find the glaciated Highlands region attractive for agriculture, recognizing that the rugged topography and generally poor soils of the region would not be productive. In New Jersey, for example, much of the far northern part of the Highlands was still not settled by the second half of the eighteenth century, with few farms being advertised for sale north of the terminal moraine by 1779. In general, the farms in the region were more than three hundred acres in the second half of the eighteenth century, indicating the need for a large area to make a living on the land, or indicating the purchase of large lots for speculation (Wacker 1973). South of the moraine, deeper soils were more attractive, and clearing began earlier. By the time of the American Revolution, most of the land was still forested, with only scattered, fairly new farms. In the century after the Revolution, however, the discovery of iron ore in the Highlands, especially magnetite, and the need for forest products to supply areas to the east led to a major onslaught on the forests. I will summarize the major uses of the land and the consequences of each for the remaining forests.

Agriculture

Old stone walls cutting through forests, abandoned homesites, often with old apple trees and other cultivated plants, and scattered dead red cedar trees under a canopy of deciduous forest are some of the indicators of the extent of agriculture in the Highlands in the middle of the nineteenth century. Using these stone walls, old maps and records, deeds, and other historic documents, one can trace the history of farming in the area. Farmers cleared all the trees from their plowed fields and pastures, selling what could be cut into usable lumber or firewood if they were close to settled areas, burning smaller wood, and often selling the ashes to help fund the establishment of the farm. Most

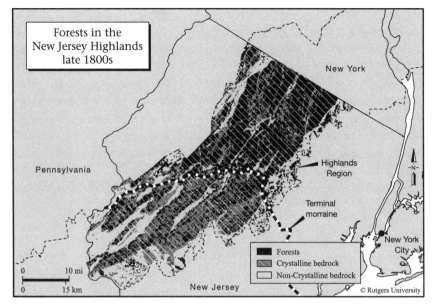

Figure 6.3. Map of New Jersey Highlands forest cover as of 1890 (darker shading) versus crystalline bedrock (slash marked). © Rutgers University.

farmers also tried to keep an area as a woodlot, although in the Highlands, where much of the land was too steep or the soil too shallow to farm, the woodlots were often larger than the cleared land. Raup (1938) estimated that only 7.5 percent of the fifteen-square-kilometer Black Rock Forest was ever cleared, for example, and this proportion is probably representative of much of the northern Highlands. Most cleared land was at lower elevations, often in stream valleys. For example, in the New Jersey Highlands in 1890, north of the terminal moraine, somewhere between 10 percent and 45 percent of the land was farmed above 200 m but 65 percent to 55 percent was farmed below that elevation (data from Smock 1900). South of the moraine, however, 70 percent to 90 percent of the land was not forested below 200 m, and even 50 percent to 60 percent above 200 m (fig. 6.3).

Agriculture affected the forest because trees were removed and replaced with crops or grazing animals, but it also affected the remaining nearby forest. At least in New Jersey, seventeenth-century laws regulated the minimum height of fences around cultivated fields, designed to keep livestock out, not in (Leaming and Spicer 1881). These roving animals, including pigs, sheep, horses, and cattle, would have greatly modified the forests in the vicinity of colonial settlements. Pigs especially were allowed to run at large, where they ate mast, and other animals browsed and grazed throughout the forest. A law in New York, intended to preserve the quality of the horse stock, forbade the release of small stallions into the forest, which indicates that most of the mares were roaming free (Laws of New-York 1691–1773). Farmers also used the forest as a source for fencing materials, firewood, and building lumber as well as for harvesting valuable plants for sale, such as ginseng (U.S. Census Bureau 1850–1890).

Farmers recognized the best soils by the kinds of trees growing in them, so their use of land selectively removed trees that grew on the best soils, leaving those that characterized poorer soils, such as chestnut oak, chestnut, and pitch pine. The use of lowlands for farms also led to drainage of marshes and, where milldams were built, to flooding of valley floors, with eventual sediment accumulation (Walter and Merritts 2008). The elimination of beavers most likely also affected the hydrology and vegetation of lowland areas, but there is no direct evidence of these impacts.

Use of the Forest Resources

To the eighteenth- and nineteenth-century owner of property in the Highlands, forested land appeared to be a vast storehouse of useful materials, available in seemingly limitless quantities. Tryon stated in 1943 that all of Black Rock Forest had been "cut hard (and usually burned) during the past 80 years," and the statement would be true for almost all the forests of the Highlands. Wood was cut for fuelwood, lumber, fencing, tanbark, charcoal, and building materials for the entire period from about 1750 into the twentieth century, and for railroad ties, utility poles, and other uses after the mid-nineteenth century. Fuelwood and lumber were always important products, but other products often produced even more income.

One of the first cash crops from the forest was bark for tanning. The major source of bark for tanneries in the early nineteenth century was oak trees (Anon. 1826). Oak trees were cut in the spring, and the bark was removed and sold to local tanneries. In 1810, the lower Hudson River area, including the Highlands, had 22 percent of New York State's tanneries, though by 1835 these had all but disappeared because of depletion of the bark supplies, that is, the oak trees that were close enough to the river to be profitable to debark (Ellsworth 1975). Similarly, of the twenty-three tanneries in Hunterdon County, New Jersey, in 1840, only seven remained by 1860 (Schmidt 1946). A large tannery in Hunterdon County used "red, white, black, pin, Spanish and chestnut oak, beech, birch and hemlock," which were running out by 1860. By the late nineteenth century, the shortage of oak bark in sufficient quantities led to a shift to using hemlock, which was still present in large stands because these generally grew in areas that were not as good farmland as oak lands. In the Highlands in general, the tanbark industry appears to have been most destructive of oak trees, although toward the end of the nineteenth century hemlocks may also have been harvested. By 1882, when the hemlock tanneries were very important in central and western Pennsylvania and New York, there were no tanneries reported in the Highlands counties (Hough 1880).

The next, and most destructive, use of the forest wood was to make charcoal. As discussed in chapter 11, the charcoal industry used all sizes and species of trees, essentially clear-cutting a large area around a charcoal "hearth" where the wood was piled and slowly burned to produce charcoal, mostly to fuel iron furnaces. The actual amounts of charcoal produced are difficult to measure because they were used directly, not ever getting into commerce to be reported in census records, but the extensive iron furnaces in the Highlands most likely cut at least half of the forest, on a roughly thirty- to forty-year rotation. Regeneration was by stump sprouts, creating the "sprout hardwoods" forest described in the early twentieth century as typical of this region. These sprouts grew very quickly, essentially crowding out any seedling growth (Raup 1938). In Pennsylvania, Illick (1914) noted that while one could not rely on sprouting for regenerating white oak, chestnut was a very vigorous sprouter, which led to an increase in the amount of chestnut in the forests at the expense of white oak.

In the United States in 1850, three out of the six biggest industries depended on forest products: the lumber industry, a direct consumer; the iron and steel industry, a consumer of charcoal; and the tanning industry, a direct consumer (Ellsworth 1975). The wealth of the nation was built on the destructive use of the forests in the nineteenth century. That forest products continued to be important into the twentieth century may be noted by some 1899 statistics from New Jersey showing that within-state users were still major consumers of wood, including domestic fuelwood with a monetary value of $2,255,000 (1899 dollars) as well as lumber ("logs and bolts at the mill") (fig. 6.4). By then new technology in transportation and utilities had created new uses for wood: railroad ties and utility poles. Because these uses required larger logs than earlier uses, they shifted the cutting cycle to a longer time period.

By the last quarter of the nineteenth century, superior sources of iron had been discovered in the Lake Superior region, and anthracite coal was replacing charcoal in the iron furnaces so much of the destructive harvesting of wood in the Highlands decreased significantly. As described in chapter 12, more productive farms were becoming available in the Midwest at this time, and many Highlands-area farmers left their farms and moved west, leaving the abandoned farms to grow back to forest. While fuelwood was still used heavily in New York for brick kilns, other uses were decreasing. Small stems that regenerated on recently cut land were cut for hoop poles for making barrels, but the directly destructive uses of the forest generally waned.

Fire

Another scourge beset these forests: fire. In a deciduous forest, fires normally burn only on the surface and move through quickly with relatively little direct damage to the forest canopy (Boerner 2005). The conditions left by the

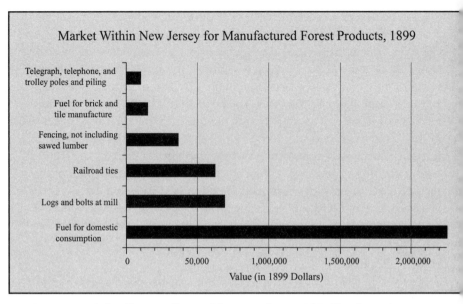

Figure 6.4. Market for manufactured forest products within New Jersey in 1899.

repeated cutting during the nineteenth century, however, had left a forest that was very inflammable, with large amounts of slash and shrubs that would have served as fire ladders to allow the fires to reach the low crowns of the trees. Illick (1914) described the landscape of Pennsylvania as "very unproductive, unsanitary, unattractive and unregulated," seriously damaged by fire and cutting. The New Jersey state geologist blamed "fires and cattle" for much of the poor regeneration of the forests in many places and observed that while fires may not kill the trees immediately, over time they will cause heart decay (Vermeule 1900). Raup (1938) also referred to many fires in Black Rock Forest. Ignition sources were almost all anthropogenic, including sparks from locomotives, carelessness (burning brush, smoking), and malicious burning (intentionally set fires). In New Jersey in 1880, for example, twenty-eight fires were attributed to sparks from locomotives, thirteen to carelessness, and seven to maliciousness (Gifford 1896). It is also possible that some of the fires of unknown origin resulted from large trees that had been struck by lightning during thunderstorms and smoldered until the surrounding brush had dried out, only then igniting a larger fire (personal communication, B. Steward, National Park Service).

The sedimentary record shows a large increase in fires after European settlement throughout the Northeast (Russell et al. 1993). This increase in fire corresponds with the decrease in hemlock and beech in the pollen record, both fire-sensitive species, and an increase in black and gray birch (*Betula lenta* and *B. populifolia*), which often respond favorably to fire. Patterson (2005) found from pollen studies that the increased amount of fire after European settlement changed the forest composition to more pine in areas with both pine and oak.

The Early Twentieth Century

The late nineteenth century to early twentieth century marked a sea change in management of the forests of the Highlands. Because of changing market pressures, there was no longer profit to be made in the destructive, frequent cutting of the forests. The condition of the forests was everywhere described as poor but recovering. While it is easy to imagine vigorous cutting of the forests during the nineteenth century, the extent and intensity of this activity is harder to envision. Even forests that grew on abandoned farm lots were logged when young, often for hoop poles, which were cut while trees were small. It seems that almost all the forests were repeatedly clear-cut for various products and often burned as well, so that the trees that were recovering in the early twentieth century were mostly stump sprouts, which most foresters described as weaker than the original, seedling-grown trees. Most descriptions indicate that seedlings had difficulty growing under the vigorous sprouts, so there was only a small proportion of trees coming from seed. There is some evidence in the pollen record and documents that the very vigorous sprouters such as chestnut had been favored by the coppice cutting, and that trees that do not sprout, such as hemlock, had been greatly diminished. Species that responded well to openings and disturbances, such as the wind-dispersed birches and red maple, had been favored, even though red maple would have been also destroyed by fires. Abandoned farms were mostly succeeding to gray birch or red cedar throughout the Highlands (Raup 1938; Vermeule 1900) (fig. 6.5).The few descriptions of swamp forests often included maples and elms, often with pine, hemlock, and sometimes tamarack.

A few old-growth forests survived into the early twentieth century, mostly in hemlock ravines that were hard to reach and had little valuable timber to make the effort worthwhile. Nichols described one that survived uncut and unburned until 1912, although logging had destroyed most of it in that year. The forest consisted mostly of very large hemlock and beech trees, with a mixture of other species, uneven in age and with numerous seedlings of the mature species (Nichols 1913). One old-growth stand of chestnut oaks, many more than three hundred years old, still characterizes a ridgetop in Pennsylvania (Mikan, Orwig, and Abrams 1994), which may indicate the aboriginal forest type on these ridges. This is also consistent with the record in the Shawangunk Mountains of chestnut oak growing primarily on ridgetops and with

Figure 6.5. Wintertime photograph of an abandoned Highlands farm regenerating back into forest circa 1910. Photo is from the foot of Mt. Dunderberg looking northeast across the frozen Hudson River to Manitou Mountain. William Thompson Howell, Highlands of the Hudson, Photography Collection, Miriam and Ira D. Wallach Division of Art, Prints and Photographs, The New York Public Library, Astor, Lenox, and Tilden Foundations.

the low numbers of chestnut oak trees in regional eighteenth-century forest surveys (7 percent), reflecting the relative rarity of this habitat.

The first major twentieth-century impact on the recovering forests was the introduction of the chestnut blight (*Cryphonectria parasitica*) from Asia. This blight spread from New York City throughout the range of the chestnut, killing all the chestnut trees. Although the chestnut trees continued to occur as small sprouts, which occasionally reached adult size and fruited, this dominant species was essentially eliminated as a forest tree. Quantitative techniques for studying forest composition and structure were just being introduced, so there is only one detailed study comparing the composition of a forest area just before the blight with that several years later, in southeastern Connecticut (Korstian and Stickel 1927; see fig. 6.6). With the loss of chestnut, a major dominant in this stand, chestnut oak became relatively more important while white and red oak became less important. This study and others that considered a qualitative estimate of the preblight composition with the postblight forest all found that it was mostly the mature trees of species that were in the forest before the blight that expanded their canopies to fill the gaps left by the chestnut, along with existing, overshadowed saplings that were released to reach the canopy, even though relative proportions of species may have changed (Good 1968).

Conclusion

Oaks, especially white oak, dominated much of the precolonial forest of the Highlands, although there were variations due to altitude, latitude, soils, and exposure. This was also the time of the Little Ice Age, so climate was somewhat cooler on average than at present. There is little evidence for any significant direct human impact on these forests except in localized areas, most likely in the larger stream valleys. Fires probably did occur, but at very long intervals and primarily during periods of significant drought and warmth. Given the structure of the forests, these were presumably surface fires that mostly burned the litter layer, and did not affect the crowns of the trees or the soils and buried seed banks. Unfortunately, we have little to no evidence of the shrubs or herbaceous layers of the forest, although anecdotal evidence

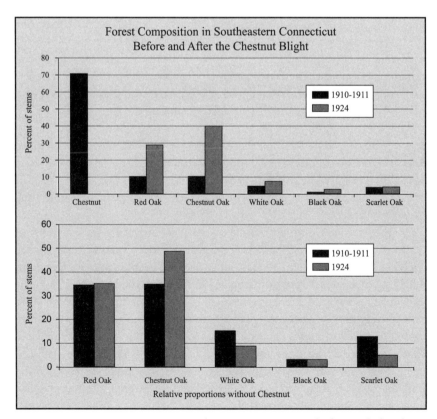

Figure 6.6. Forest composition in southeastern Connecticut before and after the chestnut blight.

suggests that the understory in the dry uplands was quite open, a natural feature of a closed-canopy forest. The amount of beech in the forests had been declining for several centuries, possibly in response to the climate of the Little Ice Age.

Overall, the evidence indicates that the forest vegetation had been in dynamic equilibrium with climate throughout the preceding millennia. Changes in climate and the consequent responses of the forest vegetation had been slow, on the order of centuries at the fastest. Disturbances were of small extent and duration, most likely the result of windstorms or insect outbreaks. The changes that followed European settlement were unprecedented in rate, extent, severity, and duration. Farmers cleared some forests completely for farms, imposing chronic soil disturbance and replacement of vegetation. Livestock, especially pigs, grazed at large in uncut forests. North of the Wisconsinan terminal moraine, pre-Revolutionary clearing for farms was more local than to the south. After the American Revolution, industrial uses of the forest for fuels and tanbark led to complete deforestation of remaining forests on a shifting or rotating basis, with never a period when the whole area was clear-cut at one time and no time when the forest soil was left completely bare. Erosion occurred, but was probably not very serious in most areas. The tree species that sprouted readily from underground stools grew vigorously after they were cut, producing a coppice or the "sprout hardwoods" forest described in the late nineteenth and early twentieth centuries. It is apparent from vegetation descriptions and from the pollen record that this process encouraged chestnut trees and discouraged hemlocks. Birch also responded favorably to this cutting. Sprouts grew vigorously enough to crowd out most seedling regeneration. South of the Wisconsinan terminal moraine, the forest was more discontinuous, contributing just 30 percent of the land cover. These woodlots were used heavily for fuelwood, fencing, and other farm essentials and as a cash crop, producing income through activities such as collecting ginseng or peeling bark.

In the late nineteenth and early twentieth centuries, fire became a major factor in these forests, eliminating fire-sensitive species such as hemlock and speeding the decline that had started earlier for beech. It may have encouraged the most fire tolerant of the oaks, the chestnut oak, as well.

There is very little direct evidence of the changes in lowland forests. One pollen study in New Jersey suggests that alder wetlands may have been converted from alder (Alnus) to ash and maple by draining, which would have changed both the hydrology and the substrate (Russell 1980), but descriptions of precolonial swamps are vague at best. The elimination of beavers and the building of permanent dams for mills would have altered the hydrology in ways that are still to be determined.

Just as the forests were beginning to recover from the destruction of the nineteenth century, a nonnative disease attacked and killed all the chestnut trees, a species that had been very prominent in the recovering forests. Other species spread their crowns to replace lost cover, and young trees in the understory accelerated their growth as well, so there was no time when there was no canopy cover, even where chestnuts formed the majority of the trees in a stand. The forests displayed remarkable resilience in the face of this dramatic die-off. Subtle effects of the preceding centuries of human impact, though, and of twentieth-century impacts such as altered atmospheric chemistry are more difficult to discern. White oak no longer was the dominant oak in these forests, chestnut had been much more important than before, hemlock and beech were less common, and chestnut oak was more important. Climate still determined what species could grow in the Highlands, but their distribution and relative importance were changed from those of the precolonial forests in ways that reflected the legacy of the centuries of unprecedented disturbances.

While one can compare the present and precolonial forests in terms of changes in hypothetical disturbance factors such as fire, it is critical to carefully evaluate the intervening processes and their legacies in terms of forest composition and structure, including the species of oaks in the forest when trying to explain the apparent lack of oak regeneration in current forests. Intervening processes such as the extensive development of sprout forests, loss of chestnut, soil depletion by overcropping, and destructive fires of the late nineteenth and twentieth centuries have left legacies the importance of which have yet to be fully evaluated.

References

Allison, T. D., R. E. Moeller, and M. B. Davis. 1986. "Pollen in Laminated Sediments Provides Evidence for a Mid-Holocene Forest Pathogen Outbreak." *Ecology* 67:1101–1105.

Anonymous. 1649. "Remonstrances of New Netherlands." In *Documents Relative to the Colonial History of the State of New York*, ed. E. B. O'Callaghan, 1:179. Albany, NY: Weed, Parsons.

———. 1826. "On the Processing, Leather-Dressing, and Dying, &c." *Journal of the Franklin Institute* 1:116–120.

Boerner, R.E.J. 2005. "Soil, Fire, Water and Wind: How the Elements Conspire in the Forest Context." In *Fire in Eastern Oak Forests: Delivering Science to Land Managers*, ed. M. B. Dickinson, 104–122. USDA Forest Service General Technical Report NRS-P-1.

Carcaillet, C., Y. Bergeron, P. H. Richard, B. Fréchette, S. Gauthier, and Y. T. Prairie. 2001. "Change of Fire Frequency in the Eastern Canadian Boreal Forests during the Holocene: Does Vegetation Composition or Climate Trigger the Fire Regime?" *Journal of Ecology* 89:930–946.

Clark, J. S., and P. D. Royall. 1996. "Local and Regional Sediment Charcoal Evidence for Fire Regimes in Presettlement North-Eastern North America." *Journal of Ecology* 84:365–382.

Clements, F. C. 1936. "Nature and Structure of the Climax." *Journal of Ecology* 24:252–284.

Cogbill, C. V., J. Burk, and G. Motzkin. 2000. "The Forests of Presettlement New England, USA: Spatial and Compositional Patterns Based on Town Proprietor Surveys." *Journal of Biogeography* 29:1279–1304.

Cronon, W. 1983. *Changes in the Land.* New York: Hill and Wang.

Davis, M. B., and R. G. Shaw. 2001. "Range Shifts and Adaptive Responses to Quaternary Climate Change." *Science* 292:673–679.

Day, G. 1953. "The Indian as an Ecological Factor in the Northeastern Forest." *Ecology* 34:329–346.

Deevey, E. S. 1939. "Studies on Connecticut Lake Sediments. I. A Postglacial Climatic Chronology for Southern New England." *American Journal of Science* 237: 691–724.

Ellsworth, L. F. 1975. *Craft to National Industry in the Nineteenth Century: A Case Study of the Transformation of the New York State Tanning Industry.* Dissertations in American Economic History. New York: Arno Press.

Fagan, B. M. 1995. *Ancient North America: The Archaeology of a Continent.* 2nd ed. London: Thames and Hudson.

Foster, D. R., and J. D. Aber, eds. 2004. *Forests in Time.* New Haven, CT: Yale University Press.

Foster, D. R., W. W. Oswald, E. K. Faison, E. D. Doughty, and B.C.S. Hansen. 2006. "A Climatic Driver for Abrupt Mid-Holocene Vegetation Dynamics and the Hemlock Decline in New England." *Ecology* 87:2959–2966.

Gardiner, R. 1746–1753, 1752–1754. "Surveys on the Wallkill." Manuscript at New Jersey Historical Society, Newark, NJ.

Gaudreau, D. C., and T. Webb III. 1985. "Late-Quaternary Pollen Stratigraphy and Isochrone Maps for the Northeastern United States." In *Pollen Records of Late-Quaternary North American Sediments,* ed. V. M. Bryant Jr. and R. G. Holloway, 247–280. Dallas: American Association of Stratigraphic Palynologists Foundation.

Gifford, J. 1896. "Report on Forest Fires for the Season of 1895." In *Annual Report of the State Geologist for the Year 1895,* 157–182. Trenton, NJ.

Gillson, L., and K. J. Willis. 2008. "Testing Sensitivity of Charcoal as an Indicator of Fire Events in Savanna Environments: Quantitative Predictions of Fire Proximity, Area and Intensity." *The Holocene* 18:279–291.

Gleason, H. A. 1926. "The Individualistic Concept of the Plant Association." *Bulletin of the Torrey Botanical Club* 53:7–26.

Good, N. F. 1968. "A Study of Natural Replacement of Chestnut in Six Stands in the Highlands of New Jersey." *Bulletin of the Torrey Botanical Club* 95:240–253.

Grimm, E. C., and G. L. Jacobson Jr. 2004. "Late-Quaternary Vegetation History of the Eastern United States." In *The Quaternary Period in the United States,* ed. A. R. Gillespie and S. C. Porter, 381–402. Amsterdam: Elsevier.

Harmon, K. P. 1968. "Late Pleistocene Forest Succession in Northern New Jersey." PhD diss., Rutgers University.

Hough, F. B. 1880. *Report upon Forestry / Prepared under the Direction of the Commissioner of Agriculture, in Pursuance of an Act of Congress, Approved August 15, 1876.* Washington, DC: Government Printing Office, 1878–1880.

Huddle, J. A., and S. G. Pallardy. 1995. "Tree Survivorship in an Oak-Hickory Forest in Southeast Missouri, USA, under a Long-Term Regime of Annual and Controlled Burns." In *10th Central Hardwood Conference Proceedings*, ed. K. W. Gottschalk and F. LO. C. Fosbroke. USDA Forest Service General Technical Report NE 1997.

Illick, J. S. 1914. *Pennsylvania Trees*. Harrisburg (Pennsylvania Department of Forestry, Bulletin 11).

Jackson, S. T., J. T. Overpeck, T. Webb III, S. E. Keattch, and K. H. Anderson. 1997. "Mapped Plant-Macrofossil and Pollen Records of Late Quaternary Vegetation Change in Eastern North America." *Quaternary Science Reviews* 16:1–70.

Korstian, C. F., and P. W. Stickel. 1927. "The Natural Replacement of Blight-Killed Chestnut in Hardwood Forests of the Northeast." *Journal of Agricultural Research* 34:631–648.

Laws of New-York from the Year 1691–1773, inclusive. Microfilm at the New York State Library, Albany.

Leaming, A., and J. Spicer. 1881. *The Grants, Concessions and Original Constitutions of the Province of New Jersey*. 2nd ed. Philadelphia: W. Bradford.

Leduc, P. 2003. Pollen Viewer 3.2, WDC for Paleoclimatology. http://www.ncdc .noaa.gov/paleo/pollen/viewer/webviewer.html.

Loeb, R. E. 1981. "Pre-European Settlement Forest Composition in East New Jersey and Southeastern New York." *American Midland Naturalist* 118:414–423.

Maenza-Gmelch, T. E.. 1997a. "Holocene Vegetation, Climate, and Fire History of the Hudson Highlands, Southeastern New York, USA." *The Holocene* 7:25–37.

———. 1997b. "Late-Glacial–Early Holocene Vegetation, Climate, and Fire at Sutherland Pond, Hudson Highlands, Southeastern New York, USA." *Canadian Journal of Botany* 75:431–439.

———. 1997c. "Vegetation, Climate, and Fire during the Late-Glacial–Holocene Transition at Spruce Pond, Hudson Highlands, Southeastern New York, USA." *Journal of Quaternary Science* 12:15–24.

Mikan, C. J., D. A. Orwig, and M. D. Abrams. 1994. "Age Structure and Successional Dynamics of a Presettlement Origin Chestnut Oak Forest in the Pennsylvania Piedmont." *Bulletin of the Torrey Botanical Club* 121:13–23.

Miller, H. 1980. "Potash from Wood Ashes: Frontier Technology in Canada and the United States." *Technology and Culture* 21:187–208.

Nichols, G. E. 1913. "The Vegetation of Connecticut. II. Virgin Forests." *Torreya* 13:199.

O'Callaghan, E. B., ed. 1853. *Documents Relative to the Colonial History of the State of New York*. Albany, NY: Weed, Parsons.

Parshall, T., and D. R. Foster. 2002. "Fire in the New England Landscape: Regional and Temporal Variation, Cultural and Environmental Controls." *Journal of Biogeography* 29:1305–1317.

Patterson, W. A., III. 2005. "The Paleoecology of Fire and Oaks in Eastern Forests." In *Fire in Eastern Oak Forests: Delivering Science to Land Managers*, ed. Matthew B. Dickinson, 2–19. Newtown Square, PA: USDA Forest Service. http://nrs.fs.fed .us/pubs/gtr/nrs_gtrP1.pdf.

Peteet, D. 2000. "Sensitivity and Rapidity of Vegetational Response to Abrupt

Climate Change." *Proceedings of the National Academy of Sciences of the United States of America* 97:1359–1361.

Raup, H. M. 1938. "Botanical Studies in the Black Rock Forest." *Black Rock Forest Bulletin 7*.

Reading, J. 1715. "Surveyor's Journal." New Jersey Historical Society, manuscript.

Russell, E.W.B. 1980. "Vegetational Change in Northern New Jersey from Precolonization to the Present: A Palynological Interpretation." *Bulletin of the Torrey Botanical Club* 107:432–446.

———. 1981. "Vegetation of Northern New Jersey before European Settlement." *American Midland Naturalist* 105:1–12.

———. 1983. "Indian-Set Fires in the Forests of the Northeastern United States." *Ecology* 64:79–88.

———. 1997. *People and the Land through Time. Linking Ecology and History*. New Haven, CT: Yale University Press.

Russell, E.W.B., and R. B. Davis. 2001. "Five Centuries of Changing Forest Vegetation in the Northeastern United States." *Plant Ecology* 155:1–13.

Russell, E.W.B., R. B. Davis, R. S. Anderson, T. E. Rhodes, and D. S. Anderson. 1993. "Recent Centuries of Vegetational Change in the Glaciated North-Eastern United States." *Journal of Ecology* 81:647–664.

Russell, E.W.B., and S. D. Stanford. 2000. "Late-Glacial Environmental Changes South of the Wisconsinan Terminal Moraine in the Eastern United States." *Quaternary Research* 53:105–113.

Schmidt, H. G. 1946. *Rural Hunterdon*. New Brunswick, NJ: Rutgers University Press.

———. 1973. *Agriculture in New Jersey*. New Brunswick, NJ: Rutgers University Press.

Smock, J. 1900. Forests of Northern New Jersey. Maps. Trenton: Geological Survey of New Jersey.

Tryon, H. H. 1943. "Practical Forestry in the Hudson Highlands." *Black Rock Forest Bulletin 12*.

United States Census Bureau. 1850–1890. Agricultural Census Returns. Washington, DC: Government Printing Office.

Vermeule, C. C. 1900. "The Forests of New Jersey." In *Annual Report of the State Geologist for the Year 1899*, 13–101. Trenton: Geological Survey of New Jersey.

Wacker, P. O. 1973. *Land and People*. New Brunswick, NJ: Rutgers University Press.

Walter, R. C., and D. J. Merritts. 2008. "Natural Streams and the Legacy of Water-Powered Mills." *Science* 319:299–304.

Watts, W. A. 1979. "Late Quaternary Vegetation Patterns of Appalachia." *Ecological Monographs* 49:427–469.

Webb, T., III. 1986. "Is Vegetation in Equilibrium with Climate? How to Interpret Late-Quaternary Pollen Data." *Vegetatio* 67:75–91.

Webb, T., III, B. Shuman, and J. W. Williams. 2004. "Climatically Forced Vegetation Dynamics in Eastern North America during the Late Quaternary Period." In *The Quaternary Period in the United States*, ed. A. R. Gillespie and S. C. Porter, 459–478. Amsterdam: Elsevier.

Whitlock, C., and P. J. Bartlein. 2004. "Holocene Fire Activity as a Record of Past

Environmental Change." In *The Quaternary Period in the United States*, ed. A. R. Gillespie and S. C. Porter, 479–490. Amsterdam: Elsevier.

Whitney, G. G. 1994. *From Coastal Wilderness to Fruited Plain*. Cambridge: Cambridge University Press.

Willis, K. J., and H.J.B. Birks. 2006. "What Is Natural? The Need for a Long-Term Perspective in Biodiversity Conservation." *Science* 314:1261–1265.

Winer, H. I. 1955. "History of the Great Mountain Forest, Litchfield County, Connecticut." PhD diss., Yale University.

7

Forest Ecology

William S. F. Schuster

Introduction

Forests are earth's dominant vegetation type and are intimately intertwined with our lives. They produce much of the oxygen we breathe, supply much of the water we drink, provide material to build the houses in which we live, and are central to many facets of human endeavor. Forests function via processes and change over timescales that can be difficult for humans to appreciate. Failures to understand forest ecosystems have underlain some of the most momentous societal collapses in history (Diamond 2005). Forests of the Highlands are of direct importance to the lives of millions of people. But some of the changes now occurring in these forests may have unprecedented impacts on humans and other organisms around the region.

Forests are more than the sum of their parts. They are ecological systems interconnected by processes such as energy flow and nutrient cycling. Natural ecosystem functions provide many services and products of value to human societies. For example, we rely on forested watersheds as sources of high-quality drinking water because of their biogeochemical cycles, which filter many substances that we consider pollutants. For another example, photosynthesis by forests absorbs enormous amounts of atmospheric carbon dioxide each year, counteracting much of the carbon dioxide released by fossil fuel combustion and slowing the rate of anthropogenic climate change. Thus alteration of forest ecosystem processes can have far-reaching and enduring consequences.

Although forest cover in the Highlands region, as in much of eastern North America, is now more extensive than in the last 150 years, abundance does not necessarily imply good health. It is increasingly clear that, in some parts of the Highlands, forest function has been substantially altered and forest health has been compromised. We need to understand what services and products we need these forests for, and we must closely monitor their health so they can provide such needs for the foreseeable future.

In the remainder of this chapter I will describe current forests of the Highlands, evaluate aspects of their health, and review some of the changes that are occurring. I will focus on key areas of ecosystem health such as energy flow, biological diversity, nutrient cycling, and disturbance regimes. I will conclude by discussing future implications of these changes and some possible responses.

Forests of the Highlands

The 250-mile-long (400+ km) Highlands province lies wholly within the "historic oak-chestnut forest" region (Braun 1967). Since the demise of the American chestnut (*Castanea dentata*), this regional forest type has often been termed "oak-hickory" despite the fact that hickories (*Carya* spp.) are only minor components of most stands. Oak trees (*Quercus* spp.) and their acorns, conversely, are iconic of the Highlands region and central to its ecology. Other abundant deciduous hardwoods in the region are red and sugar maple (*Acer rubrum* and *A. saccharum*), yellow poplar (*Liriodendron tulipifera*), hickories, birches (*Betula* spp.), ashes (*Fraxinus* spp.), and American beech (*Fagus grandifolia*). The most common conifers in the Highlands are eastern hemlock (*Tsuga canadensis*), white pine (*Pinus strobus*), and pitch pine (*Pinus rigida*). Nonnative trees that may be locally abundant include Norway maple (*Acer platanoides*), Norway spruce (*Picea abies*), tree-of-heaven (*Ailanthus altissima*), European buckthorn (*Rhamnus cathartica*), and black locust (*Robinia pseudoacacia*). The Forest Service's Forest Inventory and Analysis (FIA) database indicates that the four most common local cover types in the Highlands are white oak/red oak/hickory; red oak; yellow poplar/white oak/red oak; and red maple/lowland hardwoods (Woudenberg et al. 2009; table 7.1).

The composition and structure of current Highlands forests reflect local climate, topography, and geologic substrate as well as the sequence of historical factors described in the previous chapter: heavy cutting and clearing, conversion of much forestland to pasture and other agricultural uses, widespread abandonment of these uses, and subsequent forest regrowth. Stone walls' characteristics attest to previous land uses, with ridges and steeper slopes most often having served as woodlots while gentler slopes and valleys were more often converted to pasture or cropland. The majority of the Highlands landscape was cultivated or developed at some time in the past, and forestlands that were not converted have nearly all been repeatedly cut, and many have burned. Canopy trees in these forests today either survived or in some cases thrived as a result of this heavy disturbance and in many woodlot areas also successfully contended with naturally low levels of soil nutrients. The frequent cutting cycles of the past favored hardwoods that readily regenerate from root sprouts such as red and chestnut oak (*Quercus rubra* and *Q. prinus*). The suppression of fires through much of the twentieth century also resulted in expansion of thin-barked species such as red maple. Nonnative organisms

Table 7.1 Characteristics of Forest Inventory and Analysis (FIA) Plots around the Highlands Region (2003–2008 data)

Region	% Forested plots	Stand age (yrs)	Basal area (ft²/ac)	Wood volume*	Above-ground biomass**	Tree height (ft)	Site index (ft)
Entire Highlands	50.8	78	122.2	19.9	838	58.1	69.2
Connecticut	71.3	76	104.0	17.7	720	55.4	64.9
New York	57.9	94	103.7	19.8	898	55.8	66.5
New Jersey	62.5	80	123.5	20.4	874	60.0	64.8
Pennsylvania	34.4	72	132.1	22.1	916	60.4	80.3
Highlands N of glacial margin	69.1	83	114.0	18.4	784	56.1	63.7
Highlands S of glacial margin	35.5	72	131.1	21.4	911	59.1	78.3

* Gross cubic feet of wood in an average tree > 5 in (12.7 cm) diameter.
** Total aboveground oven dry weight in lb of an average tree 1 in (2.54 cm) diameter or larger.

began to substantially alter Highlands forests early in the twentieth century, starting with the loss of American chestnut to the Asiatic chestnut blight fungus (*Cryphonectria parasitica*). Subsequently introduced "pests" and pathogens greatly reduced American elms (*Ulmus americana*) and populations of several other native species. Many nonnative taxa have now become widespread and essentially "naturalized" in Highlands forests.

Currently about half of the Highlands region from Pennsylvania to Connecticut features forest cover (see plate 11), far less than the amount of pre-European forest cover but nearly twice as much as a century ago. Most modern forests are substantially fragmented, and the great majority are composed of individual small tracts. Highlands forests range from very young, early successional woodlands to mature forest communities up to about 150 years of age. The average age of 551 forest stands in the Highlands study area was 78.1 years, as recorded by FIA inventories between 2003 and 2008, with an average tree height of about 58 feet (17.7 meters). Well-developed forests in the Highlands have four more-or-less distinct vegetative strata: canopy, understory, shrub layer, and ground layer. Along with these four strata, numerous niches and microsites support a diverse assemblage of organisms. However, young stand age and shallow soils limit the height of many Highlands forests. Basal area of stands (the cross-sectional area of a tree measured at chest height, in this case summed across a group of trees) around the region averages 122 square feet per acre (28 square meters per hectare) with an average tree aboveground dry biomass of 838 lb (380 kg) and an average wood volume of 19.9 cubic feet (0.56 cubic meters; see table 7.1). On those areas with sufficient wood-producing capacity to be classified as timberland, the average timber tree contains about 10.5 cubic yards (8 cubic meters) of wood.

Embedded within the oak-dominated matrix in wetlands, along streams, and in flat areas with high soil moisture are found more hydrophytic forest communities characterized by trees such as red maple, shagbark hickory (*Carya ovata*), and American sycamore (*Platanus occidentalis*). Air temperatures on north-facing Highlands slopes and ravines can be several degrees cooler than on nearby south-facing slopes, and growing seasons can be as much as two weeks shorter. Some of these areas feature "northern hardwood" forest communities (variously characterized by white pine, eastern hemlock, sugar maple, beech, and yellow birch (*Betula alleghaniensis*). Differences in composition and structure also occur across the margin between the glaciated (northern) and the unglaciated (southern) sections of the Highlands, due in many cases to different soil conditions and/or contrasting land use histories (table 7.1).

North of the Glacial Margin

Most of the Highlands region north of the glacial margin is composed of rugged uplands with as much as 1,310 feet (400 meters) of local relief (see plate 12). Forest cover averages nearly 70 percent, and parks and preserved lands are common. Slopes are frequently steep with shallow, acidic, till-derived soils underlain by bedrock interspersed with rock outcrops. These conditions are more suitable for the growth of some species (e.g., chestnut and scrub oaks [*Q. illicifolia*], pitch pine) than others. Owing to the natural tendency of fires to burn uphill, upper slopes and ridges have experienced the most fires, and many now feature a high proportion of relatively fire-resistant chestnut oak. Many lower-elevation forests are former farmlands colonized by red and sugar maple, beech, hickories, basswood (*Tilia americana*), and oaks. In a few scattered valley areas where soils developed from calcareous materials, the higher pH has favored a different suite of tree species (e.g., eastern red cedar [*Juniperus virginiana*], American elm, white ash [*Fraxinus americana*], sugar maple), although most of these areas with better soils remain cultivated.

The New Jersey Highlands north of the glacial margin are 69 percent forested, with the oldest average stand age among the states at eighty-three years. White oak/red oak/hickory; yellow poplar/white oak/red oak; and chestnut oak are the most common local cover types. Upland forest understory typically features witch hazel (*Hamamelis virginiana*), mountain laurel (*Kalmia latifolia*), huckleberry (*Gaylussacia* spp.), and blueberry (*Vaccinium* spp.). Proceeding north from the glacial margin, New Jersey uplands exhibit increasing slope, more oak and less maple, and a decreasing proportion of developed land. According to FIA countywide data for all counties within the Highlands study area, the proportion of productive "timberland" peaks in Sussex County at more than 50 percent. The western Highlands in New Jersey and adjacent New York contain some of the region's most important contiguous, protected forests, with many tracts larger than one thousand acres. Between the glaciated uplands, Highlands valleys in New Jersey average 45 percent forestland and 30 percent developed land. Many valley forests are young woodland mixes of black cherry (*Prunus serotina*), red maple, and early successional and invasive species, while others are dominated by tulip poplar and sugar maple. These valley forests are often quite fragmented and contain many nonnative species but are capable of developing great stature and complexity.

New York's Highlands region, in contrast, is only 58 percent forested and is dominated by red oak; chestnut oak/black oak/scarlet oak (*Q. coccinea*); and red maple/lowland hardwoods forest types (table 7.1). Some higher-elevation and north-facing slopes in New York (as well as New Jersey) feature hemlock–northern hardwood forests with eastern hemlock, sugar maple, and occasionally American beech as well as associated trees such as yellow birch and striped maple (*Acer pensylvanicum*). A pitch pine/oak/heath community type (dominated by pitch pine, chestnut oak, and scrub oak) is sometimes present at higher elevations and on ridgetops. Forested wetlands are common and are typically dominated by red maple with other trees such as black ash (*Fraxinus nigra*) and bitternut hickory (*Carya cordiformis*), and a dense layer of shrubs such as spicebush (*Lindera benzoin*), black chokeberry (*Aronia melanocarpa*), and highbush blueberry (*Vaccinium corymbosum*). Mesic forests in lower elevations may also have elm, tulip poplar, and sugar maple. Putnam and Dutchess counties are heavily forested and over half covered in timberland while the Highlands in Rockland and Westchester counties (closer to New York City) feature more than 50 percent developed land. New York's Highlands forests have the lowest average basal area among the four states at less than 104 square feet per acre (23.8 square meters per hectare).

The Connecticut portion of the Highlands is more than 71 percent forested (table 7.1) and includes many parks and preserved lands. Common local forest types are white oak/red oak/hickory; red oak; and sugar maple/American beech/yellow birch, with significant areas of white pine and eastern hemlock forest (see plate 13). More than half of Litchfield County is productive timberland with a high volume of sawlog trees. The easternmost portion of the Connecticut Highlands study area lacks the oak dominance and bedrock outcrops characteristic of the central Highlands. The commonness of paper birch (*Betula papyrifera*), yellow birch, and understory shrubs such as nannyberry (*Viburnum lentago*) attests to the cooler northern climate of these forests.

South of the Glacial Margin

The Highlands south of the glacial margin are generally less steep and less rocky and feature less local relief and more fertile soils. Uplands cover less area than the surrounding lowlands and valleys, and the remaining forest tracts occur within a matrix of predominantly developed or cultivated lands. The area features few contiguous forests larger than one thousand acres (405 hectares), and fewer parks and preserved lands than the northern Highlands. Forest cover averages 35.5 percent, or just more than half of that north of the glacial margin, and the stands are on average eleven years younger (table 7.1). Despite their younger age, the trees are taller on average than in the northern Highlands, and stands have higher average basal area and aboveground biomass compared to stands north of the glacial margin, reflecting generally more productive growing conditions. The most common local cover types are yellow poplar; yellow poplar/white oak/red oak; white oak/red oak/ hickory; and red maple/oak. From New Jersey south through the Pennsylvania Highlands there is a trend of decreasing amount of forest cover, smaller tracts, increasing fragmentation, and less preserved and protected forestland.

The New Jersey Highlands south of the glacial margin are 48 percent forested, with high basal area, wood volume, and biomass. The most common local forest type is yellow poplar/white oak/red oak. Uplands are 58 percent forested and feature white and black oak (*Q. alba* and *Q. velutina*) with red oak, red and sugar maple, and white ash. Areas between the ridges have deep, well-drained soils often enriched by limestone bedrock. As a result, they have high agricultural resource value and are predominantly cultivated, with only 22 percent forestland. Compared to the ridges, valley forests south of the glacial margin feature less oak and more yellow poplar and black birch (*Betula lenta*).

In the Pennsylvania Highlands, Reading Prong bedrock is widely dispersed, and Highlands forests are scattered and often highly fragmented. Only 34 percent of the land is forested: Bucks, Montgomery, and Lancaster counties are less than 25 percent forested, and all other Highlands counties are less than half forested. A matrix of cultivated lands surrounds most remaining forests, interspersed with towns and developments. The uplands rise generally only 300–650 feet (100–200 meters) above surrounding lowlands and valleys. Average stand age is the youngest among the Highlands states at seventy-two years. However, site index and productivity are high with good sawtimber volume in Northampton, Chester, and Lancaster counties. Forest cover types are diverse; oaks are less dominant than elsewhere in the Highlands, and hardwoods such as tulip poplar, black gum (*Nyssa sylvatica*), and black walnut (*Juglans nigra*) are more common (see plate 14). The slightly warmer climate favors some species with mostly southern distributions (e.g., catalpa [*Catalpa bignonioides*], black gum) and fewer conifers and northern hardwood species. In the understory, blueberries and huckleberries are less common than in the northern Highlands while shrubs such as spicebush and vines such as greenbrier (*Smilax rotundafolia*) and poison ivy (*Rhus toxicodendron*) are more common.

Productivity and Diversity

All the diverse forms of life in the Highlands depend on the capture of solar energy by trees and other photosynthetic organisms. Net primary production (NPP) is the annual energy produced by photosynthesis minus that consumed in autotrophic respiration, and it represents the maximum energy available to support ecosystem food webs. Primary production can vary substantially from year to year and certainly varies spatially around the Highlands region. Measurements of net primary production in Highlands forests are relatively rare, but reported values of aboveground NPP for other temperate forest ecosystems range over an order of magnitude, from 0.2 to 1.9 lb per square yard per year (105 to 1,030 grams per square meter per year), with soil moisture, nitrogen availability, temperature, and light viewed as major controlling factors (Kloeppel, Harmon, and Fahey 2007). NPP can play a key role in regulating the size of animal populations and community biomass and can influence levels of biological diversity. Primary production is directly important to humans through impacts on wood production and the sequestration of atmospheric carbon dioxide.

Primary production in forests results in commodities such as timber, fuelwood, pulp, fruits, nuts, and greenery. Through much of the twentieth century, rates of timber removal in the Highlands were fairly low as cultivated lands returned to forest and many young forests matured. During the 1980s and 1990s the annual net growth of sawtimber and growing stock was more than twice the rate of wood removal (Phelps and Hoppe 2002). Highlands counties with the highest current volumes of sawtimber (more than five thousand board feet per acre of forest) include Connecticut's Litchfield and Hartford counties, Dutchess and Putnam counties in New York, all the New Jersey Highlands counties, and Chester and Lancaster counties in Pennsylvania. Since many trees in these forests are now reaching sawtimber size, a future increase in logging, especially for valuable oaks on private lands, is likely to occur. The 2002 Highlands regional study update concluded that half of all forest owners expect to harvest wood products in the future (Phelps and Hoppe 2002).

The regrowth of many eastern Northern American forests following extensive forest clearing in the 1800s resulted in a globally important carbon sink, slowing the rate of atmospheric CO_2 increase, thus forestalling associated climate consequences (Pacala et al. 2001; Myneni et al. 2001). Long-term data from New York's Black Rock Forest document that carbon stored in aboveground biomass nearly tripled between 1930 and 2000 (Schuster et al. 2008) (fig. 7.1). The period of highest long-term increase was from the 1930s through the early to mid-1960s, with an average annual increment of 2,675 lbs/acre (approx. 3 metric tons/hectare) of biomass. Red oak trees

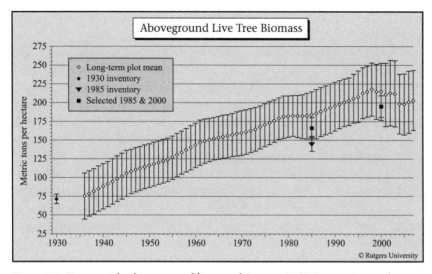

Figure 7.1. Forest-wide aboveground live tree biomass (AGB in metric tons/ hectare) in the Black Rock Forest as estimated in 1930 and 1985 inventories, mean AGB from a subset of 45 inventory plots in 1985 and 2000, and mean AGB on a series of long-term plots from 1936 to 2006. *Source*: Black Rock Forest/Schuster et al. 2008 © Rutgers University.

sequestered carbon during that period three times faster than most other species.

However, the capacity of forests to store carbon is sensitive to factors including stand age, climate, and disturbance. Some of Black Rock's maturing forests exhibited decreasing annual carbon storage after the 1960s, although other stands more than one hundred years old exhibited undiminished biomass increments (Schuster et al. 2008). Periods of widespread slow growth (1946–1954, 1960–1966, and 1979–1986) were associated with droughts and outbreaks of insect herbivores. Recently in the Black Rock Forest and elsewhere in the Highlands, there has been a wave of tree mortality, notably on poor sites between 1999 and 2005, which reduced live carbon stocks by as much as 15 percent (see fig. 7.1; Schuster et al. 2008).

The drought-prone and nutrient-poor soils that characterize many Highlands uplands limit levels of primary productivity. This is evident in the low biomass-to-stand-age ratios in Highlands regions with higher proportions of upland habitat (table 7.1). There is also a general north-to-south increase in productivity correlated with increasing temperature and growing season length and generally higher soil productivity. Some areas have lower productivity due to human-caused erosion or soil compaction. The forests with the highest productivity per acre are all south of the glacial margin (Hunterdon and Morris counties in New Jersey and Bucks and Berks counties in Pennsylvania; table 7.1).

The high habitat diversity of the Highlands (e.g., wetlands, ravines, ridges, rocky summits, talus slopes, outcrops) and the persistence of some large contiguous forest tracts have resulted in high overall biological diversity. Species diversity is generally highest in undisturbed forests with a range of habitats but can also be high in young forests with mixtures of early- and middle-successional native and nonnative species. Woody plant diversity can be locally quite high. For example fifty species of trees occur within the 3,830-acre (1,550 hectare) Black Rock Forest, and it has more than one hundred woody plant species overall (Barringer and Clemants 2003). Regional habitat and species diversity are also enhanced by the Hudson and Delaware rivers and the long, continuous ridges of the Highlands, which act as natural north–south biotic corridors.

Challenges to native species diversity in the Highlands include the absence of truly old forest and the rapid expansion of some aggressive, predominantly nonnative organisms. Some characteristic species have been eliminated across the region (e.g., American chestnut, timber wolf), and others remain seriously threatened. Disturbance often confers competitive advantages to weedy, light-loving species that can outcompete native forest species for critical resources. Plants such as Japanese barberry (*Berberis thunbergii*) and stilt grass (*Microstegium vimineum*) have specialized adaptations that enable them to thrive in areas of disturbance and tree mortality (Xu, Griffin, and Schuster 2007; Xu, Schuster, and Griffin 2007). Other abundant, invasive, nonnative plants in the Highlands include common reed (*Phragmites australis*), introduced honeysuckles (*Lonicera* spp.), purple loosestrife (*Lythrum salicaria*), Japanese bamboo (*Polygonum cuspidatum*), and garlic mustard (*Aliaria petiolata*). Even in the relatively undisturbed Black Rock Forest, introduced plants represent 20 percent of the flora (Barringer and Clemants 2003). Introduced animals that have spread throughout the Highlands include brown-headed cowbirds (*Molothrus ater*), which parasitize the nests of many forest-interior breeding birds, and the hemlock woolly adelgid insect (*Agelges tsugae*), which has devastated eastern hemlock populations.

Forest ecosystem trophic (food web) structure has been altered for more than a century owing to the aforementioned extirpation of top predators, essentially "decapitating" food webs. Large predators have not become re-established in much of the Highlands region. Some herbivore species, thus released from "top-down" population regulation, have increased severalfold, resulting in widespread problems. White-tailed deer (*Odocoileus virginianus*) populations are especially imbalanced near populated areas where hunting is restricted. Humans are affected by overabundant deer as they damage domestic plants and agricultural crops, cause motor vehicle accidents, and serve

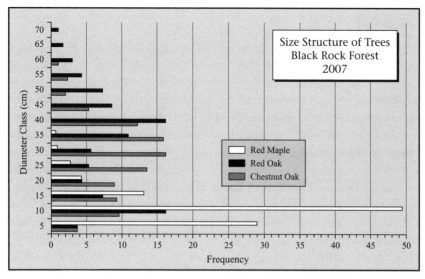

Figure 7.2. Size structure (percent frequency) of trees of three species in the Black Rock Forest showing typical paucity of small saplings. Note the small numbers of red and chestnut oak of the smallest size class of saplings (< 5 cm in diameter), which suggests future problems with successful oak regeneration.

as vectors for the spread of Lyme disease. Excessive deer are a major wildlife concern because they heavily consume acorns and food resources critical for many other animals. Excessive deer browse on seedlings, combined with heavy consumption of acorns, severely disturbs tree regeneration and community dynamics, threatening the future of many oak forests (Loftis and McGee 1992; Townsend et al. 2002; Tripler et al. 2005). This process has been shifting forest composition from preferred and browse-sensitive species to less preferred and nonbrowsed species (Romagosa and Robison 2003; Harrison and Bardgett 2004; Haas and Heske 2005). Most Highlands forest understories no longer feature the same species as the overstory, portending very different future forests (fig 7.2). FIA data for Pennsylvania indicate that one-half to two-thirds of the state's forests lack sufficient tree seedlings to regenerate these forests (McWilliams et al. 2002). Where deer populations are excessive, regeneration of native shrubs is also threatened, and populations of sensitive wildflower species have been reduced or lost completely. Areas where deer exclosures have been erected clearly document the impacts of large mammal browse on forest productivity, diversity, and regeneration. Some improvement of the situation may result from increasing populations of coyote (*Canis latrans*) and black bear (*Ursus americanus*) where sufficient forest habitat remains to sustain them.

Biogeochemical Cycling

All nutrients cycle between living organisms and the abiotic environment. Forest ecosystem productivity and health depend on these biogeochemical cycles to provide nutrients for uptake and growth. Cycling rates and nutrient availability vary widely around the Highlands, partially explaining differences in NPP. Because water is the medium in which most nutrients move, watershed inflows and outflows of these nutrients can be examined to compile biogeochemical budgets, which serve as indicators of ecosystem function and change over time. Healthy forest ecosystems typically exhibit tight, local cycling of key nutrients such as nitrogen and calcium, with minimal export in soil and stream waters (Bormann and Likens 1979; Aber et al. 2001). The major labile reservoirs of these nutrients are usually contained in organic materials, including the forest biota. Low nutrient availability in some Highlands soils can limit growth, especially in uplands with shallow soils over crystalline bedrock. In comparison, deeper soils, and especially those developed from calcareous materials or on alluvial deposits, feature higher availability of most nutrients.

Several other factors affect forest nutrient cycling and uptake. Periods of drought, especially where soils have low water-holding capacity, reduce water and nutrient uptake. Land use can substantially affect soil nutrients, with long-lasting implications for productivity and diversity (Dupouey et al. 2002). Agricultural practices can reduce soil organic-matter content by as much as 30 percent (Compton et al. 1998) and can also cause soil nutrient loss and increased erosion (Entry, Sojka, and Shewmaker 2002). The availability of nitrogen required for forest regrowth depends on the intensity of the previous agriculture, with recovery taking decades in some heavily farmed areas (Compton et al. 1998; Hooker and Compton 2003).

Forest species composition can also affect nutrient cycling (Elliott, Elliott, and Wyman 1993; Gartner and Cardon 2004). Many oaks have unique foliar and litter qualities that affect carbon and nitrogen cycling, slowing decomposition and nitrification (Finzi, Van Breemen, and Canham 1998; Lovett et al. 2004) and increasing the retention of atmospherically deposited nitrogen (Templer et al. 2005; Lovett et al. 2004). In contrast, sugar maple and white ash produce soil organic matter with low C:N ratios and high nitrification rates (Finzi, Van Breemen, and Canham 1998). The replacement of native plant species with nonnative species such as Japanese barberry can also alter forest chemical cycling and soil microbial communities (Kourtev, Ehrenfeld, and Haggblom 2002; Kourtev, Ehrenfeld, and Huang 1998). The expansion of invasive plants and the northward migration of some native forest taxa such as mulberry (*Morus rubra*) and black gum may have biogeochemical consequences deserving of further research.

Forest fires can act to enhance nutrient cycling, while fire suppression

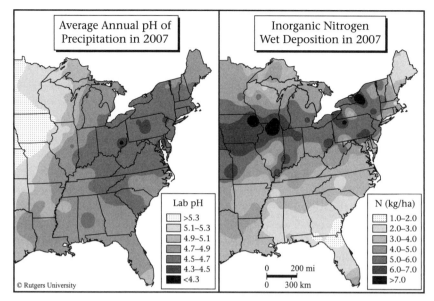

Figure 7.3. (*Left*) Isopleth map of average annual pH of precipitation in 2007 at National Atmospheric Deposition Program sites around the eastern United States. (*Right*) Isopleth map of total inorganic nitrogen deposition in precipitation in 2007 at National Atmospheric Deposition Program sites around the eastern United States. © Rutgers University.

generally retards cycling rates. But when forest canopy trees are lost to disturbance, nutrients may be leached from soils, especially if there is a lag before other trees respond with increased growth (see, e.g., Jenkins, Aber, and Canham 1999). Disturbances that reduce woody plant transpiration will at least temporarily increase soil water levels, potentially resulting in nutrient losses through leaching. Forest clear-cutting without environmental controls has been shown to trigger massive losses of nutrients (Bormann and Likens 1979). Losses of soils and nutrients from forests can dramatically reduce productivity and water quality at the same time.

A prominent feature of Highlands forest biogeochemistry is widespread soil and ecosystem acidification, with the severity inversely proportional to local acid-neutralizing capacity. Precipitation in the northeastern United States has been especially acidic since the industrial revolution, and the pH of Highlands precipitation is typically between 4.0 and 5.0 (see fig. 7.3; Shapiro 2005; Shapiro et al. 2007). Acid deposition can lower soil pH over time, causing nutrients such as nitrogen, calcium, and magnesium to bind more tightly to soil particles, reducing their availability. In highly acidified soils, aluminum availability may reach toxic levels, and aluminum may be released to stream waters (Shortle et al. 1995). Some upper watershed areas in the Highlands have become heavily acidified, resulting in strong selection for the most acid-tolerant species, such as gray birch (*Betula populifolia*).

Substantial quantities of nitrogen accompany the hydrogen ions in acid precipitation, potentially leading to forest degradation through nitrogen saturation (Aber et al. 2001). Acid precipitation in the Highlands deposits more than 4.5 lbs of nitrogen per acre per year (5 kilograms per hectare per year) (see fig. 7.3; NADP 2007), and the amount of additional "dry" deposition may be similar in magnitude (Shapiro 2005). Atmospheric inputs of nitrogen may become immobilized in soils or taken up by plants. In some cases, however, nitrogen may be exported in stream waters, especially in steep areas and during winter and early spring when biological demand for nitrogen is very low. Where nitrogen is found in any quantity in stream water, it generally indicates a problem (Aber et al. 2001). However, oak forests usually feature strong nitrogen retention (Lovett, Weathers, and Arthur 2002), and streamflow from undisturbed Highlands forests is most often very low in nitrogen.

Excess hydrogen ions from acid deposition can displace positively charged ions such as calcium, magnesium, and potassium from soil exchange sites, lowering base saturation and accelerating acidification (Likens, Driscoll, and Buso 1996; Hyman et al. 1998). Nutrient depletion from any cause (e.g., acid leaching, disturbance, heavy agricultural use) can increase forest susceptibility to a range of climatic and biotic stresses. Tree health problems can include increased vulnerability to winter injury, crown dieback, and exacerbated impacts from herbivory or disease (Lovett et al. 2006). Widespread declines of sugar maple have been linked to acid depletion of soil cations (Likens, Driscoll, and Buso 1996; Long, Horsley, and Lilja 1997; Driscoll et al. 2001). Nutrient depletion and associated tree stress can result in reduced growth and timber yield, increased mortality rates, and eventual changes in forest composition and diversity.

Disturbance Dynamics

Among the changes occurring in Highlands forests has been the alteration of disturbance regimes. Eastern deciduous forests typically cycle from open woodlands to middle-aged closed-canopy forests to old forests as shorter-lived species requiring high light are replaced by slower-growing, shade-tolerant trees with longer life spans. Disturbances such as fires, ice storms, and large windthrow events occur with characteristic frequencies, intensities, durations, and extents. These parameters of the disturbance regime determine the proportion of forest stands in any given successional "stage." Sooner or later, all stands in all forests are reset to earlier stages by disturbance.

Young Highlands forests are usually dominated by fast-growing species such as gray birch, pin cherry (*Prunus pennsylvanica*), and aspen (*Populus* spp.). These trees are eventually replaced by longer-lived species such as most of the oaks, and these in turn may eventually be replaced by the region's most shade-tolerant and long-lived taxa, such as sugar maple, beech, and hemlock. But in most of the Highlands, and a much larger surrounding area, characteristic disturbance regimes have enabled oaks to dominate for most of the last ten thousand years (Abrams 1992; Maenza-Gmelch 1997). Indeed, oak-dominated forests are the most widespread type of forest in the eastern United States.

Human activities have figured in Highlands disturbance regimes for most of the Holocene, through direct tree cutting and land clearing as well as impacts on fire dynamics. Other natural disturbance factors include windthrow, ice storms, regional droughts, flood events, and insect and disease outbreaks at irregular intervals. The natural fire regime of Highlands forests features small fires, usually ground fires that reduce fuel loads and release nutrients, and occasional larger fires during extremely dry periods that can cause widespread tree mortality, favoring fire-adapted species. These conditions have supported the regeneration of oak forests. Fire frequency appears to have increased dramatically in the Highlands following European settlement (Maenza-Gmelch 1997). Many of these fires were of low intensity and extent, but when combined with accumulated, fire-prone logging debris and dry conditions, fire intensity was occasionally high and extended over large areas. In addition to oaks, this fire regime favored most species of birch and pine at the expense of species such as sugar and red maple, beech, and hemlock. The effects on forest composition were most pronounced in frequently burned upper slope and ridge communities. Highlands fire disturbance regimes were substantially altered by the implementation of active fire suppression in the twentieth century. Fire frequency decreased dramatically afterward, and fire suppression continues to this day. Over time, in the absence of fires, oak seedlings and saplings are often outcompeted by fast-growing, fire-sensitive species such as thin-barked red maple (Chapman, Heitzman, and Shelton 2006; Drury and Runkle 2006). However, fire suppression can also lead to substantial fuel-load buildup, which potentially increases the intensity of future fires.

As a result of these changing disturbance factors, and especially owing to the historical legacy of widespread clearing followed by land-use abandonment, today's Highlands forests are overwhelmingly middle-successional. Most current stands originated between 1900 and 1960, with 85 percent of stands in the range of 40–100 years old (see fig. 7.4). Some fragments of older hemlock/beech, chestnut oak, and white oak forest up to 150 years old still remain, and individual trees can be found with ages of 200–300 years (e.g., D'Arrigo et al. 2001). But very little true old growth remains anywhere in the Highlands.

Disturbances from outbreaks of so-called forest pests and pathogens, including both native and introduced organisms, have had major impacts on these forests through history. But their rates of introduction and spread have increased in recent times, in part a consequence of increased human travel.

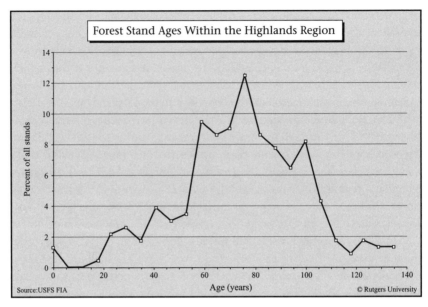

Figure 7.4. Distribution of forest stand ages among U.S. Forest Service Forest Inventory and Analysis stands within the Highlands region. © Rutgers University.

Pests and pathogens can have significant short- and long-term impacts on forest ecosystem processes such as productivity, nutrient cycling, and support of food webs. These were undoubtedly affected by the earlier pathogen-induced losses of American chestnut and American elm. Lovett and colleagues (2006) stated that "exotic insect pests and pathogens pose the most serious current threats to forests of eastern North America." The most critical biological features determining the severity of pest and pathogen outbreaks are virulence, mode of action, host specificity, and importance or uniqueness and phytosociology of the host tree (Lovett et al. 2006). Some hardwoods and conifers termed "foundation species" play particularly critical roles in regulating hydrology, fire, carbon storage, and nutrient cycling in temperate forests (Pastor and Post 1986; Houghton and Hackler 2000; Foster et al. 2002; Lovett, Weathers, and Arthur 2002; Lovett et al. 2004; Templer et al. 2005). Pest and pathogen impacts on these foundation taxa can dramatically alter ecosystem function and services (Ellison et al. 2005).

The hemlock wooly adelgid (HWA)—an introduced, foliage-feeding insect that specifically targets "foundation" eastern hemlock trees—meets the worst-case scenario for the above-listed severity factors. Highlands stands of eastern hemlock have already experienced as much as 80 percent tree mortality since the insect was first noted in this region in the 1980s (Kimple and Schuster 2002). Loss of this dominant evergreen from eastern forests is accompanied by ecological changes that affect plant, animal, and fungal populations and alter soils, diversity, trophic structure, and ecosystem processes (Jenkins, Aber, and Canham 1999; Danoff-Burg and Bird 2002; Tingley, Orwig, and Field 2002; Lewis et al. 2008). Hemlock stands provide critical winter habitat for white-tailed deer, ruffed grouse (*Bonasa umbellus*), and wild turkey (*Mealeagris gallopavo*) (McWilliams and Schmidt 1999). Hemlock loss can lead to increased stream temperatures and algae growth, which can harm aquatic invertebrates, fish, and salamanders in steams and riparian zones (Snyder et al. 2002; Brooks 2001). Eastern hemlock stands are the preferred habitat of the Canada warbler (*Wilsonia canadensis*), the hermit thrush (*Catharus guttatus*), the magnolia warbler (*Dendroica magnolia*), the solitary vireo (*Vireo solitarius*), and the black-throated green warbler (*Dendroica virens*), whose populations in Connecticut declined precipitously after hemlock mortality from HWA (Mitchell 1999; Tingley, Orwig, and Field 2002).

Significant biotic challenges are now being faced by other forest taxa that have been resilient to past perturbations. Beech bark disease, for example, is a multiorganism complex currently spreading south through the Highlands. It affects American beech trees by reducing growth and vigor, eventually leading to mortality in many trees (Houston and O'Brien 1983). Butternut canker, resulting from a fungus (*Sirococcus clavigignenti-juglandacearum*) first introduced into the United States about fifty years ago (Anderson and LaMadeleine 1978), has already killed most of the butternuts (*Juglans cinerea*) through the region. Many Highlands ash trees have been weakened and in some cases killed by "ash yellows," an incurable disease caused by a single-celled mycoplasm (Matteoni and Sinclair 1985). Emerald ash borer (*Agrilus planipennis*), a wood-boring beetle introduced from Asia that is lethal, fast acting, and specific to ash trees, is now spreading east toward the Highlands area (Tkacz, Moody, and Castillo 2007). Sugar maple trees have been killed in the New York metropolitan region by the Asian long-horned beetle (*Anoplophora glabripennis*), an introduced wood-boring insect that preferentially attacks maples but will also damage other hardwoods.

Pathogens that now threaten eastern oak forests include oak wilt fungus (*Ceratocystis fagacearum*), spreading toward the Highlands from the west, and bacterial leaf scorch (caused by *Xylella fastidiosa*), presently expanding into New York from New Jersey. Of possible future concern is *Phytophthora ramorum*, the pathogen that causes "sudden oak death" (SOD). After outbreaks of this water mold, large numbers of oak trees exhibit trunk bleeding and bole lesions, often resulting in death (Hansen, Parke, and Sutton 2005). SOD has killed hundreds of thousands of oak and tan oak trees in near-coastal locations in California and Oregon (USDA 2005), and eastern red and white oaks have both shown susceptibility to *P. ramorum* in greenhouse trials (Brasier et al. 2002; Tooley and Kyde 2003). Moreover, modeling results indicate that much of the eastern deciduous forest may be susceptible to SOD (Meentemeyer et al. 2004; Magarey, Fowler, and Randall-Schadel 2005). The USDA's "National Strategic Plan for Sudden Oak Death" states, "The oak hardwood forest is the largest forest type in the U.S., and its potential vulnerability to this pathogen is of considerable economic and ecological concern" (USDA 2005).

Many aging Highlands oak canopy trees are stressed by changing soil and climate factors and may be senescing or becoming increasingly prone to disease. Recent studies have documented an unexplained tripling of oak tree mortality and a 15 percent loss of oak canopy biomass in the Black Rock Forest since 1999 (Schuster et al. 2008). The phenomenon is consistent with "oak decline," the name for a slow-acting complex usually involving environmental stress combined with the effects of pests or pathogens, or both (Wargo, Houston, and LaMadeleine 1983). Drought often appears to be an initiating agent, and water-stressed trees become more susceptible to stem-girdling *Armillaria* fungi, which usually feed only on dead tree roots. Defoliating insects can also trigger the disease complex.

Regardless of the mode of canopy tree loss, the future of oak forests is uncertain because of widespread regeneration failure. Older oak trees have reduced propensity to sprout successfully after cutting, and overherbivory resulting from trophic imbalance, combined with fire suppression, has nearly eliminated oak regeneration by seedlings. Loss of oak forest may lead to a range of ecosystem effects such as water-quality deterioration (Lewis and Likens 2000; Lovett, Weathers, and Arthur 2002; Templer et al. 2005). Forest diversity—including animals, microbes, and subcanopy and understory plants—may be significantly affected by oak loss, potentially changing ecosystem processes if functional diversity is also altered. Losses of close associates of oaks, such as specialist ectomycorrhizal fungi and insects, will be expected, and many other insects, birds, and vertebrates that feed on oak tissues may respond negatively as well. Acorns are a critical food resource for birds and mammals during the dormant season, used to build fat reserves for winter survival, which will not be easily replaced by other foods. Loss of oak mast may prove devastating to oak-adapted wildlife, altering food webs for decades (Ostfeld, Jones, and Wolff 1996; McShea et al. 2007). Elements of the Highlands forests' disturbance regimes and their relative impacts continue to change over time, with many implications for future forest composition, structure, and ecosystem processes.

Highlands Forests and the Future

Forests act as ecological life-support systems, and humans have depended on Highlands forests for a wealth of products and supporting services over the past centuries. Chief among these has been the purification and provision of large quantities of water. Forest vegetation, roots, and litter protect soils and watersheds, control stream siltation and sedimentation, filter pollutants, and replenish groundwater. Forests also scavenge air pollutants and release much of the oxygen that humans and other resident animals breathe. They provide valuable commodities including timber and fiber, foster soil development, control local cycling of nutrients, and function in global cycles of water, carbon, and other chemicals (Dixon et al. 1994). They provide climate control and support a wealth of wildlife and biological diversity. The Highlands are particularly valued for recreation and nature enjoyment, enhancing human health, and for beautifying the landscape. But Highlands forests face a number of challenges to their health and their ability to continue to provide these ecoservices.

Only about half of the Highlands landscape is currently forested; most of these forests are highly fragmented, and many face continuing development pressure. Ongoing challenges include suppression of the natural fire regime; further ecosystem acidification and other biogeochemical changes; widespread displacement of native species by exotics; canopy tree stress and mortality from pests, pathogens, climatic stresses, and senescence; and likely future increases in logging concurrent with widespread forest regeneration failure. Highlands forests may also conceivably experience future reductions in soil and forest productivity, waves of species mortality, or loss of function as carbon sinks. Not all areas will experience all these impacts, and some will prove resistant to certain changes. But even some large, preserved Highlands forests are already experiencing a number of these impacts, and some heavily fragmented forests exhibit diminished ability to provide critical services, such as yielding clean water.

Interactions among these factors may further augment the challenges. For example, although growing conditions are generally good south of the glacial margin, this part of the Highlands faces high development pressure, which may bring further habitat loss and fragmentation. These factors combined with regeneration failure and increasing influxes of exotic species may increase the rapidity and magnitude of forest change. Further climatic changes are especially likely to exacerbate impacts of other factors.

The Highlands region experienced an overall warming of winters and summer nights during the twentieth century, with spring arriving earlier and winters becoming less snowy (Warrach et al. 2006). Further warming will especially challenge native species that are sensitive to winter temperatures and the presence or absence of snowpack (Pederson et al. 2004; Pederson 2005) and may result in loss of the region's northern hardwood forest component. Changing climate is already implicated in Highlands community composition changes: most of the species that were extirpated from the Black Rock Forest between 1930 and 2000 were northern relicts (e.g., black spruce [*Picea mariana*]), and most of the species that invaded the forest in that time were expanding their ranges from the south (e.g., red mulberry and catalpa; Schuster et al. 2008). Modeling by the U.S. Forest Service projects that if current rates of climate change continue, within the next century the Highlands climate will be unsuitable for native trees such as sugar maple and hemlock but suitable for species such as southern pines, currently growing hundreds of miles to the south (Iverson, Prasad, and Matthews 2007). Productivity, biogeochemistry, and species diversity will all be affected by compositional changes. Future climate-induced range changes will likely depend on actual rates of fossil fuel emissions (NECIA 2006).

Envisioning the Highlands in as little as fifty years into the future—after the current oak canopy is largely gone and in a warmer climate—raises several concerns. There will probably be less forested area. More species will have followed American chestnut and American elm into oblivion, and some forest types, such as northern hardwoods, may disappear from the region. We do not know which species will survive, but eastern hemlock, American beech, ash, and butternut will certainly be greatly diminished, and sugar maple populations may have declined as well. Native trees that may increase in dominance include red maple, black birch, and yellow poplar on sites with better soils. Black gum and southern hickories may increase on warmer sites, and associated species could include southern pines. Invasive trees including tree of heaven, Norway maple, and buckthorn will almost certainly have expanded substantially. These forests will represent novel forest types with uncertain implications for ecological processes and services. A general reduction in wood quality, and thus value, would appear to be a likely consequence of such a turnover. Wildlife will be considerably affected, especially by the replacement of acorns by less nutritious seeds. Many species of organisms may be extirpated, resulting in reduced native species diversity. Nutrient cycling will certainly be affected, with potentially serious consequences for surface water quality. Other implications of such a turnover for human health are uncertain, as are questions of whether these altered forests will support tourism and recreation or will increase land values in the same fashion as today's Highlands forests.

Because so many of the resources, threats, and opportunities are shared among a great many Highlands stakeholders, appropriate and effective responses will necessitate coordinated ecosystem management to conserve and restore forest health and integrity. It will be important to continue to emphasize forest conservation, exemplified by the substantial open-space acquisition and land protection already accomplished in the Highlands through conservation easements since the early 1990s (Phelps and Hoppe 2002). Further incentives that favor forest protection could prove quite beneficial. Given the key role of water in ecological health, it will be especially important to conserve forested wetlands, riparian corridors, and streamside forests. Attention should be given to further reductions of atmospheric pollutant deposition, to active ecological fire management, and to invasive species control. Native carnivore populations should be protected and enhanced, and overabundant deer populations should be reduced through cooperative programs that will restore forests' capacity for regeneration. In this way, more complete ecosystems with diverse and stable food webs may be reestablished. Native species, such as red oak, which store carbon rapidly, conserve nitrogen, and may fare well in the face of climate change (Iverson, Prasad, and Matthews 2007) should be favored and protected. Region-specific guidelines for sustainable forestry should be developed to preserve environmental quality and forest function while ensuring the continued benefits of the provision of forest products. Conservation to maintain reservoirs of native biodiversity in existing forests may provide additional benefits that we cannot yet recognize.

Reestablishment of healthy forests in degraded and heavily damaged areas should also be pursued. Trees of appropriate native species, selected in consideration of climatic and chemical challenges, should be planted in critical areas and protected from herbivory during establishment. Construction of new developments may provide additional opportunities to establish new forests. In areas where existing forest reserves can be augmented, this will serve to increase the long-term viability of native organisms and critical ecological processes, especially where new habitat corridors can be created. Purposeful native species reintroductions could also augment ecological health. Older and newly created forests alike could provide new opportunities for nature tourism, accomplished by means that will support long-term forest viability while still enhancing quality of life and providing local consumable products and other ecosystem services.

It is clear that we cannot re-create the Highlands forests of the past. We also cannot simply preserve current forests and assume that all will remain well. Essentially, we manage nearly every facet of our environment, either by our actions or by our inaction. Deeper understanding will be required to comprehend more fully the relative importance and interactions among the suite of current challenges to Highlands forests, and the consequences for ecosystem health and services. Such an understanding could enable us to develop effective response strategies for future land planning and forest management, to ensure healthy and sustainable forests for the future.

References

Aber, J., R. P. Neilson, S. McNulty, J. M. Lenihan, D. Bachelet, and R. J. Drapek. 2001. "Forest Processes and Global Environmental Change: Predicting the Effects of Individual and Multiple Stressors." *BioScience* 51:735–751.

Abrams, M. D. 1992. "Fire and the Development of Oak Forests." *BioScience* 42, no. 5: 346–353.

Anderson, R. L., and L. A. LaMadeleine. 1978. "The Distribution of Butternut

Decline in the Eastern United States." USDA Forest Service, Northeastern Area, State and Private Forestry, Rep. S-3-78.

Barringer, K., and S. Clemants. 2003. "Vascular Flora of Black Rock Forest, Orange County, New York." *Journal of the Torrey Botanical Society* 130, no. 4: 292–308.

Bormann, F. H., and G. E. Likens. 1979. *Pattern and Process in a Forested Ecosystem.* New York: Springer-Verlag.

Brasier, C. M., J. Roase, S. A. Kirk, and J. F. Webber. 2002. "Pathogenicity of *Phytophthora ramorum* Isolates from North America and Europe to Bark of European Fagaceae, American *Quercus rubra*, and Other Forest Trees," abstract, 30–31. In *Proceedings of the Sudden Oak Death, a Science Symposium,* December 15–18, Monterey, California. http://danr.ucop.edu/ihrmp/sodsymposium.html.

Braun, E. L. 1967. *Deciduous Forests of Eastern North America.* New York: Hafner Publishing.

Brooks, R. T. 2001. "Effects of the Removal of Overstory Hemlock from Hemlock-Dominated Forests on Eastern Redback Salamanders." *Forest Ecology and Management* 149:197–204.

Chapman, R. A., E. Heitzman, and M. G. Shelton. 2006. "Long-Term Changes in Forest Structure and Species Composition of an Upland Oak Forest in Arkansas." *Forest Ecology Management* 236:85–92.

Compton, J. E., R. D. Boone, G. Motzkin, and D. R. Foster. 1998. "Soil Carbon and Nitrogen in a Pine-Oak Sand Plain in Central Massachusetts: Role of Vegetation and Land-Use History." *Oecologia* 116:536–542.

Danoff-Burg, J. A., and S. Bird. 2002. "Hemlock Wooly Adelgid and Elongated Hemlock Scale: Partners in Crime?" 254–268. In *Proceedings: Hemlock Wooly Adelgid in the Eastern United States Symposium,* February. East Brunswick, NJ: USDA Forest Service.

D'Arrigo, R. D., W.S.F. Schuster, D. M. Lawrence, E. R. Cook, M. Wiljanen, and R. D. Thetford. 2001. "Climate-Growth Relationships of Eastern Hemlock and Chestnut Oak from Black Rock Forest in the Highlands of Southeastern New York." *Tree-Ring Research* 57:183–190.

Diamond, J. 2005. *Collapse: How Societies Choose to Fail or Succeed.* New York: Viking Penguin.

Dixon, R. K., S. A. Brown, R. A. Houghton, A. M. Solomon, M. C. Trexler, and J. Wisniewski. 1994. "Carbon Pools and Flux of Global Forest Ecosystems." *Science* 263:185–190.

Driscoll, C. T., G. B. Lawrence, A. J. Bulger, T. J. Butler, C. S. Cronan, C. Eagar, K. F. Lambert, G. E. Likens, J. L. Stoddard, and K. C. Weathers. 2001. "Acidic Deposition in the Northeastern United States: Sources and Inputs, Ecosystem Effects, and Management." *BioScience* 51:180–198.

Drury, S. A., and J. R. Runkle. 2006. "Forest Vegetation Change in Southeast Ohio: Do Older Forests Serve as Useful Models for Predicting the Successional Trajectory of Future Forests?" *Forest Ecology Management* 223:200–210.

Dupouey, J. L., E. Dambrine, J. D. Laffite, and C. Moares. 2002. "Irreversible Impact of Past Land Use on Forest Soils and Biodiversity." *Ecology* 83:2978–2984.

Elliott, W. M., N. B. Elliott, and R. L. Wyman. 1993. "Relative Effect of Litter and Forest Type on Rate of Decomposition." *American Midland Naturalist* 129:87–95.

Ellison, A. M., M. S. Bank, B. D. Clinton, E. A. Colburn, K. Elliott, C. R. Ford, D. R. Foster, et al. 2005. "Loss of Foundation Species: Consequences for the Structure and Dynamics of Forested Ecosystems." *Frontiers of Ecology and Environment* 3, no. 9: 479–486.

Entry, J. A., R. E. Sojka, and G. E. Shewmaker. 2002. "Management of Irrigated Agriculture to Increase Organic Carbon Storage in Soils." *Soil Science Society of America Journal* 66:1957–1964.

Finzi, A. C., N. Van Breemen, and C. C. Canham. 1998. "Canopy Tree-Soil Interactions within Temperate Forests: Species Effects on Soil Carbon and Nitrogen." *Ecological Applications* 8:440–446.

Forest Inventory and Analysis Program. 2008. "The Forest Inventory and Analysis Database: Database Description and Users Manual Version 3.0 for Phase 2, Revision 1." Washington, DC: U.S. Department of Agriculture, Forest Service. Available at http://www.fia.fs.fed.us/library/database-documentation/.

Foster, D. R., S. Clayden, D. A. Orwig, B. Hall, and S. Barry. 2002. "Oak, Chestnut and Fire: Climatic and Cultural Controls of Long-Term Forest Dynamics in New England, USA." *Journal of Biogeography* 29, no. 10–11: 1359–1379.

Gartner, T. B., and Z. G. Cardon. 2004. "Decomposition Dynamics in Mixed-Species Leaf Litter." *Oikos* 104:230.

Haas, J. P., and E. J. Heske. 2005. "Experimental Study of the Effects of Mammalian Acorn Predators on Red Oak Acorn Survival and Germination." *Journal of Mammalogy* 86:1015–1021.

Hansen, E. M., J. L. Parke, and W. Sutton. 2005. "Susceptibility of Oregon Forest Trees and Shrubs to *Phytophthora ramorum*: A Comparison of Artificial Inoculation and Natural Infection." *Plant Disease* 89:63–70.

Harrison, K. A., and R. D. Bardgett. 2004. "Browsing by Red Deer Negatively Impacts on Soil Nitrogen Availability in Regenerating Forests." *Soil Biology and Biochemistry* 36:115–126.

Hooker, T. D., and J. E. Compton. 2003. "Forest Ecosystem Carbon and Nitrogen Accumulation during the First Century after Agricultural Abandonment." *Ecological Applications* 13:299–313.

Houghton, R. A., and J. L. Hackler. 2000. "Changes in Terrestrial Carbon Storage in the United States. 1: The Roles of Agriculture and Forestry." *Global Ecology and Biogeography* 9, no. 2: 125–144.

Houston, D. R., and J. T. O'Brien. 1983. *Beech Bark Disease.* Forest Insect & Disease Leaflet 75, USDA Forest Service, Washington, DC.

Hyman, M., C. E. Johnson, S. Bailey, R. H. April, and J. W. Hornbeck. 1998. "Chemical Weathering and Cation Loss in a Base-Poor Watershed." *Geological Society of America Bulletin* 110, no. 10: 85–85.

Iverson, L. R., A. M. Prasad, and S. N. Matthews. 2007. "Modelling Potential Climate Change Impact on the Trees of the Northeastern United States." *Migration and Adaptation Strategies for Global Change* 13:517–540. doi:10.1007/s11027-007-9129-y.

Jenkins, J. C., J. D. Aber, and C. D. Canham. 1999. "Hemlock Wooly Adelgid Impacts on Community Structure and N Cycling Rates in Eastern Hemlock Forests." *Canadian Journal of Forest Research* 29:630–645.

Kimple, A., and W.S.F. Schuster. 2002. "Spatial Patterns of HWA Damage and Impacts on Tree Physiology and Water Use in the Black Rock Forest, Southern New York," In *Proceedings: Hemlock Woolly Adelgid in the Eastern United States Symposium*, 344–350, February. East Brunswick, NJ: USDA Forest Service.

Kloeppel, B. D., M. E. Harmon, and T. J. Fahey. 2007. "Estimating Aboveground Net Primary Productivity in Forest-Dominated Ecosystems." In *Principles and Standards for Measuring Primary Production*, ed. T. J. Fahey and A. K. Knapp, 63–81. New York: Oxford University Press.

Kourtev, P. S., J. G. Ehrenfeld, and M. Haggblom. 2002. "Exotic Plant Species Alter the Microbial Community Structure and Function in the Soil." *Ecology* 83:3152–3166.

Kourtev, P. S., J. G. Ehrenfeld, and W. Z. Huang. 1998. "Effects of Exotic Plant Species on Soil Properties in Hardwood Forests of New Jersey." *Water, Air and Soil Pollution* 105:493–501.

Lewis, G. P., and G. E. Likens. 2000. "Low Stream Nitrate Concentrations Associated with Oak Forests on the Allegheny High Plateau of Pennsylvania." *Water Resources Research* 36:3091–3094.

Lewis, J. D., J. Licitra, A. R. Tuininga, A. Sirulnik, G. D. Turner, and J. Johnson. 2008. "Oak Seedling Growth and Ectomycorrhizal Colonization Are Less in Eastern Hemlock Stands Infested with Hemlock Wooly Adelgid Than in Adjacent Oak Stands." *Tree Physiology* 28:629–636.

Likens, G. E., and F. H. Bormann. 1995. *Biogeochemistry of a Forested Ecosystem*. 2nd ed. New York: Springer-Verlag.

Likens, G. E., C. T. Driscoll, and D. C. Buso. 1996. "Long-Term Effects of Acid Rain: Response and Recovery of a Forested Ecosystem." *Science* 272:244–246.

Loftis, D. L., and C. E. McGee, eds. 1992. "Oak Regeneration: Serious Problems, Practical Recommendations." General Technical Report SE 84. Asheville, NC: USDA Forest Service.

Long, R. P., S. B. Horsley, and P. R. Lilja. 1997. "Impact of Forest Liming on Growth and Crown Vigor of Sugar Maple and Associated Hardwoods." *Canadian Journal of Forest Research* 27:1560–1573.

Lovett, G. M., C. D. Canham, M. A. Arthur, K. C. Weathers, and R. D. Fitzhugh. 2006. "Forest Ecosystem Responses to Exotic Pests and Pathogens in Eastern North America." *BioScience* 56:395–405.

Lovett, G. M., K. C. Weathers, and M. A. Arthur. 2002. "Control of Nitrogen Loss from Forested Watersheds by Soil Carbon: Nitrogen Ratio and Tree Species Composition." *Ecosystems* 5:712–718.

Lovett, G. M., K. C. Weathers, M. A. Arthur, and J. C. Schultz. 2004. "Nitrogen Cycling in a Northern Hardwood Forest: Do Species Matter?" *Biogeochemistry* 67: 289–308.

Maenza-Gmelch, T. E. 1997. "Holocene Vegetation, Climate, and Fire History of the Hudson Highlands, Southeastern New York, USA." *The Holocene* 7, no. 1: 25–37.

Magarey, R., G. Fowler, and B. Randall-Schadel. 2005. "Climate and Host Risk Map for Sudden Oak Death Risk (*Phytophthora ramorum*)." CPHST NAPPFAST SOD Risk Mapping Report, October 6, 2006. http://www.nappfast.org/pest%20reports/SOD.pdf.

Matteoni, J. A., and W. A. Sinclair. 1985. "Role of the Mycoplasmal Disease, Ash Yellows, in Decline of White Ash in New York State." *Phytopathology* 75:355–360.

McShea, W. J., W. M. Healy, P. Devers, T. Fearer, F. H. Koch, D. Stauffer, and J. Waldon. 2007. "Forestry Matters: Decline of Oaks Will Impact Wildlife in Hardwood Forests." *Journal of Wildlife Management* 71, no. 5: 1717–1728.

McWilliams, W. H., T. W. Bowersox, P. H. Brose, D. A. Devlin, J. C. Finley, K. W. Gottschalk, S. Horsley, et al. 2002. "Measuring Tree Seedlings and Associated Understory Vegetation in Pennsylvania's Forests." In *Proceedings of the Fourth Annual Forest Inventory and Analysis Symposium.*

McWilliams, W. H., and T. L. Schmidt. 1999. "Composition, Structure, and Sustainability of Hemlock Ecosystems in Eastern North America." General Technical Report NE-267. Durham, NH: U.S. Department of Agriculture, Forest Service, Northeastern Research Station.

Meentemeyer, R., D. Rizzo, W. Mark, and E. Lotz. 2004. "Mapping the Risk of Establishment and Spread of Sudden Oak Death in California." *Forest Ecology and Management* 200:195–214.

Mitchell, J. M. 1999. "Habitat Relationships of Five Northern Bird Species Breeding in Hemlock Ravines in Ohio, USA." *Natural Areas Journal* 19:3–11.

Myneni, R. B., J. Dong, C. J. Tucker, R. K. Kaufmann, P. E. Kauppi, L. Zhou, V. Alexeyev, and M. K. Hughes. 2001. "A Large Carbon Sink in the Woody Biomass of Northern Forests." *Proceedings of the National Academy of Sciences* 98:14784–14789.

NADP. 2007. "National Atmospheric Deposition Program 2006 Annual Summary." NADP Data Report 2007-01. Champaign, IL: NADP Program Office.

Northeast Climate Impacts Assessment (NECIA). 2006. "Climate Change in the US Northeast. Union of Concerned Scientists." Available at http://www.northeast climateimpacts.org/.

Ostfeld, R. S., C. G. Jones, and J. O. Wolff. 1996. "Of Mice and Mast: Ecological Connections in Eastern Deciduous Forests." *BioScience* 46:323–330.

Pacala, S. W., G. C. Hurtt, D. Baker, P. Paylin, R. A. Houghton, R. A. Birdsey, L. Heath, et al. 2001. "Consistent Land- and Atmosphere-Based U.S. Carbon Sink Estimates." *Science* 292:2316–2320.

Pastor, J., and W. M. Post. 1986. "Influence of Climate, Soil Moisture, and Succession on Forest Carbon and Nitrogen Cycles." *Biogeochemistry* 2:3–27.

Pederson, N. A. 2005. "Climatic Sensitivity and Growth of Southern Temperate Trees in the Eastern US: Implications for the Carbon Cycle." PhD diss., Columbia University.

Pederson, N., E. R. Cook, G. C. Jacoby, D. M. Peteet, and K. L. Griffin. 2004. "The Influence of Winter Temperatures on the Annual Radial Growth of Six Northern Range Margin Tree Species." *Dendrochronologia* 22:7–29.

Phelps, M. G., and M. C. Hoppe. 2002. "New York–New Jersey Highlands Regional Study: 2002 Update." Publication NA-TA-02-03. Newtown Square, PA: USDA Forest Service Northeastern Area State and Private Forestry.

Romagosa, M. A., and D. J. Robison. 2003. "Biological Constraints on the Growth of Hardwood Regeneration in Upland Piedmont Forests." *Forest Ecology Management* 175:545–561.

Schuster, W.S.F., K. L. Griffin, H. Roth, M. H. Turnbull, D. Whitehead, and D. T.

Tissue. 2008. "Changes in Composition, Structure, and Aboveground Biomass over Seventy-Six Years (1930–2006) in the Black Rock Forest, Hudson Highlands, Southeastern New York State." *Tree Physiology* Special Issue: "IUFRO Workshop Regional Forest Responses to Environmental Change." 28:537–549.

Shapiro, J. B. 2005. "Watershed Budgets of Chloride and Sulfate as Integrators of Ecosystem Processes." PhD diss., Columbia University, Department of Earth and Environmental Sciences, New York.

Shapiro, J. B., H. J. Simpson, K. L. Griffin, and W.S.F. Schuster. 2007. "Precipitation Chloride at West Point, NY: Seasonal Patterns and Possible Contributions from Non-seawater Sources." *Atmospheric Environment* 41:2240–2254.

Shortle, W. C., K. T. Smith, R. Minocha, G. B. Lawrence, and M. B. David. 1995. "Acidic Deposition, Cation Mobilization, and Biochemical Indicators of Stress in Healthy Red Spruce." *Journal of Environmental Quality* 26:871–876.

Snyder, C. D., J. A. Young, D. P. Lemarié, and D. Smith. 2002. "Influence of Eastern Hemlock (*Tsuga canadensis*) Forests on Aquatic Invertebrate Assemblages in Headwater Streams." *Canadian Journal of Fisheries and Aquatic Sciences* 59:262–275.

Templer, P. H., G. M. Lovett, K. C. Weathers, S. E. Findlay, and T. E. Dawson. 2005. "Influence of Tree Species on Forest Nitrogen Retention in the Catskill Mountains, New York, USA." *Ecosystems* 8:1–16.

Tingley, M. W., D. A. Orwig, and R. Field. 2002. "Avian Response to Removal of a Forest Dominant: Consequences of Hemlock Wooly Adelgid Infestations." *Journal of Biogeography* 29:1505–1516.

Tkacz, B., B. Moody, and J. V. Castillo. 2007. "Forest Health Status in North America." *The Scientific World Journal* 7, no. S1: 28–36.

Tooley, P. W., and K. L. Kyde. 2003. "Susceptibility of Some Eastern Oak Species to Sudden Oak Death Caused by *Phytophthora ramorum*." *Phytopathology* 93:S84.

Townsend, D. S., J. S. Seva, C. Hee-Seagle, and G. Mayers. 2002. "Structure and Composition of a Northern Hardwood Forest Exhibiting Regeneration Failure." *Bartonia* 61:1–13.

Tripler, C. E., C. D. Canham, R. S. Inouye, and J. L. Schnurr. 2005. "Competitive Hierarchies of Temperate Tree Species: Interactions between Resource Availability and White-Tailed Deer." *Ecoscience* 12:494–505.

USDA. 2005. "Plant Diseases Caused by *Phytophthora ramorum*: A National Strategic Plan for USDA." September 14. Washington, DC: U.S. Department of Agriculture.

Wargo, P. M., D. R. Houston, and L. A. LaMadeleine. 1983. *Oak Decline*. Forest Insect & Disease Leaflet 165. Washington, DC: USDA Forest Service.

Warrach, K., M. Stieglitz, J. Shaman, V. C. Engel, and K. L. Griffin. 2006. "Twentieth Century Climate in the New York Hudson Highlands and the Potential Impacts on Eco-hydrological Processes." *Climatic Change* 75:455–493.

Woudenberg, S. W.; Conkling, B. L.; O'Connell, B. M.; LaPoint, E. B.; Turner, J. A.; Waddell, K. L. 2009. "The Forest Inventory and Analysis Database: Database Description and Users Manual Version 4.0 for Phase 2." Gen. Tech. Rep. RMRS-GTR-245. Fort Collins, CO: U.S. Department of Agriculture, Forest Service, Rocky Mountain Research Station.

Xu, C-Y., K. L. Griffin, and W.S.F. Schuster. 2007. "Leaf Phenology and Seasonal

Variation of Photosynthesis of Invasive (*Berberis thunbergii*) Japanese Barberry and Two Co-occurring Native Understory Shrubs in a Northeastern US Deciduous Forest." *Oecologia* 154:11–21.

Xu, C-Y. W.S.F. Schuster, and K. L. Griffin. 2007. "Seasonal Variation of Temperature Response of Respiration in Invasive (*Berberis thunbergii*) Japanese Barberry and Two Co-occurring Native Understory Shrubs in a Northeastern United States Deciduous Forest." *Oecologia* 153:809–819.

8

Wetlands of the Highlands Region

Joan G. Ehrenfeld

Introduction

Wetlands are ecosystems that combine the properties of both terrestrial and aquatic environments, but they also have unique and special characteristics. Like terrestrial environments, wetlands have soils and plants, but like aquatic environments, they also have water present much of the time. Indeed, hydrology—the source, flow patterns, depth, and chemistry of the water—is the primary driving force creating the unique environment of wetlands. The presence of water in turn generates particular types of soils, and specially adapted plants tolerate these unusual conditions. The ways in which water, plants, and soils interact with each other result in a wide variety of ecological functions, many of which are highly valued by human society. As a result, wetlands receive special treatment under both state and federal law.

Wetlands constitute nearly 6 percent of the total land area of the four-state Highlands region, as designated under the Highlands Conservation Act of 2004 (192,801 acres or 78,470 hectares of wetland), and include an impressive array of biotic communities. In this chapter, a general discussion of the significance and management of wetlands precedes a description of the wetland resources of the Highlands and the current challenges to their ecological integrity.

Wetlands and Their Management

Wetlands are defined under the federal Clean Water Act of 1977 as areas that have enough water present, over a sufficiently long period, to support the plant communities that are adapted for life in saturated soils (Environmental Laboratory 1987). The delineation of wetlands that meet this definition is based on the "three-parameter" approach, where the parameters are plants, soils, and water (hydrology). This definition recognizes that wetlands are formed by the combination of particular types of plants and plant communities, particular types of soil, and the presence of water in amounts sufficient to produce those characteristic soils and plant communities. Therefore, all three elements need to be present for an area to qualify as a wetland.

Wetlands have been under the jurisdiction of the federal government through the Water Pollution Control Act of 1972 (and its successor, the Clean Water Act of 1977) since 1975, when a federal court ruling required that the Army Corps of Engineers regulate wetlands as "waters of the United States." Since then, the Army Corps and the U.S. Environmental Protection Agency (EPA), which have dual authority in enforcing the Clean Water Act, have developed extensive programs for the enforcement of Section 404 of the act, the section that mandates the permit program for dredging and filling. These programs include a technical definition of "wetlands," documents that describe the method of determining whether a wetland falls under the jurisdiction of the law (termed "jurisdictional wetlands"), and documents concerning the classification and assessment of wetlands that can support regulatory actions.

The Army Corps of Engineers, with the EPA and Fish and Wildlife Service input, has primary authority for regulating freshwater wetlands in New York, Connecticut, and Pennsylvania. However, in New Jersey, a more stringent law, the Freshwater Wetlands Act of 1978, as amended through 2008, supersedes the federal act and is the primary authority regulating wetlands. It is based on a broader definition of what constitutes "wetlands" and mandates a more comprehensive program of protection, including the provision of upland buffer areas between development and the wetland boundary. In the three other states of the Highlands region, state laws extend wetland definitions and protections, but the primary regulation of wetlands still remains under the Army Corps' enforcement of the Clean Water Act. The state laws vary in their scope, the level of government at which the laws are implemented, mitigation requirements, the use of an in-lieu-fee program, methods of enforcement, and requirements for upland buffers.

In the Highlands area of New Jersey, the Highlands Regional Master Plan requires that wetlands and riparian areas (defined as areas adjacent to and hydrologically connected with rivers and streams) have a three-hundred-foot buffer area (New Jersey Highlands Council 2008). This is a larger buffer area than is required under state or federal law. Wetlands are considered part of the "open waters" of the region, together with springs, streams, ponds, lakes, reservoirs, and impoundments. However, the jurisdictional rules concerning definition of wetland boundaries remain with the state government, which uses a more liberal definition of wetland area than does the Army Corps under the federal Clean Water Act (thus considering a larger number of sites as jurisdictional wetlands). The state Department of Environmental Protection retains authority for granting permits for wetland impacts and for approving mitigation plans. The importance of the definition of "wetland" is clearly illustrated by the fact that the Highlands Council has mapped 90,600 acres (36,667 hectares) of wetlands within its jurisdiction and a total "riparian area" that accounts for over two-fifths of the New Jersey Highlands region, whereas the National Wetland Inventory (NWI) maps include only 76,700 acre (31,041 hectares) of wetlands in New Jersey (New Jersey Highlands Council 2008).

Wetlands receive protection under both federal and state laws because they are understood to provide numerous services to society. One prominent service is the provision of habitat for many species of plants and animals (see chapters 9 and 10), including those that are harvested for products, the many species that support recreation (hunting, fishing, wildlife observation), and a disproportionately large number of threatened and endangered species, relative to their land area. Numerous rare species and rare communities are associated with Highlands wetlands (Karlin and Andrus 1988; Karlin 1989; Metzler and Tiner 1992b; Dowhan et al. 1997; Mitchell 1998; and others). Another important service is the modification of water resources, including flood storage, reduction of peak storm-water flows, the protection of stream banks, the maintenance of stream flow during low-flow conditions, and the recharge of aquifers. The improvement of water quality, including removal and sequestration of sediments, nutrients, and heavy metals and the biotransformation of toxic organic pollutants, is a third important service associated with wetlands. Finally, the storage of carbon in peat soils of bogs and fens is an increasingly important service unique to these wetlands (Mitsch and Gosselink 2000; Tiner 2005; Zedler and Kercher 2005). While no one wetland performs all these functions and services, every wetland can be expected to provide at least some of them. There is little specific data to demonstrate the ecosystem services provided by Highlands wetlands. However, the descriptions of plant communities that follow and the accounts of forest types (chapter 7), plants (chapter 9), and wildlife (chapter 10) clearly demonstrate the role of wetlands in supporting biodiversity; the analyses of water resources of the Highlands (chapter 4) demonstrate the role of wetlands in the provision of abundant supplies of clean water.

Wetland Systems of the Highlands

Wetlands throughout the region of the Highlands are classified according to the system devised and implemented in 1978 by the U.S. Fish and Wildlife Service, which was subsequently adopted by the NWI program. This classification system, termed the Cowardin system (Cowardin et al. 1979), uses a hierarchical set of categories. The first level of the hierarchy establishes five "systems" based on the major source of water, reflecting whether the water comes from marine, estuarine, riverine, lacustrine, or palustrine (wetlands with a combination of precipitation, groundwater, and surface water) sources. Within each such system, the classification hierarchy establishes several subordinate levels. Subsystems, classes, and subclasses are recognized based on several sets of criteria, including aspects of hydrology, type of substrate, and type of vegetation. According to this classification, wetlands of the Highlands region fall into three main systems: palustrine, lacustrine, and riverine; a small area of estuarine wetlands is present along the Hudson River.

Of the approximately 3.5 million acres that make up the four-state Highlands region as defined by the Conservation Act, about 5.6 percent (193,900 acres or 78,470 hectares), not including areas mapped as deep (limnetic) lake waters, is mapped as wetland by the NWI (http://www.fws.gov/nwi/). Within the Highlands ecoregion, as opposed to the larger administrative area, mapped wetlands comprise a smaller area (129,201 acres or 52,287 hectares) but a slightly larger percentage of the total ecoregion area (7 percent). The analyses below refer to areas calculated for the Conservation Act Area. The states differ from each other considerably in their total wetland area. New Jersey accounts for nearly 40 percent of the total wetland area, New York is intermediate with 29 percent of the wetland area, and Connecticut (18 percent) and Pennsylvania (13 percent) have smaller amounts. The largest difference between the Conservation Act and ecoregion boundaries of the Highlands for wetland distribution occurs in Pennsylvania. The ecoregion area (187,072 acres or 75,707 hectares) contains 1,190 acres (773 hectares) of wetland, about 1 percent of the total land area, whereas the Conservation Act area (1,384,175 acres or 560,168 hectares) contains 26,108 acres (10,566 hectares) of wetland, nearly 2 percent, or twice as much, of the total land area.

The large majority of wetland area in the Highlands is palustrine, which is defined as wetland systems that are shallow (less than 2 m), nonsaline, small, and vegetated. Palustrine wetlands typically have a combination of water sources, including precipitation, groundwater, and surface water. The palustrine wetlands include several subsystems, including shallow ponds, emergent wetlands, forested wetlands, scrub-shrub wetlands, and mixed forest-shrub wetlands. The lacustrine class includes wetlands of submerged or floating vegetation in near-shore, shallow areas on the edges of ponds and lakes. Lacustrine wetlands are primarily influenced by lake water. Riverine wetlands are those contained within a channel and influenced by moving water. Ponds are considered a subset of palustrine wetlands; they typically have submerged or floating vegetation or are largely unvegetated but have shallow water and gravelly or sandy bottoms. Along the Hudson River in New York, wetlands classified as estuarine occur; these are defined as coastal wetlands that have at least sporadic influence of salt water. The estuarine wetlands of the Hudson River have tidal water movements and have low salinity.

Within each state, the distribution of major systems is fairly similar (fig. 8.1a). Palustrine forested wetland makes up the largest category of wetland types within New Jersey, New York, and Connecticut, while in Pennsylvania there is a larger area of riverine wetland than palustrine forested wetland.

There are few patches of estuarine wetland in New York, but these patches account for a large area. Palustrine nonforested wetlands, including emergent marshes, ponds, and scrub-shrub wetlands, make up most of the rest of the wetland resource. These wetlands include almost the entire range of hydrologies mapped by the NWI; the most common hydrologies include temporarily flooded, saturated, seasonally flooded, semipermanently flooded, and permanently flooded conditions. Plant communities include deciduous forests, coniferous forests, shrublands, and wetlands with mostly dead trees (often the result of beaver activity). Ponds are as numerous as individual forested wetlands, as indicated by the large number of mapped wetland patches in this category (fig. 8.1b), but account for much less area.

Most wetlands in the Highlands are quite small. Indeed, the large majority of wetlands of all types in all states are less than 25 acres (10 hectares) (more than 94 percent of wetland polygons), and the median size of a wetland is 7 acres (3 hectares). However, there are larger wetland complexes, each consisting of several different plant communities, such as combinations of forested and emergent wetland. Several have been identified as priority wetland sites for conservation and acquisition (U.S. EPA 1994). The relatively small average size of Highland wetlands probably reflects the topographic complexity of the Highlands, with narrow valleys, riparian corridors threaded between steep slopes, and few well-developed floodplains.

There are also differences across the Highlands region in the number of wetlands found per unit of land area (wetland density). In northern New Jersey and adjacent New York, there is a high density of wetlands, with many small patches scattered across the landscape in close proximity to each other (see plate 15). In contrast, in southern New Jersey below the glacial boundary, and in Pennsylvania, there is a much lower density of wetlands. Although glaciated, wetland density in Connecticut is lower than in the northern New Jersey–southern New York region (see plate 15).

Within each wetland class and subclass, the Cowardin system defines wetland types by several "modifiers." The water regime modifiers describe differences in the depth, duration, and timing of flooding or saturation, and the presence of disturbances such as beavers, ditching, or agricultural activity that have modified the wetland hydrology. They also include different types of water chemistry, such as "acidic," as would be found in a peat bog, or "alkaline," as would be found in a calcareous fen. These modifiers to the classification system capture the diversity of wetland environments, and thus can be used as an indicator of the overall diversity of the wetland resource. There is a high diversity of wetland types throughout the region, with much of this diversity found among the emergent, forested, and scrub-shrub wetland classes.

Several of the wetland types identified by these modifiers are important to conservation. Wetlands identified as having acidic water regimes, about 237 acres (96 hectares) of the total wetland area, include a number of unusual

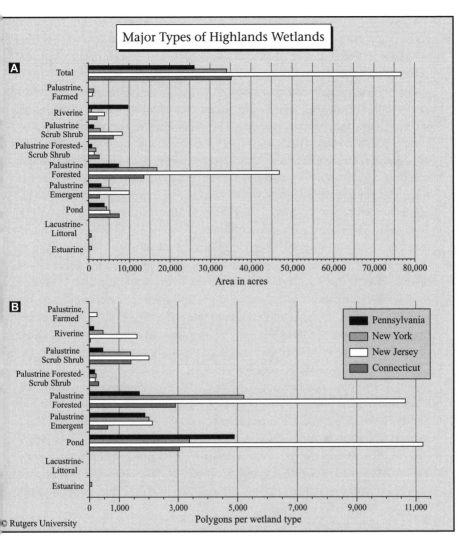

Figure 8.1. Distribution of major wetland types within each state based on the Conservation Act boundaries. Data from the National Wetland Inventory maps (http://www.fws.gov/wetlands/data/index.html). (a) Total acres per wetland system. (b) Number of polygons mapped in each wetland system. © Rutgers University.

shrubby plant communities. These wetlands, described in more detail below, share species with both the bogs of more northern and mountainous regions and with wetlands on the coastal plain, south of the Highlands region. These wetlands thus support an unusual combination of northern and southern species, and many of these species are rare, making these wetlands sites of particularly high importance for biodiversity. Similarly, the alkaline fens of the Connecticut portion of the Highlands also include numerous rare species and represent a wetland type that itself is quite uncommon.

Many wetlands in the Highlands also reflect disturbances to the natural patterns of water flow. Some of these disturbances are themselves natural and result from the activities of beavers. As mentioned in chapter 10, beavers are wetland architects, playing a key role in maintaining habitat diversity by building dams that create ponds used by other animals. Beavers account for about 4,620 acres (1,870 hectares) of wetland, including those mapped as both emergent, shrub, and forested. Most of these wetlands (75 percent) are found in Connecticut, with only two open-water ponds associated with beavers in Pennsylvania. Wetlands in the region also have been drained or ditched by humans, including 212 acres (86 hectares) of the estuarine wetlands on the Hudson River in New York. Fewer ditched wetlands are found in Pennsylvania than in the other states (8 percent of all ditched wetlands). Another set of wetlands have been formed by dikes or have been modified by the creation of dikes within or across them. The 17,361 acres (7,026 hectares) of diked or impounded wetlands include all systems and subsystems of wetlands and occur in all states. Most of the ponds (78 percent of all ponds mapped in the region) are a result of this human activity. Another 4,552 acres (1,842 hectares) of wetlands have been formed or affected by excavation. This disturbance again affects all systems and subsystems of wetlands, and is found in all states. Many of the ponds that are not associated with diking or impoundments are mapped as "excavated." These data suggest that most of the freshwater pond habitat in the Highlands has been either formed by or strongly affected by human modification of the landscape. It is likely that most of these ponds originated as dug or impounded ponds for farm use or as waterpower millponds and with time have become vegetated and taken on the attributes of wetland. Thus, about 20 percent of the wetland resource is either formed by beavers or by human activities.

Characteristics of the Wetland Resource

While upland forest may dominate the landscape, the Highlands still contain an impressive range of different types of wetland communities. The location and characteristics of the individual wetland community types are a function of the topography, glacial and land use history, underlying bedrock, and soils.

Geological Setting

Wetlands throughout the Highlands are constrained by the rugged topography, strong relief, and steep, narrow stream corridors set by the geology of the region (see chapters 1 and 2). Depressions tend to be small, or to border streams and rivers in narrow corridors, and large floodplains and meandering rivers are generally not present. Glaciation across much of the region (all of the Connecticut and New York sections and part of the New Jersey section) promoted the formation of wetlands after the ice receded. Glaciation created wetlands through several mechanisms, including the erosion of and deepening of hollows and depressions, the melting of buried ice within outwash sands and gravels, which formed troughs and kettle holes, the deposition of dense clay sediments in glacial lakes, and the deposition of compact, fine-textured basal tills that are poorly drained (Metzler and Tiner 1992b). Several glacial lakes occurred within the Connecticut portion of the Highlands region (Great Falls/Hollenbeck, Bantam, Pomperaug, Pootatuck, and Danbury), leaving behind glaciolacustrine deposits of poorly drained soils and depressions that promote wetland formation (Metzler and Tiner 1992b). South of the most recent (Wisconsin) glacial boundary in New Jersey, wetland areas reflect the effects of prior episodes of glaciations and other geomorphic processes that result in poorly drained conditions. There the topography is less steep, with fewer rock outcrops, more gentle slopes, and more land suitable for agriculture.

Wetlands of the region are also strongly affected by the nature of the bedrock. Most of the region is underlain by resistant Precambrian gneisses and schists, which produce acidic forest soils, and shallow soils in the recently glaciated regions. In sharp contrast, there are marble and limestone (carbonate rock) deposits in narrow bands throughout the region. These areas give rise to deeper, circum-neutral, base-rich soils, which in turn promote the development of wetland communities with distinctive, species-rich communities (detailed in the following).

Soils

Wetlands in the region are found on a wide range of hydric soils, including both mineral and organic soils, which represent the subset of the region's soils, as described in chapter 3, that meet the criteria of the Natural Resources Conservation Service, National Technical Committee for Hydric Soils. Overall, in the conservation area, 194 distinct hydric soil series are found; the major series types are displayed, with their total land area, in figure 8.2. New York has the lowest number of soil series but the largest number of histosols (organic soils), and it is the only state in which an organic soil has the largest area for a given soil series. No soil series is found in all four states of the region, although the most widespread soil series, the Ridgebury loam and its variants, is found in three of the four states (Connecticut, New Jersey, and New York). New Jersey occupies a clearly intermediary position because only one soil (Towhee series) is not found there; this soil is found only in Pennsylvania. Organic soils (mucks and peats) are found throughout the area, with the Catden (in New Jersey and Connecticut) and Carlisle (in New York and New Jersey) series being the most widespread organic soils, together accounting

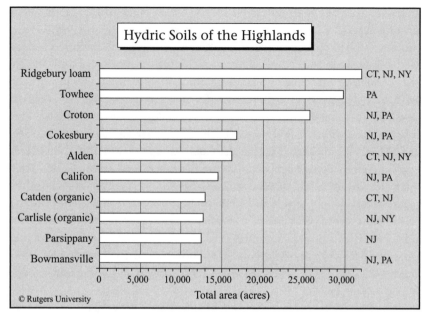

Figure 8.2. Widespread hydric soils of the Highlands region. © Rutgers University.

for 27,432 acres (11,106 hectares). Mineral hydric soils are mostly sand and silt loams; many are also stony, gravelly, or both, and some are described as extremely stony; few have clayey textures.

Wetland Communities

There have been very few published studies of wetlands throughout the region; thus there is little specific information on the structure and function of most wetland types throughout the Highlands. Most of the information available describing wetland community types has been developed for individual states, and each state has its own set of community definitions. Moreover, while some of the state reports and resources describe the general areas of occurrence of particular community types, none specifically associate community types with the Highlands ecoregion or political boundaries. Fairly recent detailed descriptions of community types are available for all four states (for Connecticut, see Metzler and Tiner 1992a; and Metzler and Barrett 2006; for New York, see Edinger et al. 2002; for New Jersey, see Breden et al. 2001; and for Pennsylvania, see Fike 1999). A more general and older set of community descriptions is available for New Jersey wetlands (Tiner 1985), and a revised and expanded classification of New Jersey communities is currently in progress (K. Walz, pers. comm.).

Some regional descriptions are also available (Barringer and Clemants 2003; and Evans, Novak, and Weldy 2003). The International Classification of Vegetation of the United States (Anderson et al. 1998; and Grossman et al. 1998) provides a framework for describing the wetland communities across the region. This comprehensive classification identifies "associations" as the basic unit for assessing and describing biodiversity. It represents a combination of dominant and characteristic species that define a recognizable grouping that occurs in a particular environment. According to this classification, there are forty-eight different wetland plant associations in the Highlands, including eighteen different forest communities, eleven different woodland and shrubland communities, and nineteen different herbaceous communities. A preliminary classification of New Jersey wetland communities of the Highlands includes twenty-six associations (K. Walz, pers. comm.).

In the following descriptions, an attempt has been made to abstract and reconcile community descriptions to give a general idea of the wetland resource across the area. While the descriptions are organized into units corresponding to the NWI mapping categories (Cowardin classes), the taxonomy follows the literature source(s) for the community description. For some states, National Vegetation Classification types have been recognized and assigned to physiographic regions (corresponding roughly to the ecoregional extent of the Highlands but not the Conservation Act area).

Lacustrine Communities. Lake-edge communities occur in a small number of locations. Small, shallow basins on granitic bedrock have acidic water with high amounts of dissolved organic carbon; they tend to be low in calcium and other cations, and they are often referred to as "bog lakes" (Edinger et al. 2002). They typically have extensive mats of *Sphagnum* moss along the shores, which in turn affect the other kinds of plants that can grow (Van Breeman 1995). Submerged and floating-leaved vegetation includes water shield (*Brasenia schreberi*), white water-lily (*Nymphaea odorata*), yellow pond-lily (*Nuphar luteum*), bladderworts (*Utricularia vulgaris, U. geminiscapa, U. purpurea*), pondweeds (*Potamogeton epihydrus, P. oakesianus*), bur reeds (*Sparganium fluctuans, S. angustifolium*), and club-rush (*Scirpus subterminalis*) (Reschke 1990). These communities are highly zoned, depending on the slope of the pond bottom and the adjoining shoreline, with varying communities found at different depths. Metzler and Barrett (2006) also describe a pickerelweed–green arrow arum (*Pontederia cordata–Peltandra virginica*) community as being abundant and associated with shallow waters on ponds and stream edges. Breden and colleagues (2001) describe several variants of this community and state that they are widespread through the region.

Palustrine Emergent Communities. Palustrine emergent communities are widespread and diverse throughout the Highlands region. In New York, palustrine emergent communities are grouped into deep-water and shallow-water assemblages (Edinger et al. 2002). Deep emergent marshes occur on both mineral and organic soils. Characteristic plants include yellow pond-lily (*N. luteum*), white water-lily (*N. odorata*), and cattails (*Typha angustifolia* and

T. latifolia). Several variants of these communities are described in Breden and colleagues (2001). These wetlands can become invaded by aggressive invasive species, including purple loosestrife (*Lythrum salicaria*) and the non-native variant of common reed (*Phragmites australis*). Shallow marshes (see plate 16), found in situations that have seasonal rather than permanent deep flooding, have a different group of species, including bluejoint grass (*Calamagrostis canadensis*), reed canary grass (*Phalaris arundinacea*), rice cutgrass (*Leersia oryzoides*), mannagrass (*Glyceria canadensis*), sedges (*Carex stricta, C. lacustris*), three-way sedge (*Dulichium arundinaceum*), bulrushes (*Scirpus cyperinus, S. atrovirens*), sweet flag (*Acorus americanus*), wild iris (*Iris versicolor*), water smartweed (*Polygonum amphibium*), marsh bellflower (*Campanula apalinoides*), and tufted loosestrife (*Lythrum thrysiflora*).

In Connecticut, a large number of palustrine emergent communities (fens) have been recognized, in particular in association with the calcareous valleys in the northern end of the Highlands region (see plate 17). Several graminoid-dominated communities, including twisted sedge (*Carex torta*) temporarily flooded grasslands occur along small, high-gradient streams, and tussock sedge (*C. stricta*) seasonally flooded grasslands occur in formerly grazed meadows; these communities are widely found throughout the region, as are *T. latifolia*–dominated grasslands and hard stem bulrush (*Schoenoplectus acutus*) communities. Similar communities, with slightly different species composition (e.g., containing bluejoint [*Calamagrostis canadensis*], reed canary grass [*Phalaris arundinacea*], bulrush [*Schoenoplectus tabernaemontani* and *S. acutus*]) are found in the southern portion of the region (Fike 1999). In Pennsylvania, a big bluestem (*Andropogon gerardii*) Indian grass (*Sorghastrum nutans*) river grassland community is found on sand and gravel deposits within rivers and riverbanks.

A bluejoint–reed canary grass wet meadow community (*Calamagrostis canadensis* and *Phalaris arundinaceae*) is widely found throughout the region (Breden et al. 2001). It is characterized by dense graminoid cover, a tussocky ground surface, and a wide range of associated shrubs, herbs, and other graminoid species.

The graminoid-dominated palustrine communities associated with the marble valleys include hairy sedge–cattail (*Carex lacustris–Typha* spp.) fens, twigrush (*Cladium mariscoides*) fens of several types, several community types with woollyfruit sedge (*Carex lasiocarpa*), mixtures of other graminoids and scattered small shrubs on deep peats, and inland sedge–bristly stalked sedge–yellow sedge (*C. interior–C. leptalea–C. flava*) grasslands on silt loam soils (Metzler and Tiner 1992a; and Metzler and Barrett 2006). In Pennsylvania an open sedge fen community containing *C. stricta, C. prairea, C. lacustris* is associated with calcareous substrates, and a golden saxifrage (*Chrysosplenium americanum*)–sedge community with a diverse groups of graminoids and forbs is found at alkaline seeps. Several other saxifrage-graminoid communities have been recognized in the Pennsylvania Highlands area (Fike 1999). The calcareous fens, seeps, and other wetlands throughout the Highlands are notable for their diverse plant communities, which include numerous rare and endangered species. They also are reported to contain an unusually high diversity of insects; Dowhan and colleagues (1997) note that more than five hundred species of Lepidoptera (butterflies and moths) and fifty species of Odonata (dragonflies) have been recorded for the wetlands in northwest Connecticut. Bog turtles (*Clemmys muhlenbergii*), listed as threatened under the federal Endangered Species Act, are also associated with these wetlands.

Palustrine Scrub-Shrub Communities. There are a large variety of shrub-dominated wetlands that occur in an equally wide variety of hydrogeomorphic positions and that often grade into emergent-dominated or tree-dominated communities. They occur on a wide variety of both mineral and organic soils, often on the edges of ponds. Characteristic plants include meadow-sweet (*Spiraea latifolia*), steeple-bush (*Spiraea tomentosa*), several species of dogwood (*Cornus joemina* ssp. *racemosa, C. amomum*), swamp azalea (*Rhododendron viscosum*), highbush blueberry (*Vaccinium corymbosum*), maleberry (*Lyonia ligustrina*), smooth alder (*Alnus serrulata*), spicebush (*Lindera benzoin*), willows (*Salix bebbiana, S. discolor, S. lucida, S. petiolaris*), wild raisin (*Viburnum cassinoides*), buttonbush (*Cephalanthus occidentalis*), sweet pepperbush (*Clethra alnifolia*), and arrowwood (*Viburnum recognitum*) in various combinations (Lynn and Karlin 1985; Breden et al. 2001). A particular type of tall shrub community is well developed in Harriman State Park; this community is referred to as a "highbush blueberry bog thicket" in the New York community classification (Reschke 1990; Evans, Novak, and Weldy 2003) and is recognized by the New York Heritage Program as a "significant natural community." This community type is often found adjacent to dwarf shrub communities (see plate 18). Highbush blueberry (*V. corymbosum*) creates a tall thicket, and sweet pepperbush (*Clethra alnifolia*), swamp azalea (*R. viscosum*), cinnamon fern (*Osmunda cinnamomea*), several species of *Carex*, and stunted red maples (*A. rubrum*) are also present, above a mat of *Sphagnum* mosses ("saturated shrub alliance" of Breden et al. 2001). It is absent from the calcareous valleys.

Metzler and Barrett (2006) describe several other types of shrub wetland found in the Connecticut portion of the region. Speckled alder–willow communities (*Alnus incana, A. rugosa, A. serrulata*, and *Salix* spp.) occur along streams and as an ecotone between forested wetlands and open water, and experience seasonal flooding. Another widespread shrub wetland community is the common buttonbush (*Cephalanthus occidentalis*) shrubland. This wetland type is found along pond borders and in undrained depressions with seasonal flooding. The wettest shrub community described for Connecticut (and probably also characteristic of Highlands wetlands through New Jersey) is the swamp loosestrife (*Decodon verticillatus*) community. This shrub is found in permanently to semipermanently flooded areas of shallow water, such as pond and lake edges. In Pennsylvania several other types of shrub swamp occur (Fike 1999). Shrublands, which are found along riverbank floodplains or on gravel bars, include black willow scrub-shrub wetlands and poison sumac (*Toxicodendron vernix*)–red cedar (*Juniperus virginiana*)–bayberry (*Myrica pensylvanica*) fens, located on calcareous areas within the Conservation Act boundaries.

In the marble valleys of the northern portion of the Connecticut Highlands, several types of shrub fen communities are found on wet organic soils. Shrub wetlands on carbonate-derived soils are characterized by shrubby cinquefoil (*Dasiphora floribunda*). Associated species include the northern bog birch (*Betula pumila*), willows, hairy sedge (*Carex lacustris*), dogwoods (*C. amomum* and *sericea*), alders (*Alnus* spp.), and poison sumac (*T. vernix*). It is likely that similar communities occur on the carbonate areas of New Jersey.

The "dwarf shrub bog" or "low shrub bog" community, a community type typical of northern boreal ecosystems (see plate 18), is considered rare. These communities have peat soil with low nutrients and highly acidic soil and pore water. They have been described for Connecticut (Metzler and Barrett 2006), New York (Edinger et al. 2002; Evans, Novak, and Weldy 2003), and adjacent New Jersey (Lynn and Karlin 1985; Breden et al. 2001). They are dominated by leatherleaf (*Chamaedaphne calyculata*), which may account for more than 50 percent of the plant cover, and a mat of several *Sphagnum* species. Other species present include sheep laurel (*Kalmia angustifolia*), bog laurel (*K. polifolia*), huckleberry (*Gaylussacia baccata*), highbush blueberry (*V. corymbosum*), cranberries (*Vaccinium oxycoccus* and *V. macrocarpon*), swamp loosestrife (*Decodon verticillatus*), and threeseeded sedge (*Carex trisperma*) as well as carnivorous plants, including pitcher plant (*Sarracenia purpurea*) and sundews (*Drosera* spp.). Occasional white pine (*Pinus strobus*), black spruce (*Picea mariana*), and tamarack (*Larix laricina*) trees may also be found.

The dwarf shrub bogs occurring along the New Jersey–New York border have been well documented (Lynn and Karlin 1985; Karlin and Andrus 1988). Karlin and Andrus (1988) recorded all the known shrub bogs near the New Jersey–New York border, recording five sites in the Highlands region. These wetlands are botanically noteworthy because they contain the southernmost locations of several species typically associated with northern peatlands. The dwarf shrub community usually occurs as a small area within larger peatland complexes of forested (conifers) or tall shrub communities, often as the ecotone between the taller woody communities and open water (small ponds). Their water chemistry indicates there is little or no mineral-rich groundwater present, just mineral-poor rainwater (ombrotrophic status) (Mitsch and Gosselink 2000), because calcium concentrations in both the bog mat and the adjoining open water are less than 2 mg/l, and pH values are very low (3.2–4.2). While some species associated with northern bogs are found in some sites (e.g., *Andromeda glaucophylla, Kalmia polifolia, Sphagnum riparium*), other species found in or near these communities, including *Chamaecyparis thyoides, Clethra alnifolia, Peltandra virginica, R. viscosum, Sphagnum flavicomans*, and *S. torreyanum*, are more common to the south or to the coastal plain (Karlin and Andrus 1986; Karlin and Lynn 1988). Thus, based on this description and regional descriptions from New York and Connecticut, it seems possible that there is a gradient in species composition of this community through the Highlands region, with northern New Jersey representing a transition area between communities dominated by purely northern species and those with a mixture of northern and southern species.

Deciduous Forested Swamps. Forested wetlands dominated by deciduous broad-leaved species are the most abundant type of wetland throughout the Highlands. The most commonly encountered swamp forest is one dominated by red maple (*Acer rubrum*) (see plate 19). Forests in which *A. rubrum* is the dominant or codominant species account for most of the deciduous forested swamp wetland area. These wetlands can have a varied composition of trees, shrubs, and herbaceous plants (Golet et al. 1993; Ehrenfeld in press). They are classified as variants of seasonally flooded cold-deciduous forests dominated by *A. rubrum* and *Fraxinus pennsylvanica*, and saturated cold-deciduous forests dominated by *A. rubrum* and *Nyssa sylvatica* (Breden et al. 2001). Golet and colleagues (1993) state that commonly associated species in the canopy include yellow birch (*Betula alleghaniensis*), black gum (*Nyssa sylvatica*), white ash (*Fraxinus americana*), eastern white pine (*Pinus strobus*), American elm (*Ulmus americana*), and eastern hemlock (*Tsuga canadensis*). Pin oak (*Quercus palustris*) and swamp white oak (*Quercus bicolor*) are found in New Jersey wetlands but less commonly north of this area; conversely, hemlock and pine are less common in the New Jersey wetlands than farther north. Golet and colleagues (1993) also note that these communities occur in a wide variety of hydrogeomorphic positions, including hillside seeps and drainageways, in shallow depressions along intermittent streams, in undrained basins on glacial deposits of till that experience prolonged periods of saturation or shallow flooding, and in alluvial habitats on river terraces and oxbows. The latter generally have shorter hydroperiods of flooding or saturation than the basin sites and have a more diverse plant community. An analysis of red maple swamps in the adjoining northern Piedmont of New Jersey (Ehrenfeld 2005, 2008) showed that these communities are diverse, with about three hundred species noted. Although these studies focused on Piedmont swamps, it is likely that the same factors found to structure variations in communities, including soil nutrient content, pH, soil texture (percent clay), and hydrogeomorphic position, are similarly important in the Highlands.

Numerous variants of red maple swamps have been described for the

Highlands region (Reschke 1990; Metzler and Tiner 1992a; Edinger et al. 2002; and Breden et al. 2001). These authors note that species richness is higher in swamps on calcareous sites, and these wetlands may have northern white cedar (*Thuja occidentalis*) and tamarack (*Larix laricina*) present, particularly on organic soil and in the northern portion of the region. Hemlock (*T. canadensis*) may be intermixed with the hardwoods throughout the region. A "red maple–skunk cabbage" community is found on both acidic and calcareous soils in several hydrogeomorphic settings. A continuous layer of skunk cabbage (*Symplocarpus foetidus*) is a distinguishing characteristic of this community. The "red maple–highbush blueberry" community is also found in a wide variety of settings; it is associated with low-nutrient conditions, and the tree canopy is more strongly dominated by red maple than in the other community types described above. Understory species characteristic of acidic soils form a well-developed understory; these species include several shrubs (*V. corymbosum, R. viscosum, I. verticillata*), sedges, and ferns (especially royal fern, [*Osmunda regalis*], marsh fern [*Thelypteris palustris*], and cinnamon fern [*Osmunda cinnamonea*]) (plate 19). A more open red maple woodland, termed the "red maple seasonally flooded woodland," is also present in nutrient-rich calcareous lowlands, in silty loam soils, or in organic soils. These swamps have an understory of willows (*Salix* spp.), alder (*A. incana*), and nannyberry (*Viburnum lentago*). Finally, a red maple–dominated open forest with an understory of tussock sedge (*C. stricta*) is found throughout the region. These communities occur on spring-fed slopes or on lowland sites with flooding or saturation for most of the growing season.

Floodplain and riparian forests have a different species composition, with silver maple (*Acer saccharinum*), red maple (*A. rubrum*), sycamore (*Platanus occidentalis*), cottonwood (*Populus deltoides*), butternut (*Juglans cinerea*), black willow (*Salix nigra*), bitternut hickory (*Carya cordiformis*), white ash (*Fraxinus americana*), black ash (*F. nigra*), and basswood (*Tilia americana*) (Edinger et al. 2002). In a study of riparian wetlands in the New Jersey Highlands, Hatfield, Moran, and Schramm (2006) recorded more than three hundred species, with about fifty to seventy species occurring per site.

In Pennsylvania, Fike (1999) describes several forested wetland types not found in the more northern parts of the region. These include a "bottomland oak-hardwood forest," dominated by *Q. palustris, Q. bicolor, A. rubrum*, and *U. americana*; a sycamore (*P. occidentalis*)–river birch (*Betula nigra*)–box elder (*A. negundo*) floodplain forest; and a silver maple (*A. saccharinum*) floodplain forest. All these types are broadly distributed throughout the Pennsylvania Highlands and are probably also well represented in the southern portion of New Jersey.

Needle-leaved Forested Communities. Forested wetlands with a predominance of needle-leaved trees are also found throughout the region, albeit at lower frequencies than deciduous forested wetlands. There are several different wetland types that occur. In Connecticut and extending into the north-ernmost parts of the New Jersey Highlands, black spruce (*Picea mariana*) woodlands or bog are found on saturated, acidic organic soils (peats) often associated with dwarf shrub communities (plate 18). These communities have strong affinities to northern and boreal bog forests. However, in some stands, pitch pine (*Pinus rigida*) may also be present. These bog forests are characterized by an open black spruce canopy, with mixtures of other spe-cies, a dense understory of mountain holly (*Nemopanthus mucronatus*), high-bush blueberry (*V. corymbosum*), sheep laurel (*Kalmia angustifolia*), and cran-berry (*V. macrocarpon*). A continuous layer of *Sphagnum* mosses is also usually present.

Another conifer-dominated type of wetland that is found throughout the northern portion of the Highlands is the hemlock (*T. canadensis*) seasonally flooded forest. This wetland community is found in valley locations that stay wet throughout the summer and have organic soils. The ground surface has a pronounced pit-and-mound microtopography, and *Sphagnum* spp. are promi-nent on the ground surface. Ferns (*Osmunda* spp.), several species of shrubs, most notably great rhododendron (*Rhododendron maximum*) but also sweet pepperbush (*C. alnifolia*), winterberry (*I. verticillata*), and highbush blueberry (*V. corymbosum*), among others, are found sparsely under the dense coniferous canopy. These swamp forests may also have some deciduous trees (yellow birch [*Betula alleghaniensis*] and red maple [*A. rubrum*]) mixed among the hem-locks (Evans, Novak, and Weldy 2003).

Northern white cedar (*Thuja occidentalis*) seasonally flooded forests are found in small numbers in the marble valleys of the northern end of the region. The understory in these wetlands tends to be sparse in density but diverse in composition with a large number of herbaceous species, many of which are not found in other wetland community types (e.g., marsh blue violet [*Viola cucullata*], wild sarsaparilla [*Aralia nudicaulis*], marsh marigold [*Caltha palustris*], goldenthread [*Coptis trifolia*], and others). Also rare are satu-rated red spruce forests (*Picea rubens*). These wetlands are found on cold, wet depressions on peat soils in Connecticut. Mountain laurel (*Kalmia latifolia*), mountain holly (*N. mucronatus*), and highbush blueberry (*V. corymbosum*) are associated species.

Near the New Jersey–New York border, there are several rare occurrences of southern Atlantic white cedar (*Chamaecyparis thyoides*) (Edinger et al. 2002). Lynn (1984) documented the occurrence of an unusually large (150 acres, or 61 hectares) stand of this species, which is primarily found on the coastal plain near Little Cedar Pond in Sterling Forest, adjacent to the New York–New Jer-sey border. The stand contained a few individuals of black spruce (*P. mariana*), white pine (*P. strobus*), tamarack (*L. laricina*), and red maple (*A. rubrum*), thus creating an unusual combination of northern and southern or coastal species. The sparse shrub layer is dominated by highbush blueberry (*V. corymbosum*).

Several other small stands of *C. thyoides* are found adjacent to nearby ponds, and a more extensive stand is located in Wawayanda State Park. There are also two small occurrences of this community in Putnam County, New York, at Brewster Pond and Tonetta Cedar Swamp (Dowhan et al. 1997).

Estuarine Wetlands. Wetlands mapped as "estuarine" by the National Wetlands Inventory within the Highlands region include a number of freshwater and brackish tidal emergent marshes located along the Hudson River. Iona Island Marsh and Constitution Marsh are ranked as priority sites of the New York/New Jersey Harbor Estuary program (Dowhan et al. 1997). These marshes are typified by graminoid communities dominated by narrow-leaved cattail (*Typha angustifolia*), *Scirpus* spp., intermixtures of emergent species (*Nuphar* spp., *Pontederia cordata*, and *Peltandra virginica*), and a number of other species. They grade into tall shrub swamps, and red maple–dominated wetland forests (as described earlier; Arrigoni et al. 2008). These marshes, which range in salinity from freshwater to oligohaline marshes, have received considerable scientific attention, mostly focused on nutrient dynamics (e.g., Pace, Findlay, and Fischer 1998; Templer, Findlay, and Wigand 1998; Connors et al. 2000; Meyerson et al. 2000; Findlay et al. 2002).

Management Issues: Threats and Opportunities

Beyond the direct destruction of wetlands for development or expanding agriculture and the indirect effects of adjacent urban and agricultural land use (Zedler and Kercher 2005), several other management issues should be briefly mentioned. Sustaining the rich biotic diversity of both common and rare wetland communities in the face of exotic species invasions and the direct and indirect effects of urban development is an ongoing challenge.

Exotic Species Invasions

After destruction associated with urban development, the invasion of exotic species is probably the most important threat to these wetlands (Houlahan and Findlay 2004a). As with other aspects of Highlands wetlands, there is little quantitative data available, and much of what data exist is not specific to the Highlands or to wetlands. However, a few studies indicate the scope of the problem. For example, Laba and colleagues (2008) used remote sensing to show that in Iona Marsh and Piermont Marsh, *Phragmites australis* covers 23 percent and 65 percent of the vegetated marsh area, respectively. Lathrop, Windham, and Montesano (2003) also used remote sensing (sequential analyses of aerial photos) to measure the rate of expansion of the *Phragmites* populations in these wetlands (1.17 hectares/yr and 5.37 hectares/yr in 1991, respectively). *Phragmites* is also widespread in the inland wetlands of Harriman State Park in New York; efforts to quantify the extent of this invasion are currently under way (E. McGowan, pers. comm.). The presence of *Phragmites* within shrub swamps has also been found to interfere with breeding by the threatened blue-winged warbler (J. L. Confer, pers. comm.).

Many other exotic invasive plant species are reported for the areas within the Highlands. The Invasive Plant Atlas of New England (see Mehrhoff 2009) gives species lists for Connecticut counties in the Highlands, and the Invasive Plant Council of New York State maintains lists of species in the New York region (New York State 2007). There are no corresponding data sources for New Jersey and Pennsylvania. Qualitative observations suggest that Japanese stilt grass (*Microstegium vimineum*) is widespread in many types of wetlands throughout at least the New Jersey and New York portions of the Highlands, and that Japanese barberry (*Berberis thunbergii*) is also present in many forested wetlands of this area. However, it is hard to assess the extent of invasion and the degree to which the presence of these species affects community integrity, species of concern, or ecosystem services.

Protection and Management

There is no comprehensive assessment of wetland status and trends within the Highlands region. The most recent national assessment (Dahl 2005) reported that 61 percent of freshwater wetland losses between 1998 and 2004 were due to urban development. Within states, urban development is also identified as a primary threat (Hasse and Lathrop 2010; Connecticut Department of Environmental Protection 2009). However, the extent of threats from urban development in different portions of the Highlands region is not well known. The adoption of a regional plan for the New Jersey Highlands (New Jersey Highlands Council 2008), the strict controls of New Jersey's Freshwater Wetlands Act, and a three-hundred-foot buffer provision in the Highlands Regional Plan are likely to mitigate development impacts in that state at least. In New York much of the Highlands region is contained in several large state parks (Sterling, Harriman, Bear Mountain), affording protection to the large range of wetlands found there.

As reviewed earlier, there are significant controls on wetland development in all four states that make up the Highlands region, including requirements for mitigation of losses through wetland creation, restoration, and enhancement. However, as has been extensively documented (NRC 2001; Turner, Redmond, and Zedler 2001; Zedler 2004; Matthews and Endress 2008), performance of mitigation wetlands is often poor, and mitigation wetlands often do not replace forested wetland types, rare ecosystems, or wetland communities developed on organic soils. As documented above, there are several wetland types distributed throughout the Highlands region that have exceptionally high value for their overall species diversity; many of these occur on organic soils. It is crucial that management agencies target these high-value wetland types for careful preservation, as the ability to restore or create them is very poor.

Conclusions and Research Needs

The Highlands contain an impressive range of wetland communities, ranging across all categories of nonmarine wetlands, as mapped by the National Wetland Inventory. This diversity of wetlands results from the combination of high topographic relief, the presence of both glaciated and unglaciated landscapes, the presence of both acidic and alkaline bedrock, and the location of the region at a biogeographic junction between northern, coastal, and southern biomes. These wetlands harbor many rare and endangered species of both animals and plants. While this biological resource is reasonably well protected by state and federal law, there remain significant threats, including effects from changes in land use that indirectly cause degradation of ecological integrity (Houlahan and Findlay 2004b; Houlahan et al. 2006).

This review also demonstrates the need for expanded research of wetland resources in the Highlands. Although there have been excellent analyses and descriptions of communities and wetlands in individual states, there is no coordination clearly linking individual community descriptions and conservation assessments in one state with others (a task well beyond the scope of this brief review). In addition, differences in the definitions of wetland types, both ecological and regulatory, across the four states of the region make comparisons difficult. A comprehensive analysis of community composition and environmental settings would facilitate better conservation and management of wetlands across the region.

This review of species composition and community types of wetlands throughout the Highlands region suggests that there are multiple biogeographic gradients across the region. Clearly, Connecticut and New York wetlands have more affinities with northern wetlands while Pennsylvania wetlands have more affinities with those in coastal and southern regions. However, the patterns are more complex because many communities have unusual mixtures of species from different biogeographic regions. The few published studies of wetlands and species at the New York–New Jersey border area (Lynn 1984; Lynn and Karlin 1985; Karlin and Andrus 1986, 1988; Karlin and Lynn 1988) suggest that complex biogeographic patterns among many taxa and communities are present but remain to be described and analyzed.

As climate changes, the need for continuous corridors to permit northward migration of species is urgent (Burkett and Kusler 2000; Wilson et al. 2005). The wetlands of the Highlands region already evidently express a gradient in biogeographic composition. Therefore, they may permit or facilitate migration of species with changing climate, evidenced by species mixtures that are already present. However, research is urgently needed to understand how existing community composition facilitates or interferes with migration and alterations of species' ranges.

As noted, one of the main reasons for the high diversity of communities and species in Highlands wetlands is the juxtaposition of both acidic and carbonate terranes. Both areas possess communities that are identified by management agencies as of high value and high priority for conservation; both, but especially the communities on carbonate areas, possess rare and threatened species. However, little is known of the relative sensitivity of these high-value communities to disturbance from changes in adjoining land use (i.e., nutrient or toxic pollution, alterations in hydrology) or climate change. The carbonate-based communities in particular are mostly found along lowlands and may be especially susceptible to disturbance from changes in adjoining land use. Exotic species invasion represents another major stressor encroaching on Highlands wetlands. Although anecdotal and informal observations suggest that invasion is widespread and poses serious threats to these ecosystems, there is no data on extent or impact that can be used to evaluate this problem. Research is needed to understand how these communities respond to stressors, and to identify which stressors are most serious in threatening their community structure and ecosystem function.

While it is widely appreciated that wetlands provide a range of ecosystem services that have high value to society, both in dollar and nondollar terms, there is very little information available to assess the types and extents of services provided by Highlands wetlands. Clearly, they are important in supporting wildlife and rare and endangered species of both plants and animals, and in moderating water flows. However, research addressing biotic, hydrologic, and water-quality functions of the different types of wetlands, in different regions, is needed to help guide management and conservation.

Acknowledgments

I am deeply grateful to the following colleagues for assistance in obtaining the information used in compiling this chapter: John Bognar and Zhang Yang of the Rutgers Center for Remote Sensing and Spatial Analysis; John Confer, Edwin McGowan, Kenneth Metzner, William Moorehead, Ann Rhoads, William Schuster, Lesley Sneddon, and Kathleen Strakosch Walz.

References

Anderson, M., P. Bourgeron, M. T. Bryer, R. Crawford, L. Engelking, D. Faber-Langendoen, M.Gallyoun, et al. 1998. *International Classification of Ecological Communities: Terrestrial Vegetation of the United States*. Volume II: *The National Vegetation Classification System: List of Types*. Arlington, VA: The Nature Conservancy.

Arrigoni, A., S. Findlay, D. Fischer, and K. Tockner. 2008. "Predicting Carbon and Nutrient Transformations in Tidal Freshwater Wetlands of the Hudson River." *Ecosystems* 11:790–802.

Barringer, K., and S. Clemants. 2003. "Vascular Flora of Black Rock Forest, Orange County, New York." *Journal of the Torrey Botanical Society* 130, no. 4: 292–308.

Breden, T., Y. Alger, K. Strakosch Walz, and A. G. Windisch. 2001. *Classification of Vegetation Communities of New Jersey.* 2nd ed. Trenton: New Jersey Department of Environmental Protection, New Jersey Natural Heritage Program.

Burkett, V., and J. Kusler. 2000. "Climate Change: Potential Impacts and Interactions in Wetlands of the United States." *Journal of the American Water Resources Association* 36:313–320.

Connecticut Department of Environmental Protection. 2009. "Statewide Inland Wetlands and Watercourses Activity Reporting Program: Status and Trends Report for the Year 2005." Bureau of Water Protection and Land Reuse Inland Water Resources Division. Available at http://www.ct.gov/dep.

Connors, L. M., E. Kiviat, P. M. Groffman, and R. S. Ostfeld. 2000. "Muskrat (*Ondatra zibethicus*) Disturbance to Vegetation and Potential Net Nitrogen Mineralization and Nitrification Rates in a Freshwater Tidal Marsh." *American Midland Naturalist* 143:53–63.

Cowardin, L. M., V. Carter, F. C. Golet, and E. T. LaRoe. 1979. "Classification of Wetlands and Deepwater Habitats of the United States." Washington, DC: Office of Biological Services, U.S. Fish and Wildlife Service, U.S. Department of the Interior.

Dahl, T. 2005. "Status and Trends of Wetlands in the Conterminous United States 1998–2004." Washington, DC: U.S. Department of the Interior, Fish and Wildlife Service.

Dowhan, J., T. Halavik, A. Milliken, A. MacLachlan, M. Caplis, K. Lima, and A. Zimba. 1997. "Significant Habitats and Habitat Complexes of the New York Bight Watershed." Charlestown, RI: U.S. Fish and Wildlife Service, Southern New England–New York Bight Coastal Ecosystems Program.

Edinger, G. J., D. J. Evans, S. Gebauer, T. G. Howard, D. M. Hunt, and A.M.O. Edinger, eds. 2002. *Ecological Communities of New York State.* 2nd ed. A revised and expanded edition of Carol Reschke's *Ecological Communities of New York State.* (Draft for review.) Albany: New York Natural Heritage Program, New York State Department of Environmental Conservation.

Ehrenfeld, J. G. 2005. "Vegetation of Forested Wetlands of Urban and Suburban Landscapes in New Jersey." *Journal of the Torrey Botanical Society* 132:262–279.

Ehrenfeld, J. 2008. "Exotic Invasive Species in Urban Wetlands: Environmental Correlates and Implications for Wetland Management." *Journal of Applied Ecology* 45:1160–1169.

Ehrenfeld, J. G. In press. "Northern Red Maple and Black Ash Swamps." In *Wetland Habitats of North America: Ecology and Conservation Concerns*, ed. Darold P. Batzer and Andrew H. Baldwin. University of California Press.

Environmental Laboratory. 1987. "Corps of Engineers Wetlands Delineation Manual." Technical Report Y-87-1, Vicksburg, MS: U.S. Army Engineer Waterways Experiment Station. NTIS No. AD A176 912.

Evans, D. J., P. G. Novak, and T. W. Weldy. 2003. "Rare Species and Ecological Communities at Harriman State Park." Unpublished report to the New York State Office of Parks, Recreation and Historic Preservation. Albany: New York Natural Heritage Program.

Fike, J. 1999. *Terrestrial and Palustrine Communities of Pennsylvania.* Harrisburg: Pennsylvania Department of Conservation and Natural Resources and The Nature Conservancy.

Findlay, S.E.G., E. Kiviat, W. C. Nieder, and E. A. Blair. 2002. "Functional Assessment of a Reference Wetland Set as a Tool for Science, Management and Restoration." *Aquatic Sciences* 64:107–117.

Golet, F. C., J. K. Calhoun, W. R. DeRagon, D. J. Lowry, and A. J. Gold. 1993. "Ecology of Red Maple Swamps in the Glaciated Northeast: A Community Profile." Biological Report 12. Washington, DC: U.S. Fish and Wildlife Service.

Grossman D. H., D. Faber-Langendoen, A. S. Weakley, M. Anderson, P. Bourgeron, R. Crawford, K. Goodin, et al. 1998. *International Classification of Ecological Communities: Terrestrial Vegetation of the United States.* Volume I: *The National Vegetation Classification System: Development, Status, and Applications.* Arlington, VA: The Nature Conservancy.

Hasse, J., and R. Lathrop. 2010. "Changing Landscapes in the Garden State: Urban Growth and Open Space Loss 1986 through 2007." New Brunswick, NJ: Center for Remote Sensing and Spatial Analysis, Rutgers University.

Hatfield, C. A., J. Moran, and J. Schramm. 2006. "Wetland Biological Indicators for New Jersey. Case Study: Forested Riparian Wetlands in the Highlands of New Jersey." New Brunswick, NJ: Rutgers University in conjunction with NJDEP.

Houlahan, J. E., and C. S. Findlay. 2004a. "Effect of Invasive Plant Species on Temperate Wetland Plant Diversity." *Conservation Biology* 18:1132–1138.

———. 2004b. "Estimating the 'Critical' Distance at Which Adjacent Land-Use Degrades Wetland Water and Sediment Quality." *Landscape Ecology* 19:677–690.

Houlahan, J. E., P. A. Keddy, K. Makkay, and C. S. Findlay. 2006. "The Effects of Adjacent Land-Use on Wetland Species Richness and Community Composition." *Wetlands* 261:79–96.

Karlin, E., editor. 1989. "New Jersey's Rare and Endangered Plants and Animals." Mahwah: School of Theoretical and Applied Science, Ramapo College of New Jersey.

Karlin, E. F., and R. E. Andrus. 1986. "Sphagnum Vegetation of the Low Shrub Bogs of Northern New Jersey and Adjacent New York." *Bulletin of the Torrey Botanical Club* 113:281–287.

———. 1988. "The Sphagnum Species of New Jersey." *Bulletin of the Torrey Botanical Club* 115:168–195.

Karlin, E. F., and L. M. Lynn. 1988. "Dwarf-Shrub Bogs of the Southern Catskill Mountain Region of New-York State: Geographic Changes in the Flora of Peatlands in Northern New Jersey and Southern New York." *Bulletin of the Torrey Botanical Club* 115:209–217.

Laba, M., R. Downs, S. Smith, S. Welsh, C. Neider, S. White, M. Richmond, W. Philpot, and P. Baveye. 2008. "Mapping Invasive Wetland Plants in the Hudson River National Estuarine Research Reserve Using Quickbird Satellite Imagery." *Remote Sensing of Environment* 112:286–300.

Lathrop, R. G., L. Windham, and P. Montesano. 2003. "Does Phragmites Expansion

Alter the Structure and Function of Marsh Landscapes? Patterns and Processes Revisited." *Estuaries* 26:423–435.

Lynn, L. M. 1984. "The Vegetation of Little Cedar Bog, Southeastern New York." *Journal of the Torrey Botanical Society* 111:90–95.

Lynn, L. M., and E. F. Karlin. 1985. "The Vegetation of the Low-Shrub Bogs of Northern New Jersey and Adjacent New York: Ecosystems at Their Southern Limit." *Bulletin of the Torrey Botanical Club* 112:436–444.

Matthews, J. W., and A. G. Endress. 2008. "Performance Criteria, Compliance Success, and Vegetation Development in Compensatory Mitigation Wetlands." *Environmental Management* 41:130–141.

Mehrhoff, L. 2009. "Invasive Plant Atlas of New England." http://nbii-nin.ciesin.columbia.edu/ipane/.

Metzler, K., and J. P. Barrett. 2006. "The Vegetation of Connecticut: A Preliminary Classification." Hartford: State Geological and Natural History Survey of Connecticut, Connecticut Department of Environmental Protection.

Metzler, K., and R. W. Tiner. 1992a. "Wetlands of Connecticut." Hartford: State Geological and Natural History Survey of Connecticut and U.S. Fish and Wildlife Survey National Wetlands Inventory.

———. 1992b. "Wetlands of Connecticut." Hartford: State Geological and Natural History Survey of Connecticut.

Meyerson, L. A., K. Saltonstall, L. Windham, E. Kiviat, and S. Findlay. 2000. "A Comparison of *Phragmites australis* in Freshwater and Brackish Marsh Environments in North America." *Wetland Ecology and Management* 9:89–103.

Mitchell, R. S. 1998. "Sterling Forest: A Botanical Bonanza." *NYFA Newsletter* 9:1–3.

Mitsch, W., and J. G. Gosselink. 2000. *Wetlands.* 3rd. ed. New York: Van Nostrand Reinhold.

New Jersey Highlands Council. 2008. "Highlands Regional Master Plan." Chester, NJ.

New York State. 2007. "New York State Early Detection Invasive Plants by Region. Assessment of Naturalized Invasive Plants REGION: Lower Hudson." New York: State of New York.

NRC. 2001. *Compensating for Wetland Losses under the Clean Water Act.* Washington, DC: National Academy Press.

Pace, M. L., S.E.G. Findlay, and D. Fischer. 1998. "Effects of an Invasive Bivalve on the Zooplankton Community of the Hudson River." *Freshwater Biology* 39:103–116.

Reschke, C. 1990. "Ecological Communities of New York State." Latham: New York Natural Heritage Program, New York State Department of Environmental Conservation.

Templer, P., S. Findlay, and C. Wigand. 1998. "Sediment Chemistry Associated with Native and Non-native Emergent Macrophytes of a Hudson River Marsh Ecosystem." *Wetlands* 18:70–78.

Tiner, R. 1985. "Wetlands of New Jersey." Newton Corner, MA: U.S. Fish and Wildlife Service, National Wetlands Inventory.

———. 2005. *In Search of Swampland.* 2nd ed. New Brunswick, NJ: Rutgers University Press.

Turner, R. E., A. M. Redmond, and J. B. Zedler. 2001. "Count It by Acre or Function—

Mitigation Adds Up to Net Loss of Wetlands." *National Wetlands Newsletter* 2:5–6, 15–16.

U.S. Environmental Protection Agency (EPA). 1994. "EPA Priority Wetlands for the State of New Jersey." New York: U.S. EPA Region 2.

Van Breeman, N. 1995. "How *Sphagnum* Bogs Down Other Plants." *Trends in Ecology and Evolution* 10:270–275.

Wilson, R. J., D. Gutierrez, J. Gutierrez, D. Martinez, R. Agudo, and V. J. Monserrat. 2005. "Changes to the Elevational Limits and Extent of Species Ranges Associated with Climate Change." *Ecology Letters* 8:1138–1146.

Zedler, J. B. 2004. "Compensating for Wetland Losses in the United States." *Ibis* 146:92–100.

Zedler, J. B., and S. Kercher. 2005. "Wetland Resources: Status, Trends, Ecosystem Services and Restorability." *Annual Review of Environment and Resources* 30:4.1–4.36.

9

An Overview of the Vascular Plants of the Highlands and the Threats to Plant Biodiversity

Gerry Moore and Steven Glenn

Introduction

As a young boy growing up in southern New Jersey in the 1970s (Millville, Cumberland County), author Gerry Moore would occasionally make trips to the Highlands region of northern New Jersey with friends of his family who were amateur naturalists and photographers. These trips were often-times made in the spring to see spring ephemerals in bloom, such as cut-leaved toothworts (*Cardamine concatenata*), Virginia spring beauty (*Claytonia virginica*), Dutchman's breeches (*Dicentra cucullaria*), trout lily (*Erythronium americanum*), and bloodroot (*Sanguinaria canadensis*). The group would also make trips to look for rare species, hiking into rich woodlands in search of showy lady's slipper (*Cypripedium reginae*) (see plate 20), Oswego tea (*Monarda didyma*), and Canada violet (*Viola candensis*). Open roadside areas provided excellent habitat for wildflowers such as wild lupine (*Lupinus perennis*).

Some of these botanical experiences from the 1970s can be repeated today. There are still plenty of places to see excellent displays of spring ephemerals. However, it is highly unlikely a visitor will be able to find the showy lady's slipper, the vast majority of its former haunts in the Highlands being lost to development and habitat alteration (see Snyder 2000). Furthermore, finding rarities along the roadside is increasingly difficult, as increased maintenance (e.g., mowing) and planting of nonnative grasses along roadsides severely limits the ability of many of our native wildflowers to grow there. In 1881, botanist Nathaniel Lord Britton, in his *Preliminary Catalogue of New Jersey*, characterized wild lupine as "quite common throughout the state," and as recently as the 1970s wild lupine could readily be found along many road-sides in New Jersey. Today, it is increasingly difficult to find and is tracked as a rare species in New Jersey, New York, and Pennsylvania (NatureServe 2009).

On these early trips, Moore also took delight in noting some of the non-native exotics that were becoming established in the flora, such as garlic mus-tard (*Alliaria petiolata*), Japanese barberry (*Berberis thunbergii*), and Oriental bittersweet (*Celastrus orbiculatus*). At the time, most botantists did not view these plants as harmful to the environment but rather as simply something new to see. These days, these nonnative exotics are all too easy to find: indeed, they have become so common that they are often regarded as threats to the native flora. This chapter provides an overview on the status of the vegetation of the Highlands region in Connecticut, New Jersey, New York, and Pennsylvania, with an emphasis on current threats to the native flora. It also provides management and regulatory recommendations to better protect the native plant diversity present in the Highlands.

Efforts and Methods Used to Document the Plants of the New Jersey Highlands Region

The flora of the New York Metropolitan region, including the Highlands area, has been studied for more than 250 years. Early botanists who explored the region included John Bartram, William Bartram, Cadwallader Colden, Jane Colden (daughter of Cadwallader Colden), and Carl Linnaeus's student Peter Kalm. Cadwallader Colden published what is probably the first formal account of the region's flora with his *Plantae coldenhamiae* (1743, 1751.). By the mid-1700s, much of the region's flora had been documented, as indicated by the fact that of the roughly three thousand species known from the region, approximately one-half were described in Linnaeus's *Species plantarum* (1753).

Following this period of general documentation, botanists focused on writing regional floras, such as Michaux's *Flora boreali-americana* (1803), Persoon's *Synopsis plantarum* (1805–1807), Pursh's *Flora americae septentrionalis* (1814), and Nuttall's *Genera of North American Plants* (1818). More recent regional flora manuals include Fernald's *Gray's Manual of Botany* (1950) and Gleason and Cronquist's *Manual of Vascular Plants of Northeastern United States and Adjacent Canada* (1991). Besides these regional manuals, numerous regional floras, catalogs, and checklists from the New York metropolitan region have also been published, including Torrey (1819), Leggett (1870–1874), Willis (1874), Bishop (1885), Britton (1881, 1889), Britton et al. (1888), Graves et al. (1910), Taylor (1915, 1927), House (1924), Gleason (1935), Anderson (1989), Hough (1983), Mitchell and Tucker (1997), and Schmid and Kartesz (1994).

While there have been numerous efforts to document the flora of the individual Highlands states of Connecticut, Pennsylvania, New Jersey, and New York (e.g., Britton 1881, 1889; Porter 1903; Graves et al. 1910; Hough 1983; Robichaud and Buell 1983; Robichaud Collins and Anderson 1994; Anderson 1989; Mitchell and Tucker 1997; Rhoads and Block 2007; Weldy and Werier 2009), there has never been an effort to catalogue all the plant species found within the Highlands region. This is in contrast to another major ecoregion in the area, the Pinelands of New Jersey, which has been the subject of numerous research efforts focusing on its vegetation (e.g., Stone 1911; Harshberger 1916; Forman 1979).

One problem, of course, is that the Highlands region has not been recognized with official boundaries until relatively recently with the passage of the federal Highlands Conservation Act in 2004. Furthermore, in New Jersey, the federal act boundaries differ somewhat from those established through the passage of the state's Highlands Water Protection and Planning Act. Another problem is the complexity of the federal and state boundaries (for New Jersey) for the Highlands that frequently run through parts of counties and municipalities. For example in New Jersey, the official Highlands boundaries span parts of seven counties (i.e., Bergen, Hunterdon, Morris, Passaic, Somerset, Sussex, and Warren) and eighty-eight municipalities. Such complex boundaries create difficulties in using what published information is available on the flora because the location data are oftentimes not precise enough to determine if a given plant species has been recorded within the Highlands region. For example, Abraitys's (1980, 1981) and Schaefer's (1949) respective checklists of the plants of Hunterdon County, New Jersey, and Northampton County, Pennsylvania, lack precise location data for each species that would allow one to determine if a record is within the Highlands region. Since both these counties lie only partly within the Highlands region, these lists cannot be used in compiling a list of Highlands plants without further research. Location data given on the collection labels of many herbarium specimens present similar problems.

Nonetheless, there is an important need to have a list of the plants of the Highlands region. Plants are one of three criteria—the others being soils and hydrology—used in delineating wetlands (Environmental Laboratory 1987). Plant species also provide important insight into land-use history and soil types for a given region. Indeed a well-trained local botanist can, through inspection of a plant list for an area, usually predict the presence of wetlands, soil types, and land-use histories for a site without ever visiting it.

Furthermore, the Highlands also support populations of many rare, threatened, and endangered species of plants that are in need of immediate protection. The New Jersey Highlands Act and its regulations protect rare, threatened, and endangered plant species as recognized by the New Jersey Natural Heritage Program (Snyder 2009). Regulated activities are prohibited if they would adversely affect any rare, threatened, or endangered plant species. Statewide regulations in Connecticut, Pennsylvania, and New York also provide various degrees of protection to populations of endangered, threatened, and rare plant species. Therefore, a list of rare, threatened, and endangered species that have been reported from the Highlands needs to be developed. Such a list is essential in the development of educational programs for environmental regulators and consultants on the correct identification and proper delineation of critical habitats for these species.

On the other side of the abundance spectrum, as recounted in chapters 7 and 8, ecologists are now recognizing the significant impacts that nonnative invasive plants are having on the landscape, including the Highlands region. Such species can dominate areas, creating monocultures where there was once species diversity. As a result of these impacts, ecologists, botanists, and environmentalists are now recognizing the need to develop official lists of invasive plants species, regulate their possession, and develop programs that seek to remove and limit the spread of invasive species.

In addressing these needs, scientists at Brooklyn Botanic Garden, working in collaboration with other botanists, ecologists, and conservationists, including staff from the Connecticut, New Jersey, New York, and Pennsylvania Natural Heritage Programs and The Nature Conservancy, compiled the following for the Highlands region: (1) a list of rare, threatened, and endangered species (see appendix 9.1 below), and (2) a list of potentially invasive species (see appendix 9.2 below). The New York Metropolitan Flora (NYMF) project's database has been one major source of data. In 1989 Steve Clemants of the Brooklyn Botanic Garden founded the NYMF with the goal of documenting all vascular plants that grow without cultivation in the New York metropolitan area. The range of NYMF includes all counties within roughly a 50-mile radius of New York City, including all of Long Island, northern New Jersey (south to Mercer and Monmouth counties), part of southeastern New York (Orange, Putnam, Rockland counties), and Fairfield County, Connecticut. The region covers approximately 7,650 square miles and includes all the New Jersey Highlands and part of the New York Highlands region. The procedure used for the mapping of occurrences breaks down the NYMF range into 964 five-by-five kilometer cells or blocks, and, as far as possible, every record is assigned to one of these blocks. The database for NYMF—AILANTHUS—is composed of records from three sources: (1) collections made in the field and stored at regional herbaria; (2) observations made in the field by reliable local botanists; and (3) published information. These data are used to generate distribution maps for all species occurring in the NYMF range.

Using the Brooklyn Botanic Garden's plant species database, AILANTHUS, in consultation with other flora publications and resources (e.g., Britton 1881, 1889; Porter 1903; Graves et al. 1910; Hough 1983; Robichaud and Buell 1983; Robichaud Collins and Anderson 1994; Anderson 1989; Mitchell and Tucker 1997; Rhoads and Block 2007; Weldy and Werier 2009), scientists at the Brooklyn Botanic Garden are preparing a comprehensive list of all vascular plant species reported from the Highlands region. To date the authors have documented the occurrence of approximately twenty-seven thousand species from the Highlands region of Connecticut, New Jersey, New York, and Pennsylvania, of which approximately 30 percent are not native to the area. This list will be submitted for publication to *Bartonia*, the journal of the Philadelphia Botanical Club.

The Flora of the Highlands Region

The flora of the Highlands region is considerably diverse, with 1,540 vascular plant species documented from the Highlands region of New Jersey alone. Based on the 2,696 species reported from the state by Anderson (1989), this number represents 56 percent of the state's flora, while the Highlands region in New Jersey (ca. nine hundred square miles) covers only 12 percent of New Jersey (Robichaud Collins and Anderson 1994). Similar comparisons are currently being conducted for the states of Connecticut, New York, and Pennsylvania. This diverse flora is a result of the Highlands region having a considerably varied landscape with elevation ranging from 350–1,500 ft, rugged ridges and valleys, frequent rock outcroppings, and glacial lakes (Robichaud Collins and Anderson 1994). These features combined with variations in bedrock, soil types, and drainage are responsible for the diverse flora present in the Highlands.

However, the features noted in the Highlands are not unique to the Highlands region or to the larger New England Uplands province. As a result, the vegetation of the Highlands, unlike other ecoregions, such as the New Jersey Pinelands, is not strikingly different from that noted in the adjacent Ridge and Valley and Piedmont landform provinces. Likewise species that are regionally endemic to the Highlands are lacking. This is in sharp contrast to the Pine Barrens of New Jersey, which has many species, such as pine barrens reed grass (*Calamovilfa brevipilis*), thread-leaved sundew (*Drosera filiformis*), New Jersey rush (*Juncus caesariensis*), sandwort (*Minuartia caroliniana*), bog asphodel (*Narthecium americanum*), pyxie *(Pyxidanthera barbulata)*, Knieskern's beaked rush (*Rhynchospora knieskernii*), curly grass fern (*Schizaea pusilla*), and turkeybeard (*Xerophyllum asphodeloides*), that are generally not found elsewhere in the state.

Similarly a high diversity but lack of unique types can be found in the natural communities reported from the Highlands. For example, of the fifty-eight nonmarine natural communities that Breden (1989) recognized in his classification for New Jersey, twenty-one were reported (36 percent of the total) as occurring in the New Jersey Highlands: streamside/lakeside shrub swamp, river bar community (possibly in Highlands), inland graminoid marsh, inland noncalcareous pond shore, glacial bog, robust emergent marsh, northern New Jersey shrub swamp, floodplain forest, hardwood conifer swamp, inland Atlantic white cedar swamp, inland red maple swamp, black spruce swamp (possibly in Highlands), silicaceous rock outcrop community, limestone glade, ridgetop pitch pine–scrub oak forest, talus slope community, silicaceous riverside outcrop community, dry-mesic inland mixed oak forest, mesic hemlock hardwood forest, chestnut oak forest, and terrestrial cave. Of these twenty-one community types in the Highlands, only the limestone glade was reported to be limited to the Highlands region. For further discussions on the ecology of forests and wetlands of the Highlands, see chapters 7 and 8 in this volume.

While the general features of the Highlands are not distinct enough from those of the adjacent provinces to create a unique flora, some distinctions can be made. For example, the ridges and valleys in the Highlands differ from those found in the Ridge and Valley province in the parent rock types and the generally broader ridges and narrower valleys with steeper slopes (Robichaud Collins and Anderson 1994). Probably because of these distinctions, some plant species are found more frequently in the Highlands than in other provinces. A review of the NYMF-AILANTHUS database showed the following seventeen species to occur more frequently in the New Jersey Highlands than in other provinces (e.g., Ridge and Valley, Piedmont, coastal plain): striped maple (*Acer pensylvanicum*), climbing fumitory (*Adlumia fungosa*), rock harlequin (*Corydalis sempervirens*), beaked hazelnut (*Corylus cornuta*), bush honeysuckle (*Diervilla lonicera*), Labrador tea (*Ledum groenlandicum*), fly honeysuckle (*Lonicera canadensis*), Bishop's cap (*Mitella diphylla*), black spruce (*Picea mariana*), red spruce (*Picea rubens*), rock crowfoot (*Ranunculus micranthus*), eastern wild gooseberry (*Ribes rotundifolium*), red elderberry (*Sambucus racemosa*), twisted stalk (*Streptopus lanceolatus*), hobblebush (*Viburnum lantanoides*), downy arrow-wood (*Viburnum rafinesquianum*), and barren strawberry (*Waldsteinia fragaroides*). This list is by no means comprehensive, because it is limited to the region of the Highlands within New Jersey and is biased toward woody species. To date, these having been more intensively surveyed by Brooklyn Botanic Garden staff (Moore et al. 2002).

Some distribution patterns do deserve further comment. Taylor (1915) and others (Britton 1884, 1887; Harper 1905, 1906) have noted the occurrence of several species that commonly occur on the coastal plain but that also occur in the Highlands region (and north and west of the Highlands region). As Taylor (1915) noted, this pattern is particularly striking when the species are generally absent in the intervening Piedmont province, the physiographic region between the coastal plain and the Highlands (Robichaud Collin and Anderson 1994). Species that fit this category include dragon's mouth orchid (*Arethusa bulbosa*), Atlantic white cedar (*Chamaecyparis thyoides*), three-way sedge (*Dulichium arundinaceum*), cotton-grass (*Eriophorum virginicum*), swamp pink (*Helonias bullata*) (see plate 22), pitcher plant (*Sarracenia purpurea*), and large cranberry (*Vaccinium macrocarpon*). Usually species with this pattern are much more frequent in the Coastal Plain. However, in some cases the reverse is true, the species being much rarer on the Coastal Plain. Species that fit this pattern include sweet gale (*Myrica gale*), mountain holly (*Nemopanthus mucronatus*), rosebay (*Rhododendron maximum*), and arrow-grass (*Scheuzeria palustris*).

Rare, Threatened, and Endangered Plant Species

The Highlands Water Protection and Planning Act of New Jersey protects the habitats of all species tracked as rare, threatened, or endangered by the New Jersey Natural Heritage Program. Currently, the program tracks 296 species as rare, threatened, or endangered that have records from within the Highlands region. Furthermore, another 329 species have been reported from the Highlands and are tracked as rare, threatened, or endangered by the Connecticut, New York, and Pennsylvania Natural Heritage programs, for a total of 626 species. The habitats in which these species are found run the gamut from dry, open fields and forested uplands to open wetland marshes and forested swamps and lakes. In many cases rare plants can occur in habitats that have been created by humans, such as roadsides and ponds.

Of the 626 rare, threatened, or endangered species, 21 are globally rare or potentially globally rare based on the rankings given by NatureServe (2009) (all are listed in appendix 9.1 below). Two of these species, swamp pink (*H. bullata;* see plate 22) and small whorled pogonia (*Isotria medeloides*), are federally threatened. Another species reported from the Highlands, Schweinitz's waterweed (*Elodea schweinitzii*), may be extinct throughout its reported range of New York and Pennsylvania (the report from New Jersey is probably an error; see NatureServe 2009). However, it is not clear if it represents a true species or a hybrid between two other species of waterweed: common waterweed (*Elodea canadensis*) and free-leaved waterweed (*E. nuttallii*) (Saint John 1965; Cook and Urmi-Konig 1985; Gleason and Cronquist 1991).

Whereas Schweinitz's waterweed may be lost, two other rare plant species that occur in the Highlands—mountain doll's daisy (*Boltonia montana*) (Townsend and Caraman-Castro 2006) and Rezniceck's sedge (*Carex rezniceckii*) (Werier 2006)—were only recently described. In each case, the original material used to prepare the original descriptions included material from the Highlands. Also in each case, material of the species was known long before its original description, the new species being the result of taxonomic revision as broadly circumscribed species were treated more narrowly, with some of the material now being treated as new species. While it is generally thought that the description of new species is an endeavor that is now limited to the tropics, these two recent descriptions from the Highlands show that this is not always the case, even for well-studied groups, such as flowering plants (angiosperms).

Invasive Plant Species of the Highlands Region

While the previous discussion on rare species can be discouraging as we witness the decline of so many of our native plants, the precipitous spread of many nonnative plant species is equally alarming. The spread of invasive species is a major threat to biodiversity, perhaps second only to habitat destruction. Invasive plant species can cause extensive and oftentimes irreversible damage and alteration to ecosystems, which can lead to the reduction or extirpation of populations of native species (Clout, Lowe, and IUCN/SSN 1996).

Hardly any habitats in the Highlands are immune from invasive plants. Upland fields and roadsides that once supported populations of many native wildflowers are now dominated by the Eurasian mugwort (*Artemisia vulgaris*). Some rich woodlands that once were bedecked with beautiful displays of native spring wildflowers are now dominated by Old World herbs, such as garlic mustard (*Alliaria petiolata*), Japanese stiltgrass (*Microstegium vimineum*), and lesser celandine (*Ranunculus ficaria*). Many open wet marshes that once supported a diversity of native hydrophytes are now a near monoculture of the Eurasian purple loosestrife (*Lythrum salicaria*) (see plate 21). Some ponds and rivers that once supported only populations of native aquatics, such as water lilies (*Nymphaea, Nuphar*), are now choked with aquatic invasives from the Old World, such as the Eurasian water chestnut (*Trapa natans*) and the European water milfoil (*Myriophyllum spicatum*).

In addition to introducing (sometimes intentionally, other times inadvertently) these invasive plant species, humans also, through their disturbance of the landscape, are contributing to the further spread of invasive plants. In comparing the performance of co-occurring native and alien invasive plants, Dahler (2003) concluded: "There appear to be few 'super-invaders' that have universal performance advantages over co-occurring natives; rather, increased resource availability and altered disturbance regimes associated with human activities often differentially increase the performance of the invaders over that of the natives." In areas with low nutrient-resource availability, such as the New Jersey Pinelands, human disturbance that does not result in increased nutrient-resource availability does not usually result in increased establishment and spread of invasive species (Bien, Spotila, and Gordon 2009), while disturbance that does increase nutrient-resource availability does result in an increase in exotics (Zampella and Laidig 1997). In the Highlands, there is oftentimes a naturally high nutrient-resource availability (e.g., rich soils) along with frequent human disturbances, some of which further contribute to nutrient-resource availability. As a result, invasive plants are a serious problem in the Highlands. Indeed, in some of the most heavily disturbed areas, nonnatives can predominate in all layers of vegetation. For example, one can experience a forested region in which the tree layer consists of tree of heaven (*Ailanthus altissima*), Norway maple (*Acer platanoides*), and sycamore maple (*Acer pseudoplatanus*); the shrub layer of nonnative honeysuckles (*Lonicera* X *bella, L. maackii, L. morrowii*) and Japanese barberry (*B. thunbergii*); vines of porcelain berry (*Ampelopsis brevipedunculata*) and Oriental bittersweet (*C. orbiculatus*), and herbs of garlic mustard (*A. petiolata*) (see plate 23), Japanese stiltgrass (*M. vimineum*), and lesser celandine (*R. ficaria*).

In addition to exotic plants, another strong indicator of human-disturbed habitats is overabundant wildlife (Stromayer et al. 1998). This overabundant wildlife, especially white-tailed deer (*Odocoileus virginianus*), which may selectively browse native species over nonnative species (Boulton 2005), may be furthering the decline of native species and the concomitant increase in nonnative species. The expanding populations of nonmigratory Canada goose (*Branta canadensis*) are also seriously disturbing vegetation in some areas.

While invasive plants and the threats they pose to ecosystems present great challenges to ecologists and environmentalists, the more recently introduced invaders pose significant challenges to the plant taxonomists and field botanists who are charged with correctly identifying them, even though these newcomers are oftentimes not included in regional identification manuals (e.g., Fernald 1950; Gleason and Cronquist 1991). For example, several years ago Brooklyn Botanic Garden scientists began noticing a woody *Aralia* spreading rapidly in the New York metropolitan area, including the Highlands. Using regional manuals (e.g., Fernald 1950; Gleason and Cronquist 1991), they found that the material readily keyed to *Aralia spinosa*, a species native to the eastern United States but not generally observed north of Delaware and Pennsylvania. Brooklyn Botanic Garden staff therefore thought they might have an example of a southern plant species, possibly aided by global warming, pushing northward into the New York metropolitan area. However, further examination of the material and consultation of other literature conclusively showed the material to belong *Aralia elata*, a species native to Asia (Moore, Glenn, and Ma 2009).

Even more problematic is when a single species is both native and nonnative. Common reed (*Phragmites australis*) is a grass common in open, disturbed wetlands throughout the Highlands and surrounding regions. In general, the species is commonly thought of as a serious invasive. However, the local material actually consists of native (*Phragmites australis* subsp. *americanus*) and nonnative material (*Phragmites australis* subsp. *australis*) introduced from Eurasia (Saltonstall 2002, 2003; Saltonstall, Peterson, and Soreng 2004). The nonnative subspecies is treated as invasive (Connecticut Invasive Plants Council 2004; Jordan 2009; Pennsylvania Department of Conservation and Natural Resources 2009), while the native subspecies is much rarer, being tracked as possibly extirpated in Connecticut, critically imperiled in Pennsylvania, and rare in New York (NatureServe 2009; Young 2008).

The threat invasive species pose to the environment is recognized through two federal executive orders, 11987 (signed by President Jimmy Carter in 1977) and 13112 (signed by President Bill Clinton), stating the need for a national policy preventing the introduction of nonnative species and controlling those nonnative invasive species that have already become established. In 2004 New Jersey governor James McGreevey signed Executive Order 97 establishing a New Jersey Invasive Species Council charged with developing an invasive species management plan, including the recommendation of possible legislative or regulatory actions. Nonetheless, New Jersey, like many states, still lacks an official list of invasive species. The problem of invasive plants in New Jersey is overviewed by Snyder and Kaufman (2004). Connecticut does have an official list of invasive plant species (Connecticut Invasive Plants Council 2004), and Pennsylvania maintains an unofficial list (Pennsylvania Department of Conservation and Natural Resources 2009).

In 2008 New York established through legislation the New York State Invasive Species Council (ISC) with a charge to develop a list of invasive plant species for eventual adoption. A subcommittee of the ISC has drafted a protocol (see Jordan, Moore, and Weldy 2008; Jordan 2009) for evaluating the invasiveness of nonnative species to be used by the ISC in its preparation of an invasive plant species list for New York. This protocol is based on other systems (e.g., Carlson et al. 2008; Morse et al. 2004; Randall et al. 2008) and defines an invasive plant as one that is "1) nonnative to the ecosystem under consideration, and 2) whose introduction causes or is likely to cause economic or environmental harm or harm to human health" (Federal Executive Order 13112). Under the protocol, invasiveness of nonnative species is assessed using four broad categories: (1) ecological impact, (2) biological characteristics and dispersal ability, (3) ecological amplitude and distribution, and (4) feasibility of control. Based on a species score in these four broad categories, the species is assigned an invasiveness ranking of very high, high, moderate, or insignificant.

Using data obtained from this process for New York and reviewing data and information from the New York Metropolitan Flora Program and from other sources (e.g., Connecticut Invasive Plants Council 2004; Snyder and Kaufman 2004; Pennsylvania Department of Conservation and Natural Resources 2009) for nonnative plant species from the Highlands, a list of fifty-eight invasive or potentially invasive species for the Highlands region has been developed (all are listed in appendix 9.2 below). It should be noted that until a formal regional process is established, this list must be taken as preliminary.

An understudied issue is how the increased maintenance and planting of roadsides is contributing to the spread of nonnative species. Roadside habitats (and those of other rights-of-way, such as railroad and power lines) oftentimes are in an early stage of succession (e.g., woody vegetation limited or absent) and as a result oftentimes support populations of plant species that prefer early stages of succession—conditions that were once maintained by natural disturbances such as fire. However, current roadside maintenance practices have changed dramatically from the past and frequently involve the planting of nonnative species, such as fescues (*Festuca* spp.) and crown vetch (*Coronilla varia*), which can dominate the roadsides to the exclusion of many native species. A further threat to the native species is the more advanced roadside mowing equipment that allows for more extensive and complete mowing of the roadsides. In many areas these changes in practices have had dramatic effects, as many roadsides that once supported populations of native species are now well-manicured linear lawns of nonnative species. The effects of roadside maintenance practices in another region, the New Jersey Pinelands, have recently been reviewed by Van Clef (2009).

Conclusions and Recommendations

Assessing the current state of the vegetation of the Highlands can be discouraging, especially for those of us who remember an earlier time when things were much different. An example of the decline of a native species and the increase of a similar invasive species can be seen in the bittersweets (*Celastrus*). Maps generated from the NYMF-AILANTHUS database document the decline of the native American bittersweet (*Celastrus scandens*) and the rapid expansion of the invasive Oriental bittersweet (*Celastrus orbiculatus*) (see plate 24). The spread of development and invasive species can seem unstoppable, with the result of this "double whammy" being a landscape of developments surrounded by seas of invasive plants.

Nonetheless, there are some facts that allow us to see the glass as half full. First, while the number of rare species tracked by local Natural Heritage Programs continues to rise, the number of extirpations of species remains low. Furthermore, while the numbers of nonnative species introduced and acreage covered by invasive species continue to rise, there remain large areas of relatively undisturbed land in the Highlands that are minimally affected by invasive plants. These data suggest that ecologists and environmentalists still have the native biological resources and intact ecosystems with which to work.

To prevent the bleak "developments surrounded by seas of invasive plants" scenario, a comprehensive management plan is needed for the Highlands that works toward preserving the native flora and limiting the spread of the non-native invasive flora. From a regulatory perspective, this means vigorously protecting from development existing populations of rare native plant species. It also means controlling the selling, planting, and possession of invasive plants species to prevent further introductions into the environment.

Regulation must also be accompanied by careful management. Simply protecting rare plants from encroaching development will not ensure their survival, because many populations without management will succumb to succession processes, be they from other native plants or nonnative invasive plants. Efforts to eradicate existing populations of invasive plants are also sorely needed in many areas. Formation of groups such as Invasive Species Strike Teams should be promoted to assist with this. Further management efforts should work toward avoiding disturbance regimes that aid the spread of invasive plants and the decline of nonnative plants, such as disturbances that increase nutrient availability and roadside mowing during the growing season.

Much more basic research is also needed in this effort. Fieldwork is needed to better understand the complete distributions of many of our native plants species, including rare species. Proper identification and assessment of nonnative species as invasive before they spread throughout the landscape is also needed. Currently, species are oftentimes not assessed as invasive until they have already spread throughout the landscape (see the distribution map of *Celastrus orbiculatus* in plate 24). Geographic information system technology is now being used to develop distribution maps that project where an invasive species may spread based on correlating the plant's known occurrences with other factors, such as geology, soil, and land-use history (Ibáñez et al. 2009). This same technology could also be used to identify areas for de novo searching of rare plant species. Furthermore, research is also needed on a number of issues not addressed in this chapter, including the impacts the following are having on Highlands native vegetation: (1) decline of native and spread of nonnative pollinators (Buchmann, Nabhan, and Mirocha 1997; Stokes, Buckley, and Sheppard 2002); (2) spread of other nonnative species, such as earthworms (Gundale 2002; Gundale, Jolly, and DeLuca 2005), and (3) global warming (McKenney et al. 2007).

In summary, the native vegetation of the Highlands region, while not unique, is quite diverse. This pattern simply reflects the diversity of features and community types within the Highlands but lack of features and community types that are unique to the region. The native vegetation is threatened by development and the spread of invasive species. Further efforts are needed in regulation, management, and research to ensure the adequate protection of the native plant resources of the Highlands of Connecticut, New Jersey, New York, and Pennsylvania.

Acknowledgments

The Connecticut (Karen Zyko), New Jersey (Robert Cartica, David Snyder, and Elena Williams), New York (Tara Salerno and Steve Young), and Pennsylvania (Kierstin Carlson) Natural Heritage Programs are thanked for the preparation of lists of rare, threatened, and endangered species used in appendix 9.1. Steve Clemants and Jinshuang Ma are thanked for their help with the preliminary research for this chapter.

References

Abraitys, V. A. 1980. "Check-List of the Flora of Hunterdon County, New Jersey." *Bartonia* 47:23–30.

———. 1981. "Additions to the Flora of Hunterdon County, New Jersey." *Bartonia* 48:11.

Anderson, K. 1989. *A Check List of the Plants of New Jersey.* Mount Holly: Rancocas Nature Center, New Jersey Audubon Society.

Bien, W. F., J. R. Spotila, and T. Gordon. 2009. "Distribution Trends of Rare Plants at the Warren Grove Gunnery Range." *Bartonia* 64:1–18.

Bishop, J. 1885. "A Catalogue of All Phaenogamous Plants at Present Known to Grow without Cultivation in the State of Connecticut." *Report of the Connecticut Board of Agriculture* 18:317–332.

Boulton, J. L. 2005. "Invasive Plants, Deer and Forest Regulation: Observations from Southeastern Vermont." In *Changing Forest—Changing Times.* Proceedings of the New England Society of American Foresters 85th Winter Meeting, ed. L. S. Kenefec and M. J. Twery. United States Department of Agriculture, Forest Service, Northeastern Research Station. General Technical Report NE-325.

Breden, T. F. 1989. "A Preliminary Natural Community Classification for New Jersey." In *New Jersey's Rare and Endangered Plants and Animals,* ed. E. F. Karlin, 157–191. Mahwah, NJ: Institute for Environmental Studies.

Britton, N. 1881. *Preliminary Catalogue of the Flora of New Jersey.* Geological Survey of New Jersey. New Brunswick, NJ: Rutgers College.

———. 1884. "On the Existence of a Peculiar Flora on the Kittatinny Mountains of North-Western New Jersey." *Bulletin of the Torrey Botanical Club* 11:126–128.

———. 1887. "Note on the Flora of the Kittatinny Mountains." *Bulletin of the Torrey Botanical Club* 14:187–189.

———. 1889. *Catalogue of Plants Found in New Jersey.* New Brunswick: Geological Survey of New Jersey, Rutgers College.

Britton, N. L., A. Brown, A. Hollick, J. F. Poggenburg, T. C. Porter, and E. E. Sterns. 1888. *Preliminary Catalogue of Anthophyta and Pteridophyta Reported as Growing Spontaneously within One Hundred Miles of New York City.* New York: Torrey Botanical Club.

Buchmann, S. L., G. B. Nabhan, and P. Mirocha. 1997. *The Forgotten Pollinators.* Washington, DC: Island Press.

Carlson, M. L., I. V. Lapina, M. Shephard, J. S. Conn, R. Densmore, P. Spencer, J. Heys, J. Riley, and J. Nielsen. 2008. *Invasiveness Ranking System for Non-native Plants of Alaska.* Technical Paper R10-TPXX, USDA. Anchorage: Forest Service, Alaska Region.

Clout, M., S. Lowe, and the IUCN/SSC Invasive Species Specialist Group. 1996. *Draft IUCN Guidelines for the Prevention of Biodiversity Loss Due to Biological Invasion.* Gland, Switzerland: International Union for the Conservation of Nature.

Colden, C. 1749, 1751. "Plantae coldenhamiae in provincia noveboracensi americes sponte crescentes." *Acta Societatis Regiae Scientiarum Upsaliensis* 1743:81–136 (1749 ed.); 1744–1750: 47–82 (1751 ed.).

Connecticut Invasive Plants Council. 2004. "Connecticut Invasive Plant List." Connecticut Public Act 03–136.

Cook, C.D.K., and K. Urmi-Konig. 1985. "A Revision of the Genus *Elodea* (Hydrocharitaceae)." *Aquatic Botany* 21:111–156.

Dahler, C. C. 2003. "Performance Comparisons of Co-occurring Native and Alien Invasive Plants: Implications for Conservation and Restoration." *Annual Review of Ecology, Evolution and Systematics* 34:183–211.

Environmental Laboratory. 1987. *Corps of Engineers Wetlands Delineation Manual.* Technical Report Y-87-1. Vicksburg, MI: U.S. Army Engineer Waterways Experiment Station.

Fernald, M. L. 1950. *Gray's Manual of Botany.* New York: American Book Co.

Forman, R.T.T., ed. 1979. *Pine Barrens Ecosystem and Landscape.* New York: Academic Press.

Gleason, H. A. 1935. *Plants of the Vicinity of New York.* 1st ed. New York: Hafner Publishing Co. (rev. ed. 1947 and 1962).

Gleason, H. A, and A. Cronquist. 1991. *Manual of the Vascular Plants of the Northeastern United States and Adjacent Canada.* 2nd ed. Bronx: New York Botanical Garden.

Graves, C. B., E. H. Eames, C. H. Bissell, L. Andrews, E. B. Harger, and C. A. Weatherby. 1910. "Catalogue of the Flowering Plants and Ferns of Connecticut Growing without Cultivation." *State Geological and Natural History Survey Bulletin,* no. 14.

Gundale, M. J. 2002. "The Influence of Exotic Earthworms on the Soil Organic Horizon and the Rare Fern *Botrychium mormo.*" *Conservation Biology* 16:1555–1561.

Gundale, M. J., W. H. Jolly, and T. H. DeLuca. 2005. "The Susceptibility of a Northern Hardwood Forest to Exotic Earthworm Invasion." *Conservation Biology* 19: 1075–1083.

Harper, R. M. 1905. "Coastal Plain Plants in New England." *Rhodora* 7, no. 76: 69–80.

———. 1906. "Further Remarks on the Coastal Plain Plants of New England, Their History and Distribution." *Rhodora* 8, no. 86: 27–30.

Harshberger, J. 1916. *The Vegetation of the New Jersey Pine Barrens.* Philadelphia: Christopher Sower Co.

Hough, M. 1983. *New Jersey Wild Plants.* Harmony, NJ: Harmony Press.

House, H. D. 1924. "Annotated List of the Ferns and Flowering Plants of New York State." *New York State Museum Bulletin* 254:1–759.

Ibáñez, I., J. A. Silander Jr., A. Wilson, N. LaFleur, N. Tanaka, and I. Tsuyama. 2009. "Multi-variate Forecasts of Potential Distribution of Invasive Plant Species." *Ecological Applications* 19, no. 2: 359–375.

Jordan, M. J. 2009. "Identifying the Invaders: Understanding the 'Do Not Sell' List of Non-native Plants." *Long Island Botanical Society Newsletter* 19, no. 3: 17, 19–21.

Jordan, M. J., G. Moore, and T. W. Weldy. 2008. *Invasiveness Ranking System for Non-native Plants of New York.* Cold Spring Harbor, NY: The Nature Conservancy; Brooklyn: Brooklyn Botanic Garden; Albany, NY: The Nature Conservancy.

Leggett, W. 1870–1874. "A Revised Catalogue of Plants Native and Naturalized, within Thirty-three Miles of New York." *Bulletin of the Torrey Botanical Club,* vols. 1–5, various pages.

Linnaeus, C. 1753. *Species plantarum*. Stockholm.

McKenney, D. W., J. H. Pedlar, K. Lawrence, K. Campbell, and M. F. Hutchinson. 2007. "Beyond Traditional Hardiness Zones: Using Climate Envelopes to Map Plant Range Limits." *BioScience* 57, no. 11: 929–937.

Michaux, A. 1803. *Flora boreali-americana*. 2 vols. Paris.

Mitchell, R. S., and G. C. Tucker. 1997. "Revised Checklist of New York State Plants." *New York State Museum Bulletin* 490:1–400.

Moore, G., S. Glenn, and J. Ma. 2009. "Distribution of the Native *Aralia spinosa* and Non-native *A. elata* (Araliaceae) in the Northeastern United States." *Rhodora* 111:145–154.

Moore, G., A. Steward, S. Clemants, S. Glenn, and J. Ma. 2002. "An Overview of the New York Metropolitan Flora Project." *Urban Habitats* 1:17–24.

Morse, L. E., J. M. Randall, N. Benton, R. Hiebert, and S. Lu. 2004. "An Invasive Species Assessment Protocol: Evaluating Non-native Plants for Their Impact on Biodiversity." Ver. 1. Arlington, VA: NatureServe.

NatureServe. 2009. "An Online Encyclopedia of Life." http://www.natureserve.org/explorer/.

Nuttall, T. 1818. *The Genera of North American Plants*. 2 vols. Philadelphia.

Pennsylvania Department of Conservation and Natural Resources. 2009. "Invasive Plants in Pennsylvania." www.dcnr.state.pa.us/forestry/wildplant/invasivelist.aspx.

Persoon, C. H. 1805–1807. *Synopsis plantarum, seu enrichidium botanicum*. 2 vols. Paris.

Porter, T. C. 1903. *Flora of Pennsylvania*. Boston: Ginn & Company.

Pursh, F. 1814. *Flora Americae septentrionalis*. 2 vols. London.

Randall, J. M., L. E. Morse, N. Benton, R. Hiebert, S. Lu, and T. Killeffer. 2008. "The Invasive Species Assessment Protocol: A Tool for Creating Regional and National Lists of Invasive Nonnative Plants That Negatively Impact Biodiversity." *Invasive Plant Science and Management* 1:36–49.

Rhoads, A. F., and T. A. Block. 2007. *The Plants of Pennsylvania*. Philadelphia: University of Pennsylvania Press.

Robichaud, B., and M. F. Buell. 1983. *Vegetation of New Jersey*. New Brunswick, NJ: Rutgers University Press.

Robichaud Collins, B., and K. Anderson. 1994. *Plant Communities of New Jersey*. New Brunswick, NJ: Rutgers University Press.

Saint John, H. 1965. "Monograph of the Genus Elodea, Part 4: The Species of Eastern and Central North America." *Rhodora* 67, no. 769: 1–35.

Saltonstall, K. 2002. "Cryptic Invasion by a Non-native Genotype of the Common Reed, *Phragmites australis*, into North America." *Proceedings of the National Academy of Sciences (U.S.A.)* 99, no. 4: 2445–2449.

———. 2003. "A Rapid Method for Identifying the Origin of North American *Phragmites* Populations Using RFLP Analysis." *Wetlands* 23, no. 4: 1043–1047.

Saltonstall, K., P. M. Peterson, and R. J. Soreng. 2004. "Recognition of *Phragmites australis* subsp. *americanus* (Poaceae: Arundinoideae) in North America: Evidence from Morphological and Genetic Analyses." *Sida* 21, no. 2: 683–692.

Schaefer, R. L. 1949. "The Vascular Flora of Northampton County, Pennsylvania." PhD diss.. University of Pennsylvania, Philadelphia.

Schmid, J. A., and J. T. Kartesz. 1994. *Checklist and Synonymy of Higher Plants in New Jersey and Pennsylvania with Special Reference to Their Rarity and Wetland Indicator Status*. Media, PA: Schmid & Co.

Snyder, D. B. 2000. "One Hundred Lost Plants Found." *Bartonia* 60:1–22.

———. 2009. *Special Plants of New Jersey*. Trenton: New Jersey Department of Environmental Protection, Division of Parks and Forestry, Office of Natural Lands Management, Natural Heritage Program.

Snyder, D., and S. R. Kaufman. 2004. *An Overview of Nonindigenous Plant Species in New Jersey*. Trenton: New Jersey Department of Environmental Protection, Division of Parks and Forestry, Office of Natural Lands Management, Natural Heritage Program.

Stokes, K. E., Y. M. Buckley, and A. W. Sheppard. 2002. "A Modelling Approach to Estimate the Effect of Exotic Pollinators on Exotic Weed Population Dynamics: Bumblebees and Broom in Australia." *Diversity and Distributions* 12, no. 5: 593–600.

Stone, W. 1911. "The Plants of Southern New Jersey." Annual Report for 1910, Part II. Trenton: New Jersey State Museum.

Stromayer, K.A.K., R. J. Warren, A. S. Johnson, P. E. Hale, C. L. Rogers, and C. L. Tucker. 1998. "Chinese Privet and the Feeding Ecology of White-Tailed Deer: The Role of an Exotic Plant." *Journal of Wildlife Management* 62, no. 4: 1321–1329.

Taylor, N. 1915. "Flora of the Vicinity of New York." *Memoirs of the New York Botanical Garden*, vol. 51.

———. 1927. "The Vegetation of Long Island." *Brooklyn Botanical Garden Memoirs* 3:1–151.

Torrey, J. 1819. *A Catalogue of Plants Growing Spontaneously within Thirty Miles of the City of New York*. Albany: Lyceum of Natural History of New York.

Townsend, J. F., and V. Caraman-Castro. 2006. "A New Species of Boltonia (Asteraceae) from the Ridge and Valley Physiographic Province, U.S.A." *Sida* 22:873–886.

Van Clef, M. 2009. *Best Management Practices for Pine Barrens Roadside Plant Communities*. Report prepared for the Pinelands Preservation Allaince. Great Meadows, NJ: Ecological Solutions, LLC.

Weldy, T., and D. Werier. 2009. *New York Flora Atlas*. [S. M. Landry and K. N. Campbell (original application development), Florida Center for Community Design and Research. University of South Florida]. Albany: New York Flora Association. http://newyork.plantatlas.usf.edu/.

Werier, D. 2006. "*Carex reznicekii*, a New Widespread Species of *Carex* Section *Acrocystis* (Cyperaceae) from Eastern North America." *Sida* 22:1049–1070.

Willis, O. 1874. *Catalogue of Plants Growing without Cultivation in the State of New Jersey*. 1st ed. New York: J. W. Schermerhorn.

Young, S. M., ed. 2008. *New York Rare Plant Status Lists, June 2008*. Albany: New York Natural Heritage Program. http://www.dec.ny.gov/docs/wildlife_pdf/nynhprpsl.pdf.

Zampella, R. A., and K. J. Laidig. 1997. "Effect of Watershed Disturbance on Pinelands Stream Vegetation." *Journal of the Torrey Botanical Society* 124, no. 1: 52–66.

Appendix 9.1 List of 21 Globally Rare, Threatened, and Endangered Plant Species Reported from Connecticut, New Jersey, New York, and Pennsylvania

Scientific name	Common name	State protection status[a]
Agalinis auriculata	earleaf false foxglove	PA-E; G3
Bidens bidentoides	estuarine beggars ticks	NY-SC; G3G4
Bidens hyperborea var. *hyperborea*	estuary beggars ticks	NY-E; G4T2T4
Boltonia montana	mountain doll's daisy	NJ-SC; G1G2
Cardamine longii	Long's bittercress	NJ-E, NY-T; G3
Carex polymorpha	variable sedge	NJ-E, PA-E[b]; G3
Eleocharis aestuum	tidal spikerush	NY-SC[c]; G3
Elodea schweinitzii	Schweinitz's waterweed	PA-SC[b]; GH
Eriocaulon parkeri	Parker's pipewort	NY-SC[b]; G3
Helonias bullata	swamp pink	NJ-E; US-T; G3
Isotria medeoloides	small whorled pogonia	CT-E, NJ-E, PA-E, US-T; G2
Malaxis bayardii	Bayard's adder's-mouth orchid	NJ-E, NY-E; G1G2
Mitella prostrata	creeping bishop's cap	NJ-SC; G1G3
Panax quinquefolius	American ginseng	CT-SC, NJ-SC; G3G4
Polemonium vanbruntiae	Van Brunt's polemonium	NJ-SC[b], PA-E; G3G4
Pseudognaphalium helleri ssp. *micradenium*	Heller's cudweed	NY-E; G4G5T3?
Pycnanthemum clinopodioides	basil mountain-mint	CT-E, NJ-E, NY-E, PA-SC[b]; G2
Pycnanthemum torrei	Torrey's mountain-mint	NJ-E, NY-E, PA-E; G2
Triphora trianthophora	three-birds orchid	NJ-E, NY-E[c], PA-E; G3G4
Trollius laxus ssp. *laxus*	American globe flower	CT-T, NJ-E; NY-SC, PA-E; G4T3

State or Federal (U.S.) Designations

E   The species is listed as endangered in that state or the United States.
T   The species is listed as threatened in that state.
SC   "Special concern." The species is not listed as endangered or threatened but is tracked by the state Heritage Program.

Global Element Ranks (as Ranked by the Nature Conservancy)

G1   Critically imperiled globally because of extreme rarity.
G2   Imperiled globally because of rarity.
G3   Either very rare and local throughout its range or found locally.
G4   Apparently secure globally, although it may be quite rare in parts of its range, especially at the periphery.
G5   Demonstrably secure globally, although it may be quite rare in parts of its range, especially at the periphery.
GH   Of historical occurrence throughout its range.
GU   Possibly in peril range-wide but status uncertain; more information needed.
GNR Species has not yet been ranked.
T   The infraspecific taxon is being ranked differently than the full species; numerical ranking scheme similar to that for G above.

Note: To express uncertainty, the most likely rank is assigned and a question mark added (e.g., G2?). A range is indicated by combining two ranks (e.g., G1G2).

(*continued*)

[a] List of states in which the species is tracked by the Heritage Program and has been recorded from the Highlands region in that state. The absence of a state from the third column can mean several things, including that the species is (1) not known from that state; (2) known from that state but is not tracked as rare, threatened, or endangered by the state Heritage program; (3) known from that state, is tracked as rare, threatened, or endangered, but is not known from the Highlands region of that state, or (4) not recognized as taxonomically distinct by the state Heritage Program. Note that this list may change in the future with new species added and other species removed as their status changes.

[b] The species is believed to be extirpated from the state.

[c] The record for this species from the Highlands region has yet to be confirmed.

Appendix 9.2 List of 58 Invasive or Potentially Invasive Species Known from the Highlands Region

Acer platanoides	*Frangula alnus (Alnus frangula)*
Acer pseudoplatanus	*Heracleum mantegazzianum*
Alianthus altissima	*Humulus japonicus*
Alliaria petiolata	*Hydrilla verticillata*
Ampelopsis brevipedunculata	*Hydrocharis morus-ranae*
Anthriscus sylvestris	*Iris pseudacorus*
Aralia elata	*Lespedeza cuneata*
Artemesia vulgaris	*Ligustrum obtusifolium*
Arthraxon hispidus	*Lonicera japonica*
Berberis thunbergii	*Lonicera maackii*
Cabomba caroliniana	*Lonicera morowii/tatarica*
Cardamine impatiens	*Lysimachia nummularia*
Carduus nutans	*Lysimachia vulgaris*
Celastrus orbiculatus	*Lythrum salicaria*
Centaurea stoebe ssp. *micranthos* s.l.	*Microstegium vimineum*
(*C. biebersteinii, C. diffusa, C. maculosa*	*Myriophyllum aquaticum*
misapplied, *C. xpsammogena*)	*Myriophyllum spicatum*
Cirsium arvense (C. setosum, C. incanum,	*Persicaria longiseta*
Carduus arvensis, Serratula arvensis)	*Persicaria perfoliata*
Clematis terniflora	*Phalaris arundinacea (nonnative material)*
Cynanchum louiseae (C. nigrum, Vincetoxicum	*Phellodendron amurense/japonicum*
nigrum)	*Phragmites australis* ssp. *australis*
Cynanchum rossicum (C. medium, Vincetoxicum	*Potamogeton crispus*
medium, V. rossicum)	*Pueraria montana*
Dioscorea polystachya (D. batatas)	*Ranunculus ficaria*
Egeria densa	*Rhamnus cathartica*
Elaeagnus umbellata	*Rhodotypos scandens*
Euonymus alatus	*Rosa multiflora*
Euonymus fortune	*Rubus phoenicolasius*
Euphorbia cyparissias	*Salix atrocinerea/cinerea*
Euphorbia esula	*Trapa natans*
Fallopia japonica/sachalinensis/ ✕ bohemica	

10

Wildlife of the Highlands

Elizabeth A. Johnson

Introduction

The four-state Highlands region is characterized by a diverse array of natural and man-made communities, from rocky outcrops to boggy seeps, from large lakes to small seasonal pools, and from extensive forests and wetlands to agricultural fields. These various communities and their plant life in turn support abundant and diverse animal life—both vertebrate and invertebrate, common and rare. The wildlife of the Highlands region is protected and managed by the individual state agencies charged with their care. Each state maintains a list of endangered and threatened species (species in danger of extirpation or extinction or those close to becoming endangered), as well as species thought to be in decline (species of conservation concern; see appendix 10.1). This chapter will introduce some of the rare species as well as common wildlife of the Highlands, with an emphasis on terrestrial and aquatic habitats and the species they support.

Animals of Deciduous and Coniferous Forests of the Highlands

The Highlands region is perhaps best known today for its extensive oak-hickory and mixed deciduous forests. The health and integrity of these large, intact forest communities is vital to the survival of many animal species, but none more so than the birds that nest in the interiors of forests. These species include songbirds such as the scarlet tanager (*Piranga olivacea*), wood thrush (*Hylocichla mustelina*), red-eyed vireo (*Vireo olivaceus*), and eastern wood pee-wee (*Contopus virens*). Also found in these forests are raptors, such as the sharp-shinned hawk (*Accipiter striatus*), Cooper's hawk (*Accipiter cooperii*), northern goshawk (*Accipiter gentilis*), red-shouldered hawk (*Buteo lineatus*), and broad-winged hawk (*Buteo platypterus*). A dense forest understory offers good habitat for such ground nesters as the ovenbird (*Seiurus aurocapillus*), which forages in decaying leaf litter for beetle grubs and other invertebrates. The extensive canopy provides nesting sites for the cerulean warbler (*Dendroica cerulea*), which prefers to glean tiny caterpillars from the upper branches. Raptors prey on the abundant small mammals in the forest and seek out the larger trees capable of supporting their heavy nests.

The unbroken canopies of these expansive forests are an important deterrent to various predators and nest parasites that prefer more open-edge habitats. Nest and egg predators such as the raccoon (*Procyon lotor*), striped skunk (*Mephitis mephitis*), and house cat (*Felis catus*) are rarely found in the largest patches of contiguous forests; instead they flourish along the edges of smaller woodlands. The great horned owl (*Bubo virginianus*), a raptor and songbird predator that also prefers edge habitat, has limited the ability of red-shouldered hawks to nest successfully in fragmented, more open forests in New Jersey (Liguori 2003b). Likewise, the cowbird (*Molothrus ater*), an important nest parasite, frequents forests and field edges but avoids deeper forests. Cowbirds opportunistically deposit their eggs in the nests of other birds and cause the failure of 20 to 50 percent of the nests of their unwitting hosts' own young (Askins 2000).

Half of the birds that nest in the Highlands are neotropical migrants—birds that migrate south each fall to spend the winter months in Central and South America, returning the following spring to breed (USDA Forest Service 2002). For this reason, the quality of both their summer nesting and wintering habitats are important to their survival. Located along the Atlantic flyway, the larger blocks of forest are also critically important to birds in transit on their spring migration to breeding areas farther north. The Hudson River valley is especially noted as a movement corridor during both the spring and fall migrations. Some of the best-known viewing areas during fall migration are at Hook Mountain and along the Hudson River and cliff slopes near upper Nyack, New York (Burger and Liner 2005), and at Scotts Mountain, New Jersey.

The extensive Highlands forests are also home to a variety of wide-ranging mammals such as the black bear (*Ursus americanus*), bobcat (*Lynx rufus*) (see plate 25), river otter (*Lutra canadensis*), and gray fox (*Urocyon cinereoargenteus*). The largest of these—black bears and bobcats—have substantial home ranges and rely on the vast expanses of contiguous forests to provide adequate food and shelter. Corridors between individual patches of forest are also vital for safe passage because these animals often move great distances during the year. For example, male black bears have home ranges that extend eight to twenty-five square miles, and bobcats can move up to twelve miles in a single night (Whitaker and Hamilton 1998). Bobcats have become more numerous thanks to efforts from state wildlife agencies in Pennsylvania and New Jersey, which afforded protection from trapping for almost thirty years.[1] In addition to restoration efforts, New Jersey provided even stronger protection measures by adding bobcats to their state endangered species list in 1991 (Schantz and Valent 2003a). An animal that most people never see in the wild, bobcats favor deep woods interspersed with open glades, swamps, dense thickets, or rocky outcrops and ledges that can be used for denning and resting areas. Owing in part to the protection of many large forest tracts in the Highlands, other carnivores such as the fisher (*Martes pennanti*) have moved back into the northernmost sections. In fact, fishers are expanding statewide in Pennsylvania following reintroduction efforts in the north central part of the state, and may also be moving northward from the mountains of West Virginia and western Maryland (C. Eichelberger, pers. comm., July 2009).

Smaller mammals, such as the eastern chipmunk (*Tamias striatus*), southern flying squirrel (*Glaucomys volans*), and eastern gray squirrel (*Sciurus carolinensis*), flourish on the nuts provided by a variety of oak, beech, and hickory trees. Perhaps the least known of the woodland mammals are the mice, shrews, and voles, which are nocturnal and have been little surveyed. One of the more widespread of these is the short-tailed shrew (*Blarina brevicauda*) (Cinquina 1965), a feisty little animal with poor eyesight that uses echolocation to navigate and to find prey. When it bites a worm or even a smaller mammal, powerful toxins in its salivary glands immobilize the prey for future consumption (Whitaker and Hamilton 1998).

Nine species of bats can be found in the Highlands and are best observed at dusk as they venture out on their evening forays to feed. Although many of the region's bats migrate south or hibernate inside caves or outcrops during the winter, they rely heavily on forests during the spring and summer months. Trees are frequently used as roosting sites, resting places, and even as maternity colonies, and they also shelter the insects on which the bats feed. Bats may live up to twenty-five years or more, often using the same roost trees, hibernation sites, and feeding areas throughout their lives. The rarest of the bats in the Highlands region is the Indiana bat (*Myotis sodalis*), a federally listed endangered species. Although its range extends from New England to Kentucky, this bat is vulnerable to disturbance because it can hibernate only in locations that meet its exacting temperature and humidity requirements. Some of the largest Indiana bat hibernation locations are in abandoned iron mines in the Highlands. These bats, along with many other bat species, are important for insect control because they feed on a variety of insects such as moths, mosquitoes and other flies, and beetles (Hartmaier and Beans 2003, USFWS 2007). In recent years, populations of cave-hibernating bats throughout the Northeast, including the Highlands region, have been decimated by white-nose syndrome, the cause of which has not been positively identified as of the publication date.

Surprisingly, the most common vertebrate animal of Highlands' forests

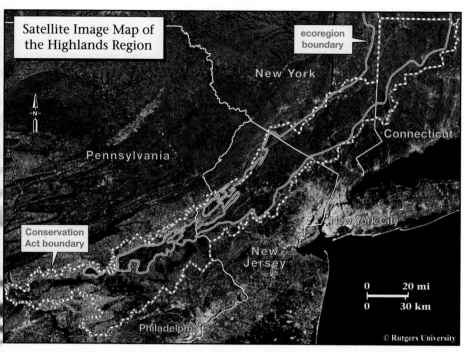

Plate 1 Satellite image map of the Highlands region. © Rutgers University.

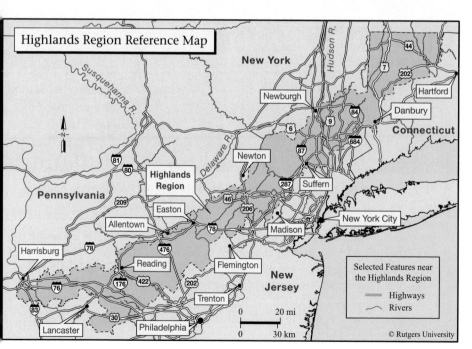

Plate 2 Highlands region reference map. © Rutgers University.

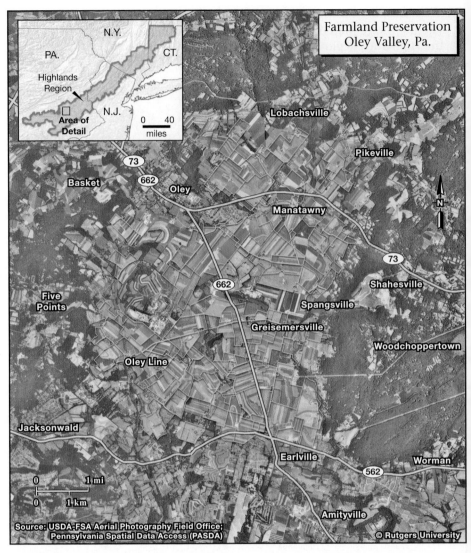

Plate 3 Nestled within the fork of the Reading Prong of the Pennsylvania Highlands, the Oley Valley is an area of prime agricultural soils that is intensively farmed. The yellow highlighted areas represent lands protected by a farmland preservation easement. Note that the crystalline bedrock uplands have remained in forestland, which shows up as dark green in this natural-color aerial photograph. *Air photo source*: USDA-FSA Aerial Photography Field Office. *Preserved farms source*: Pennsylvania Spatial Data Access. *Place names source*: U.S. Geological Survey.

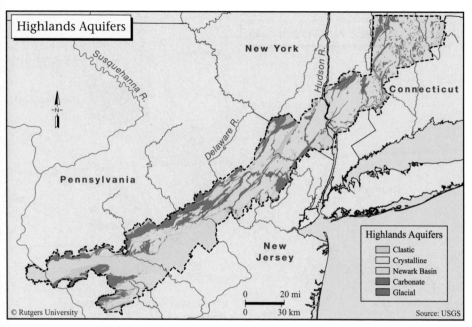

Plate 4 Map of Highlands aquifers. © Rutgers University.

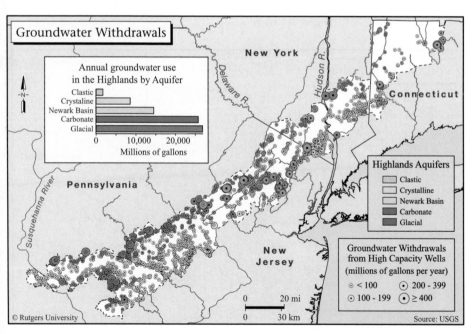

Plate 5 Map of groundwater withdrawals from major water-supply wells, circa 2000. *Source*: USGS. © Rutgers University.

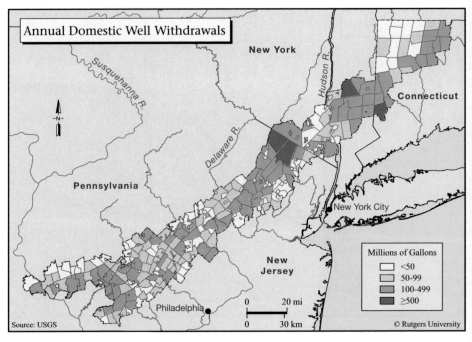

Plate 6 Map of estimated annual domestic well withdrawals by municipality, circa 2000. *Source*: USGS. © Rutgers University.

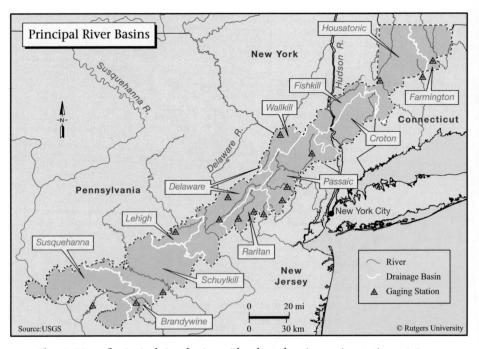

Plate 7 Map of principal river basins with selected major gaging stations. © Rutgers University.

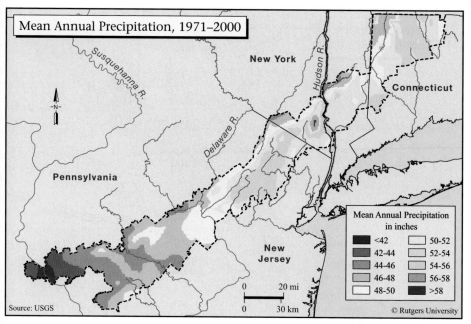

Plate 8 Map of mean annual precipitation, 1971–2000. *Source*: USGS. © Rutgers University.

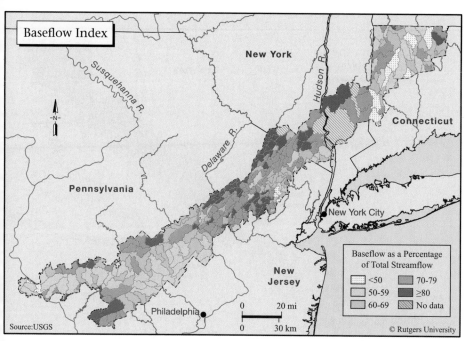

Plate 9 Map showing the baseflow index in the Highlands. *Source*: USGS. © Rutgers University.

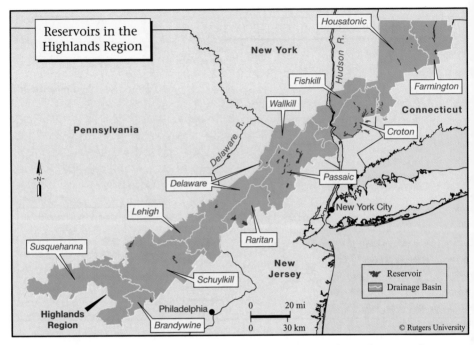

Plate 10 Major drinking water supply reservoirs and principal river basins in the Highlands region. © Rutgers University.

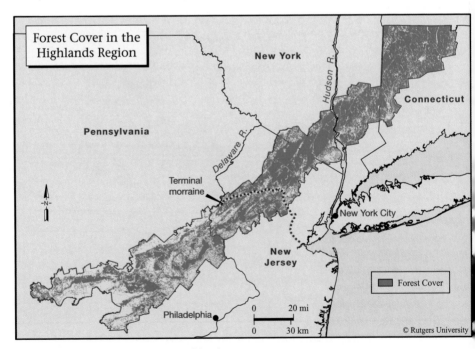

Plate 11 Forest cover in the Highlands region. © Rutgers University.

Plate 12 Oak-dominated ridgetop and slope forests in the New York Highlands. Photo by William Schuster.

Plate 13 Connecticut Highlands forest near Granby. Note northern hardwoods, eastern hemlock, and dense ericaceous understory. Photo by William Schuster.

Plate 14 Pennsylvania Highlands forest near Furnace Hills. Note tulip poplar and black cherry along with red oak and red maple. Photo by William Schuster.

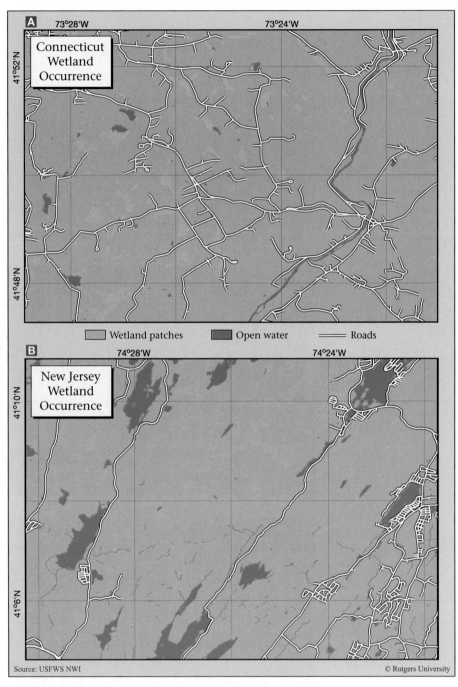

A

73°28'W   73°24'W

41°52'N

Connecticut
Wetland
Occurrence

41°48'N

☐ Wetland patches   ■ Open water   —— Roads

B

74°28'W   74°24'W

41°10'N

New Jersey
Wetland
Occurrence

41°6'N

Source: USFWS NWI   © Rutgers University

Plate 15 Typical examples of wetland occurrences in Connecticut and New Jersey. *Source*: USFWS NWI. © Rutgers University.

Plate 16 Shallow emergent marsh (Wawayanda State Park, N.J.). Photo by Joan Ehrenfeld.

Plate 17 Calcareous fen community (sloping fen in Sharon, Conn.). Photo by William Moorehead.

Plate 18 Dwarf shrub–leatherleaf bog with beaver lodge (Edison Bogs, N.J.). Photo by Joan Ehrenfeld.

Plate 19 Red maple–highbush blueberry community (Pyramid Mountain, N.J.). Photo by Joan Ehrenfeld.

Plate 20 Lady's slipper (*Cypripedium reginae*). Photo by Gerry Moore.

Plate 21 Eurasian purple loosestrife (*Lythrum salicaria*). Photo by Gerry Moore.

Plate 22 Swamp pink (*Helonias bullata*). Photo by Gerry Moore.

Plate 23 Garlic mustard (*Alliaria petiolata*). Photo by Gerry Moore.

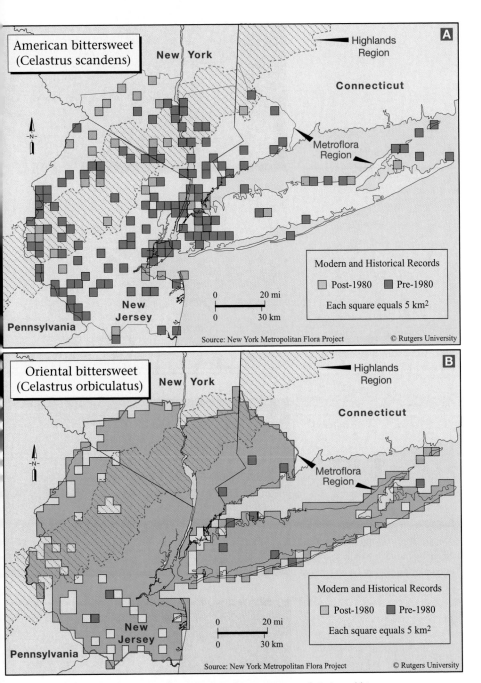

Plate 24 Distribution maps for American bittersweet and Oriental bittersweet occurring in the NYMF range. *Source*: New York Metropolitan Flora Project. © Rutgers University.

Plate 25 Bobcat (*Lynx rufus*).
Photo by Mick Valent.

Plate 26 Golden-winged warbler (*Vermivora chrysoptera*).
Photo by Cal Vornberger.

Plate 27 Needham's skimmer dragonfly (*Libellula needhami*).
Photo by Lloyd Spitalnik, LLoyd spitalnikphotos.com.

Plate 28 Courting pair of timber rattlesnakes (*Crotalus horridus*). Photo by Melissa Craddock.

Plate 29 Hopewell Furnace and Cast House, part of the historic reconstructed buildings at the Hopewell Furnace National Historic Park. The furnace was built into the side of the hill with the charcoal and ore house (on upper slope) connected to the stone furnace by a covered ramp. The white-sided wood frame building surrounding the furnace chimney is the Cast House. Photo credit: National Park Service, Hopewell Furnace National Historic Site, Pa.

Plate 30 Tuyere entrance with pipe to tub bellows. Photo credit: National Park Service, Hopewell Furnace National Historic Site, Pa.

Plate 31 Front of furnace inside Cast House. Note that the metal "furnace cupola," in front of the furnace hearth on the casting bed, is not original and is used by the National Park service for demonstrations. Photo: National Park Service, Hopewell Furnace National Historic Site, Pa.

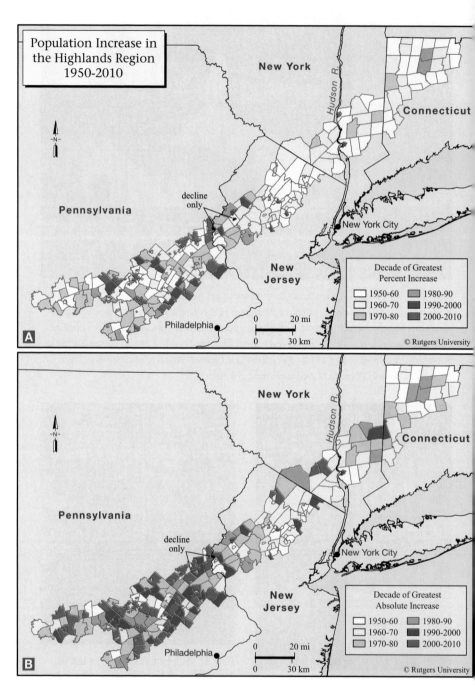

Plate 32 Map of population change at a municipal scale, 1950–2010, showing the decade of greatest percent change (*top*) and the decade of greatest absolute increase (*bottom*). © Rutgers University.

Plate 33 Early Mt. Gretna postcard, "An Early Morning Row, Lake Conewago, Mt. Gretna, Pa." Mt. Gretna Historical Society.

Plate 34 Mt. Gretna Hall of Philosophy. Mt. Gretna Historical Society.

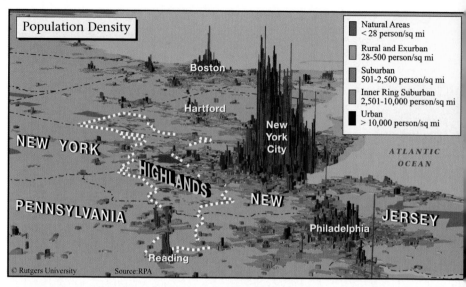

Plate 35 Population density of the mid-Atlantic and southern New England urban areas in proximity to the Highlands region. *Source*: RPA. © Rutgers University.

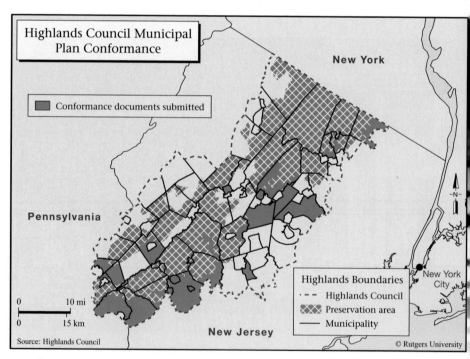

Plate 36 Map of New Jersey municipalities' conformance to the Regional Master Plan of the Highlands Water Protection and Planning Council. Conformance is mandatory in the preservation area, voluntary but encouraged through incentives in the planning area.

may not be a bird or mammal but a slender forest floor salamander—the red-backed salamander (*Plethodon cinereus*) (Burger 1935; Burton and Likens 1975). These inconspicuous but actively territorial animals spend much of their time under forest logs or rocks, emerging on rainy nights to search for worms, beetles, and other invertebrates of the forest floor. Many a Highland hiker has also encountered the red eft (*Notopthalmus viridescens*), a bright orange salamander often seen crawling about during and after a rain. The eft is actually the juvenile, land-dwelling stage of the red-spotted newt. As adults, newts live in ponds or slow-moving water. In the spring, females attach eggs singly to pond vegetation; after hatching and a brief larval period, the animal metamorphoses into the red eft and spends two to four or more years living on land. Highly toxic to other animals, their bright orange skin may serve as a warning to birds and other predators, protecting the small juvenile salamanders from being eaten during this terrestrial phase.

Invertebrate life abounds in the forests of the Highlands. Familiar to many are the vocal insects—the cicadas of early summer and the katydids and snowy tree crickets (*Oecanthus fultoni*) that herald the coming of fall with their late-summer choruses. There are several species of cicadas in the Highlands. Annual cicadas (five *Tibicen* species, which are brown with green markings) first emerge in late June and July, while the periodical cicadas (*Magicicada septendecim*, which are brown with red eyes) emerge at the end of May after spending thirteen or seventeen years underground, feeding on the tree sap from tree rootlets. The region's last big emergence was in 2004, and new emergences are expected in various parts of the Highlands in 2013 and 2021 (Elliot and Herschberger 2007). Many butterflies frequent forest paths and other forest openings, including spring azure (*Celastron ladon*), eastern comma (*Polygonia comma*), question mark (*Polygonia interrogationis*), mourning cloak (*Nymphalis antiopa*), northern pearly eye (*Enodia anthedon*), and several hairstreaks and duskywings. At night, the magnificent luna (*Actias luna*) and polyphemus moths (*Antheraea polyphemus*) can sometimes be found flying to porch lights.

Coniferous forests of hemlock, pine, or spruce provide moist, shady habitat for a different suite of animals. More than 120 vertebrate species, including nearly 90 species of birds, frequent eastern hemlock forests (DeGraaf et al. 1992; Ward et al. 2004). Some species, such as the Blackburnian warbler (*Dendroica fusca*), black-throated green warbler (*Dendroica virens*), dark-eyed junco (*Junco hyemalis*), and Acadian flycatcher (*Empidonax virescens*), actually prefer coniferous trees for nesting (Martin, Zim, and Nelson 1951; Tingley et al. 2002). Hemlock seeds are relished by the American goldfinch (*Carduelis tristis*), ruffed grouse (*Bonasa umbellus*), pine siskin (*Carduelis pinus*), crossbills (*Loxia* spp.), black-capped chickadee, and mammals such as the American red squirrel (*Tamiasciurus hudsonicus*) (Martin, Zim, and Nelson 1951). Hemlocks also attract white-tailed deer (*Odocoileus virginianus*) and porcupine (*Erethizon dorsatum*), which forage on hemlock foliage and bark. The deer and porcupine also find abundant cover in the rhododendron and laurel thickets that often grow in the tree's shade (Ward et al. 2004). The northern flying squirrel (*Glaucomys sabrinus*) also prefers old-growth coniferous forests, feeding on cones as well as on fungi and lichens (Whitaker and Hamilton 1998). In the Highlands this squirrel is found only in the northernmost sections in New York and western Connecticut.

Animals of Highlands Grasslands

Grassland habitats have always been part of the Highlands landscape, although they were not extensive when early explorers first reached the region in the 1600s. At that time, seasonal burning by Native Americans kept some areas open, as did beaver activity and occasional hurricanes (Askins 2000). Grassland habitat increased substantially during the late 1700s and 1800s as forests were burned and cleared for agriculture, settlement, and to fuel homes and the iron industry, although today they are on the decline as Highlands forests have regrown and farmlands have been converted to development. With the availability of abundant fields, grazing lands, and meadows during the height of land clearing, numbers of many grassland-nesting bird species also increased. These species included grasshopper sparrow (*Ammodramus savannarum*), bobolink (*Dolichonyx oryzivorus*), meadowlark (*Sturnella magna*), vesper sparrow (*Pooecetes gramineus*), savannah sparrow (*Passerculus sandwichensis*), and upland sandpiper (*Bartramia longicauda*). Each species has specific habitat requirements, including size of open field and height and species of grass. The grasshopper sparrow, for example, prefers to nest in large fields of one hundred or more contiguous acres that have short to medium-high bunch grasses interspersed with patches of bare ground (Liguori 2003a). These sparrows construct well-camouflaged, dome-shaped nests in thick vegetation on the ground. Occasionally in winter, northern songbirds such as the snow bunting (*Plectrophenax nivalis*), Lapland longspur (*Calcarius lapponicus*), and water pipit (*Anthus spinoletta*) will descend on Highlands grasslands. These large, sudden appearances occur when food supplies in the birds' home territory are in short supply and they move south in search of new resources for the winter.

The region's grasslands also provide important habitat for some raptors that prefer open country. American kestrels (*Falco sparverius*), or sparrow hawks, are small falcons that rely on extensive grasslands to support the small mammals and insects on which they feed. These raptors can often be seen hovering low over fields in search of their prey. While the American kestrel breeds in parts of the Highlands region, other raptors use Highlands grasslands more as overwintering habitat. The northern harrier (*Circus cyaneus*), the rough-legged hawk (*Buteo lagopus*), and, occasionally, the short-eared owl

(*Asio flammeus*) visit to take advantage of the abundant rodent populations living in open fields.

Recent surveys conducted by federal and state wildlife agencies and local Audubon societies have shown a steady decline in the number of breeding grassland bird species throughout their entire range, including the Highlands. These population reductions are most likely due to the decline of traditional agriculture along with the intensification of current agricultural practices, conversion of agricultural lands to development, and regrowth of substantial amounts the region's forests over the last one hundred years. Today the Highlands support only small populations of grassland birds, primarily in the areas of Stewart Airport, Wallkill valley farmlands, Shawangunk grasslands, Croton Point in New York, Pohatcong grasslands in New Jersey, Litchfield agriculture lands (e.g., Topsmead State Forest) in Connecticut (Burger and Liner 2005), and Middle Creek Wildlife Management Area in Pennsylvania. Farmland preservation and the implementation of compatible farming and other habitat management practices coupled with habitat restoration are important to the continued survival of these species in the Highlands.

Highlands grassland habitats also support populations of many invertebrate species. On a summer day in an old field, one might see or hear several species of grasshoppers, a few dozen bee species pollinating blooming wildflowers, crickets, orb weaver spiders, praying mantises, numerous moths, butterflies such as the monarch (*Danaus plexippus*), common wood nymph (*Cercyonis pegala*), tiger swallowtail (*Papilio glaucus*), orange sulphur (*Colias eurytheme*), pearl crescent (*Phyciodes tharos*), great spangled fritillary (*Speyeria cybele*), silver-spotted skipper (*Epargyreus clarus*), and many species of folded-winged grass skipper. One of the rarest is the arogos skipper (*Atrytone arogos arogos*), listed as endangered in New Jersey; in fact, the New Jersey Highlands populations are the only ones remaining in the northeastern United States. This small, light orange butterfly is found in abandoned agricultural fields, power line rights-of-way, and dry fields dominated by little bluestem grass (*Schizachyrium scoparius*), its larval food plant (Golden and Tesauro 2003). The regal fritillary (*Speyeria idalia*), another grassland-dependent butterfly, is declining across much of its range and has vanished from the Highlands—mainly because of loss of habitat (Vaughan and Shepherd 2005). Other rare or declining insects of the region include bumblebees, with three species—the yellow-banded bumblebee (*Bombus terricola*), the rusty-patched bumblebee (*Bombus affinis*), and their associated social parasite, Ashton's bumblebee (*Bombus ashtoni*)—recently proposed for listing as species of special concern in Connecticut (State of Connecticut 2009). Once abundant throughout the northeastern United States, these bumblebee species have not been observed or collected since the 1990s, their disappearance most likely due to introduced disease from European bumblebees brought to the area by commercial greenhouse growers (Thorp and Shepherd 2005).

Animals of Highlands Old Fields, Shrublands, and Other Early Successional Habitats

Open, nonforested habitats of the Northeast have declined by 98 percent over the past sixty years with almost one-quarter of this loss occurring in shrubland communities (Tefft 1996), and similar trends have occurred in the Highlands region. Much of this decline is due to forest regrowth associated with the decline in agriculture, as well as to the conversion of abandoned farmland to residential or other development. Shrublands typically consist of overgrown weedy fields where scattered shrubs or woody plants less than ten feet tall have grown among open patches of grasses and flowering plants. Common species include sumac (*Rhus* spp.), red cedar (*Juniperus virginiana*), shrubby dogwoods (*Cornus* spp.), and thickets of blackberry (*Rubus* sp.). Shrublands have always been part of the landscape, growing up in old beaver meadows or in forest clearings created by windstorms (tornadoes, occasional hurricanes), fire, or even by serious insect infestations that kill overstory trees. Today some of the best places to find these early successional habitats are along power line rights-of-way, or in abandoned farmlands and regenerating clear-cuts. While rarely considered of interest by most people, these shrubby fields are essential to the survival of many animal species (Fuller and DeStefano 2003).

Bird species that benefit from or even require shrubland habitats include the golden-winged warbler (*Vermivora chrysoptera*), yellow-breasted chat (*Icteria virens*), white-eyed vireo (*Vireo griseus*), brown thrasher (*Toxostoma rufum*), and field sparrow (*Spizella pisilla*). Of the many bird species that inhabit shrubland communities, twenty-two are undergoing serious population declines (Askins 2000; Tefft 1996). The rarest of the Highlands species is the golden-winged warbler, a small, grayish white bird with a black mask, yellow cap, yellow wings, and a distinctive "bee-buzz-buzz" song (see plate 26). Golden-winged warblers build their nests on the ground, concealed in vegetation. Where their ranges overlap, they can be outcompeted by the more common blue-winged warbler (*Vermivora pinus*), which also nests in old fields. In addition, the two species often interbreed, and the resulting hybridization is contributing to the decline of the golden-winged warbler as a distinct species. Yet in the New York Highlands, where some of the most thorough studies of the golden-winged warbler have been conducted, both bird species have occurred together for more than one hundred years. This coexistence is possibly due to habitat segregation, where some golden-winged warblers have taken to nesting in red maple swamp forests (Burger and Liner 2005; Confer, Barnes, and Alvey 2010).

Mammals such as the common woodchuck (*Marmota monax*) and eastern cottontail rabbit (*Sylvilagus floridanus*) also favor scrubby fields, where they make their burrows or nests and find succulent grasses on which to feed. In addition to sharing the same habitat, cottontails frequently overwinter in old woodchuck burrows (Whitaker and Hamilton 1998). The rare New England cottontail (*Sylvilagus transitionalis*) can be found east of the Hudson River in a few locations in the New York and Connecticut Highlands as well as northward into Maine. This rabbit population has declined significantly, most likely owing to the loss of thickets as the region's forests have regrown and to competition for habitat with the eastern cottontail, which was periodically introduced by hunting clubs into New England states between 1900 until the 1960s (Whitaker and Hamilton 1998; USFWS 2006).

Many reptile species frequent old fields and shrubby areas, relying on the sunny openings at different times of the year for basking, foraging, and egg laying. The eastern box turtle (*Terrapene carolina*) and wood turtle (*Glyptemys insculpta*) visit old fields in search of earthworms and berries (Mitchell, Breisch, and Buhlman 2006). Aquatic turtles, such as the painted turtle (*Chrysemys picta*) and snapping turtle (*Chelydra serpentina*), deposit their eggs in nests dug in bare soil adjacent to their wetland habitats. Black racers (*Coluber constrictor constrictor*) and milk snakes (*Lampropeltis triangulum*) feast on the abundant small rodents that also live in old fields and shrublands.

Some of the rarest shrub communities in the Highlands are found on the ridgetops of its mountains: Canaan, Bear, and Mohawk mountains in Connecticut; Bearfort in New Jersey; and Schunemunk (or Schunnemunk) in New York. The plants and animals of these ridgetops are adapted to dry, nutrient-poor soils, and wind and ice damage from winter storms may help to maintain the shrub community by limiting tree growth (Motzkin, Orwig, and Foster 2002). Characterized by low-growing heaths, thickets of scrub oaks, and pitch pine trees, these plant communities support populations of rare butterflies and moths, such as the Gerhard's underwing moth (*Catocala herodias gerardi*), found in Connecticut, and other insects, such as spider wasps, ant lions, robber flies, ants, ground beetles, and spiders. In fact, some of these ridgetop shrub communities harbor many of the same plants and insects found in the sand-plain pitch pine–scrub oak barrens of the river valleys and coastal areas (Wagner, Nelson, and Schweitzer 2003).

Highlands Aquatic and Wetland Habitats

As briefly touched on in chapters 4 and 8, the aquatic systems of the Highlands—rivers, creeks, lakes and ponds, and freshwater wetlands—serve as vital habitat and support a varied assemblage of animal life. Streams are characterized by their flowing water. Small, headwater streams usually have fast riffles often interspersed with deeper pools, while larger downstream sections (reaches) are wider and slower, with more uniform flow. Water temperature, chemistry, the amount of oxygen dissolved in the water, and the substrate vary among streams and even along the length of individual streams. These factors determine whether (and which) fish and other aquatic animals can live in a particular aquatic habitat. In faster-moving, oxygen-rich waters, native brook trout (*Salvelinus fontinalis*) and other species of non-native trout are found, along with other cool-water-loving fish such as slimy sculpin (*Cottus cognatus*) and several dace species. Small invertebrates such as flat, water penny beetle larvae (*Psephenus* spp.) cling to the rocks, while in slower-moving, more tranquil sections whirligig beetles (*Dineutes discolor*) congregate and water striders (*Gerris remigis*) glide about the water's surface. Stone fly and mayfly nymphs graze on algae and other plants and insects along the stream bottom while some caddis fly larvae filter plankton from the water as it drifts by.

The largest rivers of the Highlands also harbor unique fish species. The Delaware, Hudson, and Susquehanna are home to anadromous fish, fish that spawn in freshwater but spend most of their lives in salt water. A good example is the American shad (*Alosa sapidissima*). Young shad hatch from eggs deposited in the upper reaches of the rivers, swim downstream in the fall, and then spend a few years in the ocean. When mature, the shad often return to the same river in which they were born and swim upstream to spawn as river water temperatures warm up in the spring. Atlantic sturgeon (*Acipenser oxyrinchus*) and striped bass (*Morone saxatilis*), which live in the deeper, wider river mouths, have a similar life cycle. In contrast, American eels (*Anguilla rostrata*), long, slender, snakelike fish, are catadromous, meaning that they spend most of their lives in freshwater and return to salt water to spawn. Eels spawn in the Sargasso Sea, a calm, warm area in the middle of the North Atlantic Ocean. Once hatched, the young eels (called *leptocephali*) drift in northerly currents and transform into glass eels as they near the river mouths of northeastern North America. At this point in their lives they actively swim and enter the streams, where they mature and repeat the cycle, spending years or even decades in freshwater. A number of Highlands streams support eel populations.

Freshwater mussels are another important component of aquatic biodiversity (Christian and Harris 2008). Owing to their filter-feeding lifestyle, these hard-shelled mollusks are generally found in unsilted, free-flowing water; in turn, mussels serve an important role in helping to strain and clean the water column. These mollusks have a fascinating reproductive cycle; female mussels release parasitic larvae, called glochidia, which must attach to fish to survive (Barnhart, Haag, and Roston 2008). Some mussel species have very specific host fish requirements and in some cases have evolved elaborate morphological and behavioral displays to attract the host fish. Within the space of several weeks, the larvae mature, drop off the fish, and settle into the stream bottom to start life as young mussels. Owing to their sensitivity to sedimentation, pollution, habitat alterations (e.g., dam construction and the straightening of stream corridors), and their reliance on fish hosts, native freshwater mussels are among the most imperiled species in the United States (Williams et al. 1993). Some mussel species, such as eastern elliptio (*Elliptio complanata*), are commonly found across a range of aquatic habitats in the Highlands, while others, such as the brook floater (*Alasmidonta varicosa*), are more restricted to creeks and small rivers with a stable substrate (Cordeiro and Bowers-Altman 2003). Because of its declining status, the brook floater is a federal species of concern and is considered imperiled or critically imperiled across the four Highlands states (NatureServe 2009).

The nonflowing (lentic) waters of lakes and ponds are usually formed in basins or depressions on the landscape, in contrast to the flowing waters of streams. Ponds typically are defined as small water bodies shallow enough for light to penetrate to the bottom such that plants can grow anywhere across the bottom, whereas lakes can be quite deep and large. Many lakes and ponds formed naturally on the landscape from past beaver activity or in glacial depressions where they intersect the water table, but others are man-made, including farm ponds, old gravel pits, and larger reservoirs. (e.g., Clinton Reservoir in New Jersey, Barkhamsted Reservoir in Connecticut, and Nockamixon Reservoir in Pennsylvania). Regardless of their origin, these lakes and ponds (as well as the larger reaches of slow-moving rivers) host an array of fish that thrive in the warmer waters. Such fish include yellow perch (*Perca flavescens*), many species of sunfish (e.g., large- [*Micropterus salmoides*] and smallmouth bass [*M. dolomieu*], crappies [*Pomoxis* spp.] and pumpkinseed [*Lepomis gibbosus*], catfishes [*Ictalurus* sp., *Amieurus* spp.], white sucker [*Catostomus commersonii*], common carp [*Cyprinus carpio*], killifishes [(*Fundulus* spp.], northern pike [*Esox lucius*], pickerels [*Esox* spp.]), and a score of minnow species, small members of the family Cyprinidae. These minnows, which are found in all habitats from headwater riffles to large lakes and the main channels of the large rivers, include daces (*Rhinichthys* spp.), shiners (*Notropis* spp.), and chubs (*Semotilus* spp.), and each inhabits a relatively narrowly defined habitat, which partly explains their abundance and diversity (Smith 1985). In ponds and the shallower waters of most lakes, invertebrates such as pond snails creep slowly about, scraping algae off plant leaves and stems in the water, while case-building caddis fly larvae, protected in their constructed tubes of leaves, small sticks, or stones, filter plankton from the water.

Wetlands, often closely connected with lakes, ponds, and streams, range in size and character from small areas of moist soil and sphagnum moss to extensive swamp and marsh complexes covering thousands of acres—and all can be found within the Highlands region (see chapter 8). The largest forested wetlands, such as Great Swamp in New York, provide excellent breeding habitat for red-shouldered hawks and barred owls (*Strix varia*), which require large wet forests in which to successfully raise their young. Although great blue herons (*Ardea herodias*) stealthily hunt for fish in a variety of aquatic habitats—streams, ponds, or swamps—they also depend on forested wetlands because they construct their nests high atop trees. Other tree-dependent wetland birds include cavity-nesting ducks such as the wood duck (*Aix sponsa*) and common merganser (*Mergus merganser*). Purple finches (*Carpodacus purpureus*), magnolia warblers (*Dendroica magnolia*), and other northern breeding birds nest preferentially in the region's coniferous-dominated swamps and bogs. Cattail marshes and other open wetlands—Quakertown Swamp and Great Marsh in Pennsylvania and White Memorial Foundation in Connecticut, for example—harbor secretive birds such as the least bittern (*Ixobrychus exilis*) and Virginia rail and sora (*Rallus limicola* and *Porzana carolina*, respectively).

Perhaps the best-known mammal of pond and swamp is the beaver (*Castor canadensis*). Almost extirpated from the region during the late 1800s owing to unregulated market trapping for the European hat trade, reintroduction efforts, protection from trapping, and recolonization from other states have allowed them to make a comeback. Beavers are wetland architects, playing a key role in maintaining habitat diversity by building dams that create ponds used by other animals. River otter, mink (*Mustela vison*), muskrat (*Ondatra zibethicus*), and the star-nosed mole (*Condylura cristata*) are just a few of the other mammals adapted to wetland habitats in the Highlands.

Some of the most characteristic—as well as the noisiest—inhabitants of freshwater habitats are frogs. As tadpoles, these amphibians filter-feed on algae suspended in the water column, or they scrape algae and bacterial debris that cling to leaves and rocks at the bottom of small ponds, swamps, or bogs. Once metamorphosed into adult frogs, they become carnivorous, feeding mostly on insects and other invertebrates. The wood frog (*Lithobates sylvaticus*) and spring peeper (*Pseudacris crucifer*) are the first to emerge in early spring from their hibernation sites under leaves on the forest floor. Both species are relatively freeze-tolerant (to 20°F) due to the presence of protective glucose molecules in their bodies. In fact, they can survive freezing of about 50 percent of their total body-water content (Hammerson 2004; Storey and Storey 1996). They are therefore able to hibernate near the surface of the ground, ready at first spring thaw to "awaken" and migrate to nearby breeding ponds to mate. Thus, the peeper's shrill call and the ducklike quack of the wood frog are among the first sounds of spring. Peepers lay their minute eggs singly on submerged vegetation, while wood frogs and many other frogs lay their eggs in gelatinous masses buoyed by the water column. Later in the season, as nighttime temperatures rise into the 50s in April and early May, pickerel frogs (*Lithobates palustris*) and American toads (*Anaxyrus americanus*) emerge from hibernation, adding to the chorus. Finally, on warm humid nights in May and June, come the bubbly trills of gray tree frogs (*Hyla versicolor*), the insectlike clicks of cricket frogs (*Acris crepitans*), which are heard only in a few places in the Highlands, and the characteristic summer "songs" of bullfrogs (*Lithobates catesbeianus*) and green frogs (*Lithobates clamitans*).

Another group of animals dependent on aquatic habitats such as wetlands are dragonflies and damselflies, the Odonata. Like amphibians, they have an aquatic larval stage (nymph) that lasts anywhere from a few months to a year or two. When ready to transform into an adult, the nymph typically crawls out of the water onto a plant stem or rock and pulls itself out of its old, split "shell" (exoskeleton). After expanding and hardening its soft, damp wings for several hours, it flies off to begin its life as an adult. One uncommon damselfly of the Highlands is the New England bluet (*Enallagma laterale*), which lives in shallow, boggy wetlands, where it lays its eggs on the leaves of water shield (*Brasenia shreberi*) or other floating or emergent vegetation. There are a few scattered populations in the Highlands region.

Many reptiles also require freshwater wetlands. The rarest and smallest turtle of the Highlands is the bog turtle (*Glyptemys muhlenbergii*), known by its dark, compact shell and the large, reddish orange or yellow patch behind each eye. It is found in the more open portions of spring-fed sphagnum bogs or limestone fens that have soft muddy bottoms into which it can burrow. Bog turtles can sometimes be found basking on tussocks or searching under streamlet vegetation for insects, larvae, crayfish, mollusks, or worms. Many of the best bog-turtle habitats in the Highlands are actually wet meadows that have been kept open by livestock grazing. The bog turtle is considered endangered by states throughout its northern range. It is included on the federal threatened species list because of its restricted habitat requirements and the increasing loss of that habitat as well as degraded wetland conditions and illegal collecting (Gibbs et al. 2007; Liguori and Tesauro 2003).

Another rare turtle of the Highlands is the Blanding's turtle (*Emydoidea blandingii*), which has a large, hinged, helmet-shaped bottom shell and a bright yellow throat. Although primarily a midwestern species, the Blanding's turtle is known to inhabit a few wetlands in the Hudson valley section of the New York and Connecticut portions of the Highlands. Long lived, reaching fifty to seventy years of age, these turtles prefer sizable, semipermanent wetlands with a diversity of watercourses, both shallow and deep, and thick shrubby vegetation. They feed on crayfish and other invertebrates, tadpoles, frogs, small fish, berries, and vegetation. Also a protected species, the Blanding's turtle is vulnerable to nest predation by raccoons, skunks, and other predators as well as heavy road traffic and poor water quality (Gibbs et al. 2007).

Vernal ponds are unique wetlands that are actually dry for a portion of the year. Typically they fill with water from winter rains and snowmelt and dry out during the summer months. In the Highlands, they are often formed from kettle holes created during past glacial activity. Because they dry out each year, vernal ponds are generally free of fish, which makes them safer habitat for mole salamanders to reproduce. The mole salamanders include the spotted, blue spotted, marbled, and Jefferson's salamanders—*Ambystoma maculatum, A. laterale, A. opacum,* and *A. jeffersonianum,* respectively. They live most of the year in forests under logs or in thick leaf litter, or in the burrows of other animals, emerging during early spring evenings (or fall in the case of *A. opacum*) during rain, when they migrate to vernal ponds to breed. Other amphibians also use these ponds—namely, spring peepers, wood frogs, and toads. Spotted turtles (*Clemmys gutatta*) travel throughout these pond complexes feasting on salamander egg masses while box turtles visit occasionally, seeking cool, moist conditions during hot summer days (Mitchell, Breisch, and Buhlman 2006). Shrews and other mammals as well as birds such as the common yellowthroat (*Geolypis trichas*) can often be found at the water's edge. The ponds support a diverse aquatic invertebrate assemblage, which includes the intriguing fairy shrimp (*Eubranchipus* spp.), a small reddish crustacean. Fairy shrimp can readily be seen in early spring swimming upside down near the water's surface, rapidly moving their eleven pairs of legs as they absorb oxygen from the water. Fairy shrimp feed on bacteria and microplankton filtered from the water column.

The Highlands region includes some brackish marshes and intertidal mudflats, the most extensive of which is Iona Marsh, along the Hudson River shallows just south of Beacon, New York. The mudflats exposed at low tide provide important feeding areas for migratory shorebirds in spring and fall. Uncommon birds, such as the least bittern, nest in the marshes, and more common species such as northern water snakes (*Nerodia sipedon*), muskrats, snapping turtles, and green frogs call these wetlands home. Needham's skimmer dragonfly (*Libellula needhami*), typically a more southern species, can also be found hunting for insect prey among the reeds and cattails (see plate 27). A host of overwintering bird species rely on the extensive marsh habitats, among them waterfowl such as mergansers (*Mergus* spp.), canvasbacks (*Aythya valisineria*), mallards (*Anas platyrhynchos*), and common goldeneyes (*Bucephala clangula*). Bald eagles (*Haliaeetus leucocephalus*) roost on the trees on the river side of Iona Island during the winter and feed along the Hudson River and the nearby Croton Reservoir (USFWS 1999). In fact, this lower section of the Hudson River is one of the most critical bald eagle overwintering sites in New York State.

Headwater seeps are wetland areas where groundwater flows to the surface to become the beginning of streams. They typically have water flow most of the time and are home to animals such as the northern red (*Pseudotriton ruber*) and spring salamanders (*Gyrinophilus porphyriticus*) and dragonflies such as the arrowhead spiketail (*Cordulegaster obliqua*). Northern water shrews (*Sorex palustris albibarbis*) frequent such seep habitats, while Louisiana waterthrush (*Seiurus motacilla*) and mourning warblers (*Oporornis philadelphia*) often nest nearby. In addition, seeps located in forest areas provide important ice-free watering sites for many animals, and they are often the first areas in the forest to become green in the spring and provide food. One of the rarest of the Highlands seep dwellers is the gray petaltail dragonfly (*Tachopteryx thoreyi*), whose larvae develop in these small, inconspicuous wetlands. Generally a southern species, the gray petaltail reaches its northern limit in southern New York and occurs in the Highlands region only in New Jersey and New York.

Rocky Outcrops

Rocky outcrops are found along the Hudson River bluffs and the interior ridges of the Highlands, extending from the Taconic Mountains to Breakneck Ridge (New York), at higher elevations of Morris County to Scotts Mountain (New Jersey), and into Pennsylvania along South Mountain and farther south. Rocky outcrops are often used as nesting sites by the common raven (*Corvus corax*), which in recent years has made a comeback in the region, and the peregrine falcon (*Falco peregrinus*), now found on the cliffs of the eastern Highlands such as in New York's Fahnestock and Hudson Highlands state parks (Burger and Liner 2005).

These rocky outcrops with their associated talus (boulder fields at the toe of the cliff) provide critical habitat components for a number of reptile species. Five-lined skinks (*Plestiodon fasciatus*) and eastern fence lizards (*Sceloporus undulatus*) bask on warmed rocks, and snakes such as northern copperheads (*Agkistrodon contortrix*) and timber rattlesnakes (*Crotalus horridus*) rely on these habitats for basking, gestating, and denning. In fact, the Highlands are a stronghold for timber rattlesnakes in the mid-Atlantic region (see plate 28). During the winter months, the rattlesnakes gather in communal dens (sometimes referred to as hibernacula), which are often located within these rocky outcrop areas. During the rest of the year, an individual may travel one to two miles away from the den site. Timber rattlesnakes require large mature forests where they spend much of their time camouflaged on the forest floor, waiting in ambush for an eastern chipmunk or white-footed mouse (*Peromyscus leucopus*) to scurry past (Peterson and Fritsch 1986; Schantz and Valent 2003b).

One mammal that is a rocky outcrop habitat specialist is the Allegheny woodrat (*Neotoma floridana magister*). Once found along the Appalachian Mountains from Tennessee to southeastern New York State, it has disappeared from most of the Highlands region, with only one northern population remaining in the nearby Palisades of New Jersey and the rest in the westernmost sections of the Highlands in Pennsylvania. Its near disappearance has been attributed to several factors, including habitat fragmentation and a reduction in food supply due initially to the loss of the American chestnut (*Castanea dentata*), followed by a more recent oak mortality caused by gypsy moths (*Lymantria dispar*). Another factor is the introduction of the raccoon roundworm (*Baylisascaris procyonis*), which has decimated populations throughout their range (Valent 2003).

Caves and Abandoned Mines

There are not many natural caves in the Highlands, because any that might have formed in the limestone bedrock most likely collapsed under the weight of the glaciers that covered the region more than ten thousand years ago. The caves that do exist are commonly found in calcium-rich deposits of igneous rocks. However, the Highlands are well known for the iron deposits that were mined during the Revolutionary War—and even into the twentieth century (see chapter 11). The abandoned mines have provided important habitat for a number of Highland bat species, specifically the little brown bat (*Myotis lucifugus*) and the Indiana bat. The Durham mine in Pennsylvania has been home to more than ten thousand hibernating bats each year and is one of the largest such sites in that state (C. Butchkoski, pers. comm., August 2010). The Hibernia mine in New Jersey has also been an important bat hibernation site. Both of these caves are gated with special bars that allow bats to enter and exit freely but prevent people from entering the caves and disturbing the bats.[2] Additionally, northern red salamanders or two-lined salamanders (*Eurycea bislineata*) may inhabit the damp openings of caves, especially if there is flowing water or seepage. Common species of crickets, snails, and other invertebrates also often frequent cave openings. Porcupines and other wildlife may also occasionally seek shelter in shallow caves.

Threats to Species and Habitats

Since the arrival of the first settlers in the Highlands region in the early 1600s, numerous species have vanished from the area. Some of these losses were due directly to overhunting for food or sport, including the now-extinct passenger pigeon (*Ectopistes migratorius*). Others were bounty-hunted as "varmints," particularly the timber wolf (*Canis lupus*) and cougar (*Puma concolor*). Overhunting also contributed to the disappearance or near disappearance of white-tailed deer, black bear, turkey, and beaver, whose numbers have since rebounded with forest regeneration, legal protection, and reintroductions.

Wildlife populations have also declined because changes in their habitats left them without suitable places to shelter, find food, and raise young. Extensive land clearing in the early 1700s destroyed intact forests that were home to many species. At the same time, such clearing created great swaths of open habitat that were colonized by grassland-nesting birds. With forest regrowth and the conversion of farmland to development, these open grasslands and fallow agricultural fields have disappeared and, along with them, many of the open-country birds, insects, and other animals that rely on these habitats. In more recent times, wetlands have been filled, ditched, or drained (see chapter 8) and streams dammed or channelized. With such changes in habitat, a few wildlife species benefit, but most decline or disappear.

Despite recent great strides in conservation, land protection, and habitat restoration by governmental agencies, nongovernmental organizations, and citizens, there are still threats to the vertebrate and invertebrate life of the Highlands. The most significant threat to biodiversity within the Highlands region today is loss of habitat, including its degradation and fragmentation. When habitats are converted for development, agriculture, or resource extraction, many fields and forests are destroyed outright as land is cleared or paved over, resulting in the death of many of the individual animals living there. Conversions leave adjacent portions of habitat intact in a piecemeal fashion, leading to habitat degradation and fragmentation where larger tracts of forest or grassland are divided into smaller patches of open land separated by roads, lawns, buildings, or other development. Many animals require large habitat blocks to meet their needs for food and shelter, and the conversion of deep forest into smaller isolated woodlots, for instance, renders the altered habitats unsuitable for these specialists. The environmental characteristics of forests change as they become smaller, altering vegetation and microclimates. The smaller size also allows access by certain predators that otherwise would not be found in a larger forest. Once habitats are fragmented, some animals may search for more suitable places to live, but they rarely find safe passage, encountering predators and vehicles as they cross lawns and roads. Any individuals that remain in the smaller habitat remnant ultimately become isolated from others of their kind, unable to reproduce and maintain a viable population.

Fragmentation especially affects animals that use many different habitats throughout the year, depending on their needs—for nesting, foraging, estivating (a kind of dry weather "hibernation"), or hibernating during the winter months. For example, wood turtles emerge from their stream-bank hibernation sites in the spring, foraging far and wide through both forest and field in search of food, sometimes traveling up to two miles or more from their overwintering sites. On hot summer days, they may return streamside. During the June nesting season, female wood turtles seek open fields in which to dig their nests and deposit their eggs, the warmth of the sun being the only source of incubation heat for the developing embryos (Liguori 2003c). Each habitat along with the ability to move among them is key to the survival and reproduction of wood turtles, as is the case with many other animal species.

Habitats may also change because of natural succession, with grassy fields reverting to shrublands and then to mature forest. In an intact landscape, natural disturbances can set back this succession to create new early-stage habitats. Fires lead to sunny clearings in forests, while beaver activity forms new ponds and open meadows. Unfortunately, fragmentation and development disrupt these natural processes that shape and maintain the landscape. Dams, levees, and water-diversion projects prevent flooding and change the nature of many streams. Fire suppression is the norm where development has encroached into fire-adapted landscapes. In addition, habitat restoration that calls for prescribed burning or restoration of a natural stream by periodic flooding is often at odds with the wishes of those who have moved into these areas.

Incompatible land management can also render habitats unsuitable for some wildlife. For example, birds and other species that depend on open grasslands are affected by early-season mowing for hay as well as by the conversion of pasturelands to row crops (such as corn or soybeans) and the reduction of acreage that is allowed to lie fallow from year to year. Recent changes in power line maintenance requirements that promote intensive cutting or increased use of herbicides can be harmful to the wildlife associated with the more open habitats that these rights-of-way provide (Relyea 2005). Some forestry practices also create early successional habitats and a mosaic of different-age stands across the landscape, to the benefit of many species. However, in larger forests clear-cutting or even selective cutting may allow the encroachment of invasive species and can significantly alter forest microclimates. This, in turn, may adversely affect forest-nesting neotropical migrant birds, as well as woodland salamanders that depend on a closed canopy to maintain essential soil-moisture conditions.

Invasive, nonnative animal and plant species are the second-most prevalent threat to Highlands habitats, both terrestrial and aquatic. Forests have been under siege for years. The chestnut blight fungus (*Cryphonectria parasitica*), accidentally introduced to this country in the early 1900s, essentially wiped out the American chestnut, a dominant forest tree, by 1940. The chestnut's loss affected many species, including the passenger pigeon. The spread of gypsy moths throughout the eastern United States, beginning in the early 1900s, also altered forest composition and affected oak-dependent species. In recent years, the hemlock wooly adelgid insect (*Adelges tsugae*) has devastated large areas of hemlock forests in the Highlands and is expanding its range. This will have far-reaching effects on the animals that depend on the cones as food as well as on the moist forest floor or coldwater stream conditions that hemlock shade provides.

Unfortunately, new introductions and invasions continue. In the mid-Atlantic region of the United States, the Asian long-horned beetle (*Anoplophora glabripennis*), which was introduced in wooden packing material from China, is currently restricted to the New York–New Jersey Piedmont and coastal plain regions. However, it could spread into the Highlands, where it would have dire consequences for the oak/hickory/maple forest. Also moving closer to the region is the emerald ash borer (*Agrilus planipennis*), accidentally introduced from Asia into the midwestern United States in 2002.

Indiscriminate use of pesticides to combat forest pests can create more problems. DDT, Sevin, and Dimilin (in certain places) were used heavily over the past fifty years to control gypsy moths in forested regions of the Highlands, with immediate impacts to many forest butterflies and moths. Fortunately, use of these pesticides through widespread aerial application has been severely curtailed, if not banned in the region over the past twenty years. In addition, the use of integrated pest management practices (IPM) and less-toxic pesticides such as Btk (*Bacillus thuringiensis* var. *krustaki*) has further minimized the risk to nontarget Lepidoptera and other insect populations (Schweitzer, Minno, and Wagner forthcoming). Another threat to the integrity of forest habitats is the recent growth in numbers of nonnative earthworms that degrade the natural organic layer in the upper soil. Originally from Europe and Asia, these earthworms were first introduced to the Northeast in potting soil and ship ballast, and they have spread in recent years, partly from the sale of worms for gardening and as fish bait. Most native earthworms that may have lived in the area were eradicated ten thousand years ago during the last Ice Age as glaciers scoured the landscape. Consequently, until recently the primary decomposers in Highlands forests have been bacteria and fungi, and the primary nutrient cyclers have been other invertebrates such as ants. Many plants and animals depend on a thick, spongy layer of decomposing vegetation found in leaf litter. High numbers of nonnative earthworms rapidly remove this duff, which alters nutrient availability for plants. In addition, this loss of the forest litter layer leads to a decline in invertebrate abundance and the salamanders that depend on them as prey (Maerz, Nuzzo, and Blossey 2009).

Invasive nonnative plants can be problematic for wildlife when they change soil chemistry to make the soil less habitable to native forest plants, as do Japanese barberry (*Berberis thunbergii*) and stiltgrass (*Microstegium vimineum*) (Ehrenfeld, Kourtev, and Huang 2001). Some invasive plants can also affect groundwater levels and change the makeup of microhabitats on which many animal species depend. Purple loosestrife (*Lythrum salicaria*) and common reed (*Phragmites australis*) degrade wetlands by overgrowing the open tussocks used by bog turtles for basking and nesting sites. In addition, the accumulation of dead stems firms up the soft muddy substrate in which the turtles burrow. The nonnative garlic mustard (*Alliaria petiolata*) poses a significant threat to populations of the checkered white butterfly (*Pontia protodice*). Larvae hatching from eggs deposited on this ubiquitous plant develop poorly or do not grow at all (Golden and Tesauro 2003; Wagner 2007). Invasive plants, such as autumn olive (*Elaeagnus umbellata*) and multiflora rose (*Rosa multiflora*), crowd out the little bluestem grass that supports skipper butterflies, such as cobweb (*Hesperia metea*) and arogos skippers (Wagner 2007). In aquatic systems, the nonnative water chestnut (*Trapa natans*) forms dense mats that crowd out native vegetation and block sunlight, thus altering water chemistry by reducing the water's dissolved oxygen content (Swearingen et al. 2002). Such changes modify the habitat to the detriment of dragonfly species like the spadderdock darner (*Rhionaeschna mutata*) (A. Barlow, pers. comm., August 2010).

Development and its associated human activity also change relationships between and among species by favoring more "human-adapted" animal species over others. Predatory house cats, raccoons, skunks, red foxes (*Vulpes vulpes*), black bears, coyotes (*Canis latrans*), and birds such as crows (*Corvus* spp.) benefit from handouts from human beings, whether intentional or not. Although many are native, higher populations of these predators can be a significant problem for many wildlife species, especially ground-nesting birds. Some of these predator species also can be considered problematic for humans. As more people move into the Highlands region, for example, reports of human–bear interactions have increased. Conflicts most often occur when new development is close to or encroaches on optimum bear territory (Rohrbach 2005). Additionally, many people feed bears—intentionally with handouts or unintentionally with bird feeders, garbage, or pet food—and this causes some bears to habituate to people as a source of food. Strategies are especially needed for improving the ongoing and long-term relationships between people and predators.

Another animal that has benefited greatly from human habitat alterations is the white-tailed deer. Deer numbers have rebounded from the decimation caused by market and subsistence hunting of the early 1900s and as their habitat has recovered from deforestation, primarily to support agriculture and iron smelting, during the late nineteenth century. This growth in deer numbers has also been attributed to additional factors including increased suburban development, which has fragmented larger forests into smaller woodlots with plenty of edge, creating prime deer habitat. Despite expanded hunting opportunities designed to control deer numbers, these small suburban habitat patches often serve as refugia from hunting. The result of such high deer numbers is severe overbrowsing of the forest, causing the removal of forest shrubs and herbs, which in turn has negative effects on many other forest animals and plants (Rooney and Waller 2003; Herr 2007). For example, nesting and migrating birds that depend on vegetative cover to provide foraging sites or protection from predators cannot find suitable habitat (McShea and Rappole 2000).

Pollution remains a major concern in the Highlands region. Acid precipitation, for instance, not only harms aquatic systems but also degrades upland habitats in part by leaching calcium from the soil and reducing its availability for soil and litter invertebrates and for the birds that feed on them (Hames et al. 2002). Mercury emitted from power plants is taken up by forest soil invertebrates as they feed. This leads to a magnified accumulation of mercury in the tissues of insect-feeding birds such as thrushes, with harmful reproductive effects (Evers 2005).

Aquatic ecosystems are affected by both point- and nonpoint-source pollution. Point-source pollution comes from one source, such as a discharge pipe. Today, the greater threat in the Highlands is nonpoint-source pollution, or overland runoff from farms, roads, and suburban yards, which carries heavy metals, road salt, oil, dust, pet waste, fertilizers, pesticides, and even household pharmaceuticals and personal care products into waterways (see chapter 4 for a more detailed discussion). These pollutants threaten all Highlands aquatic ecosystems and their inhabitants, with amphibians being particularly vulnerable owing to their permeable skin.

Light and noise pollution also pose increasing threats to wildlife as more people recreate in and move to the Highlands. Artificial lighting at night seriously affects animal navigation, reproduction, and courtship (Longcore and Rich 2004). In addition, most animals rely on hearing to communicate, avoid predators, and find food. For these reasons, noise from lawn mowers, leaf blowers, recreational vehicles, power-generating stations, and increased traffic flow can negatively affect the long-term survival of certain species by forcing them to alter their natural behavior or move to less-optimal habitat (Habib, Bayne, and Boutin 2006; Turina and Barber 2008).

Perhaps the biggest "wildcard" faced by all wildlife in the Highlands is climate change. Scientists predict warmer temperatures and more severe droughts and floods for the region. A changing climate may alter the fine-tuned relationships among species. For example, plants may bloom before their insect pollinators are active, and birds may migrate earlier, before their insect food is available on their nesting grounds. In response to changing environmental conditions, many animals will seek more suitable habitat, but other protected areas may not exist or may not be reachable because of a lack of viable connections between habitats. Conservation planning will need to be adaptive, with a longer-term vision that incorporates future climate changes into recommended conservation actions. This should include protection of the "green infrastructure" necessary to accommodate the needs of plants and wildlife to adapt to changing conditions.

Despite these ongoing challenges to biodiversity, many species in the Highlands are making a comeback. Habitat protection and restoration efforts over the past forty years and longer have led to some great successes. As mentioned earlier, wild turkey, black bear, beaver, and bobcat numbers have rebounded in the past one hundred years, and fishers are returning. In addition, new arrivals such as the coyote are moving into the region. Originally found in the midwestern and western states, coyotes have moved east to the Highlands area over the past seventy years, taking over the niche vacated when the wolf was eliminated from the region more than one hundred years ago (Whitaker and Hamilton 1998).

Bald eagles depend on sections of the Hudson Highlands as overwintering sites and in recent years have expanded their nesting range into the area. The osprey (*Pandion haliaetus*) is another bird of prey once adversely affected by pesticide use that has made a comeback with the ban on DDT and other organochlorine pesticides. Ospreys are now thriving in the Highlands region, mainly along its larger rivers (e.g., Delaware, Hudson) and around larger lakes and reservoirs (e.g., Clinton Reservoir, New Jersey). Many of the larger silk and sphinx moths are now found regularly in parts of the Highlands region, due in part to the changeover to IPM for pest control (Schweitzer personal communication).

Conclusions

The wealth of habitats in the Highlands support an important and diverse array of animal species, each with its own ecological needs. Protection and management of Highlands habitats must consider that most species depend on multiple habitats throughout their lives, that maintaining connectivity among habitats is critical, and that it is important not only to conserve the rarest Highlands inhabitants but also to keep common species common.

Additionally, the integrity of the Highlands plant and animal communities, both terrestrial and aquatic, is key to the maintenance of ecological processes and water quality of the region. This not only benefits wildlife but also protects the well-being of its human inhabitants. In fact, the biodiversity of the Highlands—its plants, animals, and natural communities—provides not only ecosystem services, such as water purification, soil creation, and pollination, but also food, fuel, building materials, and other natural resources. Perhaps more important, Highlands landscapes—the wetlands, expansive forests, and rocky outcrops, and the variety of plant and animal inhabitants they support—offer stunning beauty along with the thrill of encounters with wildlife in the natural world. We have made a great start in protecting Highlands landscapes across four state boundaries. With continued conservation efforts and with the help of citizens who value this diversity, the wildlife of the Highlands will continue to thrive.

Acknowledgments

Sincere thanks to everyone who provided background information, reviewed and improved text, and edited materials, including Sally Anderson, John Ascher, Allen Barlow, Chanda Bennett, Jeanette Bowers, Fiona Brady, Cal Butchkoski, Patrick Comins, John Confer, Bob Daniels, Emile DeVito, Terry Dickert, Jenny Dickson,

Charlie Eichelberger, Dave Jenkins, Fred Koontz, Roger Latham, Betsy Leppo, John Maerz, Ed McGowan, Mike Nichols, Paul Novak, Sally Ray, Laura Saucier, Kris Schantz, Dale Schweitzer, James Smith, Jennifer Stenzel, Jim Thorne, Mick Valent, David Wagner, John Waldman, Sharon Wander, Wade Wander, John Waldman, David Wagner, Judy Wilson, and staff of the New York and New Jersey Natural Heritage Program. Thank you also to Melissa Craddock, Lloyd Spitalnick, Mick Valent, and Cal Vornberger for generously sharing their photographs.

Notes

1. There is now a carefully regulated trapping season on them in Pennsylvania.

2. The arrival of white-nose syndrome has been decimating these cave bat populations at the time of this writing.

References

Askins, R. A. 2000. *Restoring North America's Birds: Lessons from Landscape Ecology.* New Haven, CT: Yale University Press.

Barnhart, M. C., W. R. Haag, and W. N. Roston. 2008. "Adaptations to Host Infection and Larval Parasitism in Unionoida." *Journal North American Benthological Society* 27, no. 2: 370–394.

Burger, J. W. 1935. "*Plethodon cinereus* (Green) in Eastern Pennsylvania and New Jersey." *The American Naturalist* 69, no. 725: 578–586.

Burger, M. F., and J. M. Liner. 2005. *Important Bird Areas of New York: Habitats Worth Protecting.* Albany, NY: Audubon.

Burton, T. M., and G. E. Likens. 1975. "Salamander Populations and Biomass in the Hubbard Brook Experimental Forest, New Hampshire." *Copeia* 3:541–546.

Christian, A. D., and J. L. Harris. 2008. "An Introduction to Directions in Freshwater Mollusk Conservation: Molecules to Ecosystems." *Journal of the North American Benthological Society* 27, no. 2: 349–369.

Cinquina, J. 1965. "Mammals." In *A Natural History of the Northern New Jersey Highlands (Morris, Passaic and Sussex Counties)*, ed. J. Cinquina. Oak Ridge, NJ: Highlands Audubon Society.

Confer, J. L., K. W. Barnes, and E. C. Alvey. 2010. "Golden- and Blue-Winged Warblers: Distribution, Nesting Success, and Genetic Differences in Two Habitats." *Wilson Journal of Ornithology* 122:273–278.

Cordeiro, J., and J. Bowers-Altman. 2003. "Freshwater Mussels of the New York Metropolitan Region and New Jersey: A Guide to Their Identification, Biology, and Conservation." Center for Biodiversity and Conservation, American Museum of Natural History, New York. http://cbc.amnh.org/mussel/index.html.

DeGraaf, R. M., M. Yamasaki, W. B. Leak, and J. W. Lanier. 1992. "New England Wildlife: Management of Forested Habitats." *General Technical Report NE-144.* Radnor, PA: U.S. Department of Agriculture, Forest Service, Northeastern Research Station.

Ehrenfeld, J. G., P. Kourtev, and W. Huang. 2001. "Changes in Soil Functions Following Invasions of Exotic Understory Plants in Deciduous Forests." *Ecological Applications* 11:1287–1300.

Elliot, L., and W. Herschberger. 2007. *The Songs of Insects*. New York: Houghton Mifflin Company.

Evers, D. C. 2005. *Mercury Connections: The Extent and Effects of Mercury Pollution in Northeastern North America*. Gorham, ME: BioDiversity Research Institute.

Fuller, T. K., and S. DeStefano. 2003. "Relative Importance of Early-Successional Forests and Shrubland Habitats to Mammals in the Northeastern United States." *Forest Ecology and Management* 185:75–79.

Gibbs, J. P., A. R. Breish, P. K. Ducey, G. Johnson, J. L. Behler, and R. C. Bothner. 2007. *The Amphibians and Reptiles of New York State*. New York: Oxford University Press.

Golden, D. M., and J. Tesauro. 2003. "Arogos Skipper." In *Endangered and Threatened Wildlife of New Jersey*, ed. Bruce Beans and Larry Niles. New Brunswick, NJ: Rutgers University Press.

Habib, L., E. M. Bayne, and S. Boutin. 2006. "Chronic Industrial Noise Affects Pairing Success and Age Structure of Ovenbirds *Seiurus aurocapilla*." *Journal of Applied Ecology* 44:176–184.

Hames, R. S., K. V. Rosenberg, J. D. Lowe, S. E. Barker, and A. A. Dhondt. 2002. "Adverse Effects of Acid Rain on the Distribution of the Wood Thrush *Hylocichla mustelina* in North America." *Proceedings of the National Academy of Science* 99, no. 17: 11235–11240.

Hammerson, G. A. 2004. *Connecticut Wildlife—Biodiversity, Natural History, and Conservation*. Lebanon, NH: University Press of New England.

Hartmaier, B., and B. E. Beans. 2003. "Indiana Bat." In *Endangered and Threatened Wildlife of New Jersey*, ed. Bruce Beans and Larry Niles. New Brunswick, NJ: Rutgers University Press.

Herr, B. 2007. "Butterflies: Canaries of the Meadows." *American Butterflies* 15, no. 1–2 (Spring–Summer): 4–11.

Liguori, S. 2003a. "Grasshopper Sparrow." In *Endangered and Threatened Wildlife of New Jersey*,. ed. Bruce Beans and Larry Niles. New Brunswick, NJ: Rutgers University Press.

———. 2003b. "Red-Shouldered Hawk." In *Endangered and Threatened Wildlife of New Jersey*,. ed. Bruce Beans and Larry Niles. New Brunswick, NJ: Rutgers University Press.

———. 2003c. "Wood Turtle." In *Endangered and Threatened Wildlife of New Jersey*,. ed. Bruce Beans and Larry Niles. New Brunswick, NJ: Rutgers University Press.

Liguori, S., and J. Tesauro. 2003. "Bog Turtle." In *Endangered and Threatened Wildlife of New Jersey*, ed. Bruce Beans and Larry Niles. New Brunswick, NJ: Rutgers University Press.

Longcore, R., and C. Rich. 2004. "Ecological Light Pollution." *Frontiers in Ecology and the Environment* 4:191–198.

Maerz, C. J., V. Nuzzo, and B. Blossey. 2009. "Declines in Woodland Salamander Abundance Associated with Nonnative Plant and Earthworm Invasions." *Conservation Biology* 23:975–981.

Martin, A. C., H. S. Zim, and A. L. Nelson. 1951. *American Wildlife and Plants—a Guide to Wildlife Food Habits*. New York: Dover Publications.

McShea, W. J., and J. H. Rappole. 2000. "Managing the Abundance and Diversity of

Breeding Bird Populations through Manipulation of Deer Populations." *Conservation Biology* 14, no. 4: 1161–1170.

Mitchell, J. C., A. R. Breisch, and K. A. Buhlman. 2006. *Habitat Management Guidelines for Amphibians and Reptiles of the Northeastern United States.* Technical publication HMG-3. Montgomery, AL: Partners in Amphibian and Reptile Conservation.

Motzkin, G., D. A. Orwig, and D. A. Foster. 2002. "Vegetation and Disturbance History of a Rare Dwarf Pitch Pine Community in Western New England, USA." *Journal of Biogeography* 29:1455–1467.

NatureServe. 2009. "NatureServe Explorer: An Online Encyclopedia of Life." http://www.natureserve.org/explorer/.

Peterson, R. C., and R. W. Fritsch II. 1986. "Connecticut's Venomous Snakes: The Timber Rattlesnake and Northern Copperhead." Department of Environmental Protection Bulletin 111. Hartford: State Geological and Natural History Survey of Connecticut.

Relyea, R. A. 2005. "The Lethal Impact of Roundup on Aquatic and Terrestrial Amphibians." *Ecological Applications* 15, no. 4: 1118–1124.

Rohrbach, T. 2005. "Spatial Analysis of Human–Black Bear Conflicts in Northwestern New Jersey." Master's thesis, Rutgers University, New Brunswick.

Rooney, T. P., and D. M. Waller. 2003. "Direct and Indirect Effects of White-Tailed Deer in Forest Ecosystems." *Forest Ecology and Management* 181:165–176.

Schantz, K., and M. Valent. 2003a. "Bobcat." In *Endangered and Threatened Wildlife of New Jersey*, ed. Bruce Beans and Larry Niles. New Brunswick, NJ: Rutgers University Press.

———. 2003b. "Timber Rattlesnake." In *Endangered and Threatened Wildlife of New Jersey*, ed. Bruce Beans and Larry Niles. New Brunswick, NJ: Rutgers University Press.

Schweitzer, D. F., M. Minno, and D. L. Wagner. Forthcoming. "Rare, Imperiled and Poorly Known Moths and Butterflies of Eastern Forests and Woodlands." Morgantown, WV: USDA Forest Service, Forest Health Technology Enterprise Team.

Smith, C. L. 1985. "The Inland Fishes of New York State." Albany: New York State Department of Environmental Conservation.

State of Connecticut. 2009. "Department of Environmental Protection Endangered, Threatened and Species of Special Concern. Proposed amendments to Sections 26–306-4, 26–306-5, and 26–306-6 of the Regulations of Connecticut State Agencies." http://www.ct.gov/dep/lib/dep/public_notice_attachments/draft_regulations/regs09endangeredthreatenedspecial2009.pdf.

Storey, K. B., and J. M. Storey. 1996. "Natural Freezing Survival in Animals." *Annual Review of Ecology, Evolution, and Systematics* 27:365–386.

Swearingen, J., K. Reshetiloff, B. Slattery, and S. Zwicker. 2002. "Plant Invaders of Mid-Atlantic Natural Areas." Washington, DC: National Park Service and U.S. Fish & Wildlife Service, Washington, D.C. http://www.nps.gov/plants/alien/pubs/midatlantic/index.htm.

Tefft, B. C. 1996. "Managing Shrublands and Old Fields." In *Managing Grasslands, Shrublands, and Young Forest Habitats for Wildlife—a Guide for the Northeast*, ed. J. D. Oehler, D. F. Covell, S. Capel, and B. Long. Northeast Upland Habitat Technical Committee and the Massachusetts Division of Fisheries & Wildlife. http://www.wildlife.state.nh.us/Wildlife/Northeast_Hab_Mgt_Guide.htm.

Tingley, M. W., D. A. Orwig, R. Field, and G. Motzkin. 2002. "Avian Response to Removal of a Forest Dominant: Consequences of Hemlock Woolly Adelgid Infestations." *Journal of Biogeography* 29:1505–1516.

Thorp, R. W., and M. D. Shepherd. 2005. "Profile: Subgenus *Bombus*." In *Red List of Pollinator Insects of North America*, eds. M. D. Shepherd, D. M. Vaughan, and S. H. Black. CD-ROM Version 1 (May). Portland, OR: The Xerces Society for Invertebrate Conservation.

Turina, F., and J. Barber. 2008. "Annotated Bibliography: Impacts of Noise on Wildlife." Natural Sounds Program Center, National Parks Service. http://www.nature.nps.gov/naturalsounds/PDF_docs/wildlifebiblio_Aug08.pdf.

U.S. Department of Agriculture (USDA) Forest Services. 2002. "New York–New Jersey Highlands Regional Study: 2002 Update." NA-TP-02-03. Newtown Square, PA: USDA Forest Services.

U.S. Fish and Wildlife Service (USFWS). 1999. "Regionally Significant Habitats and Habitat Complexes of the New York Bight Watershed." Charlestown, RI: USFWS.

———. 2006. "New England Cottontail (*Sylvilagus transitionalis*)." Hadley, MA: USFWS. http://www.fws.gov/northeast/pdf/necotton.fs.pdf.

———. 2007. "Indiana Bat (*Myotis sodalis*)." Draft Recovery Plan: First Revision. Fort Snelling, MN: USFWS.

Valent, M. 2003. "Allegheny Woodrat." In *Endangered and Threatened Wildlife of New Jersey*, ed. Bruce Beans and Larry Niles. New Brunswick, NJ: Rutgers University Press.

Vaughan, D. M., and M. D. Shepherd. 2005. "Species Profile: *Speyeria idalia*." In *Red List of Pollinator Insects of North America*, ed. M. D. Shepherd, D. M. Vaughan, and S. H. Black. CD-ROM Version 1 (May). Portland, OR: The Xerces Society for Invertebrate Conservation.

Wagner, D. L. 2007. "Butterfly Conservation." In *The Connecticut Butterfly Atlas*, eds. J. E. O'Donnell, L. F. Gall, and D. L. Wagner. Bulletin No. 118. Hartford, CT: State Geological and Natural History Survey.

Wagner, D. L., M. W. Nelson, and D. F. Schweitzer. 2003. "Shrubland Lepidoptera of Southern New England and Southeastern New York: Ecology, Conservation, and Management." *Forest Ecology and Management* 185:95–112.

Ward, J. S., M. E. Montgomery, C.A.S.-J Cheah, B. P. Onken, and R. S. Coules. 2004. *Eastern Hemlock Forests: Guidelines to Minimize the Impacts of Hemlock Wooly Adelgid*. NA-TP-03-04. Morgantown, WV: USDA Forest Service.

Whitaker, J. O., Jr., and W. J. Hamilton Jr. 1998. *Mammals of the Eastern United States*. Ithaca, NY: Comstock Publishing Associates, Cornell University Press.

Williams, J. D., M. L. Warren Jr., J. S. Cummings, J. L. Harris, and R. J. Neves. 1993. "Conservation Status of Freshwater Mussels of the United States and Canada." *Fisheries* 18, no. 9: 6–22.

Appendix 10.1 List of Threatened and Endangered Animal Species Reported from Connecticut, New Jersey, New York, and Pennsylvania Highlands

Scientific name	Common name	State, federal, and global protection status[a]
Mammals		
Cryptotis parva	least shrew	PA-E; G5
Lynx rufus	bobcat	NJ-T; G5
Myotis sodalis	Indiana bat	NJ-E, NY-E, PA-E, US-E; G2
Neotoma florida magister	Allegheny woodrat	NJ-E, PA-T; G3G4
Birds		
Accipiter cooperii	Cooper's hawk	NJ-T; G5
Accipiter gentilis	northern goshawk	NJ-E; G5
Accipiter striatus	sharp-shinned hawk	CT-E; G5
Ammodramus henslowii	Henslow's sparrow	NJ-E, NY-T; G4
Ammodramus savannarum	grasshopper sparrow	CT-E, NJ-T; G5
Anas discors	blue-winged teal— nesting pop.	CT-T; G5
Aquila chrysaetus	golden eagle	NY-E; G5
Asio flammeus	short-eared owl (wintering pop. CT)	NJ-E; G5
Asio otus	long-eared owl	NJ-T; G5
Batramia longidauda	upland sandpiper	NY-T, PA-T; G5
Botaurus lentiginosos	American bittern	CT-E, NJ-E, PA-E; G4
Buteo lineatus	red-shouldered hawk	NJ-T; G5
Casmerodius albus	great egret	PA-E; G5
Circus cyaneus	northern harrier	NJ-E, NY-T; G5
Cistothorus plantensis	sedge wren	CT-E, NJ-E, PA-E; G5
Dolichonyx oryzovorus	bobolink	NJ-T; G5
Falco peregrinus	peregrine falcon	NJ-E, NY-E, PA-E, US-E; G4
Falco sparverius	American kestrel	CT-T; G5
Gallinula chloropus	common moorhen	CT-E; G5
Haliaeetus leucocephalis	bald eagle	CT-T, NJ-T, NY-T, PA-T; US-T; G5
Ixobrychus exilis	least bittern	CT-T, NY-T, PA-E; G5
Lanius ludovicianus	loggerhead shrike	NJ-E; G4
Malanerpes erythrocephalus	red-headed woodpecker	NJ-T; G5
Nyctocorax nycticoras	black-crowned night heron	CT-T, NJ-T, PA-E; G5
Nyctocorax violaceus	yellow-crowned night heron	NJ-T, PA-E; G5
Pandion haliaetus	osprey	NJ-T, PA-T; G5
Passerculus sandwichensis	savannah sparrow	NJ-T; G5
Podilymbus podiceps	pied-billed grebe	CT-E, NJ-E, NY-T; G5
Pooecetes gramineus	vesper sparrow	CT-E, NJ-T; G5
Progne subis	purple martin	CT-T; G5
Rallus elegans	king rail	PA-E; G4
Strix varia	barred owl	NJ-T; G5

(continued)

Appendix 10.1 List of Threatened and Endangered Animal Species Reported from Connecticut, New Jersey, New York, and Pennsylvania Highlands, *continued*

Scientific name	Common name	State, federal, and global protection status[a]
Tyto alba	barn owl	CT-E; G5
Vermivora chrysoptera	golden-winged warbler	CT-E; G4
Reptiles		
Crotalus horridus	timber rattlesnake	CT-E, NJ-E, NY-T; G4
Emydoidea blandingii	Blanding's turtle	NY-T; G4
Eumeces fasciatus	five-lined skink	CT-T; G5
Glyptemys insculpta	wood turtle	NJ-T; G4
Glyptemys muhlenbergii	bog turtle	CT-E, NJ-E, NY-E, PA-E, US-T; G3
Pseudemys rubriventris	red-bellied turtle	PA-T; G5
Sceloperous undulatus	eastern fence lizard	NY-T; G5
Amphibians		
Acris crepitans	northern cricket frog	NY-E; G5
Ambystoma laterale	blue-spotted salamander	CT-T (diploid pops only), NJ-E; G5
Eurycea longicauda	long-tailed salamander	NJ-T; G5
Gyrinophilus porphyriticus	northern spring salamander	CT-T; G5
Plethodon glutinosus	northern slimy salamander	CT-T; G5
Pseudacris triseriata kalmi	New Jersey chorus frog	PA-E; G4
Pseudotriton montanus montanus	eastern mud salamander	PA-E; G5
Scaphiopus holbrookii	eastern spadefoot toad	PA-E; G5
Fish		
Acipenser brevirostrum	shortnose sturgeon	NJ-E, NY-E, US-E; G3
Lota lota	burbot	CT-E; G5
Notropsis chalybaeus	ironcolor shiner	PA-E; G4
Invertebrates		
Alasmidonta heterodon	dwarf wedgemussel	CT-E, NJ-E, NY-E, US-E; G1G2
Alasmidonta undulata	triangle floater	NJ-E; G4
Alasmidonta varicosa	brook floater	NJ-E, NY-T; G3
Lampsilis abruptus	pink mucket	NY-E, US-E; G2
Lampsilis fasciola	wavy-rayed lampmussel	NY-T; G5
Lampsilis radiata	eastern lampmussel	NJ-T; G5
Lasmigona subviridis	green floater	NJ-E, NY-T; G3
Liguma nasuta	eastern pondmussel	NJ-T; G4
Margaritifera margaritifera	eastern pearlshell	PA-E; G4G5
Pleurobema clara	clubshell	NY-E, US-E; G2
Potamilus capax	fat pocketbook	NY-E, US-E; G1G2

(*continued*)

Appendix 10.1 List of Threatened and Endangered Animal Species Reported from Connecticut, New Jersey, New York, and Pennsylvania Highlands, *continued*

Scientific name	Common name	State, federal, and global protection status[a]
Insects		
Amblyscirtes vialis	common roadside skipper	CT-T; G4
Anarta luteola	noctuid moth	CT-E; G5
Atrytone arogos arogos	arogos skipper	NJ-E, NY-E; G3
Bolaria selene myrina	silver-bordered fritillary	NJ-E; G5
Calephelis borealis	northern metalmark	CT-E, NJ-E; G3G4
Callophrys hesseli	Hessel's hairstreak	CT-E, NY-T; G3G4
Callophrys irus	frosted elfin	CT-T, NJ-E, NY-T; G3
Catocala herodias gerhardi	Herodias underwing	CT-E; G3
Cordulegaster erronea	tiger spiketail	CT-T; G4
Enallagma minisculum	little bluet	NY-T; G4
Erynnis lucilius	columbine duskywing	CT-E; G4
Erynnis persius persius	Persius duskywing	CT-E, NY-T; G5
Euphyes bimacula	two-spotted skipper	CT-T; G4
Euphyes dion	sedge (Dion) skipper	CT-T; G4
Gomphus adelphus	mustached clubtail	CT-T; G4
Gomphus descriptus	harpoon clubtail	CT-T; G4
Gomphus quadricolor	rapids clubtail	CT-T; G3G4
Grammia speciosa	bog tiger moth	CT-E; G5
Hemaris gracilis	slender clearwing	CT-T; G3G4
Hetaerina americana	American rubyspot	CT-T; G5
Hybomitra frosti	horsefly	CT-T; GNR
Hybomitra longiglossa	horsefly	CT-E; GNR
Itame sp. 1 nr. *inextricata*	barrens itame	CT-T; G3G4
Leucorrhinia glacialis	crimson-winged whiteface	CT-T; G5
Metarranthis apiciaria	barrens metarranthis moth	CT-E; G1G3
Mitoura hesseli]	Hessel's hairstreak	CT-E; G3G4
Neonympha mitchellii mitchellii	Mitchell's satyr	NJ-E, US-E; G2
Papaipema appassionata	pitcher plant borer	CT-E; G4
Papaipema leucostigma	columbine borer	CT-T; G4
Phyllonorycter ledella	Labrador tea tentiform leafminer	CT-E; GNR
Pontia protodice	checkered white	NJ-T; G4
Psectraglaea carnosa	pink sallow	CT-T; G3
Pyrgus syandot	Appalachian grizzled skipper	NJ-E; G1G2
Speyeria atlantis	Atlantis fritillary butterfly	CT-T; G5

(*continued*)

Appendix 10.1 List of Threatened and Endangered Animal Species Reported from Connecticut, New Jersey, New York, and Pennsylvania Highlands, *continued*

State or Federal (U.S.) Designations

E   The species is listed as endangered in that state or the United States.

T   The species is listed as threatened in that state.

SC   "Special concern." The species is not listed as endangered or threatened but is tracked by the state Heritage Program.

Global Element Ranks (as Ranked by the Nature Conservancy)

G1   Critically imperiled globally because of extreme rarity.

G2   Imperiled globally because of rarity.

G3   Either very rare and local throughout its range or found locally.

G4   Apparently secure globally, although it may be quite rare in parts of its range, especially at the periphery.

G5   Demonstrably secure globally, although it may be quite rare in parts of its range, especially at the periphery.

GH   Of historical occurrence throughout its range.

GNR   Global rank not yet assessed.

GU   Possibly in peril range-wide but status uncertain; more information needed.

Note: To express uncertainty, the most likely rank is assigned and a question mark added (e.g., G2?). A range is indicated by combining two ranks (e.g., G1G2).

[a] List of states in which the species is tracked by the Heritage Program and has been recorded from the Highlands region in that state. The absence of a state from the third column can mean several things, including that the species is (1) not known from that state; (2) known from that state but is not tracked as rare, threatened, or endangered by the state Heritage program; (3) known from that state, is tracked as rare, threatened, or endangered, but is not known from the Highlands region of that state, or (4) not recognized as taxonomically distinct by the state Heritage Program. Note that this list may change in the future with new species added and other species removed as their status changes.

    There are many species that are considered species of special concern by various states and others not listed that are tracked by the state natural heritage programs that are not on this list.

Part IV

People and the Land

When considering the lush forested vistas of the present-day Highlands, it is easy to overlook this region's previous incarnation as a center of early American industry. Chapter 11 lays out the history of the iron industry and the Highlands' role in helping to forge America's rise as an industrial giant. The iron industry also helped shape the development of the region's rail and canal infrastructure of the nineteenth century. While most of the ironworks are long gone, the Morris Canal defunct, and the minor rail lines abandoned, the iron industry and associated transportation networks helped set the template of later urban development in the twentieth century. Not to be forgotten is the agricultural heritage of the Highlands, which was regionally significant in the nineteenth century. Chapter 12 recounts how farming across the Highlands quickly evolved from an initial subsistence phase to a commercial phase oriented to supporting the rapidly growing urban centers of the mid-Atlantic and southern New England. By the mid-1800s agriculture in the region was on the wane, afflicted by, among other troubles, increased competition from the newly settled American Midwest. While much diminished, this agricultural heritage still lives on in some of the more fertile Highlands valleys, especially in the southern Highlands of New Jersey and Pennsylvania. As introduced in part III, the agricultural and industrial abandonment of the land allowed the regrowth of the forest during the latter half of the nineteenth and into the twentieth century.

As northeastern U.S. urban populations expanded, enhanced transportation and greater amounts of leisure time enabled a return to the land—this time for recreation. The Highlands saw many "firsts" in the development of American outdoor recreation—early resort development, leadership in the state parks movement, completion of the first leg of the Appalachian Trail (chapter 13). The mid- to late twentieth century saw the beginnings of a major transformation of the Highlands. Post–World War II population growth, increasing affluence, and the birth of the state and interstate highway system unleashed a massive wave of sprawling suburbanization. Concern about the loss of the Highlands' wild and scenic character, in particular the

Hudson Highlands and Storm King as iconic American grandeur, spurred the growth of the environmental movement and the push for more stringent land-use planning. There is increasing recognition that development does not always constitute the "highest and best use" of the land and that the Highlands geology and topography put real constraints on acceptable land uses.

As discussed in chapter 14, the region serves as a test bed for multistate cooperation in the form of the four-state Highlands Conservation Area as well as state-level planning as mandated by the New Jersey Water Protection and Planning Act. As made clear in chapter 15, a failure by these aforementioned conservation initiatives and a "business as usual" continuation of existing development trends will lead to further reductions in forests and farmlands and a reduction in watershed integrity. A future vision for the Highlands is laid out, where large tracts of unfragmented forest help to sustain watershed integrity, uncluttered vistas, and thriving communities within a working landscape.

11

Ironworking in the Highlands

Theodore W. Kury and Peter O. Wacker

Introduction

When the coming of the Iron Age in the Old World supplanted the use of bronze for implements and weapons, the search for iron ores and the means to reduce them to metallic iron became of paramount importance. In the European encounter with eastern North America, iron ore was one of the valued resources. Early surveyors, frustrated at having their magnetic compasses malfunction owing to the enormous deposits of iron-rich magnetite in the Highlands (Reading Prong of the New England upland), alerted entrepreneurs to the possibilities of exploiting this resource. In addition to the ore itself, vast wooded tracts could be used for charcoal to provide the fuel for reducing the iron ore. The power needed to provide air introduced into both forge and furnace to aid combustion was readily accomplished by harnessing the abundant waterpower readily available in this humid, well-watered region. Local limestone provided the flux, which was added to the mixture of ore and charcoal to combine with impurities in the ore to render relatively pure metallic iron. The diminution of forested areas due to either clear-cutting for agriculture or overharvesting for the production of charcoal led eventually to the use of anthracite coal, readily available in the relatively nearby Lehigh Valley of Pennsylvania. This chapter delves into both the technological and cultural history of the Highlands iron industry during the eighteenth and nineteenth centuries as well as the transportation infrastructure it spawned. Selected iron industry sites are explored to further illustrate the impact that the industry had in shaping the region.

Iron Industry

Initially, iron complexes depending on charcoal had three often-complementary components: bloomeries, forges, and furnaces that were derived from English and German antecedents.[1] The first type of ironworks sited in the

Highlands as a whole, and the most common for the entire iron period, was the bloomery forge. Bloomeries consisted of one or two stone hearths or "fires." These were constructed very much like a blacksmith's forge and were accompanied by a waterwheel-driven bellows and a waterwheel-powered helve hammer (also known as a trip-hammer). The massive helve hammer was lifted by a cam (activated by a waterwheel) located between the fulcrum and the head of the hammer. The production of bar iron at a bloomery involved the acquisition of relatively rich iron ore located nearby. This was broken into small pieces and placed in a hearth along with the flux (limestone) and large quantities of charcoal. As the ore softened from the heat, forgemen worked it with a long bar until a lump of metallic iron, known as the bloom or loop, was formed. The pasty ball of iron was withdrawn from the forge proper and placed on an anvil to be pounded under the helve hammer. Successive returns to the forge for reheating and to the anvil drove out most of the impurities. The resulting bar iron was useful for local fashioning into agrarian and household utensils.

Bloomeries were relatively small enterprises, with maximum production of about one ton of bar iron per week. Bloomery bar iron brought a price much higher than pig iron but less than bar iron refined from pig iron because of the relatively larger amounts of impurities in the bloomery iron. Bloomeries were often simply referred to as forges, since their product was also bar iron. These manufactories remained economically viable well into the nineteenth century because they could take advantage of locally smaller supplies of charcoal. Thus, they were sited, in many cases, in relatively rugged, well-watered locations within the glaciated portions of the Highlands where an adequate supply of wood could be had because permanent agricultural settlement had not taken place.

The type of iron manufactory (other than the bloomery) that came to be most identified with the Highlands was the blast furnace (fig. 11.1). Although somewhat varied in size and shape, the blast furnace usually took the form of a four-sided stack of native stone (abundant in the Highlands) some twenty to thirty-five feet high and twenty to twenty-five feet square at the base. The widest portion of the inner part of the stack, or bosh, usually was about nine feet in diameter. The interior of the stack was lined with a refractory material (able to maintain itself at high temperatures), often sandstone and, later, firebrick. The stack was open at both ends and rested on a square chamber called the hearth. This was built of sandstone or firebrick. On each side of the stack were arches that extended into the masonry and helped support the structure.

The furnace was generally built near a low rise from which a wooden or log bridge was built to allow loads of iron ore, limestone, and charcoal to be placed alternately in the top of the furnace (see plate 29). An opening (tuyere)

Figure 11.1. Beckley Furnace, East Canaan, Conn., part of the Salisbury Iron District. The blast furnace has been restored and is open to the public. Note that the interior chamber of the stone stack is lined with firebrick forming the bosh, where iron ore, charcoal, and limestone flux were fired. In this restoration, the interior of the bosh (which narrows to form the crucible) and the hearth are exposed for better viewing. Photo by Richard Lathrop.

through an arch into the masonry stack (see plate 30) provided passage for air blasts pumped into the furnace by leather bellows activated by a waterwheel. Later the bellows were replaced by piston-driven wooden tubs that were also connected to a waterwheel, and later still, by a blowing engine. Once a furnace had been "blowed in" (started operating), the process was continuous. A stream of air forced by the bellows, activated by a waterwheel, entered the stack through the tuyere. The air intensified combustion of the charcoal, which melted the iron ore and limestone. The latter combined with impurities in the ore to produce slag (fused and vitrified material) that separated from the molten iron. Both molten iron and slag accumulated in the hearth before being drawn off.

In front of the furnace, either protected by a simple roof or in an enclosed structure, was the casting or molding shed or house (plate 29). On the floor of this building (see plate 31) was a bed of sand into which the molten iron from the hearth was channeled into a series of troughs, where the iron cooled and solidified into bars of "pig iron." The resulting "pig iron" was so named because the main channel of molten iron, or "sow iron," fed iron into branching channels in the sand in a pattern that resembled a sow suckling piglets. The molten iron could also be run into a series of molds to produce various iron products. Included were holloware, tools, stove plates, munitions, and the like. This was cast iron. The productive capacity of furnaces varied. The Durham Furnace in the Pennsylvania portion of the Reading Prong opposite the Musconetcong valley in the New Jersey Highlands fabricated three tons of pig iron every day. The typical work crew for such furnaces was a little over a dozen men, working in two twelve-hour shifts.

Nineteenth-century innovations greatly enhanced the efficiency and productivity of the blast furnace. Following its successful introduction at Oxford Furnace in New Jersey in the 1830s, a hot-air blast quickly replaced the older cold-air blast systems. To achieve a hot blast, air from the bellows was passed through a stove located on the top of the furnace, where it was warmed by the waste heat emitted by the furnace before it was introduced into the bosh. This technology resulted in higher smelting temperatures, increased production, and reduced the amount of charcoal fuel required. As the abundant deposits of anthracite coal in nearby Pennsylvania became easily accessible, experiments were undertaken to replace increasingly scarce charcoal with anthracite. The hotter, more consistent burning of this new fuel led to the construction of larger, higher-capacity furnaces, some attaining heights upward of forty feet with base dimensions extending to thirty feet or more, which required added support from iron rods or bands wrapped around the native stone stack.

Associated with furnaces were the refining forges, where the bars of pig iron could be made into a tougher, less brittle product. The refinery forge consisted of two hearths, covered with heaps of coals and surmounted by huge chimneys, and a massive helve hammer operated by a waterwheel. Also powered by water were bellows introducing blasts of air to each open hearth. The first hearth used in the process was known as the finery. Here the pig iron was successively reheated and hammered to remove impurities and lengthen the iron fibers (a texture caused by residual traces of slag). The result was an "ancony," a bar of wrought iron. This was flat, thick, and had a rough knob at each end. Anconies were generally reheated at the next hearth, known as the "chafery," and placed under the helve hammer to be worked into the "bar iron" of commerce.

Individual pieces of bar iron varied greatly in size but were typically about fourteen feet long, two inches wide, and one-half inch thick. This was what a blacksmith would use as raw material. Bar iron was easily marketable everywhere and could be fashioned locally into products such as anchors or converted into plates, hoops (for the ever-present casks and barrels of commerce), or straps in a rolling mill. These mills also produced rods that were then transferred to slitting mills for the manufacture of nails. The refining of pig iron into bar iron resulted in the loss of some metal, increased consumption of charcoal, and greater use of labor; thus, bar iron and its finished products sold for several times the price of pig iron.

The iron industry played a major role in transforming the Highlands landscape. Its largely self-contained communities were often referred to as "iron plantations." First, workers had to be housed and fed. For the smaller forge communities, scattered log houses would serve for housing, and food could be locally grown or acquired from local agrarian communities. Indeed, workers had their own gardens and ran livestock in the woods. Furnace activities required an even larger footprint on the landscape. There would be more houses and a "mansion" for the resident iron master. The iron master's house might be of stone construction, symbolizing the authority of the man in charge. There would be a company store where workers could get their daily necessities—possibly including liquor, but in many cases taverns and the availability of alcohol were restricted to avoid drunkenness on the job. From the beginning, the iron industry depended on waterpower, often involving impoundments and the excavation of millraces. Other industrial enterprises depending on waterpower, such as a gristmill or sawmill, might also be present. There would be coal houses for keeping the charcoal fuel dry. There generally would be a blacksmith's shop. If agriculture was being carried on by the furnace company, the landscape would reflect this with structures devoted to storage and the protection of livestock (which, in any case, was necessary owing to the need to transport raw materials and finished products by horse or ox-drawn wagon). Of course, there was also the major by-product of iron production, slag. This had to be disposed of, altering the soil composition of the iron sites, or used as fill at the site, slightly changing local topography.

The mining operations associated with furnaces also transformed the Highlands landscape. Mining usually began in the spring and carried on as long as the furnace was in blast. (Icing in the watercourse that served the furnace generally caused operations there to cease for the season.) The deposits of iron ore were opened by miners, also referred to as ore raisers in several early ledgers and help-wanted advertisements. They worked the open pits and trenches with pickaxes, pry bars, shovels, and hand drills, then washed dirt and grit from the ore and loaded it on wagons for transport to the furnace. In the earliest days, once the pits or trenches reached a depth of twenty to forty feet, the mine was abandoned and a new deposit was opened.

By the end of the eighteenth century, shaft mining had begun. Guided by

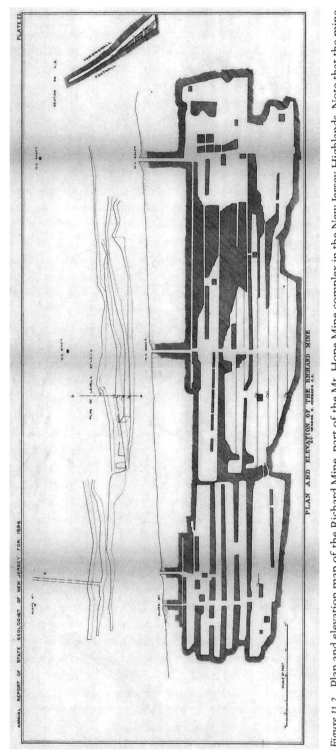

Figure 11.2. Plan and elevation map of the Richard Mine, part of the Mt. Hope Mine complex in the New Jersey Highlands. Note that the mine chambers reach a depth of nearly six hundred feet below the surface and extend horizontally for over one-third of a mile. Photo: Annual Report of the State Geologist of New Jersey for 1896. Courtesy of the NJDEP-NJGS Map Archive of New Jersey's Abandoned Mines, Trenton, NJ.

candles or lanterns, miners used black powder to construct adits (horizontal entrances), drifts (an approximately horizontal passageway), and vertical shafts from which the iron ore and rock burden was excavated. The ore was then hauled to the surface in animal-drawn carts or, later, railcars. As the mines penetrated the groundwater table, steam engines were needed to pump out the continual seepage of water. In areas of especially rich ores where mining went on over a number of years, some of the shafts became very deep and complex (fig. 11.2). If not filled in properly, these were subject to subsidence, endangering latter-day construction at the site. Trailing heaps (the residue of the mining efforts with most of the ore removed) and water-filled open pits would remain on the surface.

Charcoal was absolutely necessary because, until well into the 1840s, it was the only fuel known in America that could attain temperatures high enough to melt iron ore. Charcoal had several distinct advantages. It was almost free of sulfur, an iron contaminant, and its ash provided lime and alkalines, which supplied part of the flux needed in smelting. Depletion of forest resources eventually became a problem for the Highlands iron industry, especially where productive agricultural soils could be found southwest of the terminal moraine, bringing about a decline in the number of forges and furnaces owing to a lack of fuel.

The first step in procuring charcoal was to fell the trees, trim, and cut them into four-foot lengths called billets (fig. 11.3a). Wood chopping was an off-season activity, so temporarily unemployed furnace workers and locals involved in agriculture, usually idled during the cold season, were employed to chop the wood. The "green" wood was then allowed to properly season. Bining (1938) has an interesting discussion of the charcoal-making process. It took several colliers to "coal" felled timber—as many as a dozen to supply a furnace. The billets of wood were stacked and covered with leaves and then "dusted" with dirt to slow down the combustion (figs. 11.3b, 11.3c). Two or three master colliers supervised "helpers" who were obliged to tend the piles of wood day and night in the process of charring. Thus, they had to live onsite in impermanent structures, which were no better than hovels. After the pile was charred, the smoldering charcoal was raked out of the mound to cool (fig. 11.3d). Once the possibility of spontaneous combustion had passed, the charcoal was hauled to one or more charcoal houses near the furnace, generally constructed with thick stone walls. The charcoal house could store only a relatively small amount of charcoal, and it would not do for the charcoal to get wet, so charcoal production was an ongoing activity during the blast period. The remains of charcoal pits may still be observed in some locations where the extreme heat generated by repeatedly burning charcoal at the same place so changed soil conditions that only grasses and small shrubs characterize the later vegetative cover.

Figure 11.3. Photos of a charcoal mound constructed as a demonstration at the Hopewell Furnace National Historic Park, circa 1936. (a) Hauling the hardwood billets (note the basket for collecting charcoal in lower left of image). (b) Stacked tiers of billets. (c) Covering ("dusting") the mound with dirt before firing. (d) Raking out finished charcoal. National Park Service, Hopewell Furnace National Historic Site, Pa.

Canals and Roads

Many raw materials that the ironworks needed and their finished products had to be transported. Initially, roads were built or improved, and watercourses (such as the Hudson, Delaware, and Schuylkill rivers) were used. Viewed at first as an avenue for marketing anthracite coal in New York City, the Morris Canal, which opened in 1831 and was extended to Jersey City opposite Manhattan in 1836, spanned the New Jersey Highlands to connect the Hudson River with the Delaware River and the Lehigh Valley by way of the Lehigh Navigation Canal (fig. 11.4). The Morris Canal was an engineering marvel in its day; it climbed 760 feet from its beginning at Phillipsburg on the Delaware, opposite Easton, Pennsylvania, to its summit near Lake Hopatcong, and then

c

d

descended 914 feet to its terminus at Jersey City. In crossing the Highlands, a series of inclined planes and locks were used to raise and lower the canal boats. In all, twenty-three inclined planes and twenty-three locks made the passage feasible.

The route of the Morris Canal was of great significance later when anthracite coal from the Lehigh Valley came into wide use in the Highlands' blast furnaces. Iron production was especially favored at places such as Phillipsburg (originally Port Delaware), Stanhope, Wharton, Rockaway, Boonton, and Dover, where anthracite could be relatively inexpensively delivered to sources of rich magnetite ore. The canal boats at first were loaded at Mauch Chunk, Pennsylvania, and crossed the Delaware from Easton using a cable. Later, after the development of railroads and a bridge spanning the Delaware River, the coal was brought in by rail and the canal boats were loaded on the New Jersey side. An example of just how much coal was used early on by the iron industry was that in 1847, by no means the premier year of use, 61,951 tons of anthracite from the Lehigh Valley entered the canal at Phillipsburg to be transported across New Jersey. However, by the time the coal reached the

Hudson River to be taken by lighter (barge) across to Manhattan, only 17,883 tons remained. What should have been a major function of the canal, delivering anthracite to Manhattan, was not being served. Instead, the bulk of the coal was being "appropriated" by the iron industry.

Despite its abandonment in 1924, the canal left lasting imprints on the New Jersey Highlands. Along much of the former canal route lie remnants of the canal prism (excavation), embankments, locks, planes, and employee housing. Lake Hopatcong, originally enlarged by the construction of a dam to power the eighteenth-century Brooklyn (Brookland) forge, was further impounded behind an even larger dam, almost doubling the lake's surface area to ensure adequate water for the eastern portion of the canal. The subsequent impoundment of Lake Musconetcong ensured sufficient water for both the canal's western division and the future furnaces at Stanhope. Existing

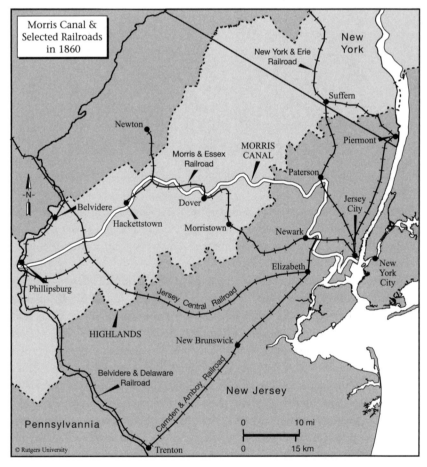

Figure 11.4. Map showing the route of the Morris Canal and important railways associated with the New Jersey Highlands iron industry, 1860. © Rutgers University.

Highland settlements such as Boonton, Rockaway, Dover, and Waterloo Village gained further prominence because of industrial development and traffic generated by the canal. Relic place-names serve to trace the canal route for the modern traveler. Port Morris, Shippenport, Port Murray, and Port Colden are today far removed from any commercial water link.

The failure of the Morris Canal to meet the demands for anthracite coal in New York City necessitated the development of an alternate means of transport. That need, as well as the need to also supply the expanding iron industry, was to be served by the railroads. Although the New Jersey railroads immediately followed the canals in establishment, their penetration of the Highlands lagged.

Railroads had several advantages over canals. The first was that water (other than that needed for servicing the steam engines) was not needed in quantity. Grade was less of an obstacle, with no need for locks to overcome gentle grades. Steep grades did not need inclined planes. They could eventually be overcome with expensive switchbacks or, later, even more expensive tunnels. Trains had a much greater capacity to move bulk cargo. Three railcars carried as much freight as the largest canal boat. Trains were also much faster. A train could move across New Jersey in eight hours; a canal boat took five days. Trains required far less manpower per unit of bulk moved and could easily be unloaded by gravity feed (with the train brought in at a higher level than the point of delivery). Frozen water, which halted canal traffic in winter, was not an issue.

The Central Railroad of New Jersey (better known as the Jersey Central) reached Phillipsburg in 1852 with the objective of picking up coal from the Lehigh Canal (fig. 11.4). Its competitor and contemporary, the Morris and Essex Railroad Company, had reached Dover by 1848 but did not push on. Also entering the competition to secure coal were the Delaware, Lackawanna & Western (the Lackawanna) and the Lehigh Valley (the Lehigh) railroads. These lines were founded by three entrepreneurs—John Blair (Blairstown and Blair Academy are namesakes) and George and Selden Scranton, who were purchasers of Oxford Furnace. Another "player" in the coal game was created with the founding of the Belvidere Delaware Railroad (the Bel-Del) in 1836. This line was also planned to reach Phillipsburg. In 1854 the Bel-Del was hauling pig iron from Phillipsburg to Trenton. At the time, a unique bilevel bridge was being built across the Delaware at Phillipsburg. The top level connected the Lehigh Valley Railroad with the Jersey Central. The lower level connected Lehigh Valley coal cars to the Bel-Del tracks.

The iron-oriented railroad network serving the Hudson Highlands was far less complex. Initial attempts at railroad building in New York followed the path of the Hudson River and Erie Canal. In 1832 a charter was granted to the New York and Erie Railroad ("the Erie") enabling it to construct a competing broad-gauge line from its eastern terminus at Piermont on the Hudson (fig. 11.4) westward to Dunkirk on Lake Erie. The main line of the Erie through the Ramapo valley was completed by the early 1840s, which allowed the two-way transport of iron ore, pig iron, and necessary supplies. Within a few years the Erie line was extended to an additional eastern terminal at Jersey City, which gave direct access to New York City. The increased use of Highlands iron ore in the blast furnaces in the Lehigh and Schuylkill valleys of Eastern Pennsylvania after the mid-nineteenth century was facilitated by linkages between the Erie and the Lackawanna and Pennsylvania railroads.

Individual Iron Sites

What follows is a discussion of subregions of the Highlands and selected individual sites where data are available and relevant to support generalizations made in the chapter introduction. However, even with relatively well-documented sites there are often temporal gaps in the record.[2]

The Pennsylvania Highlands

Pennsylvania has long occupied a leading role in the production of iron products. For much of the colonial period it ranked behind only the Chesapeake Bay area in the quantity and value of its iron products. This was in large measure due to the commercial prominence of Philadelphia and the natural resources available in eastern Pennsylvania. From the close of the Revolutionary War until well into the twentieth century, Pennsylvania held the nation's first rank in the manufacture of iron. Industrial enterprises within and adjacent to the Reading Prong were critical components of this industrial dominance.

After crossing through New Jersey, the Reading Prong extends beyond the Delaware River south of present-day Easton, Pennsylvania, as it continues a northeasterly–southwesterly trend to a vaguely defined terminus at the Schuylkill watershed. As elaborated on in chapter 1, deposits of magnetite, red hematite, and brown hematite are located all across the Highlands region. The hematite ores are concentrated along the Highlands flanks and the southern terminus. The magnetite iron deposits become sparse beyond the Delaware valley and then form significant deposits once again along the southern margins of the Reading Prong. The magnetite ore bodies in the vicinity of Cornwall, known as the Cornwall Ore Banks, were the largest and most bountiful in the entire Highlands region and were considered one of the most important east of Lake Superior (figs. 11.5 and 11.6 [location 1]) (Eggert 1994). Both strip and underground mining were used to extract iron ore from the Cornwall Ore Banks for well over two hundred years from the 1730s to 1973, when the mine ceased operation (Oblinger 1984). Owing to the paucity of large-scale ore bodies between the Delaware and Schuylkill valleys, the

Figure 11.5. Open-pit mine excavation at the Cornwall Ore Banks, Pa., circa 1880s, one of the largest and richest iron ore deposits in the eastern United States. During the 1880s steam shovels replaced hand loading of iron ore. The Pennsylvania State Archives.

iron industry became concentrated in the Delaware-Lehigh region and along the Schuylkill River.

Entrepreneurial interests from Philadelphia dominated the wave of iron manufactory construction and operation in the region prior to the Revolutionary War. Following the establishment of the initial ironworks within the Reading Prong—Rutter's forge in 1716 and the Colebrookdale Furnace near Pottstown about 1720 (fig. 11.6 [location 3])—some forty-seven ironworks were erected in eastern Pennsylvania between 1720 and 1780 (Bining 1938). Of that number, some eight furnaces and seventeen forges were concentrated in Berks County with the remainder in Chester, Lebanon, and Montgomery counties—all of these establishments having convenient overland and riverine access to Philadelphia and its domestic and export markets. The sole furnace enumerated for Bucks County was located at Durham (fig. 11.6 [location 4]) in the northern sector convenient to the Delaware River. Although the principal outlet for Durham pigs was the Philadelphia market, pig iron was also supplied in quantity to the Chelsea and Greenwich forges (fig. 11.6 [locations 5

Figure 11.6. Selected ironworks of the Highlands region (numbered sequentially from southwest to northeast): (1) Cornwall, (2) Hopewell, (3) Colebrookdale, (4) Durham, (5) Chelsea, (6) Greenwich, (7) Oxford, (8) Whippany, (9) Andover, (10) Edison, (11) Mt. Hope, (12) Hibernia, (13) Pompton, (14) Ringwood, (15) Long Pond, (16) Wawayanda, (17) Sterling, (18) Southfield, (19) Greenwood, (20) Forest of Dean, (21) West Point Foundry, (22) Philipse Iron Belt, (23) Kent, (24) Lakeville, and (25) Canaan. © Rutgers University.

and 6]) in the Musconetcong valley of New Jersey, where it was transformed into bars for market (Chelsea Forge Journal, Greenwich Forge).

Although iron manufacture in Pennsylvania diffused southward into the South Mountains and westward beyond the Susquehanna River into the Juniata region of central Pennsylvania during the early decades of the nineteenth century, the strength of the Philadelphia market continued to support the Highlands industrial sites. Reports compiled for the census of 1830 indicated that Berks County was still the home of eleven furnaces and twenty-three forges and bloomeries (McLane 1833). With the evolution of transportation and improvements in the design and fueling of the blast furnaces, the iron industry continued its growth. Lesley's survey of 1857 identified as least twenty-five furnaces (sixteen fueled by anthracite, nine by charcoal) and fourteen forges and bloomeries within or adjacent to the confines of the Reading Prong. Additionally, some eight rolling mills were found in the Pottstown-Reading area (Lesley 1866). Toward the end of the nineteenth century, further technological changes (the use of coke as fuel and the introduction of the Bessemer and open-hearth processes for steel making) and the exploitation of high-quality hematite iron ores in the Upper Great Lakes basin (e.g., the Mesabi

Iron Range of Minnesota) brought about a gradual decline in the iron industry and a shift in focus toward western Pennsylvania and the Great Lakes region. The industry maintained a presence in the Schuylkill valley through a reliance on imported foreign ores and an emphasis on steel fabrication and processing.

There is a fairly good record concerning Durham Furnace (Durham Historical Society), which was located about one and a half miles inland from the Delaware, opposite the mouth of the Musconetcong River on the Jersey side. The presence of rich iron ore there was known as early as 1698, but the site was remote from markets. A Philadelphia-based stock company established a furnace to exploit these rich ores in 1727. The size of the tracts purchased, 6,900 acres initially and expanded to 8,511 acres by 1773, indicates an interest in providing enough woodland to support sustained charcoal production and an "iron plantation," also devoted to producing food for workers and feed for livestock. Waterpower was furnished by Cook's Creek, now known as Durham Creek. A raceway three-quarters of a mile long was dug to deliver the water, which also served three nearby forges and a stamping mill. There were also dams, which served to impound water. A "mansion house" probably served to house the manager. Limestone for flux was readily available, and limestone kiln pits are still apparent on the landscape.

The Durham complex and its associated forges in the Musconetcong valley of New Jersey produced not only pig iron but also bar iron and cast-iron pans, utensils, and stove plates, including the famous "Franklin Stove." Pig iron and bar iron from the New Jersey forges crossed the Delaware at Stillwell Ferry. The famed Durham boat, invented specifically to navigate the Delaware River rapids at Trenton, conveyed these products to Philadelphia. During the Revolution, the Durham complex produced cannons, cannonballs, shot, and other military equipment for the Continental Army. The charcoal furnace "blew out" in 1791.

Furnace operations were begun again in 1849 with two new anthracite-fueled furnaces. To understand what a furnace community of this period entailed, consider the following: In 1873 fifty-eight buildings were associated with the works. These included dwellings for 125 families, with two being for superintendents. A church, a store, and a post office served the employees. There was a stone farmhouse and a large stone barn along with three smaller barns, attesting to the agricultural activities of the works and probably to the need to house horses used to haul wagons of raw materials and finished products. Immediately associated with the works were two furnaces with associated engines and machinery, a foundry building of 160 by 60 feet, and a machine shop of 300 by 50 feet, run by waterpower. This produced one hundred horsepower "at the driest time." There was also a pattern shop, case maker's shop, smith, wheelwright, and saddler's shops, stock houses, and a cart house.

In 1874 and 1875 the old works were torn down, rebuilt, and remodeled; they continued to use ore mostly from nearby mines. After struggling along at low capacity, the furnace again fell into disuse until completion of the Quakertown and Easton Railroad, which presumably delivered relatively inexpensive anthracite fuel. The works ceased operating in 1908, and the furnace was dismantled a few years afterward.

The Southern New Jersey Highlands

The general view of the settlement of the unglaciated southern New Jersey Highlands was that they were settled first by ironworkers who later were replaced by agriculturists when deforestation had removed the vital charcoal fuel source. Thomas F. Gordon in 1834 wrote that the first settlers of the Highlands were "rather manufacturers than agriculturists; and the narrow valleys of the mountain region, which contain many and excellent mill seats, were only partially tilled for the subsistence of wood cutters and bloomers. The forge was universally the precursor of the farm. The iron master occupied large tracts of land, which, when stripped of timber, were subdivided among agricultural successors, operating on the smallest scale." Current research has shown this to be not entirely true. For example, farmers were settled at the mouth of the Musconetcong River in the New Jersey Highlands by 1705, and the valley itself was being settled in the 1730s. This was up to several decades prior to the establishment of ironworks there in the 1740s and 1750s.

A long-lasting furnace located in New Jersey's southern Highlands but outside the Musconetcong valley, for which extensive records exist, was Oxford Furnace (fig. 11.6 [location 7]), established in 1742. This was located on a branch of the Pequest River near a very rich source of iron ore. Starting in 1749, Dr. William Shippen of Philadelphia purchased the furnace. His son Joseph took over the operations and built and lived in Shippen Manor, a truly impressive iron master's mansion. Production at Oxford waxed and waned over the next two centuries. In 1835 Oxford Furnace installed a "hot air apparatus," which passed air from the bellows through a stove located on the top of the furnace using waste heat to warm the air being sent into the bosh, thus creating higher smelting temperatures and saving fuel. The device did not work well at first but with tinkering finally began to produce an acceptable product using less charcoal. In 1839 the furnace was sold to George W. Scranton and Selden T. Scranton. The Scranton name, of course, became famous in iron manufacture in the Pennsylvania city that bears the family name. The Scrantons lost the property in the financial crash of 1873. The foreclosed property was sold and then saw a series of owner-operators. Although the furnace was finally closed in 1921, the iron mines operated into the 1960s. The state of New Jersey acquired the furnace and Shippen Manor but subsequently, owing to financial problems, transferred both properties to Warren County as a historical site.

Glaciated Highlands of New Jersey and New York

From the earliest colonial times, government officials and settlers held conflicting views of the Highlands north of the Pleistocene terminal moraine. To some, the rugged, forested ridges seemed incapable of sustaining permanent settlement, especially those lands not conducive to agricultural improvement or beyond the reach of convenient transportation. To others, the reports of iron ore, good falls of water for potential mill seats, and the ample forests suggested resource availability that could provide a foundation for industrial development if proper encouragement was given.

Settlers initially encroached on the glaciated portions of the Highlands when land surveyed along the Whippany River, a tributary of the Passaic, for the East Jersey Proprietors as early as 1714 was found to be sufficiently endowed with natural resources to support both farmer and iron maker. A bloomery, one of the first ironworks reported in the entire Highlands, was erected at what is now Whippany by 1720 (fig. 11.6 [location 8]). While in operation, it fashioned wrought iron into diverse agricultural implements and household articles from ores transported from the mine at Succasunna. Within a few years other bloomeries were set up nearby at Troy, Mendham, and along the lower Rockaway River. Many of these lasted only a few decades, as both iron makers and encroaching farmers cleared the land of timber.

In the following decades, stable supplies of timberland within reach of substantial iron deposits propelled entrepreneurs to venture deeper into the Highlands. Individuals and corporate interests that possessed sufficient financial resources and a knowledge of iron making took title to the large landholdings necessary to support their enterprises. Initial attention was drawn to the resource-rich lands along the then ill-defined New Jersey–New York border. Because the border between the two states was not confirmed until 1769, both the East Jersey Proprietors and holders of the Cheesecock Patent often issued competing land claims prior to that date. Between 1736 and 1740, Cornelius Board acquired several parcels of land from the East Jersey Proprietors along the Ringwood River and at the base of Sterling Lake. After Board left the area, the concern of Timothy Ward and Company erected a bloomery at Sterling by 1740 (fig. 11.6 [location 17]) and within a decade operated both a blast furnace and refining forge at the same location. In 1767 Peter Townsend took over operations at Sterling and began an association between the Townsend family and the Sterling Estate that would continue until the late nineteenth century.

In the pre–Revolutionary War era, a flourishing trade arose between the furnace and the forges that converted pig iron into bars and anchors; between the manufactory and the local populace for stoves, utensils, and implements; and between manufactories and leading market cities where ironmongers offered not only pig and bar iron but also anchors and a wide array of cast-iron products and holloware to coastwise and foreign markets. Extant Sterling accounts verify that pig and bar iron were sent to English markets in Bristol and Liverpool; that merchants in Boston, Providence, and Newport sought pig iron and anchors; and that ironmongers in the Carolinas and Bermuda desired refined iron and anchors (Kury 2005). As the industry grew, so did the reputation of its products. Frequent newspaper advertisements in Elizabeth, Newark, New York, and Philadelphia made mention of "Andover," "Mount Hope," "Hibernia," "Ringwood," and "Sterling" iron as a warranty of quality (fig. 11.6 [locations 9, 11, 12, 14, 17]).[3] Protected somewhat by the rugged terrain, the absence of significant agrarian-based settlement, and a sparse road net, ironworks in the New Jersey–New York Highlands played a significant role in support of the Continental Army during the Revolutionary War. A few, such as the Forest of Dean Furnace (fig. 11.6 [location 20]), located a few miles from West Point, were forced to close as British forces occupied nearby land or ports. Others, such as the Andover Furnace in Sussex County, were abandoned by their Loyalist owners or confiscated by Continental forces. Still other ceased operations as workers were diverted to service in the Revolutionary army.

Primary source materials from Hibernia, Mount Hope, Pompton (fig. 11.6 [location 13]), Ringwood, and Sterling indicate that large quantities of cannonballs, shells, shot, casings (carcasses) of various sizes and weights, and other ironware were produced. Often orders for munitions were followed by complaints over delayed payment or balances due. For example, in 1776 Joseph Hoff wrote that Hibernia Furnace had proofed three-pound cannon and made thirty-five tons of shot for which he requested payment of £1,000 to complete the order ("Letter Book," November 14, 1776). An account found in the National Archives in Washington, D.C., between the United States government and Mount Hope and Pompton furnaces for 1782 indicates that the two ironworks supplied more than 146 tons of shells and 54 tons of shot in that year and were owed almost £8,000 (NARA, Doc. 20435). To continue production of vital munitions, iron masters also requested exemptions from military service for their workers. At Hibernia, "haveing [sic] in our power at this time to give exemptions to 25 Men is the only thing that induces the greater part of the Men to work here that we now have . . . should that exemption be revok'd, I don't see how we should be supply'd with Workmen" ("Letter Book," March 20, 1778). The need for workmen became so desperate that representatives from Mount Hope and Hibernia traveled to Philadelphia to recruit prisoners of war and deserters ("Letter Book," July 1778).

Perhaps the most important contribution of the iron industry to the Continental cause was the production of the great chain that was placed across the Hudson River. With the fall of Forts Clinton and Montgomery there was a fear that British forces would gain control of the Hudson valley, thereby isolating Continental forces on either side of the river from each other. An earlier attempt to place a light chain between Fort Montgomery and Anthony's Nose had failed. Then Hugh Hughes, deputy quartermaster general of the Continental Army, engaged Noble, Townsend and Company (the forge and anchor works at Sterling) "to have made and ready to be delivered . . . an Iron Chain of the following Dimensions, and Quality. That is in Length five hundred Yards, each Link about two Feet long to be made of the Best Sterling Iron, two inches and one Quarter Square, or as near thereto as possible, with a Swivel to every hundred Feet, and a Clevis to every thousand Wt. in the same manner as those of the Former Chain." The contract also provided for twelve tons of anchors that were to be used in attaching the chain and log booms to the river floor (Kury 2004). The contract was completed within three months' time; the chain was successfully installed at West Point on April 30, 1778, and remained in place until the end of the war.

Despite the loss of the English market, the role of the iron industry in the new national economy was well regarded. Alexander Hamilton, as secretary of the treasury, observed in 1791 (U.S. Treasury 1827): "The manufactures of this article are entitled to pre-eminent rank. . . . They constitute, in whole or in part, the implements or materials, or both, of almost every useful occupation." Furthermore, he concluded that an expanding market and increasing prices "render[ed] it probable that the free admission of foreign iron would not be inconsistent with an adequate profit to the proprietors of iron works." At the time of the first actual census of manufacturers in 1810, it was reported that iron ranked only behind textiles, leather goods, and distilleries in total market value (Coxe 1814). Statistics compiled in conjunction with the first census placed New Jersey's share of the iron production, the bulk of it from the Highlands, third after Pennsylvania and Virginia.

The advent of the War of 1812 once again placed heavy demands on iron makers throughout the Highlands for munitions and sundry iron articles. Contemporary records of the activities at specific manufactories are not as extensive as those from the Revolutionary era; nevertheless, it may be ascertained that the production of large quantities of shot, shell, and cannonballs and the forging of anchors for the emerging U.S. Navy were among the important contributions to the war effort. Moreover, the war had demonstrated a need for permanent munitions suppliers. Soon afterward the West Point Foundry (fig. 11.6 [location 21]), which consisted of a blast furnace and cannon foundry, was erected at Cold Spring on the east side of the Hudson River. Initially reliant on iron ore supplied by mines in Putnam County's Philipse Iron Belt (fig. 11.6 [location 22]), the most prominent iron deposit in the Highlands east of the Hudson River, the foundry increasingly depended on the mines and furnaces at Southfield and Greenwood (fig. 11.6 [locations 18, 19]) in Orange County for supplies of ore and pig metal.

The years following the war proved disastrous for the iron industry in the Highlands. Iron makers found it increasingly difficult to obtain the quantities of charcoal needed for their furnaces and forges, and they sought out ever-more remote areas away from established transport networks. Industrial workers now demanded higher wages for labor in a primitive working environment as more options for employment presented themselves in nearby urban areas. Meanwhile, the British iron industry underwent a series of technological changes that greatly increased productivity and substantially reduced costs. Foremost among these were the use of steam power to generate the air blast and the substitution of coal for charcoal. Consequently, American iron makers, who had benefited from greatly inflated prices during the war, were now confronted by vigorous foreign competition that reduced prices to prewar levels or below. This competition helped spur a transformation in the domestic iron industry with the gradual switch to more efficient technology and improved transportation networks.

As previously discussed, the opening of the Morris Canal had the desired effects of increasing the availability of anthracite coal and reducing transportation costs for the iron manufacturers. The fortuitous availability of Pennsylvania anthracite dovetailed with a technological shift away from the use of charcoal as a fuel in iron production. Not only did the use of anthracite fuel lead to higher furnace temperatures that boosted efficiency and production, but it also significantly reduced labor costs—gone from the payrolls were the woodcutters, colliers, and their teamsters. Location now became a factor as well. Whereas furnaces had been situated throughout the Highlands in close proximity to mineral and forest resources, the introduction of anthracite-based technology in the manufacture of iron favored sites along the canal where iron ore from the mines could be married to Pennsylvania coal. Between 1841 and 1871 a number of furnaces were established at Boonton, Port Oram (now Wharton), Stanhope, and Hackettstown along with rolling mills and naileries. Beyond the reach of the canal, few charcoal-fueled furnaces continued to operate, although new furnaces, operational for only twenty years or so, were erected during this period at Long Pond (fig. 11.6 [location 15]) near Ringwood and at Wawayanda (fig. 11.6 [location 16]) on the extreme northwestern edge of the Highlands.

The successful use of anthracite in the iron industry and the concentration of iron furnaces along the route of the canal had a secondary effect. Mine owners reasoned that if it were possible to transport Pennsylvania coal eastward, then a return trip could carry iron ore from the Highlands westward to markets in Phillipsburg, the Lehigh Valley, and beyond. Soon ore depots were erected along the banks of the canal as roads and tramways delivered significant tonnage from the Andover, Ogden, Mount Hope, Hibernia, Dickinson, and Mine Hill ore bodies. In 1866, the peak year of operation for the canal, total shipments reached 889,220 tons, of which 459,775 tons were anthracite coal and 290,165 tons were iron ore. So much rich iron ore was being exported from New Jersey, largely to the Lehigh Valley, that a speaker before the New Jersey Historical Society in Newark advocated that New Jersey be called "The Iron State" (Miller 1855). Pennsylvania was the "Keystone State," New York was the "Empire State," but New Jersey did not yet have a nickname.

As discussed previously, the volume of products carried by the canal and the markets to which the canal was linked attracted entrepreneurs who desired to advance the cause of the railroads. The roads and tramways that formerly connected mines to the canal were now either rerouted to meet the Morris and Essex main line or replaced with narrow-gauge short-line railroads.

A similar transformation of the iron industry occurred in the Hudson Highlands. Completion of the New York and Erie Railroad main line through the Ramapo valley (extending from Suffern, New York; see fig. 11.4) provided a convenient entry point for shipments of anthracite coal. Robert Parrott and Peter Parrott, who had previously assumed control of the Greenwood Furnace and the West Point Foundry, now erected a new anthracite-fueled furnace at Greenwood by 1854. This stack, known as the Clove Furnace, may be seen on the east side of the New York State Thruway a few miles south of the Harriman exit. During the Civil War, the West Point Foundry used pig metal from the Clove Furnace and iron ore from Putnam and Orange county mines in the manufacture of the Parrott gun, an artillery piece with a reinforced hooped barrel that became a staple with the Union forces. The fortunes of the West Point Foundry declined as it faced stiffer competition from the developing steel industry in Pennsylvania and elsewhere, eventually closing in 1911.

Mining and smelting operations at the Sterling Estate were also shaped by the presence of the Erie Railroad. Ore and pig metal could now be sent at lower cost to the Erie terminal at Piermont for easy transshipment to New York City. The Sterling Mountain and Southfield Branch railroads were constructed to connect the Southfield furnaces and the Lakeville (Sterling) mines with the Erie Railroad. Although the furnaces were converted to burn cheaper anthracite fuel after the Civil War, the export of iron ore increased. In all but a single year between 1874 and 1882 more than 50 percent of the ore mined at Sterling was destined for outside markets, primarily those in the Lehigh and Schuylkill valleys of eastern Pennsylvania. The Sterling Furnace shut down in 1891, although ore was still mined and shipped elsewhere through the close of World War I (Ransom 1966).

The shift in focus from the production of pig iron to the shipment of iron ore evident at Sterling after the Civil War carried over to the New Jersey Highlands as well. Bayley (1910) noted that the census of 1880 recorded a total of 350 named mines in the New Jersey Highlands, of which only 136 were actually worked for some part of that year; the most productive mines had been leased or sold to outside interests. The tonnage reported for individual

Figure 11.7. Photo of the processing facility containing magnetic ore separator at the Edison Iron Works, Ogdensburg, N.J. Note the electrical wires in the foreground. National Park Service, Edison National Historic Site, N.J.

mines varied considerably: twenty-five mines produced 10,000 tons or more, thirty-nine produced between 1,000 and 10,000 tons, and the remainder less than 1,000 tons, some as little as 20 tons. Iron ore production in New Jersey reached a peak of 932,762 tons in 1882 before seeing a gradual decline as the richer and more easily exploited deposits in the Upper Great Lakes region started to come into production.

Just as the iron industry in the Highlands entered this downturn in the 1880s, Thomas Alva Edison, the Wizard of Menlo Park, saw a business opportunity. Edison had an idea that by using powerful crushers coupled with powerful electromagnets, he could more efficiently process and extract iron from the otherwise low-grade magnetite ores and make the failing iron mines of the Highlands profitable again. Started in 1890, the Edison Iron Works in Ogdensburg, New Jersey (fig. 11.6 [location 10]), consisted of a massive industrial complex employing hundreds of employees, many living on-site, surrounded by an extensive network of open-pit and deep-shaft mines (Johnson 2004). The ore-processing facility and associated buildings and shops were some of the first to be powered by that newly harnessed marvel, electricity (fig. 11.7). Edison's system for separating and refining iron ores did not work quite as well as envisioned. In the face of competition from richer and more easily exploited deposits in the Upper Great Lakes region, Edison's enterprise went bust. Never one to accept failure, Edison realized that the huge stone crushers and rollers built to pulverize iron ore could instead be used to crush limestone that could be processed to make cement (Josephson 1959). This cement found a ready market in nearby New York City, providing the foundations for numerous skyscrapers and the city's iconic skyline. Thus, the Edison Portland Cement Company was added to Edison's long list of successful industrial ventures. Realizing that it would be more economical to locate the processing facilities closer to the sources of limestone, Edison moved his entire complex to Stewartsville, New Jersey, and the Ogdensburg site was abandoned by the turn of the nineteenth century.

The Highlands iron industry continued to slide into the beginning of the twentieth century; with improved mining methods and increased mechanization, the few mines that remained competitive with higher-quality ore were able to maintain high rates of ore production. World War I and World War II brought increased activity, with mines reopened and production ramped up to meet added wartime demands. Iron ore production in New Jersey peaked during World War II, when extraction amounted to some 1 million tons per year, chiefly from the Mount Hope, Richard, Scrub Oaks, and Oxford mines (Shea 1977). Most of these mines were shut down by the 1960s. One of the few mines still open in the twentieth century—the New Leonard Mine, part of the Mount Hope complex (fig. 11.6 [location 11])—opened during World War II and operated at a high capacity for a number of years before closing in the early 1980s.

Connecticut Highlands

The Housatonic River valley and the uplands of northwestern Connecticut that comprise Litchfield County presented environmental challenges and opportunities similar to those of the Highlands to the southwest. Settlers first came into the region seeking fertile land for farming as available land in the rich Connecticut River valley became scarce. Finding little such land, they then turned to the available natural resources—forests, waterpower sites, and iron ore. The ores were chiefly limonite or brown hematite rather than the magnetite ores generally found in New York and New Jersey. Prior to the Revolutionary War, a sufficient number of bloomeries (19) and furnaces (3) were in operation so as to constitute the Salisbury Iron District; chief among them were a blast furnace at Lakeville (fig. 11.6 [location 24]) and several bloomeries in Canaan (fig. 11.6 [location 25]). Unlike their counterparts in Pennsylvania, New Jersey, and New York, the Salisbury iron masters were New England–oriented for both financial support and markets. Connecticut merchants provided outlets for a variety of cast-iron articles, gun barrels, anchors, and the like. After the war, rolling mills were built to furnish nails and saws.

By the end of the eighteenth century, Litchfield County was home to some fifty forges, three slitting mills, and several blast furnaces. Expanding their search for ore, Connecticut entrepreneurs crossed the border into the ridges of Dutchess and Putnam counties, New York. High-grade brown hematite ores were discovered in the Amenia area and magnetite in several places within the Philipse Ore Belt (fig. 11.6 [location 22]). In addition to the Connecticut furnaces, these ores were transported to at least three forges established in Putnam County between 1795 and 1810 (Doyle and Sypher 1994). However, only one of these New York bloomeries remained some two decades later, and future exploitation was directed toward mining (McLane 1833).

In the ensuing decades, Salisbury iron makers were buffeted by the same cycles of prosperity and decline as iron masters elsewhere. Reports gathered in conjunction with the census of 1830 identify only five furnaces and three forges operational throughout Litchfield County (McLane 1833), including three blast furnaces situated in the town of Kent (fig. 11.6 [location 23]). To grow and maintain the industry, Salisbury operators sought niche markets. Nearness to national armories and gun manufactories in the Connecticut River valley enabled them to become a principal source of gun iron. Somewhat later, Salisbury blast furnaces produced the charcoal-fueled pig iron that was much in demand by makers of cast railroad-car wheels owing to the iron's unusual toughness and ability to withstand heavy and sudden shocks (Harte 1944; R. Gordon 1996). In Lesley's survey of iron manufacturers, the Salisbury District was home to some thirteen blast furnaces, including one anthracite-fueled furnace, five charcoal-fueled hot-blast stacks, and four forges (Lesley 1866). The last of these blast furnaces, the Canaan No. 3 (fig. 11.6 [location 25]), was "blown out" in 1923 (Harte 1944).

Conclusions

Most of the iron mines in the New York–New Jersey Highlands region were shuttered by the end of the nineteenth century, although some mining activity continued past the middle of the twentieth century and large reserves of iron ore remain untouched. By the middle of the nineteenth century, other sources of more easily and relatively cheaply ("open pit") mined ore came into wide use. In many places, especially in the southern Highlands, widespread deforestation made the requisite vast amounts of charcoal difficult to obtain. The substitution of anthracite coal from the relatively nearby Lehigh Valley for the traditional charcoal, along with the improved transportation provided by canals and railroads, served to rejuvenate the Highlands iron industry for a time. As late as 1870, in New Jersey, forty-two forges were still working in Sussex and Morris counties, while ten furnaces remained in blast in Sussex, Passaic, Morris, and Warren counties. In New York's Hudson Highlands the tally was three furnaces and one forge. In the final analysis, the national financial panics of 1873 and 1893, the discovery and exploitation of high-quality surface deposits of iron ore in the Upper Great Lakes region, and the further technological shift to bituminous coal and the Bessemer converter in the making of steel rather than pig iron sealed the fate of the Highlands iron mines and brought an end to iron making there. Subsequently, workers and their families abandoned most of the associated large landholdings in the glaciated Highlands to such an extent that a mid-twentieth-century geographer included the Highlands in his study of "empty areas" in the eastern United States (Klimm 1954). Iron mining continued at a few select locations, such as Cornwall Ore Banks in Pennsylvania and the Mount Hope Mine complex in New Jersey, where the size and quality of the ore deposits warranted continued production, but even the last of these closed by the early 1980s.

The imprint of the iron industry is still evident on the present-day landscape. In a few locations one can visit the preserved remnants of once-flourishing iron plantations, such as Hopewell Furnace National Historic Site in Pennsylvania (fig. 11.6 [location 2]; plate 29). Several large state forest preserves and parks in the Highlands were assembled from lands held by the iron masters. One needs only to explore parks such as French Creek, Wawayanda, Ringwood, Sterling Forest, Harriman, and Macedonia Brook to find evidence of furnaces, forges, and associated structures moldering in the forest. The circular remains of charcoal pits may still be observed in many isolated parts of the Highlands where the extreme heat of burning charcoal so changed soil conditions that grasses and shrubs form the only vegetation cover to regenerate. Evidence of the mines themselves include tailing heaps; debris-filled trenches; water-filled open pits; and open, sealed, or water-filled shafts. The dark side to this industrial heritage is the public safety hazards caused by surface subsidence and sinkholes formed by the collapse of shafts and tunnels of abandoned mines (Shea 1977).

The iron industry and its cultural and natural historical legacy have become an indelible part of the Highlands landscape. The water impoundments that provided the necessary waterpower have become popular recreation sites, water supply reservoirs, or the locus for lakeshore communities. While some of the iron-mining villages long ago became ghost towns, others grew and diversified into other industrial and commercial enterprises or more recently morphed into residential bedroom communities. Likewise, most of the spur rail lines built to carry iron ore have been abandoned, although many of the main trunk lines are still important carriers of rail traffic. While the iron-mining industry itself is gone, the original settlements and transportation networks continue to shape modern-day development patterns.

Notes

1. The general discussion on iron making and ironworks in the Highlands region is based on works by Bartholomew and Metz (1988); Bining (1938); Boyer (1931);

DeVorsey (1954); R. Gordon (1996); Kury (1968, 1971, 2004, 2005); Muntz (1960); Ransom (1966); Swank (1884); Wacker (1968, 1975); and Wacker and Clemens (1995).

2. Depositories with substantial collections of primary resources devoted to the Highlands iron industry include the Bucks County Historical Society, Doylestown, PA; the Free Public Library of Morristown and Morris Township, Morristown, NJ; the Historical Society of Pennsylvania, Philadelphia, PA; the Hagley Museum and Library, Wilmington, DE; the New Jersey State Archives, Trenton, NJ; the New York State Archives, Albany, NY; the Orange County Historical Society, Arden, NY; and the Special Collections Department, Rutgers University Library, New Brunswick, NJ.

3. Much vital information relative to the conduct of the iron industry from pre-Revolutionary times through the early decades of the nineteenth century, including descriptions of property, employment opportunities and expectations, and products for sale, is contained in contemporary newspaper accounts. Although access to the original papers is limited to a handful of depositories, many pertinent accounts have been collected and published in Gottesman (1938–1965) and in the "Newspaper Extracts" volumes edited by Whitehead et al. (1880–1949) and Stryker et al. (1901–1907).

References

Bartholomew, C. L., and L. E. Metz. 1988. *The Anthracite Iron Industry of the Lehigh Valley*. Easton, PA: Center for Canal History and Technology.

Bayley, W. S. 1910. *Iron Mines and Mining in New Jersey*. Vol. VII. *Final Report of the State Geologist*. Trenton, NJ: MacCrellish and Quigley.

Bining, A. C. 1938. *Pennsylvania Iron Manufacture in the Eighteenth Century*. Harrisburg: Pennsylvania Historical Commission.

Boyer, C. S. 1931. *Early Forges and Furnaces in New Jersey*. Philadelphia: University of Pennsylvania Press.

Chelsea Forge Journal. "Potware Accounts, Chelsea Forge, NJ; with Wood Chopping and Charcoal Burning Records, 1780–1789." MSS, BM-223. Bucks County Historical Society, Doylestown, PA.

Coxe, T. 1814. *A Statement of the Arts and Manufactures of the United States of America, for the Year 1810*. Philadelphia: A. Cornman Jr.

DeVorsey, L., Jr. 1954. "The Growth and Distribution of Iron Manufacturing in New Jersey, 1780–1860." MA thesis, Indiana University.

Doyle, B., and S. Sypher. 1994. "Too Little, Too Late: Early Ironmaking in the Eastern Hudson Highlands." Paper presented at the Historic Ironmaking Conference, October 1–2, Arden, NY.

Eggert, G. C. 1994. "The Iron Industry in Pennsylvania." Pennsylvania Historical Studies No. 25, Pennsylvania Historical Association, Harrisburg, PA.

Gordon, R. B. 1996. *American Iron, 1607–1900*. Baltimore: Johns Hopkins University Press.

Gordon, T. F. 1834. *A Gazetteer of the State of New Jersey*. Trenton, NJ: Daniel Fenton.

Gottesman, R. S. 1938–1965. *Arts and Crafts in New York, 1726–1804*. 3 vols. New York: New-York Historical Society.

Greenwich Forge. April 6, 1779–October 2, 1780. "Forge Books of Richard Backhouse." MSS. Historical Society of Pennsylvania, Philadelphia.

Harte, C. R. 1944. "Connecticut's Iron and Copper: Part 1." 60th Annual Report of the Connecticut Society of Civil Engineers. American Society of Civil Engineers.

Johnson, R. P. 2004. *Thomas Edison's "Ogden Baby": The New Jersey & Pennsylvania Concentrating Works*. N.p.: Privately printed.

Josephson, M. 1959. *Edison: A Biography*. New York: McGraw-Hill.

Klimm, L. E. 1954. "The Empty Areas of the Northeastern United States." *Geographical Review* 44:325–345.

Kury, T. W. 1968. "Historical Geography of the Iron Industry in the New York–New Jersey Highlands, 1700–1900." PhD diss., Louisiana State University.

———. 1971. "Anthracite, Iron and the Morris Canal." *Pioneer America* 3 (July): 46–53.

———. 2004. "Revisiting the Vanished Ironworks of the Sterling Estate." *Ouray County Historical Society Journal* 33:24–41.

———. 2005. "Sterling, Southfield and Augusta: A Fresh Look at Charcoal Iron Communities in the Highlands." *Ouray County Historical Society Journal* 34:3–13.

Lesley, J. P. 1866. *The Iron Manufacturer's Guide to the Furnaces, Forges and Rolling Mills of the United States*. New York: John Wiley.

"Letter Book of Joseph and Charles Hoff—March 10, 1775 to July 10, 1778." MSS. Morristown National Historical Park, Morristown, NJ.

McLane, L. 1833. *Documents Relative to the Manufacturers in the United States*. 2 vols. Washington, D.C.: Duff Green.

Miller, J. W. 1855. "The Iron State: Its Natural Position, Power and Wealth." *Proceedings of the New Jersey Historical Society* 7:82.

Muntz, A. P. 1960. "Forests and Iron: The Charcoal Iron Industry of the New Jersey Highlands." *Geografiska Annaler* 42:315–323.

NARA. *Revolutionary War Records, 1775–1790s*. Miscellaneous Numbered Records, Record Group 93. Washington, DC: National Archives and Records Service.

Oblinger, C. 1984. *Cornwall: The People and Culture of an Industrial Camelot, 1890–1980*. Harrisburg: Pennsylvania Historical and Museum Commission.

Ransom, J. M. 1966. *Vanishing Ironworks of the Ramapos: The Story of the Forges, Furnaces and Mines of the New Jersey–New York Border Area*. New Brunswick, NJ: Rutgers University Press.

Shea, T. K. 1977. "Abandoned Magnetite Iron Mines of New Jersey." Trenton: NJ Department of Labor and Industry.

Stryker, W. S., et al., eds. 1901–1907. *Archives of the State of New Jersey: Documents Relating to the Revolutionary History of the State of New Jersey*. Second series. 5 vols. Various places: State of New Jersey.

Swank, J. 1884. *History of the Manufacture of Iron in All Ages and Particularly in the United States for Three Hundred Years, from 1585 to 1885*. Philadelphia: American Iron and Steel Association.

U.S. Treasury Department. 1827. *Alexander Hamilton's Report on the Subject of Manufactures Made in His Capacity of Secretary of the Treasury, on the Fifth of December, 1791*. 6th ed. Philadelphia: William Bowen.

Wacker, P. O. 1968. *The Musconetcong Valley of New Jersey: A Historical Geography*. New Brunswick, NJ: Rutgers University Press.

———. 1975. *Land and People: A Cultural Geography of Preindustrial New Jersey: Origins and Settlement Patterns*. New Brunswick, NJ: Rutgers University Press.

Wacker, P. O., and P.G.E. Clemens. 1995. *Land Use in Early New Jersey: A Historical Geography*. Newark: New Jersey Historical Society.

Whitehead, W. A., et al., eds. 1880–1949. *Archives of the State of New Jersey: Documents Relating to the Colonial, Revolutionary, and Post Revolutionary History of the State of New Jersey*. First series. 42 vols. Various places: State of New Jersey.

In addition to the publications cited in the text and listed above, the following websites and materials were consulted:

Durham Historical Society. "History of the Durham Furnace and Ironworks." http://www.durhamhistoricalsociety.org/history3.html.

Handouts prepared for Ironmasters Conference, May 16–17, 1998, in Falls Village, CT.

New Jersey Department of Environmental Protection. "Abandoned Mines of New Jersey." 1:24,000 map. New Jersey Geological Survey. http://www.state.nj.us/dep/njgs/geodata/dgs03–2.htm.

12

Agriculture and Urban Development Patterns in the Highlands

Richard G. Lathrop Jr.

Introduction

Prior to European settlement, Native American tribal groups, most notably the Lenni Lenape, inhabited the Highlands (Kraft 2001). Compared with the dramatic changes that followed, the Native Americans had a light touch upon the land. With the advent of European colonization, the Highlands underwent a major transformation as the land was cleared to support the fledgling iron industry and agriculture. By the mid-1800s much of the Highlands was either actively farmed or repeatedly cut over for timber or charcoal. As technology and transportation changed, these industries changed, as did their imprint on the landscape. By the late nineteenth century, the heyday of the iron industry had passed and agriculture was in decline. Abandoned lands were soon reclaimed by forest by the early twentieth century. The Highlands remained a largely rural area of forests and fields until the mid-twentieth century and post–World War II suburban expansion. The advent of major interstate highway construction that first started in the 1950s brought the Highlands within commuting distance of the Philadelphia–New York City–Hartford metropolitan regions. Since the 1950s, portions of the Highlands have undergone dramatic human population growth and suburban expansion. Chapters 6 and 11 examine the region's forest history and the iron industry in greater detail, but this chapter will focus on the land-use implications of agriculture and urban development. I will start by tracing the history of farming in the Highlands before charting the post–World War II trends in population growth and associated urban development.

Agriculture Land Use Post–European Settlement to Present Day

As the name of the region implies, the Highlands are noted for their rugged upland topography, conditions not generally conducive to farming. However, the broader region encompassed within the boundaries of the

Highlands Conservation Act of 2004 includes the river valleys nestled between the Highlands ridges as well as the more rolling terrain of the adjacent Piedmont (to the south) and Valley portion (to the north) of the Ridge and Valley physiographic provinces. In the unglaciated portions of the southern Highlands, described in chapter 3, these lowland areas are blessed with prime agricultural soils derived from the limestone and sedimentary bedrock rather than the igneous and metamorphic rocks of the true Highlands backbone. The major river systems such as the Susquehanna, Delaware, and Hudson provided early avenues for European settlement of the arable lands in the southern Highlands and on the fringes of the northern Highlands (Fletcher 1950; Hedrick 1933; Wacker 1975). In many cases, these earliest agricultural settlements were in the river and stream valleys previously farmed by Native Americans decades earlier. While these areas were beginning to be cleared and settled in the early 1700s, the interior portions of the Highlands remained in frontier status for decades longer (Wacker 1975; Russell 1976). The settlement pattern in the rugged interior was governed more by the emergence of the iron industry spurred on by the demand for Revolutionary War munitions and subsequent industrial development than by agriculture. In many instances, employees on the larger iron "plantations" cleared land for farms and pasture to provide a local source of food, fiber, and fodder (Ransom 1966; Rutsch 1999).

Eighteenth- and nineteenth-century agriculture in the Highlands region shared many similarities to agriculture elsewhere in the northeastern United States. By the early 1800s the initial "frontier" phase of clearing and subsistence agriculture was over, and commercial agriculture was on the rise (Schmidt 1973; Danhof 1969). Wheat was an important early crop; it was in high demand, transported well, and provided a comparatively good return in relation to the effort expended (Favretti 1976; Fletcher 1950; Gates 1960; Hedrick 1933). This bountiful harvest was often short-lived because wheat was hard on the land through a combination of soil erosion and nutrient depletion and was also susceptible to introduced diseases and pests. To keep their land productive, farmers soon realized the need to rotate crops as well as apply fertilizer and other amendments to replenish depleted soil nutrients (Danhof 1969; Stoll 2002). In addition to livestock manure and guano, the application of gypsum and lime became a standard farming practice by the 1830s (Fletcher 1950, 1955; Danhof 1969). Local deposits of gypsum and limestone were in ready supply in the valleys that bound the Highlands (Schmidt 1973; Danhof 1969). To improve its availability for plant uptake, limestone (calcium carbonate) was burned in special limekilns constructed for this purpose to form lime (calcium oxide) (Fletcher 1955). These kilns can still be found today, often overgrown and tumbling down.

Crops and livestock came and went with the vagaries of market forces, technological innovation, and new consumer demands. While fruit orchards have long been an important component of Highlands agriculture, the fruit industry has gone through booms and busts over the years. In the eighteenth and early nineteenth centuries, much of the apple crop was pressed and fermented into hard cider and the peach crop turned into brandy (Favretti 1976; Hedrick 1933; Russell 1976; Schmidt 1973). With the improvement of transportation in the latter half of the nineteenth century, fresh fruit increasingly found its way to city markets. In response to this demand, apple, peach, pear, and plum orchards covered thousands of acres across the Highlands (Favretti 1976; Fletcher 1955; Russell 1976; Schmidt 1973). Nowhere was this boom, and later bust, more striking then in New Jersey. In the 1880s, peach orchards covered large sections of Hunterdon, Warren, and Sussex counties; by the latter 1890s farmers were ripping out their trees (Schmidt 1972, 1973). Agricultural census figures for the Highlands counties of New Jersey show upward of 3.8 million trees in 1890, but the number was down to thirty thousand by the turn of the twentieth century (NASS 2009). The Highlands counties of Pennsylvania experienced a later boom and bust of apple and, to a lesser extent, peach growing in the early 1900s (Fletcher 1955). While fruit orchards persisted as a viable form of agriculture well into the first quarter of the twentieth century, the present-day orchard industry is only a shadow of what it was at its peak (NASS 2009).

After the initial phase of small-grain farming that so depleted the thin soils, extensive areas of the more marginal uplands were converted to pasture for sheep. By 1840, more than one hundred thousand sheep grazed in the Highlands counties of New Jersey (Schmidt 1973). Sheep raising rapidly lost favor with the rise in competition from western states and the decline in wool prices. Between 1840 and 1850, the number of sheep in the Highlands counties of Pennsylvania decreased more than 60 percent (Fletcher 1950). Similar declines were experienced in Connecticut (Russell 1976). Whereas some of the most marginal pastureland was among the first to be abandoned (after which it began a natural succession back to forest), in many Highlands locations sheep were replaced by cows. During the first half of the nineteenth century, dairying as a specialized form of farming combined the production of butter, cheese, and milk with the fattening of beef (Fletcher 1955; Danhof 1969). Butter and cheese were less perishable and more easily transported to urban markets than fluid milk, so butter and cheese were the primary dairy products. Goshen, in the heart of Litchfield County, Connecticut, was a major center of cheese production and export in the first half of the nineteenth century (Favretti 1976; Russell 1976). Although still hilly, this region of the Connecticut Highlands is covered with an irregular veneer of till and other glacial deposits, and the gravelly loam is admirably suited for pasture and dairying.

The ubiquitous dairy barn and accompanying silo surrounded by fields and pasture, the postcard image of a Highlands farm, is a creation of the latter half of the nineteenth century and early twentieth century. Starting in the mid-1800s, technological innovation, improved transportation, burgeoning urban populations, and changing eating habits led to a shift in the dairy industry with increased production of milk for urban consumption. With ready proximity to the large urban markets of Philadelphia and New York City, the dairy industry swelled across the Highlands (Dillon 1941; Favretti 1976; Fletcher 1955; Gates 1960; Hedrick 1933). Demand for milk was further bolstered with the founding of the New York Condensed Milk Company by Gail Borden in 1857 and with the opening of condensing factories at several locations in the New York and Connecticut Highlands (Frantz 1951). The rise of dairying brought other changes; with hay and alfalfa grown for forage and corn for silage, all phases of production could be contained on one operation (Russell 1976). Although declining, dairying remains the most prominent form of agriculture across the southern Highlands farm belt of Pennsylvania and New Jersey. Elsewhere in the Highlands, the dairy industry is struggling to hold on. The huge dairy barns and silos are empty, replaced by equestrian stables. The fields, if not abandoned, are planted in hay or turned over to horticultural industries that support a growing suburbia with sod, nurseries, or Christmas trees. Many of these farms have ultimately been converted to "McMansions."

Swine production has always been an important component of Pennsylvania agriculture (Watts 1925). In portions of Lancaster and Berks counties, where the present-day landscape is dotted with the long narrow barns of confined hog operations, the overall number of hogs and pigs exceeds that of cows (NASS 2009). Changing economic factors and technological innovations have led to the increased concentration of livestock operations, both swine and cattle, to the point where the traditional system of recycling manure back onto the cropland and pasturelands is maxing out. With the increasing concentration of animals and feed imported from elsewhere (rather than grown on the farm itself), too much manure is being produced relative to the capacity of the land to assimilate the nutrients, leading to major problems with polluted runoff (Kellogg et al. 2000). While seemingly far upstream, what happens in the Highlands has great implications to the downstream estuaries of Chesapeake and Delaware bays, the lower Hudson River, and Long Island Sound. A major focus of the Chesapeake Estuary Program has been to improve agricultural management practices in the Susquehanna River watershed with the objective of reducing the excess nutrient produced in runoff from intensive agriculture in areas such as Lancaster County (Chesapeake Bay Program 2008).

Agricultural land surveys undertaken by the U.S. Department of Agriculture since 1850 provide a rich source of data for examining the extent of agricultural land use in the broader Highlands region (NASS 2009). The numbers of farms and acres in active farmland (i.e., harvested crop and pastureland)

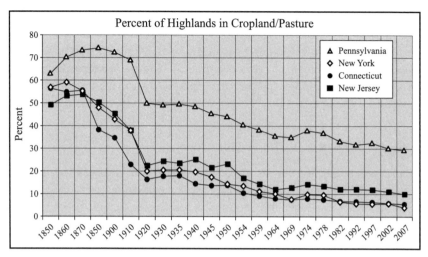

Figure 12.1. Graph of Highlands cropland and pasture cover, 1850–2007.
Source: NASS 2009.

peaked in the late 1800s, followed by a rapid decline in the Great Depression of the 1930s (fig. 12.1). These patterns track elsewhere in the northeastern United States. Significant portions of the land that was cleared for agriculture by the mid-nineteenth century were progressively abandoned during a period of nationwide agricultural readjustment spurred by increased competition brought on by the opening of the American Midwest, changing labor markets, and expanding lifestyle choices brought on by industrialization (Schmidt 1973; Bell 1989; Russell 1976). Farming stabilized, if not rebounded slightly, during the late 1930s and into the 1940s, then entered another period of decline before stabilizing somewhat in the 1970s. Across the entire 150-year period of the agriculture census record, the Highlands counties of Connecticut, New Jersey, and New York have experienced a 50 percent to 80 percent decline of farmland compared to the peak acreages in the late 1800s. Owing to the consolidation of farms over the period, the decline in the number of farm families has been even more dramatic, with decreases of 80 percent to 90 percent.

These post–World War II trends mirror what was happening elsewhere in the northeastern United States (Bell 1989; Russell 1976) as well as more broadly across the United States (Zelinsky 1962; Danbom 1995). Today, active farmland comprises only a comparatively minor proportion (less than 10 percent) of the Highlands in Connecticut, New Jersey, and New York. With nearly a third of the land still actively farmed, the Pennsylvania Highlands remain a more pastoral landscape, with prime agricultural soils and some of the best farming areas in the state in the counties of Berks and Lancaster. Farmland preservation efforts have been especially active in these counties, with approximately 16 percent of farmland preserved from development with agricultural conservation easements (Tyrrell et al. 2010). In some locations, such as the Oley Valley of Berks County, nestled between the hills of the Reading Prong, there is a large concentration of preserved farmland parcels that will hopefully serve to protect the integrity of the existing agricultural landscape (see plate 3).

Suburbanization of the Highlands

While the agricultural census records document the decline in the number of farms in the Highlands from the late 1800s onward, the U.S. census records reveal a steady rise in Highlands human population (fig. 12.2) (U.S. Census of Population and Housing 2002; 2011). The Pennsylvania Highlands region saw a doubling of population in the first half of the twentieth century and continued to climb steadily post-1950. At nearly 1.4 million people in 2010, the Pennsylvania Highlands were almost double the population of the New Jersey Highlands, the next most populous of the four state regions. Starting in 1950, the New Jersey and New York Highlands experienced a rapid rate of population growth that moderated somewhat after 1970, with the two states tracking closely together. With the smallest population at slightly over 300,000 people in 2010, the Connecticut Highlands have experienced slower but steady growth over the time period. Closer examination of municipal-level census data reveals that much of the growth in the years prior to 1950 is accounted for by the cities and larger towns rather than the more rural townships. The urban centers were the home of factories and mills that attracted the sons and daughters of farming families as well as newly arrived immigrants (Danbom 1995; Russell 1976). For example, Torrington, Connecticut, a collection of mill towns on the Naugatuck River in central Litchfield County, doubled in population between 1890 and 1900, from 6,000 to 12,000. In its role as a leading rail transportation hub for anthracite coal, Reading, Pennsylvania (of the board game Monopoly fame), became a major city with more than 15,000 inhabitants by 1850 (the forty-third-largest city in the United States at the time) and swelled to over 110,000 by 1930 as its industrial base expanded (Gibson 1998). Like that of many other northeastern Rust Belt cities in the last quarter of the twentieth century, Reading's population stagnated (falling off the top one hundred list by 1960), eventually decreasing to 81,000 by 2000 (though the more recent 2010 census shows a slight uptick to 88,000 residents).

The rise of the automobile ushered in the next phase of Highlands land-use history. The Taconic State Parkway, opened in 1927 in Westchester County, New York, was one of the first roadways designed specifically to provide automobiles a scenic, rapid route into the Highlands. In 1927 the Regional Plan Association completed its first plan for the greater New York City metropolitan

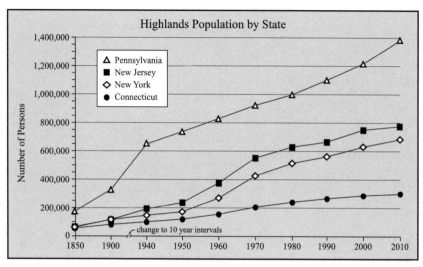

Figure 12.2. Population trends for the Highlands region within the four Highlands states, 1850–2010. Note that the expanded time scale after 1940, with 10-year increments, makes the post-1950s growth appear less dramatic. *Source:* U.S. Bureau of the Census.

region, recommending the construction of a network of expressways to link the center city and its larger metropolitan region (Lewis and Goodrich 1974). Similar expressways were also in the works in the Philadelphia metro region. The establishment of the federal interstate highway system brought a spate of construction of major highways crisscrossing the Highlands in the 1950s and 1960s that continued into the 1990s: the Pennsylvania Turnpike Schuylkill Expressway (Route I-76); the Pennsylvania Turnpike Northeast Extension (Route I-476); the New York State Thruway, Interstate Routes 78, 80, 84, 287, and 684. Post–World War II population growth coupled with auto-based commuting initiated the spread of suburbia up into and beyond the Highlands.

Closer examination of the U.S. census data for the past several decades shows that the rate of Highlands population growth declined steadily in Connecticut and oscillated in New York and New Jersey, while Pennsylvania continued to climb at a growth rate of over 10 percent (fig. 12.3). Overall, each state's Highlands population grew faster than that of the state as a whole, though as of the 2010 census, the rates of population growth in New Jersey and Connecticut were converging on the statewide rates. From 1970 to 1990, Highlands housing grew much faster than population, with fewer people living in each house (fig. 12.3). However, while this trend has been on a general downward trajectory across the Highlands region, New York and Connecticut showed an uptick in the percent increase in the number of Highlands housing units during 2000 to 2010. In all but one case, the percent increase in the number of housing units regionally outstrips the statewide totals. While

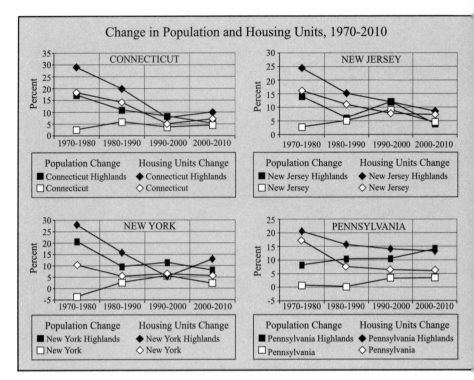

Figure 12.3. Plot of percent change in population and housing units for the four Highlands states (1970–2010) by within-state Highlands region and state overall.

it is still too early to make definitive conclusions, it is worth noting that during the 2000 to 2010 time period, the growth rate in both the population and number of housing units in the New Jersey Highlands dipped to levels lower than the other states' Highlands regions. As recounted in more detail in chapter 14, it was during this same time period that the state of New Jersey passed the Highlands Water Protection and Planning Act (in 2004) instituting stringent urban growth controls.

Mapping the decade of the greatest percentage as well as the greatest absolute population increase for the individual Highlands municipalities reveals that the spatial pattern of population growth has varied greatly across the four-state Highlands region (plate 32). A majority of the municipalities in Connecticut and New York exhibited their peak years of growth in the decades of the 1950s to 1970s, although the areas around Torrington in Connecticut and Monroe in New York appear to be more recent hot spots of growth. Nowhere in the Highlands region is the impact from the earlier phase of post–World War II suburbanization more dramatic than Rockland County, New York, which increased more than 285 percent, from 55,000 people in 1950 to more than 210,000 by 1980.

Later stages of suburban-exurban sprawl from the New York City metro urban core are evident in the growth experienced in the southwestern New Jersey Highlands. These western rural townships, along with a few select eastern and central municipalities with ready access to Interstates 78, 80, and 287, show up as hot spots of growth in the last two decades of the twentieth century and into the next. Bisected by I-78, Greenwich Township in the western Highlands of Warren County exhibited a 130 percent population increase between 1990 and 2000. The Pennsylvania Highlands show a number of municipalities that have experienced their peak percentage increase as well as peak absolute increase in population between 1980 and 2010. A number of these growth hot spots are on the leading edge of Highlands fronting the Philadelphia metro region in such municipalities as Perkiomen Township in Montgomery County, with a more than 200 percent increase in population between 2000 and 2010, or on the far side of the central spine of the Highlands in the I-78 travel corridor, such as the Bethlehem area in Northampton County or Lower Macungie Township in Lehigh County.

The northeastern Pennsylvania Highlands (Northampton, Lehigh, and Bucks counties) and the neighboring Lehigh Valley (outside the Highlands proper) are prime examples of the expansion of the New York metro region's "commutingshed." Attracted by lower housing prices and the promise of "getting more house for your money," newcomers have spurred a development boom over the past two decades. However, these new Pennsylvania residents are often still tethered to jobs back in the New York City metro region. In 2005, during a typical morning peak-commuting period, more than 8,500 vehicles from Pennsylvania commuted eastward across the New Jersey Highlands over I-78 to destinations across New Jersey and into New York (NJTPA 2008). By the time I-78 leaves the Highlands, it picks up more than 10,000 additional New Jersey vehicles commuting eastward. Although many of these cars might be continuing far eastward toward New York City, a large number diverge to destinations within or near the Highlands. The decentralization of corporate office complexes, light industry, and the "second wave" of commercial development that follows residential development out into the suburbs and the exurbs beyond has further blurred the boundaries between the "rural" Highlands and the major metropolitan areas of Philadelphia, northern New Jersey, New York City, and Hartford.

Maps of land use and land cover produced from satellite and aerial photographic imagery provide a bird's-eye view of landscape change over the last several decades. Data sets produced as part of the U.S. Forest Service–sponsored Highlands Regional Study (Lathrop, Hatfield, and Tulloch 2003; Tyrrell et al. 2010) suggest that urban developed-land coverage in the Highlands portion of each of the four states has been increasing between 1 and 2 percent per year during the most recent periods of record (CT = 2,210 acres/yr or 2.2 percent between 1995 and 2002; NJ = 3,300 acres/yr or 1.9 percent; NY =

Table 12.1. Land-Cover-Change Estimates Derived from the USFS-Sponsored Highlands Study between 1980s–1990s and 2000s

Connecticut

	1985 (acres)	1995 (acres)	2002 (acres)	1985–2002 % change
Land cover class				
Developed	94,641	102,773	118,267	+25.0
Ag/grass	61,500	61,500	48,016	−21.9
Barren	3,148	3,774	4,707	+49.5
Forest	467,976	459,186	457,167	−2.3
Wetland	23,105	23,191	23,894	+3.4
Water	27,068	27,014	25,386	−6.2
Total	677,438	677,438	677,437	

Pennsylvania

	1992 (acres)	2001 (acres)	1992–2001 % change
Land cover class			
Developed	347,443	390,593	+12.4
Ag/grass	545,730	493,165	−9.6
Barren	11,874	12,594	+6.1
Forest	442,709	444,726	+0.5
Wetland	21,825	27,202	+24.6
Water	13,112	14,413	+9.9
Total	1,382,693	1,382,693	

New Jersey

	1984 (acres)	1995 (acres)	2000 (acres)	1984–2002 % change
Land cover class				
Developed	180,823	177,263	193,769	+7.2
Ag/grass	135,053	128,917	122,528	−9.3
Barren	3,227	4,235	5,687	+76.2
Forest	379,423	382,289	373,351	–1.6
Wetland	65,081	69,619	68,684	+5.5
Water	24,362	25,922	24,227	-0.6
Total	787,969	788,245	788,246	

New York

	1984 (acres)	1995 (acres)	2000 (acres)	1984–2002 % change
Land cover class				
Developed	113,966	152,936	162,664	+42.7
Ag/grass	57,865	43,709	41,670	−28.0
Barren	4,296	3,772	3,962	−7.8
Forest	377,545	354,590	347,828	−7.9
Wetland	35,166	33,867	33,501	−4.7
Water	40,724	40,759	40,007	−1.8
Total	629,562	629,633	629,632	

Note: Developed category includes development-associated lawns and park areas. The increase in wetland area observed in Connecticut and Pennsylvania may be attributable to mapping differences between wet and dry years.

1,945 acres/yr or 1.3 percent; PA = 4,795 acres/yr or 1.4 percent) (table 12.1). The increase in urban developed land has resulted in the loss of farm- and forestland across the region. All four states experienced a loss of farmland over the 1980s to 2000s period. While the amounts of forest- and wetland showed a slight uptick between 1984 and 1995 in New Jersey, presumably owing to natural succession on abandoned farmland, forest- and wetland coverage declined between 1995 and 2002. In New York and Connecticut forest area declined, while in Pennsylvania forest area appears to have increased between 1984 and 1995, presumably owing to the abandonment of farmland and the resulting natural succession.

Comparing the increases in population with the urban developed land-cover-change figures, one can estimate the actual footprint of cleared, developed land per the average new housing unit. For example, in the New Jersey Highlands between 1990 and 2000, approximately 17,171 acres were developed (Lathrop, Hatfield, and Tulloch 2003), accommodating 29,881 new housing units and 78,423 new people; this equates to approximately 0.6 acre per housing unit or 4.6 people per acre of developed land. In reality, the amount of land consumed per new house is somewhat higher when one considers the full lot size rather than the amount of cleared land (as mapped in the land-cover-change data sets) and the fact that most of the New Jersey Highlands region is zoned at 2 acres per housing unit. Most of this urbanization is occurring one house or small subdivision at a time, here and there across the landscape; taken in aggregate, the implications are significant.

Conclusions

Over the past several centuries of settlement, development, and in some cases abandonment, the Highlands landscape has undergone many transformations in land use and land cover. Since the 1970s, the four-state Highlands region has shown a sizable growth in human population, with increases on the order of 40 percent to 60 percent. Representing the expanding outer edge of the Philadelphia–New York to Hartford metropolitan "commutingshed," the Highlands population in each state grew faster than that of the state as a whole. While the rate of growth in the Connecticut Highlands has slowed steadily over the period, and has oscillated in New York and New Jersey, the rate in Pennsylvania has continued to climb. From 1970 to 1990, housing grew much faster than population in all four states, with fewer people living in each house. However, this trend has been stabilizing since 1990, although the percent increase in the number of Highlands housing units still outstrips the statewide totals. As a direct result of this increasing population, the amount of urban developed land has increased, transforming the Highlands' once largely rural landscapes.

Over the past several centuries, Highlands farmers have benefited from close proximity to a large and wealthy metropolitan region at which to market their varied harvest. However, with suburban and exurban development increasing everywhere in the Highlands, there is greater direct competition for a scarce resource: buildable land. Soaring land values coupled with the conflicts caused by encroaching urban development have made it difficult to continue farming successfully over the long term (Adelaja and Schilling 1999). The result has been that many farms have gone under. Many landowners have discontinued farming activities, and farms have been replaced by residential and commercial development. However, while the NASS statistics (fig. 12.1) suggest that the loss of farmland has somewhat stabilized across the Highlands region, the land-cover-change data paint a different picture, recording continued erosion in active farmland acreage. Nevertheless, expansion of farmland preservation policies, the societal push for more locally grown food, and the farming community's demonstrated resilience and innovation in adapting to changing technology and markets suggest that farming will continue to play a vital role in the Highlands in the coming decades, although on reduced acreage.

As detailed in chapters 6 and 7, Highlands forests have expanded greatly since the mid- to late 1800s through their regeneration on abandoned farmland and the cessation of widespread charcoal and fuelwood harvesting. While forest is still the most dominant land cover across most of the Highlands, the most recent land-cover-change data suggest that we have turned a corner; rather than increasing, forests are now decreasing in area. Even more troubling is the documented increase in the rate of deforestation as forests are cleared and converted to suburban residential and commercial development at a faster pace. While it is easy to understand why so many people have been attracted to the amenities of a rural home among the scenic forested ridges and valleys of the Highlands, there is a downside. Forests and wetlands play a vital role in the landscape because of all the attendant ecosystem services that they provide, such as watershed protection, carbon sequestration, wildlife habitat, and recreation, to name just a few (Costanza et al. 1997, 2006; Millennium Ecosystem Assessment 2005a, 2005b). As elsewhere around the world, we are coming to appreciate the vital role that forests play in supporting our global ecosystem, just as we are cutting them down with increasing rapidity.

The explosion of suburban to exurban development is a nationwide phenomenon from the lake country of the northern Midwest to the foothills of the Rocky Mountains, the pine flats of the southeast to the forested hills of the Highlands. This land-use trend is especially pronounced in areas with appealing natural settings that have varied topography and water areas along with quality-of life-amenities such as outdoor recreation opportunities that are within commuting distance of major metropolitan areas or areas attractive to active senior citizens (McGranahan 1999; Alig, Kline, and Lichenstein 2004; Stein et al. 2005). This development is displacing farms and forestlands, ranch lands, and wildlife habitat. Land-use patterns and economies centered on their local natural-resource base are being replaced by those of amenity-driven "quality of lifers" tied into a larger regional, if not globalized, economy. The ongoing pattern of development as documented by the USFS Highlands Regional Study provides clear evidence that the Highlands are part of this larger national trend. While the natural-resource-based economy of the Highlands was always tied to neighboring metropolitan areas through the export of iron, water, timber, and agricultural products, the Highlands remained somewhat physically and culturally removed. With the advent of modern interstate highways and the preeminence of the automobile in American life, rather than a landscape apart, the Highlands are increasingly being subsumed within the larger mid-Atlantic metropolitan region.

Acknowledgments

I would like to express my sincere gratitude to Carolyn Ferwerda, who was instrumental in compiling the U.S. Census and National Agricultural Statistics data as well as developing the graphics and maps. Many thanks to John Bognar for his assistance polishing the maps. I also want to acknowledge Mary Tyrrell, Myrna Hall, and Joel Stocker for providing the land-use and land-cover data for Pennsylvania and Connecticut.

References

Adelaja, A. O., and B. J. Schilling. 1999. "Innovative Approaches to Farmland Preservation." In *Contested Countryside: The Rural Urban Fringe in North America*, ed. O. Furuseth and M. Lapping. New Brunswick, NJ: Rutgers University Press.

Alig, R. J., J. D. Kline, and M. Lichenstein. 2004. "Urbanization on the U.S. Landscape: Looking Ahead in the 21st Century." *Landscape and Urban Planning* 69:219–234.

Bell, M. 1989. "Did New England Go downhill?" *Geographical Review* 79, no. 4: 450–466.

Chesapeake Bay Program. 2008. "Chesapeake Bay 2007 Health and Restoration Assessment." CBP/TRS-291–08 EPA-903-R-08–002, March. http://www.chesapeakebay.net/content/publications/cbp_26038.pdf.

Costanza, R., R. d'Arge, R. de Groot, S. Farber, M. Grasso, B. Hannon, K. Limburg, et al. 1997. "The Value of the World's Ecosystem Services and Natural Capital." *Nature* 387:253–260.

Costanza, R., C. Wilson, A. Troy, A. Voinov, S. Liu, and J. D'Agostino. 2006. "The Value of New Jersey's Ecosystem Services and Natural Capital." Trenton: New Jersey Department of Environmental Protection. http://www.nj.gov/dep/dsr/naturalcap/nat-cap-2.pdf.

Danbom, D. B. 1995. *Born in the Country: A History of Rural America*. Baltimore: Johns Hopkins University Press.

Danhof, C. H. 1969. *Change in Agriculture: The Northern United States, 1820–1870*. Cambridge, MA: Harvard University Press.

Dillon, J. J. 1941. *Seven Decades of Milk: A History of New York's Dairy Industry*. New York: Orange Judd Publishing.

Favretti, R. J. 1976. "Highlights of Connecticut Agriculture." Storrs: University of Connecticut Cooperative Extension Service.

Fletcher, S. W. 1950. *Pennsylvania Agriculture and Country Life: 1640–1840.* Harrisburg: Pennsylvania Historical and Museum Commission.

———. 1955. *Pennsylvania Agriculture and Country Life: 1840–1940.* Harrisburg: Pennsylvania Historical and Museum Commission.

Frantz, J. B. 1951. *Gail Borden: Dairyman to a Nation.* Norman: University of Oklahoma Press.

Gates, P. W. 1960. *The Farmer's Age: Agriculture 1815–1860.* Vol. 3 of *The Economic History of the United States.* New York: Holt, Rinehart and Winston.

Gibson, C. 1998. "Population of the 100 Largest Cities and Other Urban Places in the United States: 1790 to 1990." Population Division Working Paper No. 27. Washington, DC: U.S. Bureau of the Census. http://www.census.gov/population/www/documentation/twps0027.html.

Hedrick, U. P. 1933. *A History of Agriculture in the State of New York.* Albany: New York State Agricultural Society.

Kellogg, R., C. Lander, D. Moffitt, and N. Gollehon. 2000. "Manure Nutrients Relative to the Capacity of Cropland Pastureland to Assimilate Nutrients: Spatial and Temporal Trends for the United States." NPS00–0579, Natural Resources Conservation Service and ERS, December. http://www.nrcs.usda.gov/technical/NRI/pubs/manntr.html.

Kraft, H. C. 2001. *The Lenape-Delaware Indian Heritage: 10,000 B.C.–A.D. 2000.* Stanhope, NJ: Lenape Books.

Lathrop, R., C. Hatfield, and D. Tulloch. 2003. "Section 2: Land Resources." In "New York–New Jersey Highlands Regional Study Technical Report," NA-TP-04–03, ed. M. Hoppe. Newtown Square, PA: USDA Forest Service.

Lewis, H. M., and E. P. Goodrich. 1974. *Highway Traffic. Regional Survey.* Vol. 3 of *Regional Plan of New York and Its Environs.* New York: Arno Press (orig. pub. 1927).

McGranahan, D. 1999. "Natural Amenities Drive Rural Population Change." Agricultural Economic Report No. AER781. Washington, DC: Economic Research Services, USDA.

Millennium Ecosystem Assessment. 2005a. *Ecosystems and Human Well-being: Synthesis.* Washington, DC: Island Press. http://www.millenniumassessment.org/en/index.aspx.

Millennium Ecosystem Assessment. 2005b. *Ecosystems and Human Well-being: Wetlands and Water Synthesis.* Washington, DC: World Resources Institute. http://www.millenniumassessment.org/documents/document.358.aspx.pdf.

National Agricultural Statistics Service (NASS). 2009. "Census of Agriculture: 2007." Washington, DC: U.S. Department of Agriculture. http://www.agcensus.usda.gov/Publications/2007/Full_Report/index.asp.

North Jersey Transportation Planning Authority (NJTPA). 2008. "I-78 Transit Study: Final Report." Prepared by Dewberry, Inc., and Urbitran Associates. http://www.njtpa.org/Plan/Need/Corridor/I78/documents/FinalReport-I78–032008.pdf.

Ransom, J. M. 1966. *Vanishing Ironworks of the Ramapos: The Story of the Forges, Furnaces and Mines of the New Jersey–New York Border Area.* New Brunswick, NJ: Rutgers University Press.

Russell, H. S. 1976. *A Long Deep Furrow: Three Centuries of Farming in New England*. Hanover, NH: University Press of New England.

Rutsch, E. S. 1999. "The Story of Ironmaking Bloomery Forges at Picatinny Arsenal." Vicksburg, MS: U.S. Army Engineer Research and Development Center, Waterways Experiment Station.

Schmidt, H. G. 1972. *Rural Hunterdon: An Agricultural History*. New Brunswick, NJ: Rutgers University Press.

————. 1973. *Agriculture in New Jersey: A Three-Hundred-Year History*. New Brunswick, NJ: Rutgers University Press.

Stein, S. M., R. E. McRoberts, R. J. Alig, M. D. Nelson, D. M. Theobald, M. Eley, M. Dechter, and M. Carr. 2005. "Forests on the Edge: Housing Development on America's Private Forests." USDA Forest Service General Technical Report PNW-GTR-636.

Stoll, S. 2002. *Larding the Lean Earth: Soil and Society in Nineteenth-Century America*. New York: Hill and Wang.

Tyrrell, M. L., M. H. Hall, S. Myers, J. Cox, E. Hawes, L. Yocom, S. Price, T. Worthley, and J. Stocker. 2010. "Part 4: Growth and Impact Analysis." In "Highlands Regional Study: Connecticut and Pennsylvania 2010 Update," NA-TP-01–10. ed. M. Barnes. Newtown Square, PA: USDA Forest Service. http://na.fs.fed.us/pubs/stewardship/highlands_regional_study_ct_pa_10_print.pdf.

U.S. Census of Population and Housing. 2002. "Measuring America: The Decennial Censuses from 1790 to 2000." Washington, D.C.: U.S. Census Bureau. http://www.census.gov/prod/www/abs/decennial/.

U.S. Census of Population and Housing. 2011. "2010 Redistricting Data Release." Washington, D.C. : U.S. Census Bureau. http://2010.census.gov/2010census/data/redistricting-data.php.

Wacker, P. O. 1975. *Land and People: A Cultural Geography of Preindustrial New Jersey: Origins and Settlement Patterns*. New Brunswick, NJ: Rutgers University Press.

Watts, R. L. 1925. *Rural Pennsylvania*. New York: MacMillan.

Zelinsky, W. 1962. "Changes in the Geographic Patterns of Rural Populations in the United States, 1790–1960." *Geographical Review* 52, no. 4: 492–524.

In addition to the works cited throughout the text, the following websites and other materials were consulted:

NYCroads. "The Roads of Metro New York." www.nycroads.com/roads.

Pennsylvania Department of Transportation. ftp.dot.state.pa.us/public/pdf/BPR_pdf_files/MAPS/statewide/TYPE15.pdf.

Pennsylvania Highways. www.pahighways.com/interstates/.

"Thruway History: The Beginning." The Upstate New York Roads Site. http://www.upstatenyroads.com/thruway-history1.shtml.

13

Open Space and Recreation in the Highlands

Daniel Chazin

Introduction

Situated near the populous Philadelphia–New York–Hartford metropolitan region, the Highlands have long been treasured as a recreational outlet and source of spiritual renewal by the citizens of the region. The preservation of acreage in the Highlands was motivated by the desire to protect open space, preserve scenic beauty, and establish new recreational opportunities. The Highlands also served a pivotal (and often underappreciated) role as the formative ground for a number of ideas and movements that spread throughout the country and had a major impact on our national land preservation and environmental policies.

Early Recreational History of the Highlands (1800s)

There is evidence of recreational uses of the Highlands as early as the eighteenth century. Some of these were passive uses such as hiking and hunting (i.e., they involved minimal development and left the land relatively undisturbed), but in the nineteenth century, many facilities were built in the Highlands—in New Jersey, New York, and Pennsylvania—for active recreation (involving more intensive development such as hotels, amusement parks, and camps).

About 1810, the Heath House—described as "a renowned spa [and] summering place for the elite who desired escape from the cities' heat"—was established on Schooleys Mountain in Morris County, New Jersey. Another famous hotel at Schooleys Mountain was the Belmont House, whose register "gathered such names as Goulds, Vanderbilts, Astors and Roosevelts." Schooleys Mountain remained a popular destination until the twentieth century (Washington Township Historical Society 1976).

Nearly ninety years later, Lake Hopatcong became a favorite destination for recreation, with rail lines bringing people from the cities to the lake for a day or weekend. The largest lake in New Jersey, Lake Hopatcong was raised by twelve feet about 1830 so it could serve as the single largest source of water for the Morris Canal. When the Central Railroad of New Jersey reached the lake in 1882, it realized the lake's potential for recreation, and it soon began running excursion trains to Nolan's Point. The Lackawanna Railroad, whose line touched the southern end of the lake, soon followed. By 1900, there were more than forty hotels and rooming houses at Lake Hopatcong. Of these, the most prestigious was the Hotel Breslin, completed in 1887. The Bertrand Island Amusement Park opened on the lake in 1924. Lake Hopatcong remained a major recreational destination until the Depression of the 1930s and the onset of World War II. The last hotel on the lake was destroyed by fire in 1972. Today, Lake Hopatcong has evolved into a year-round residential community.

The Highlands in New York were also developed for recreational uses during the mid-nineteenth century, a period when epidemics were prevalent in New York City. The Hudson Highlands were viewed as a "healthful mountain countryside" that offered "the conditions for good health." Many New Yorkers flocked to the Highlands—considered to offer the "nearest mountain air"—in an attempt to escape the ravages of the diseases that plagued the city (Dunwell 2008). Cornwall, on the west side of the Hudson, was a popular destination. The well-known writer Nathaniel Parker Willis spent the summer of 1851 at the Sutherland House in Cornwall, and he publicized the benefits of the area. While there were only a handful of boardinghouses in Cornwall when Willis stayed there in 1851, there were dozens of them twenty years later. Another important destination in the Highlands was Cozzens Hotel, which opened on the grounds of West Point in 1849 and moved in 1861 to a promontory on the Hudson in adjacent Highlands Falls (Dunwell 2008).

A favorite destination of nineteenth-century hikers in the Hudson Valley was Mount Beacon, which towers over the city of the same name along the shore of the Hudson River. The mountain is named after the beacons lit there during the Revolutionary War to warn the Americans of the approach of British troops. In the 1830s, "the ascent of Mount Beacon was praised as 'worthwhile' and easily accomplished 'by the help of some boy-guide, to be picked up at the 'Corners'" (Waterman and Waterman 2003). On Memorial Day in 1902, the Mt. Beacon Incline Railway opened, carrying passengers to the crest of the 1,540-foot mountain. The 65 percent grade was the steepest of any inclined railway in the world. Patrons could spend the day at The Casino, a restaurant and dance hall, or even stay overnight at the Beaconcrest Hotel. More than 60,000 people rode the railway during its first season, and the number had increased to 110,000 twenty years later. The hotel was destroyed by fire in 1932 and was never rebuilt.

The scenic and tranquil hills of the Pennsylvania Highlands were the site of a summer recreational colony established toward the end of the nineteenth century. When Robert H. Coleman, owner and operator of the Cornwall

Iron Furnace, constructed a railroad in 1883 from Lebanon south to Cornwall and Conewago (west of Elizabethtown), in the southwestern corner of the Pennsylvania Highlands, he selected a particularly scenic spot along the rail line as a station stop and recreation area (Bitner 1990). Named Mount Gretna, the area was cleared to create a park, and Conewago Creek was dammed in 1885 to create Lake Conewago (see plate 33). In 1889 a four-mile-long narrow-gauge railroad was built to carry tourists to the top of the nearby Governor Dick Hill (named for a local eighteenth-century woodcutter and charcoal burner dubbed "Governor" Dick by his friends). Beginning in 1892 Mount Gretna played host to the Pennsylvania Chautauqua Society and camp meeting of the United Brethren during the summer months, with small cottages built to serve the summer residents. Several buildings for public gatherings, including a Hall of Philosophy (see plate 34) and a Tabernacle, were also constructed, and restaurants and hotels were established. Mount Gretna continued as a popular summer resort until the advent of World War II. Today, it has evolved into a center for arts and culture and a year-round residential community (Bitner 1990).

Another recreational use of the Highlands during the nineteenth century was as a site for youth camps. In 1885 Sumner Dudley, known as the "grandfather of the camping movement," took 7 teenage boys from the Newburgh YMCA on a one-week camping excursion to nearby Orange Lake. The following year, the camp was moved to Wawayanda Lake in the Highlands of New Jersey, and 12 boys attended. This camp is considered to be one of the first youth camps in the United States. By 1889 there were 65 boys at the camp. As the number of boys increased, the campsite became too small, and in 1891 the camp was moved to Lake Champlain in the Adirondacks, but a Jersey Boys' YMCA camp was reestablished on Wawayanda Lake in 1901. In the summer of 1913 there were about 360 boys and men at the camp, with 158 boys of ages twelve to fourteen and 102 boys between fifteen and seventeen years of age (the remainder were over eighteen); a news article about the camp described its location as "perhaps the most inaccessible spot in the State." The camp remained there until 1919, when a new camp opened in Andover, New Jersey.

In sum, although the Highlands began to be used for recreational purposes in the nineteenth century, most such uses were active rather than passive. Moreover, the recreational uses were primarily private, mainly for-profit operations, and little thought was given to the preservation of lands for public use.

The State Parks Movement in the Highlands

By the start of the twentieth century, industrial development of the Highlands had declined. Many iron furnaces throughout the Highlands were abandoned in the second half of the nineteenth century. The West Point Foundry along the Hudson River in Cold Spring closed in 1911, and a chemical factory at Manitou was also abandoned about this time. As a result, the population of the Hudson Highlands had decreased to about a quarter of its Civil War–era levels, and the area "was reverting to wilderness" (Dunwell 2008). Around this time, the nature of the recreational uses of the Highlands began to change from active to passive. In addition, the preservation of lands for scenic and recreational purposes began.

One of the first hikers to explore the rejuvenated Highlands was William Thompson Howell (1873–1916), who would often hike as much as thirty miles a day, no matter what the weather (fig. 13.1). Described by one writer as "the poet laureate of the Hudson Highlands" who "marshaled public opinion to the cause of conservation," Howell proposed that the Highlands should be preserved in their natural state. Arguing against the development of facilities for active recreation in the area, Howell contended "there is something more at stake here than the preservation of the scenery. . . . There is a wild charm and isolation about the Highlands that will fly forever when the 'improvements' begin to come in" (Waterman and Waterman 2003). Although

Figure 13.1. Photo of William Thompson Howell (on right) hiking with companion, circa 1910. Photo: William Thompson Howell, Highlands of the Hudson, Photography Collection, Miriam and Ira D. Wallach Division of Art, Prints and Photographs, The New York Public Library, Astor, Lenox, and Tilden Foundations.

his vision of the Highlands was not fulfilled, his published diaries, *The Hudson Highlands*, inspired generations of hikers and helped spur the protection of the area (Howell 1933–1934).

The most notable conservation effort at the dawn of the twentieth century was the establishment of the Palisades Interstate Park Commission to protect the Palisades of the Hudson (Binnewies 2001). Largely through the efforts of the New Jersey Federation of Women's Clubs, this bistate commission was established in 1900, and it acquired lands along the New Jersey Palisades, primarily with private funds (Myles and Chazin 2010). Although the commission's jurisdiction did not initially extend to the Highlands, the scope of its authority was later expanded, and the commission soon became a critical party in the effort to preserve the Highlands from inappropriate development.

In 1907 Dr. Edward Partridge, a Manhattan physician who had a summer home on Storm King Mountain, organized the Association for the Protection of the Highlands of the Hudson, which campaigned for the establishment of a national park in the area. At Dr. Partridge's behest, the American Scenic and Historic Preservation Society proposed legislation to safeguard the Hudson Highlands. It drafted a bill that would create a 122-square-mile park on both sides of the Hudson, from Peekskill Bay on the south to Newburgh Bay on the north (Dunwell 2008).

When their efforts to create a national park in the Highlands proved unsuccessful, these groups turned to the state government. The Hudson-Fulton Commission, which had been established to organize efforts to commemorate the tricentennial of Henry Hudson's landmark voyage up the Hudson in 1609, endorsed two bills: the Bennett bill, which proposed the creation of a park on a half-mile-wide strip of land along the Hudson, from Jones Point to Storm King; and the Wainwright bill, which proposed the creation of a state forest reserve encompassing about seventy-five thousand square miles on each side of the river. However, these efforts did not achieve any meaningful success. The Bennett bill failed to pass the legislature, and while the Wainwright bill was enacted in 1909, the area on the east shore of the Hudson was not included, and the legislation permitted the harvesting of trees in the seventy-five-square-mile Highlands of the Hudson Forest Preserve that was established on the west side of the Hudson (Dunwell 2008).

Although legislation failed to achieve the preservation of parkland in the Hudson Highlands at the start of the twentieth century, private philanthropy stepped in to create what is now known as Harriman–Bear Mountain State Parks—the first major piece of open space in the Highlands to be preserved as parkland. The initial piece of land for these parks was a gift of Mary Averell Harriman, the widow of financier and railroad magnate Edward Harriman, in 1910. The catalyst for the establishment of these parks was, ironically, a proposal made in 1908 to relocate the Sing Sing Prison to Bear Mountain.

The state purchased a 740-acre tract at the base of Bear Mountain, and work began on the construction of the new prison (Myles and Chazin 2010). Those who loved the beauty of the Highlands were outraged at this proposal. Among the opponents who fought it was Dr. Partridge, who had advocated the establishment of a national preserve in the Highlands. In a September 1908 article titled "The Fight to Save the Beauties of the Hudson," the *New York Times* noted that the prison could be a "mixed blessing" since it was projected that only thirty-three acres would be needed for the prison, "while the rest, it is promised, will practically be a park" (New York Times 1908).

In December 1909 Mary Harriman proposed to donate to the state ten thousand acres of her estate for a park, along with $1 million to administer the park, provided that additional funds were raised from other sources, that the jurisdiction of the Palisades Interstate Park Commission (established in 1900 as a bistate agency to protect the Palisades in New Jersey) was extended northward, and that the prison project was discontinued. The various conditions were soon met, and on October 29, 1910, Mary Harriman's son W. Averell presented the Palisades Interstate Park Commission with a check for $1 million and a deed for the ten thousand acres of land, which was dedicated as Harriman State Park. The land previously acquired by the state at Bear Mountain for the now-abandoned prison was designated Bear Mountain State Park, which was opened to the public on July 5, 1913 (Binnewies 2001; Myles and Chazin 2010).

Under the leadership of general manager and chief engineer Maj. William A. Welch, Harriman–Bear Mountain State Parks were developed extensively for both active and passive recreation. These parks became a model emulated in other states, and Major Welch was known as the "father" of the state park movement and one of the pioneers in the national park movement. One of the first structures built in the park for public recreation—the Bear Mountain Inn—opened in 1915. Built of rustic stone and timber and with furnishings of American chestnut, the architecture of this landmark building greatly influenced the design of park structures throughout the country. Boy Scout camps for the scouts of New York City were established in the parks beginning in 1913 (Myles and Chazin 2010; Waterman and Waterman 2003). By 1927 the Boy Scout camps were moved to the Ten Mile River Scout Reservation in Sullivan County, but many more children's camps were built in the 1930s through the efforts of the Civilian Conservation Corps (Myles and Chazin 2010).

A four-thousand-acre tract of Highlands land in Litchfield County, Connecticut, was dedicated in 1913 as a nature preserve by Alain Campbell White and his sister, May. The son of a wealthy New York real estate magnate whose family estate was on Bantam Lake, White was inspired to preserve the entire surrounding area to ensure that its natural beauty would not be marred. He established the White Memorial Foundation, dedicated to recreation, education, conservation, and research, and acquired neighboring properties, which he dedicated as a nature preserve (Libov 1988). During White's lifetime, the property was managed as a private preserve, but it was subsequently opened to public use. White also donated thousands of acres to the state of Connecticut for parkland. In 1918 he gave fifteen hundred acres to create Macedonia Brook State Park, which was later enlarged to twenty-three hundred acres to become one of Connecticut's largest state parks. The Appalachian Trail originally went through this park, but it was relocated in the 1980s to another route. Other parks and forests established through donations by White and his foundation include Kent Falls State Park, Mohawk State Forest, Campbell Falls State Park, and Peoples State Forest (Brenneman 2009). These parks form the core of public open space in the Connecticut Highlands to the present day.

The Rising Popularity of Hiking and the Establishment of Marked Hiking Trails

Recognizing the importance of establishing and maintaining a network of hiking trails in the new Harriman–Bear Mountain State Parks, the first general manager of the parks, Maj. William A. Welch, began informal talks in the summer of 1920 with the hiking clubs to enlist them in an effort to create a system of marked trails in the parks. The first trail map of the parks was published that same year. On the evening of October 19, 1920, representatives of the major clubs met at the log cabin atop Abercrombie & Fitch's store (the leading sporting goods outfitter at the time) and agreed to form a permanent federation of hiking clubs, to be known as the Palisades Interstate Park Trail Conference (renamed the New York–New Jersey Trail Conference in 1922) (Waterman and Waterman 2003; Scherer 1995). With the encouragement of Major Welch, the Trail Conference promptly started work on several important long-distance trails that crisscrossed the park. The first major trail completed (in the spring of 1921) was the twenty-four-mile-long Tuxedo–Jones Point Trail (now known as the Ramapo-Dunderberg Trail). The Tuxedo–Jones Point Trail was soon followed by the Arden-Surebridge Trail (1921), the Tuxedo–Mount Ivy Trail (1923), the Appalachian Trail (1923–1924), and the Suffern–Bear Mountain Trail (1927) (Myles and Chazin 2010; Waterman and Waterman 2003; Scherer 1995). Most of the trails that presently exist in Harriman–Bear Mountain Parks were built in the 1920s, and they represent the first trail network in the Highlands. The Trail Conference was responsible for the creation of hiking trails not only in Harriman–Bear Mountain Parks but throughout other areas of the Highlands (as well as elsewhere) in southern New York and northern New Jersey. According to Raymond Torrey, a leader of the Trail Conference, the trails were laid out "to include the highest scenic qualities: directness of route, supplies of water . . . and occasional ledges and cliff climbs to make the routes interesting" (Scherer 1995).

The *New York Walk Book* by Raymond Torrey, Frank Place, and Robert L. Dickinson was published in 1923. This was the first guidebook to hiking in the New York–New Jersey Highlands. At the time, few marked hiking trails existed, and most of the book was devoted to a description of hiking routes on old woods roads and unmarked paths. Subsequent editions of the book contained mostly descriptions of marked trails; the book is now in its seventh edition. In addition to promoting the growing popularity of hiking as a form of passive outdoor recreation, the *New York Walk Book* informed readers on the region's natural and cultural history and celebrated the region's scenic beauty with Dickinson's wonderful pen-and-ink drawings (Figure 13.2) (Scherer 1995).

During the 1920s, most hikers lived in New York City, and few had cars. Railroads were the primary means of transportation to the trailheads, and many hiking clubs were formed. The Appalachian Mountain Club (AMC), one of the oldest conservation organizations in the United States, formed a New York chapter in 1912 (Waterman and Waterman 2003). Subsequently, AMC chapters were also formed in Connecticut and in the Delaware valley area of New Jersey and Pennsylvania. Chapters of the Green Mountain Club and of the Adirondack Mountain Club were also formed in the New York City area. Some clubs allowed only males (e.g, the Fresh Air Club) or only females (e.g., the Inkowas Club) to join, and many clubs were "restricted" (no Jews or blacks allowed). New clubs were formed to accommodate those who were denied membership in the more established clubs. Many of the clubs also built and maintained trails (Waterman and Waterman 2003).

During the 1920s, Dr. Will Monroe, a professor at the Montclair Normal School, a New Jersey college, established an extensive network of trails in the Wyanokies of New Jersey. The New York Section of the Green Mountain Club, which Monroe organized, maintained the trails. The area was also the site of a camp established by the Nature Friends, a German-speaking group, which had more than one hundred cabins and a four-hundred-foot-long swimming pool, fed by a natural stream (Waterman and Waterman 2003; Chazin 2004).

In a 1921 article published in the *Journal of the American Institute of Architects*, Benton MacKaye proposed the creation of a 2,000-mile trail that would extend along the crest of the Appalachian Mountains from Maine to Georgia. At a meeting held on April 25, 1922, the New York–New Jersey Trail Conference met with MacKaye and enthusiastically endorsed the concept of an Appalachian Trail. Scouting of the route from Connecticut to the Delaware River soon began, and by January 1924 a 20-mile section of the Appalachian Trail (AT) was opened from Bear Mountain to Arden, at the western end of Harriman State Park. This was the first section to be completed of this landmark trail, which today extends 2,170 miles from Mount Katahdin in Maine to Springer Mountain in Georgia (Anderson 2002; Scherer 1995).

Figure 13.2. "Our Best Wild Up and Down Country," print from the *New York Walk Book* by Robert L. Dickinson. New York–New Jersey Trail Conference, *New York Walk Book.*

Other portions of the AT through the Highlands were built a few years later. West of Harriman State Park, the AT was routed through the then–privately owned Sterling Forest before dipping south into New Jersey. Rather than following the Highlands southwest across New Jersey and into Pennsylvania, the AT headed west, parallel to the New Jersey–New York state line, to reach the Kittatinny Ridge just north of High Point. It then followed the Kittatinny Ridge southwest to cross the Delaware River at the Water Gap and continue down the Blue Mountain ridge in Pennsylvania. Where permissions from private landowners could not be obtained, the trail was routed along roads. Work on the AT east of the Hudson River, from the Bear Mountain Bridge to Connecticut, was begun by Murray Stevens in 1927–1928 and completed in 1930 (Waterman and Waterman 2003). In Connecticut, the AT route was scouted and built by Ned Anderson, a local farmer, with the assistance of a local Boy Scout troop that he had organized. By 1933 the AT was completed from New York to the Massachusetts border (Waterman and Waterman 2003).

Expansion of the Parks—1920 to 1960

A favorite haunt of William Thompson Howell, Storm King—which rises abruptly from sea level at the Hudson River to a height of thirteen hundred feet—has long been a landmark for travelers along the Hudson (fig. 13.3). In 1922 Dr. Ernest Stillman donated about eight hundred acres on Storm King Mountain to the Palisades Interstate Park Commission to preserve the scenic

beauty of the Storm King Highway, which opened the same year. A network of hiking trails was developed in this park, which offers spectacular views over the Hudson River and the East Hudson Highlands, and the park has been expanded to about eighteen hundred acres (Chazin 2005).

In 1928 Dr. Ernest Stillman set aside the adjacent thirty-eight-thousand-acre Black Rock Forest as a research and demonstration forest. He also built trails through the forest and invited hikers to enjoy them and the Trail Conference to maintain them. Upon his death in 1949, he bequeathed the property to Harvard University. Today, the Black Rock Forest Consortium manages the land (Chazin 2005). Although the primary mission of Black Rock Forest has always been scientific study rather than recreation, the trails and woods roads of Black Rock Forest remain open to hikers, and swimming is permitted in one of its ponds. Hunting and fishing are also allowed, but only for members of the private Black Rock Game Club.

As was the case throughout the Highlands, vast tracts of land in northwestern Connecticut were owned by the iron companies, who used them to provide the charcoal needed to fuel their furnaces. With the demise of the iron industry in the latter half of the nineteenth century, the iron companies sought to divest themselves of these cut-over forest lands. In 1927 the state of Connecticut purchased three thousand acres from an iron company to create the Housatonic State Forest. Expanded to ten thousand acres by subsequent purchases, the forest offers a variety of recreational activities. The Connecticut Forest & Park Association (CFPA) has been instrumental in the establishment of other parks and forests in the Connecticut Highlands (Milne 1995; Brenneman 2009). It partnered with the White Memorial Foundation in 1921 to preserve twenty-nine hundred acres as Mohawk State Forest.

Figure 13.3. Photo of Storm King Mountain, at the northern gate of the Hudson Highlands, taken from Little Stony Point, circa 1910. William Thompson Howell, Highlands of the Hudson, Photography Collection, Miriam and Ira D. Wallach Division of Art, Prints and Photographs, The New York Public Library, Astor, Lenox, and Tilden Foundations.

In 1924 CFPA was instrumental in coordinating donations from a number of civic groups and individuals (including the White Memorial Foundation) to purchase and preserve the Peoples State Forest (Landgraf 2005). And in 1929 CFPA established the Blue-Blazed Hiking Trail System, which traverses public and private lands throughout Connecticut (Waterman and Waterman 2003; Milne 1995).

In 1929 Dr. Ernest Fahnestock donated twenty-four hundred acres of land in the East Hudson Highlands to the State of New York in memory of his brother, Maj. Clarence Fahnestock. Through acquisition of adjoining property, Fahnestock State Park now includes more than twelve thousand acres (Chazin 2005). It contains an extensive network of hiking trails, including a section of the Appalachian Trail. In the summer, swimming is permitted on a beach on Canopus Lake.

Bull Hill (Mount Taurus), just north of Cold Spring, was acquired by the Hudson River Stone Company in 1931. It opened a quarry on the west side of the mountain, facing the Hudson River. Citizens were outraged at the gash on the face of the mountain created by the quarry, and Governor Franklin D. Roosevelt appointed a committee to explore fund-raising to enable the state to acquire the land. But the committee was not successful in its efforts, and the quarrying continued (Dunwell 2008).

Frustrated at the inability of the state to stop the destruction, a group of influential citizens established the Hudson River Conservation Society in 1936. Recognizing that the purchase of the Bull Hill quarry would only result in the establishment of another quarry on a different parcel, the society began to identify potential quarry sites and to negotiate with the owners to place deed restrictions on their property that would prevent such an undesirable use. By 1938 the society had succeeded in preserving 2,350 acres in this manner. It also raised funds that enabled it to purchase about 250 acres on the northwest face of Breakneck Ridge and donate the property to the state. The rugged trail up Breakneck Ridge has become one of the most popular hiking trails in the Highlands, offering spectacular views over the Hudson River. In 1939 the same group succeeded in preserving land adjacent to Anthony's Nose, another popular destination for hikers, which overlooks the east end of the Bear Mountain Bridge. Although the owners of the quarry on Bull Hill rejected a purchase offer as too low, the quarrying operations ended in 1944 and the land subsequently was acquired by the state and added to Hudson Highlands State Park (Dunwell 2008).

Although the 1923 edition of the *New York Walk Book* included a "New Jersey Highlands and Ramapo River" chapter, most of the routes described required hikers to follow woods roads or streams. There were few trails in the area, and nearly all of the land was privately owned. This began to change in the 1930s. In 1936 Abram Hewitt's son, Erskine, donated the Ringwood Manor house and 95 surrounding acres to the State of New Jersey. His nephew, Norvin Green, donated additional property, bringing the total to 579 acres (Chazin 2004). Then, in 1946, Norvin Green gave the state more than 4,000 acres in the Wyanokies, which became Norvin Green State Forest. Most of the trail network created in the 1920s by professor Will Monroe and the Green Mountain Club was now situated on public land.

Around 1930 many volunteers took it upon themselves to create new hiking trails in Harriman–Bear Mountain State Parks, with the result that there were many conflicting and confusing routes. To resolve what became known as "The Great Trail War," the New York–New Jersey Trail Conference was reactivated in April 1931 with Raymond Torrey as its chair, and it was agreed that all trails and relocations had to be approved by the Trail Conference. Another "Trail War" developed in 1937, but it was soon resolved through efforts of the Trail Conference (Waterman and Waterman 2003; Scherer 1995).

The creation of the Civilian Conservation Corps and the Works Progress Administration during the Great Depression of the 1930s facilitated the construction of new roads and recreational facilities in Harriman–Bear Mountain State Parks (Binnewies 2001; Myles and Chazin 2010). Many children's camps were built in the park during this period. When the park was established, it had only fourteen lakes. Another twenty-two lakes were built, and some of the others were enlarged to provide swimming and boating opportunities for the children attending these camps. Roads were constructed into the interior of the park to provide access to the camps, and a scenic drive known as the Perkins Memorial Drive was built to enable visitors to drive to the summit of Bear Mountain and enjoy the scenic views.

During this period, new state parks were also established in Pennsylvania on lands that had formerly been denuded by clear-cutting. The Hopewell Furnace ironworks had been erected in the Highlands of southeast Pennsylvania in 1771. To provide the furnace with charcoal, the timber in the area was repeatedly cut. Only after the furnace closed in 1883 did a second-growth forest begin to cover the land. In the 1930s, the federal government acquired property in the area as part of a national project to reclaim marginal lands, and the Civilian Conservation Corps built recreation sites and camping areas. In 1946 most of the property was transferred to the Commonwealth of Pennsylvania, which established French Creek State Park. This 7,526-acre park offers many recreational opportunities, including hiking, bicycling, horseback riding, and camping. Boating and fishing are allowed at two lakes, a pool is provided for swimming, and hunting is allowed in most of the park as well as on adjacent state game lands (SGL). The federal government retained the furnace site itself, which is now administered by the National Park Service as the Hopewell Furnace National Historic Site.

Farther west, the Pennsylvania Highlands are locally known as the Furnace Hills because of their proximity to the Cornwall and Speedwell iron furnaces, both of which were principally owned by the Coleman family. These wooded ridges were heavily cut over as a source of charcoal to fuel the furnaces (Bitner 1990). In 1934 Clarence Schock acquired a 1,105-acre parcel surrounding one of the higher peaks—Governor Dick Hill above the resort village of Mount Gretna. He donated the land to the school district of the borough of Mount Joy in 1953 as a playground and public park. When the school district sought to be relieved of its responsibilities for the land in 1998, the Clarence Schock Foundation and the county of Lebanon were appointed cotrustees of the land, which is now known as the Park at Governor Dick. The summit has long served as a favored destination of hikers because it provides expansive views of the Pennsylvania Highlands and the neighboring Lancaster and Lebanon valleys. A sixty-six-foot-high concrete-and-steel observation tower was erected in 1954, replacing earlier wooden observation towers. This tower still stands today. An extensive network of trails for hiking, biking, and horseback riding crisscrosses the park and the adjacent 2,800 acres of State Game Lands (SGL) 145. The Pennsylvania Game Commission manages another 10,500 acres of state game lands (SGL 156 and 46) in the Furnace Hills as public hunting and recreation lands.

From Parks to Open Space: The Evolution of an Idea—1960 to the Present

The fight over a proposed development at Storm King Mountain helped crystallize the growing recognition of the Highlands as a scenic landscape of national significance. In 1962 the Consolidated Edison Company proposed to construct a large pumped-storage hydroelectric plant on lands owned by the Palisades Interstate Park Commission at the base of Storm King Mountain, with power lines extending across the river to Putnam County. At the same time, the Central Hudson Gas and Electric Company proposed the establishment of a similar plant at the base of Breakneck Ridge. The Con Edison plan was initially met with opposition from the Palisades Interstate Park Commission, the Hudson River Conservation Society, and the West Point Military Academy. However, when Con Edison agreed to move the plant to private land on the north face of Storm King and to put the transmission lines under the Hudson River, these groups dropped their objections to the plan. Others did not, however. A leader in the fight against the plant was Leo Rothschild, conservation chairman of the New York–New Jersey Trail Conference, who decried "the desecration of the northern gate of the Hudson Highlands." The Scenic Hudson Preservation Conference was formed in 1963 to fight this proposed intrusion on the beauty of the Highlands (Dunwell 2008).

Despite opposition from environmentalists, in 1965 the Federal Power Commission (FPC) granted Con Edison a license to construct the plant (Dunwell 2008). Later the same year, the United States Court of Appeals for the Second Circuit reversed the FPC's decision, ruling that the FPC "must include as a basic concern the preservation of natural beauty." After holding additional extensive hearings, the FPC issued a decision in 1970, again granting a license to Con Edison to construct the plant. But more legal challenges were raised, and the leadership of Con Edison changed. Its new chairman, Charles Luce, decided to consider a mediated settlement. Finally, in 1980, a settlement was announced that provided for the pumped-storage project to be abandoned, with the land acquired by Con Edison for the project to be donated to the Palisades Interstate Park Commission and the town of Cornwall (Dunwell 2008). The *New York Times* characterized the settlement as "a peace treaty for the Hudson" (New York Times 1980).

The landmark decision of the Second Circuit in *Scenic Hudson Preservation Conference v. Federal Power Commission* established the right of citizen groups to sue a government agency to protect natural resources and scenic beauty. Not only did the decision lead to the abandonment of the proposed power plant, but it also set a national precedent for environmental issues and is credited with launching the modern environmental movement (Dunwell 2008).

In the first half of the twentieth century, many of the parks in the four-state Highlands region resulted from private donations by wealthy individuals.

During this period, comparatively few parks were purchased with public funds. Starting in the 1960s, however, the trend shifted with the rise of publicly funded open-space preservation programs.

One of the first major acquisitions by the New Jersey Green Acres program (established in 1961) was the 4,000-acre area surrounding Wawayanda Lake, purchased in 1963 from the New Jersey Zinc Company, which had proposed subdividing the acreage for development. Another 3,200 acres were added to Wawayanda State Park in 1966, and subsequent acquisitions have brought it to its present-day size of 17,500 acres (Chazin 2004). Today Wawayanda State Park contains a network of trails, mostly old woods roads. Most of the trails are open to mountain bikes as well as foot travel. The centerpiece of the park is the 255-acre Wawayanda Lake, which offers swimming and boating in season.

During the 1960s and 1970s, the state of New Jersey and the county of Bergen acquired lands in the Ramapo Mountains that had been privately owned. In 1964 Ringwood State Park was expanded by the acquisition of a 541-acre tract that included Shepherd Lake. The park's size was increased again in 1966, when a 1,000-acre tract containing Skylands Manor was purchased from Shelton College, and in 1972, when the Bear Swamp Lake area was acquired from the private Bear Swamp Club. In 1976 the estate of the late Clifford F. MacEvoy, south of Ringwood State Park, was acquired by the state and became Ramapo Mountain State Forest. Next, in 1978, the Green Engineering Camp of Cooper Union, which contained several trails laid out by the former Cooper Union Hiking Club, was added to Ringwood State Park. The 1981 acquisition of the 540-acre Muscarelle Tract closed the gap between Ringwood State Park and Ramapo Mountain State Forest. In 1972 Bergen County acquired the 2,145-acre Ramapo Valley County Reservation in Mahwah (Chazin 2004).

In the late 1970s, under the leadership of Frank Oliver of the New York–New Jersey Trail Conference, the Youth Conservation Corps constructed a network of trails in the area, which incorporated many of the former carriage roads (Chazin 2004). Following the acquisition of Camp Glen Gray by Bergen County in 2002, the trails in the area were revitalized under the leadership of John Moran, North Jersey Trails chair of the New York–New Jersey Trail Conference. Mountain bikes are allowed on many of the former carriage roads surrounding Skylands Manor, while other trails are for hiking only. Shepherd Lake is a popular destination for swimming and picnicking in the summer.

The 5,283-acre Nockamixon State Park—the second-largest state park in the Pennsylvania Highlands—was first proposed in 1958 by the Army Corps of Engineers. Tohickon Creek was dammed, forming the 1,450-acre Lake Nockamixon (the largest lake in southeastern Pennsylvania), and the park was opened to the public in 1973. The lake is popular for boating and warmwater fishing. Trails are available for hiking, bicycling, and horseback riding, and a pool is provided for swimming. About 3,500 acres are open to hunting, with an additional 2,000 acres of SGL situated just northeast of the park.

In 1900, to protect the sources of its water supply, the city of Newark acquired fifteen thousand acres in Morris, Passaic, and Sussex counties (later enlarged to thirty-five thousand acres). For many years, the property was closed to most recreational uses, including hiking. A major policy change occurred in 1974, when the property was opened to recreational use by the public through a controlled-access-by-permit program. The Newark Watershed Conservation and Development Corporation was assigned to manage the property, and various recreational uses are now allowed (Chazin 2004). A volunteer group was asked to create a twenty-five-mile hiking trail network on watershed property, which is also open to hunting and horseback riding. More recently, sections of the Highlands Trail have been routed over watershed property. Unlike the practice in most other public lands in the area, hiking in the watershed is not permitted during hunting season (except on Sundays and other times during the hunting season when hunting is not allowed).

Located in the heart of the New Jersey Highlands, Morris County has developed an extensive network of public parks that preserve scenic features and offer many recreational opportunities to the public, including hiking, bicycling, and camping. The 3,042-acre Mahlon Dickerson Reservation is the largest Morris County park, and it offers year-round hiking and camping opportunities, with a section of the Highlands Trail traversing the reservation. Other noteworthy Morris County parks include Mount Hope Historical Park, whose trails pass by numerous iron mine shafts (active from about 1850 to 1958); Pyramid Mountain Natural Historic Area, which features Tripod Rock, a unique glacial erratic perched on three smaller boulders; and Black River County Park, which includes a remote, wild stretch of the Black River (Chazin 2004).

In 1995 the Morris Land Conservancy (now the Land Conservancy of New Jersey) enlisted the aid of the New York–New Jersey Trail Conference to construct a trail that would link the public open spaces in the Farny Highlands in Morris County. Over the next decade, the Trail Conference was able to secure public access to certain private lands in the area, including the Jersey City and Newark Watersheds. Trail Conference volunteers have since constructed a thirty-two-mile network of trails in the area (Chazin 2004).

In addition to acquiring lands for parks and forests, state agencies have acquired lands to promote a diversity of wildlife, with hunting permitted in season. In New Jersey, several of these wildlife management areas (Berkshire Valley, Black River, and Wildcat Ridge) are located in the Highlands, primarily in Morris County. Hiking is also a permitted use, and a developed trail system has been established in Wildcat Ridge (Chazin 2004). In the Pennsylvania Highlands, various parcels of SGL provide thousands of acres of public hunting lands that are protected as open space.

In the late 1980s a proposal was put forth to develop Sterling Forest, the largest remaining undeveloped, privately owned tract of land in the New York metropolitan area. As discussed in chapter 14, a group called the Public-Private Partnership to Save Sterling Forest was formed to spearhead efforts to protect this property, and both private and public funds were raised to secure the future of the largest parcel of open space in the New York metropolitan area still in private hands. In February 1998 the major portion of more than fifteen thousand acres was acquired by the Palisades Interstate Park Commission and opened to the public as Sterling Forest State Park (Chazin 2005). Subsequent acquisitions have expanded the size of the park. A network of woods roads and trails crisscrosses the property, and various recreational activities, including hiking, bicycling, and cross-country skiing, are permitted. Hunting is allowed in season by permit.

Standing somewhat isolated on the northwest flank of the Highlands in Orange County, New York, Schunemunk Mountain has one of the largest elevation differences from base to summit of any of the Highlands peaks. The mountain is located just west of the New York Thruway, where thousands of drivers and passengers view its steep and rocky slopes every day. Formerly owned by the Star Expansion Company, which permitted a network of hiking trails to be established on this 1,664-foot-high mountain, Schunemunk Mountain was acquired in 1996 by The Open Space Institute, which sold it to the state of New York in 2004. It is now a state park administered by the Palisades Interstate Park Commission (Chazin 2005).

To highlight the scenic beauty of the Highlands region and strengthen efforts to preserve this important natural resource, the New York–New Jersey Trail Conference, together with the Highlands Coalition, decided to establish a Highlands Trail, which extends for more than 150 miles—from Cornwall Landing on the Hudson River to Pohatcong Township on the Delaware River at the New Jersey–Pennsylvania boundary. A ribbon-cutting ceremony in May 1995 celebrated the opening of the first stretch of the trail. To date, more than 100 miles of this trail, which incorporates a number of preexisting trails but also includes many new trail sections, have been completed. Another ribbon-cutting ceremony was held in May 2009 to celebrate the crossing of the trail over the Delaware River and the start of construction of a 100-mile route through the Highlands of Pennsylvania. The Trail Conference is working on an extension of the trail through the Highlands east of the Hudson River toward Connecticut, and it is hoped that the trail will eventually extend into the Connecticut Highlands. The Trail Conference has also been working on developing other new trails in the Highlands, such as the Iron Belt Trail, which would connect the Appalachian Trail with the Highlands Trail in Morris and Sussex counties in New Jersey. In addition, the Trail Conference has cooperated with government agencies to acquire lands for these trails.

In the 1920s, when a hiking trail network was being formed in Harriman–Bear Mountain State Parks, Major Welch recognized the unsuitability of the existing network of woods roads as hiking trails, and he encouraged the hiking clubs to develop new routes that would emphasize attractive footpaths and scenic views. As a result, Harriman today has an extensive network of foot trails and is probably the favorite destination of most hikers in the New York metropolitan area. By contrast, when Sterling Forest State Park was formed in 1998, a detailed planning process for trails was established. The process has been mired in bureaucratic delays; at present, many designated trails in Sterling Forest are multiuse trails that follow unattractive, eroded woods roads. Moreover, the Cedar Pond area—considered by many to be the most beautiful part of the park—has been entirely closed off to public use on environmental grounds. As a result, visits to the park by the public have been far below what was anticipated. In 2009 the New York State Office of Parks, Recreation and Historic Preservation issued its Final Trails Plan for the park. It authorized the establishment of a number of new trails, including the Bare Rock Trail, a footpath that leads to a spectacular viewpoint. It is hoped that the opening of this and other attractive hiking-only trails will result in greater appreciation by the public of the natural resources of Sterling Forest State Park.

Conclusions

For more than two hundred years, the Highlands have played an important role in providing recreational opportunities for residents of the populous Philadelphia–New York–Hartford metropolitan region. In the nineteenth century, private interests built hotels, camps, and other facilities for active recreation. Then, in the twentieth century, the focus began to shift toward passive recreations such as hiking. At first, private individuals donated thousands of acres in the Highlands as parklands. Later, with the establishment of state Green Acres programs and, more recently, the provision of federal funding, thousands of additional acres of public open space and parklands have been acquired through public funding or public–private partnerships. As iron mining and other industrial uses of the Highlands declined, much land that formerly supported these uses has been reforested and is now dedicated to recreation and conservation. Today, recreational opportunities in the Highlands include hiking, bicycling, horseback riding, camping, boating, swimming, hunting, and fishing. The Highlands Coalition, a coalition of nearly two hundred conservation organizations and land trusts, continues to work to identify and preserve key tracts of open space across the four-state Highlands region.

In addition to serving as a recreational resource to regional residents, the Highlands have played a pivotal role in the development of outdoor recreation and open-space preservation across the United States. The Highlands were the locus of a number of events and ideas that spread nationwide, including the first summer resort (at Schooleys Mountain, New Jersey); establishment of the first summer youth camps; fostering of the state parks movement (through the innovative leadership of Maj. William Welch, first general manager of Harriman–Bear Mountain State Parks); construction of the first section of the Appalachian Trail (at Harriman–Bear Mountain State Parks); and the birth of the modern environmental movement in the wake of the fight to preserve Storm King Mountain and the scenic beauty of the Hudson Highlands.

References

Anderson, L. 2002. *Benton MacKaye: Conservationist, Planner, and Creator of the Appalachian Trail*. Baltimore: Johns Hopkins University Press.

Binnewies, R. O. 2001. *Palisades: 100,000 Acres in 100 Years*. Hudson Valley Heritage Series, No. 1. Palisades Interstate Park Commission, Bear Mountain, NY. New York: Fordham University Press.

Bitner, J. 1990. *Mt. Gretna, a Coleman Legacy: A History of Mt. Gretna and the Coleman Dynasty*. 3rd ed. Mt. Lebanon, PA: Lebanon County Historical Society.

Brenneman, R. L. 2009. "Rescuing Connecticut: A Story of Land-Saving Actions." In *Twentieth-Century New England Land Conservation: A Heritage of Civic Engagement*, ed. C.H.W. Foster. Cambridge, MA: Harvard University Press.

Chazin, D., ed. 2004. *New Jersey Walk Book: A Companion to the New York Walk Book*. 2nd ed. Mahwah, NJ: New York–New Jersey Trail Conference.

———, ed. 2005. *New York Walk Book: A Companion to the New Jersey Walk Book*. 7th ed. Mahwah, NJ: New York–New Jersey Trail Conference.

Dunwell, F. F. 2008. *The Hudson: America's River*. New York: Columbia University Press.

Howell, W. T. 1933–1934. *The Hudson Highlands: William Thompson Howell Memorial*. Repr. 1982, New York: Walking News Press.

Landgraf, Walt. 2005. "History of Peoples State Forest." Stone Museum, Pleasant Valley, CT. Originally published in the *Squire's Tavern Quarterly*, published by the Barkamsted Historical Society. http://www.stonemuseum.org/history_of_peoples.htm.

Libov, C. 1988. "The View from the White Memorial: The Legacy of a Man before His Time." *New York Times*. July 17, p. CN2.

Milne, G. M. 1995. *Connecticut Woodlands: A Century's Story of the Connecticut Forest & Park Association*. Rockfall: Connecticut Forest and Park Association.

Myles, W. J., and D. Chazin. 2010. *Harriman Trails: A Guide and History*. 3rd ed. Mahwah, NJ: New York–New Jersey Trail Conference.

New York Times. 1908. "The Fight to Save Beauties of the Hudson." September 20, p. SM5.

———. 1980. "A Peace Treaty for the Hudson." December 20, p. 24.

Scherer, G. D. 1995. *Vistas & Vision: A History of the New York–New Jersey Trail Conference*. New York: New York–New Jersey Trail Conference.

Torrey, R., F. Place, and R. L. Dickinson. 1923. *New York Walk Book*. New York: American Geographical Society.

Washington Township Historical Society. 1976. "This Is Washington Township: A Brief Historical Record, 1730–1976." Washington, Morris County, New Jersey. www.washingtontwplibrary.org/WT%20History%20Scans/ThisIsWT.pdf.

Waterman, L., and G. Waterman. 2003. *Forest and Crag: A History of Hiking, Trail Blazing and Adventure in the Northeast Mountains*. Boston: Appalachian Mountain Club.

In addition to the publications cited in the text and listed above, the following websites and other materials were consulted:

Clarence Schock Memorial Park. "Park at Governor Dick." http://parkatgovernor d ick.org/dnn/History/tabid/55/Default.aspx.

Connecticut Department of Environmental Protection. "Connecticut State Forests— Seedling Letterbox Series Clues for Housatonic State Forest." http://www.ct .gov/dep/cwp/view.asp?A=2697&Q=322824.

Frost Valley YMCA. "About Camp History." http://www.frostvalley.org/about/camp-history.html.

Hudson Fisheries Trust. "Home Port: Beacon, New York." http://www.fisheries trust .org/beacon.htm.

Lake Hopatcong Commission. "Historical Perspective of Lake Hopatcong. http:// www.lakehopatcong.org/history%20of%20Lake%20Hopatcong.htm.

Mount Beacon Incline Railway Restoration Society. "Incline History." http://www .inclinerailway.org/history_construction.htm.

National Park Service. 2009. "Hopewell Furnace National Historic Site." http://www .nps.gov/hofu/index.htm.

Pennsylvania Department of Conservation and Natural Resources. "French Creek State Park." http://www.dcnr.state.pa.us/stateparks/parks/frenchcreek.aspx.

———. "Nockamixon State Park." http://www.dcnr.state.pa.us/stateparks/parks/ nockamixon.aspx.

Pennsylvania Game Commission. "State Game Lands." http://www.portal.state.pa .us/portal/server.pt/community/pgc/9106.

White Memorial Conservation Center, Litchfield, Connecticut. http://www.white memorialcc.org/about_wmcc.html.

14

Land-Use Planning and Policy in the Highlands

Robert Pirani, Thomas A. Gilbert, and Corey Piasecki

The use of land—public or private, large or small—is a product of three factors: the larger regional or metropolitan economy, which creates the market for existing or new uses; decisions made by the individual property owner, who can be driven by factors both economic and personal; and public policy, by which elected officials set a planning and regulatory framework that reflects the will of their constituents and various vested interests. Decisions about land use in the Highlands—a regional landscape that is also the aggregate of many individual properties—are no different. This chapter outlines the context and options for land-use planning and open-space conservation in the Highlands, and describes how these policies and practices have been implemented since the late 1980s.

Regional Context for Conservation

More than 27 million people live in the forty-five counties that comprise the New York, Philadelphia, and Hartford metropolitan regions—the population centers that provide the land use and economic context for the Highlands.[1] Approximately two-thirds of those people live either in the urban centers at the core of these regions (New York City, Philadelphia, and Hartford) or in the densely developed "inner-ring" counties such as Bergen, Western Essex, and Union in New Jersey. The remaining one-third reside in "outer-ring" counties, where much of the land remains undeveloped. The Highlands are located within these outer-ring counties (see plate 35).

Land-use change in the Highlands continues to be driven by the decades-long shifts in population to the communities at the edges of these metropolitan areas. For the past sixty years, the population has been consistently moving from the urban core toward first the inner ring (from 1950 to 1980) and now the outer ring of suburban and rural counties. As detailed in chapter 12, the towns that encompass the four-state Highlands region saw their population increase, often at a much higher rate of growth than in the urban core or in the four states as a whole. While growth in New York City, Philadelphia, Hartford, and other cities and inner-ring suburbs has been driven most recently by new immigrants, growth in the outer ring of suburbs seems to be driven more by intraregional movement of former core and inner-suburb residents. Development in the Highlands consists primarily of low-density one- to five-acre building lots. Because of the sharp increase of these low-density land uses, the amount of urbanized land in the four-state Highlands area increased sharply in roughly twenty years, about 27 percent.[2]

These trends are driven by many interrelated causes: the out-migration of population from urban and inner-suburban communities; the desire for bigger homes and yards; the growing importance of environmental quality to home buyers; and the ability of developers to satisfy these market forces in formerly rural towns with available land and fewer development restrictions. But perhaps the most important driver is the shift of employment and retail centers from the cities and inner suburbs to locations along the various interstate highways throughout the region, especially I-287, I-78, and I-84 among others. This locational shift has allowed employees to increase the spending power of their housing dollars by purchasing larger homes in the outer suburbs.

While it satisfies a market demand for large-lot housing, there are many external impacts associated with this pattern of urban sprawl. Locating development far from existing urban areas generally means that it is far from available infrastructure such as mass transit or even road systems with the capacity to handle higher volumes of traffic. Other important issues associated with sprawl include inefficiencies in land and energy use, fiscal inequities, and racial and economic segregation. In the Highlands, sprawling development also has the immediate and visible impact of paving as well as fragmenting wildlife habitat, recreational and scenic resources, and productive agricultural lands.

Land-Use Decision Making in the Highlands

Managing the use of land and preventing sprawling patterns of growth from disrupting the Highlands' natural and cultural resources is the responsibility of private landowners and federal, state, and especially local government. Landowners can have very different goals for their property. As Highlands communities have suburbanized, the property characteristics and motivation of landowners have generally changed as well, from farmers and other large landowners actively managing their land, to developers purchasing property with the intent of building homes and businesses, to home owners on smaller residential lots concerned about protecting community character and their property value. While landowners are often excellent stewards of their own property, they generally do not have the motivation or the resources to conserve their land and its natural resources in perpetuity.

To protect lands and waters in the Highlands for conservation purposes, especially where public access is desired, government can purchase and manage property. New Jersey in particular has a long and successful tradition of such state and local programs. These include the state's Green Acres program, which traditionally has relied on state environmental bonds to finance state and local acquisition; a farmland preservation program that purchases development rights to active agricultural lands; and the Environmental Infrastructure Trust, which provides funding and financial instruments for clean water infrastructure to acquire upstream watershed lands, sometimes with matching support from public and private water purveyors. Local and county governments, through sources such as the Morris County Preservation Trust and government's ability to tap real estate transfer taxes, also provide funds. Private philanthropy, through outright grants or donations or through sales of property at bargain prices, can also contribute.

State and local funds are complemented by federal sources. The Forest Legacy program purchases development rights from working forests. The United States also purchases land to create or expand federally designated properties such as the U.S. Fish and Wildlife Service's Wallkill Refuge or the National Park Service's Appalachian Trail. All these programs work in concert with private land conservancies, such as the Trust for Public Land, that can effectively approach and negotiate with landowners.

Such programs are quite effective at ensuring that land will be managed for conservation purposes. But their ability to effect such change across an expansive landscape such as the Highlands is limited. Land acquisition programs are based on conservation priorities, available funding, and—usually— the ability and willingness of landowners to sell their property. For a region shaping open space such as the Highlands, the combination of high-priority areas and a fragmented landscape of smaller property owners means that available funds will never match the conservation need. The Regional Plan Association and Highlands Coalition had estimated in 2005 that about three hundred thousand acres of unprotected, high-priority lands existed in the New Jersey Highlands alone (Regional Plan Association and Environmental Defense 2006). At an average $6,000 to $12,000 an acre, the roughly $3 billion of funding required to purchase such land exceeds the ability of all levels of government to finance it in the near term; New Jersey Future estimated that programs in the Highlands were able to contribute about $100 million a year (New Jersey Future 2005). Moreover, even if such funding was made available, there is no guarantee that owners of the highest-priority properties would be willing to sell or that it would be administratively feasible to purchase and manage so many smaller properties.

The government can also protect lands and water by regulating land use and the impacts to land and water that result from development. Under the "home rule" philosophy in place in the Highlands states, local government has the primary authority for determining the use and appropriate density of development, the subdividing of property to create residential building lots, and the review of building site plans. Federal and state government regulations are responsible for ensuring the safety of drinking and other water resources and protecting the habitat of endangered species and other species of special concern. They regulate the use of lands of special state or federal concern, such as wetlands or stream buffers. While some states, such as New Jersey, have state planning offices with legislative mandates to coordinate the various levels of government, this is atypical. New York, Pennsylvania, and Connecticut provide only technical assistance and advisory policies to local governments.

The overlapping nature of these responsibilities makes protection of large, complex landscape resources a challenge. At the heart of this challenge is the coordination of municipal goals and land-use decisions with broader regional concerns. Towns can be concerned with conservation but also act to provide and protect housing and businesses. Their decisions are most often driven by local fiscal concerns because towns and local school boards derive the majority of their budgets from local property and sales taxes. The four-state Highlands region is home to 315 municipalities, each with its own financial agenda, credo, politics, and land-use agenda.

Models for Regional Land-Use Cooperation

Protecting regional landscapes such as the Highlands requires some common ground between federal, state, and local government and private landowners. There are a number of models for coordinating tools such as land acquisition and local land-use powers with broader regional, state, and federal conservation concerns. A cooperative framework can provide the foundation on which to build a process that balances regional and local interests and resources and provides mutually beneficial decisions over time (Nolon 1999).

Intergovernmental agreements vary in their degrees of authority. These have been described as ad hoc, where no development plan exists; advisory, where a region has a master plan but no regional authority; supervisory, where there is a plan governed by a regional implementation strategy and developed jointly with local governments; and authoritative, where there is a regional authority with the ability to require and enforce modifications in local plans and codes to ensure consistency with a regional plan (Hitchings 1998).

Ad Hoc

An example of the ad hoc approach to conservation planning is the Memorandum of Understanding signed by federal, state, and local agencies for the purpose of coordinating existing efforts and exploring joint initiatives to protect California's Santa Ana River watershed (Santa Ana Watershed Project Authority 1974). The group is facilitated and self-selecting; anyone can participate. It does not vote, require consensus, make recommendations, or advocate positions. Rather, it uses a scoping process to address identified concerns, issues, opportunities, and action-oriented initiatives. There is no single comprehensive plan but rather ad hoc actions.

Another example of an ad hoc group is the Hudson River Valley National Heritage Area. Its mission is to recognize, preserve, protect, and interpret the nationally significant cultural and natural resources of the Hudson River valley. It accomplishes this goal by working with a large management committee that identifies interpretive themes and enhances opportunities for collaboration between related partners and resources. The partnership created by the federal Highlands Conservation Act (described in detail below) could also be considered ad hoc. Federal and state agencies, together with elected officials, local governments, the Highlands Coalition, and other civic leaders, work collaboratively to identify conservation land acquisitions eligible for funding under the act.

Another example is the Spruce Run Smart Growth Initiative. The initiative seeks to prevent the degradation of and loss of water supply to the Spruce Run Reservoir by acquiring critical lands in the watersheds that feed it (US EPA 2003). Its members, five municipalities and the New Jersey Water Supply Authority, intend to develop mutually beneficial approaches to protecting the reservoir and watersheds. The result will be a set of recommendations to municipal planning boards and governing bodies that should be incorporated into master plans and municipal ordinances as appropriate.

Advisory

A more proactive yet nonauthoritative approach is the advisory system demonstrated by New Jersey's Rockaway River Cabinet. Membership is composed of participants from federal, county, and local government agencies, and nongovernmental partners. The cabinet's purpose is to offer expertise and guide participating municipalities in decision making. Among other objectives, the cabinet provides strategies for the protection and redeveloping of properties as well as educational and outreach programs to encourage stakeholder participation.

Another example of an established body that provides ongoing comprehensive information in an advisory way is the Delaware Valley Regional Planning Commission (DVRPC). Federal law requires the creation of metropolitan planning organizations to coordinate federally funded transportation-planning programs. In addition to its federally designated role in transportation, the DVRPC seeks to foster regional cooperation in the nine-county, two-state Philadelphia metropolitan area on a voluntary basis. DVRPC provides technical assistance to member governments and serves as a forum through which city, county, and state representatives can come together to address key issues of regional significance such as open space, economic development, housing, and land-use planning. Member governments' contributions to a comprehensive planning fund provide support for DVRPC staff and consultants.

Supervisory

States in the Highlands region allow for two or more municipalities to enter into agreements to jointly make land-use decisions. The premise is that certain activities have impacts beyond the boundaries of a single municipality (Boniface 1999). For example, in New Jersey, state legislation allows for municipalities to create a "joint environmental commission for the protection, development or use of natural resources located within their combined territorial boundaries" to establish, maintain, and improve a public recreation system, which includes open space, and to create joint regional planning boards.[3] Joint commissions can propose a zoning ordinance that is satisfactory to the participating municipalities. "For instance, where a wetland or aquifer is located within multiple jurisdictions, a joint commission could propose a standard wetlands ordinance and a single, shared enforcement officer. The same approach could be taken with steep slope ordinances, visual buffer regulations, etc." (ibid.). "Complimentary ordinances serve to conform development to standards that are mutually agreeable to neighboring municipalities by presenting developers and review boards a standard set of criteria with which to conform their proposals. Municipalities cannot adopt a joint ordinance or zoning code because such an ordinance or code has the force of law, and one municipality cannot enforce a law outside of its own particular jurisdiction. But if two municipalities agree to adopt separate ordinances with similar provisions, they have accomplished the same goal" (Stinson 1996).

A second supervisory avenue toward compatibility in intermunicipal land-use regulation is the formation of a joint review board. Two or more municipalities may choose to form a planning review board with representation from each municipality. The board would review applications in accordance with the laws of the municipality where the project is proposed. If the municipalities have similar ordinances, the review board can review projects with a more unified vision. However, even if the municipalities do not have such regulatory coordination, the representation of municipalities facilitates a regional perspective in the board's review process (Stinson 1996).

One example of a joint review board is the Somerset County Inter-Municipal Policy Agreement (New Jersey), which recognizes that certain "Projects of Regional Significance" could have substantial and far-reaching effects on public health, safety, or welfare beyond the jurisdiction in which it is located. "All planning boards will voluntarily agree to a detailed analysis of how their respective master plans and zoning ordinances are consistent with County and adjacent municipal plans . . . and work cooperatively to resolve conflicts and seek greater regional consistency and harmony in furtherance of the general public interest" (Somerset County Planning Division 2007).

Another example of the supervisory approach is the growth management strategy adopted by the San Diego Association of Governments in California. The regional comprehensive plan, adopted in 2004, provides guidelines for changes in the cities' and county's general and community plans (San Diego Association of Governments 2004). The plan contains an incentive-based approach to encourage and channel growth into existing and future urban areas and smart-growth communities. Local and regional agencies self-certify the status of the regional growth management strategy in their jurisdictions on a biennial basis—a public hearing allows the city, county, and regional agency to examine whether each jurisdiction and agency is doing its part.

In New York, the Hudson River Valley Greenway Communities Council has called together local, county, and state governments; the business environmental and agricultural communities; and residents of the valley to jointly plan for the environmental, heritage, and economic development needs of the area. The long-term goal is the development of an overall greenway plan and construction of the Hudson River Trail. The council's authorization comes from state legislation. The council comments on projects that are of regional significance. It also comments at the request of local governments. Entering into the compact provides municipalities indemnity from the state in the event of lawsuits resulting from the adoption of greenway plans; preference for state funding for infrastructure and land acquisition needs identified in local greenway plans; expedited review for projects in development zones identified in greenway plans; and authority for the municipality to charge impact fees to developers and to devise other innovative zoning techniques.

The 1997 NYC Watershed Memorandum of Agreement (MOA) was signed by New York City; New York State; the U.S. Environmental Protection Agency (EPA); watershed counties, towns, and villages; and certain public interest groups. This partnership enabled New York City to receive from EPA a waiver of the federal requirement that it filter water from its Catskill/Delaware supply. The MOA established the institutional framework and relationships needed to implement the range of protection programs identified as necessary by the city, state, and EPA. During this period, seventy-nine municipalities—counties, towns, and villages—in the Catskill, Delaware, and Croton basins all decided, through their elected officials, to sign the agreement, thereby jointly committing to the program's various initiatives and organizations, including implementing the rules and regulations under which the NYC Department of Environmental Protection regulates discharge of pollutants into the source waters from both point and nonpoint sources and minimizes adverse impacts of erosion. The MOA also established a land acquisition program and created a variety of means of promoting appropriate economic development, including the Catskill Watershed Corporation, the Watershed Agricultural Council, and the Watershed Protection and Partnership Council. The headwaters of the Croton basin are in the New York Highlands, as is a distributing reservoir that temporarily holds Delaware basin water.

Authoritative

Conserving resources on the scale of the Highlands has generally required additional state and federal commitments to use all their financial and legal incentives and regulatory powers. These incentives and powers include:

- State legislative authority that establishes a specific entity with the ability, clear legal authority, and independence to protect resources over time.
- Clear primary and secondary goals that protect water and other natural resources while accommodating sustainable growth within these resource constraints.
- Identification of core preservation and compatible growth areas, including areas that are to be immediately and fully protected and the criteria by which additional core preservation areas and compatible growth areas shall be identified.
- State regulatory and financial powers to restrict or prohibit development in designated protection and preservation areas and to foster development where it is appropriate. This could include additional planning and regulatory requirements, such as land-use regulations, transfer of development rights programs, capacity analyses, performance standards, municipal incentives, equitable taxing arrangements, state indemnification and legal representation, and targeted use of state infrastructure investments to foster development in appropriate locations.
- Creation of a regional plan that identifies any additional core preservation areas, conservation areas, and the compatible growth areas; delineates how the preservation mechanisms authorized in legislation are to be implemented; notes any specific additional planning and regulatory requirements, such as land-use regulations, capacity analyses, and performance standards; and includes an assessment of the overall level of growth that is compatible with land resource preservation and protection goals.
- Consistent and coordinated efforts with local government and other state agencies. Local governments would be required to conform local plans and ordinances with the regulations, practices, and standards identified in the regional plan. Incentives (land acquisition/infrastructure money, property tax mitigation, legal indemnification, technical and financial assistance, and authorization for growth management tools) should be offered to towns that adopt consistent plans. The entity should have the ability to complement and engage regulatory authority held by other levels of government. This should include joint permitting, joint

enforcement, and the power to review (and deny) public development/ capital projects.

- Innovative legal and financial means to ensure the equity in land of property owners in the core preservation areas, including prioritization of core lands for acquisition and authorization of a regional transfer of development rights program and bank.

The New Jersey Pinelands Commission, the Long Island Pine Barrens Commission, and the Cape Cod Commission are all examples of entities with such high-level of authority. Created by federal or state legislation, these commissions develop land-use regulations in accordance with a comprehensive management plan that delineates priority preservation areas as well as growth areas.

The New Jersey Pinelands Commission, created by federal and state legislation, oversees county and municipal master plans. Land-use ordinances are required to be in conformance with the comprehensive management plan and are subject to approval by the commission. Once they are approved, the municipality is responsible for administering the ordinances with the commission's oversight. Because ecosystem boundaries rarely correspond to political boundaries, the cooperation of various levels of government was essential (Good and Good 1984).

The Long Island Pinelands Commission, created by the New York state legislature, also oversees the development and implementation of a comprehensive master plan. After passing the Pine Barrens Act, the legislature passed a statewide Environmental Protection Act providing long-term funding to various conservation efforts, including the Pine Barrens project, allowing for funding a number of activities from landfill closure to waterfront-planning efforts and Central Pine Barrens planning.

The Cape Cod Commission, a regional land-use-planning regulatory agency, was created by an act of the Massachusetts General Court in 1990. Similar to the other commissions, the Cape Cod Commission reviews projects that may affect regional issues identified in the act, including water quality, traffic flow, historic values, affordable housing, open space, natural resources, and economic development. Developments of regional impact (DRIs) are referred to the commission for review. The legislation also calls for the nomination and creation of districts of critical planning concern (DCPC), which allow for increased scrutiny and protection for portions of Cape Cod. Backing up the whole process is a host of technical information supplied by the commission staff that helps in technical review of DRIs and DCPCs.

As noted earlier, regional cooperation has occurred in the Highlands in all four states and at a variety of scales. But only New Jersey's Highlands Water Protection and Planning Act and that Highlands Council that it created follow in the tradition of these authoritative models. As described in the following, its creation and structure was unique to the state, to the Highlands, and to the political dynamics of the moment.

Toward Regional Conservation for the Highlands

Concern over the future of the Appalachian Highlands dates back to the early years of the twentieth century when Benton MacKaye suggested a series of protected forests all along the eastern seaboard (along with his landmark proposal for the federal Appalachian Trail). Large state and national forests were created during this time as well.

Although there were numerous conservation initiatives in the area throughout the twentieth century, they were galvanized on a regional basis in the late 1980s with the proposed development of Sterling Forest, a unique twenty-thousand-acre tract containing the largest intact forest in the Highlands and straddling both the New York–New Jersey border and the Appalachian Trail. The forest's single owner started planning a new community with more than fourteen thousand housing units and 2 million square feet of commercial development.

Most of the forest was located in New York State, but its pristine streams all drained into New Jersey's drinking water reservoirs. Passaic County responded directly to the possibility of development by condemning the two thousand acres in New Jersey. The Palisades Interstate Park Commission (PIPC), a bistate entity, and the New York–New Jersey Trail Conference convened the Public-Private Partnership to Save Sterling Forest, a civic coalition to campaign for preservation of the forest in New York State. This partnership of national and local conservation organizations, including the Trust for Public Land, Environmental Defense, Passaic River Coalition, and Regional Plan Association, ultimately persuaded private individuals and philanthropies, the states of New Jersey and New York, and the federal government to combine resources. A willing-seller transaction resulted in the creation of Sterling Forest State Park in 1998.

The successful, decade-long effort to protect the twenty-thousand-acre Sterling Forest raised immediate questions about conservation of land and water resources throughout the Highlands landscape. The Regional Plan Association (RPA), in its 1996 regional plan, had proposed making the Highlands a greenbelt around the core cities and suburbs of New York, New Jersey, and Connecticut. RPA, the Trust for Public Land, and many other members of the Sterling Forest partnership were also participants in the Highlands Coalition, a New Jersey–based alliance founded originally by the New Jersey Audubon, the New Jersey Conservation Foundation, and several grassroots organizations. Flush with the success of Sterling Forest, coalition leaders reached out to organizations in Connecticut and Pennsylvania to create a new four-state Highlands coalition to address these broader concerns.[4] The coalition took on the task of building a regional identity for the Highlands and engaging local, state, and federal leaders in the protection of the full four-state landscape.

One important technique was the successful engagement of the federal government in Highlands conservation, through the offices of the USDA Forest Service, Northeastern Area State and Private Forestry. Alerted by local advocates and congressional leaders to the concern over loss of natural resources, the Forest Service prepared a 1992 Highlands Regional Study and a 2002 Update. The 1992 Regional Study (Michaels et al. 1992), funded by Congress and the efforts of Rep. Peter Kostmeyer (D-PA), documented the national significance of the New York–New Jersey Highlands, raising its visibility and setting the stage for the extraordinary $17.5 million appropriation from the Land and Water Conservation Fund for Sterling Forest. Rep. Rodney Frelinghuysen (R-NJ) secured federal funds for the 2002 "New York–New Jersey Highlands Regional Study Update," which contains a detailed geographic information system assessment that identifies which Highlands resources are most significant, locates them on the landscape, and documents how these resources are likely to change in the future. It also identifies possible conservation strategies to be undertaken by the Forest Service and its partners to protect these resources. Much of research documented elsewhere in this book is based on the Regional Study. But most critically, the Highlands Study Update has provided the context for important and recent policy initiatives at the federal and state level.

Federal Highlands Conservation Legislation

The Highlands Stewardship Act. With the U.S. Forest Service beginning the process of updating the 1992 study of the New York–New Jersey Highlands, Rep. Ben Gilman (R-NY) held a Highlands Preservation Summit at the Bear Mountain Inn in New York in October of 2000 (Phelps and Hoppe 2002). On the heels of this summit, Representative Gilman convened a Highlands Preservation Initiative Work Group consisting of representatives from the U.S. Forest Service, the Palisades Interstate Park Commission, the Highlands Coalition, the Farm Bureau, Regional Plan Association, the New Jersey Builders Association, and other regional stakeholders. The group met throughout 2001 and developed consensus on a series of recommendations that became the basis of federal legislation, the Highlands Stewardship Act.

In July of 2002, Representative Gilman introduced the Highlands Stewardship Act, H.R. 5146, describing it as, "a new, cooperative approach to addressing urban sprawl in our Highlands region; an area which includes critical water supplies for three of our Nation's largest metropolitan areas."[5] He also said the act "recognized the national significance of the Highlands region, builds upon the work of the USDA Forest Service Highlands Regional Study and Update . . . and relies on the partnership needed between Federal, State, local and private entities to meet the present and future needs of this important region." Sen. Jon Corzine (D-NJ) introduced companion legislation in the Senate.[6]

The act authorized the secretaries of agriculture and interior to establish and map a "Highlands Stewardship Area" within the four-state Highlands region, a new federal designation not previously authorized or in existence. It also authorized the establishment of an Office of Highlands Stewardship within the U.S. Department of Agriculture to implement the strategies of the 1992 and 2002 U.S. Forest Service studies of the region, and the formation of a Highlands Stewardship Area Work Group consisting of public and private stakeholders in the region to advise the Office of Highlands Stewardship. The act authorized $25 million annually over ten years from the Land & Water Conservation Fund (LWCF) to provide federal matching funds to assist eligible nonfederal entities in "protecting, conserving, or preserving the natural, forest, agricultural, recreational, historical, or cultural resources of the Stewardship Area" (U.S. Congress, House 2002, HR 5146 IH). The act was introduced late in the 107th Congress, which concluded without acting on the legislation.

The Highlands Conservation Act. With the retirement of Rep. Ben Gilman at the close of the 107th Congress, Rep. Rodney Frelinghuysen (R-NJ) stepped forward as the new sponsor of the Highlands Stewardship Act in the 108th Congress, which he introduced on May 6, 2003, as H.R. 1964.[7] Sen. Jon Corzine again introduced companion legislation in the Senate. Although the legislation as introduced was virtually identical to the legislation introduced in the 107th Congress, significant changes were made to the act as it went through the legislative process, resulting in the Highlands Conservation Act that was signed into law on November 30, 2004.[8]

The House Subcommittee on National Parks, Recreation, and Public Lands held a hearing on the bill on June 17, 2003. On October 29, 2003, the full House Resources Committee met to consider the bill. Rep. Richard Pombo (R-CA) offered an amendment in the nature of a substitute that renamed it the Highlands Conservation Act, eliminated the Office of Highlands Stewardship, reduced the authorization of appropriations for land conservation partnership projects from $25 million annually to $10 million annually over ten years, and included language that private property rights will be protected by including safeguards for landowners. The bill, as amended, was ordered favorably reported to the House of Representatives by voice vote.[9]

On November 21, 2003, the act was agreed to by voice vote under suspension of the rules. During the floor debate before the vote, Rep. Richard Pombo (R-CA), a well-known and vocal proponent of private-property rights, said, "I will tell my colleagues, on any legislation like this in the future that we choose to move through the Committee on Resources, we will use this bill as a template, as a way to get things done in a bipartisan way in trying to move forward with a Federal and a local partnership in protecting lands that are environmentally sensitive and that are important, but at the same time protecting the property rights of those individual owners, which is something that is extremely important to me."[10]

The Senate Subcommittee on Public Lands and Forests held a hearing on H.R. 1964 on March 24, 2004. On September 15, 2004, the Senate Committee on Energy and Natural Resources approved H.R. 1964 with amendments, including striking the LWCF as the designated source of funds for land conservation partnership projects, replacing the written description of the area with a map of the Highlands region (see plate 2), and directing the U.S. Forest Service to complete a study of the lands within the mapped boundaries of the region in the States of Connecticut and Pennsylvania.[11] On October 10, the full Senate approved H.R. 1964 by unanimous consent. On November 17, the House of Representatives approved H.R. 1964 as amended by the Senate under suspension of the rules. President George W. Bush signed H.R. 1964 into law on November 30, 2004.[12]

The first funds appropriated under the Highlands Conservation Act came in FY2007, when the Bush administration provided $2 million for land conservation partnership projects under the act through the LWCF after the 109th Congress approved a series of continuing resolutions, which left the administration with discretion over allocation of LWCF funds. In FY2008 Congress appropriated $1.75 million for land conservation partnership projects through the LWCF. In FY2009 funding for the act was reduced to $1.5 million, but then increased to $4 million in FY2010, the largest annual appropriation to date. The early record of appropriations for the Highlands Conservation Act suggests that the primary challenge in implementation will be securing funds at or close to the $10 million authorized annually at a time when there are severe pressures on the federal budget and declining funds for federal land conservation programs. However, federal Highlands studies and legislation also provided an impetus for action at the state level to protect the Highlands, especially in New Jersey.

New Jersey State Legislation to Protect the Highlands

Early Initiatives.   Discussions at the state level in New Jersey regarding the need for a regional approach to protect the Highlands began in 1989 when Governor Thomas Kean signed Executive Order 224 creating a Skylands Greenway Task Force. The task force, led by New Jersey Audubon, released "A Plan for Action" report in 1992, which recognized the need for a regional planning entity and improvements to land-use planning and natural resource management in the Highlands. It called for the designation of a Highlands National Stewardship Area and the establishment of a federally authorized Highlands Regional Council (Skylands Greenway Task Force 1992). The Forest Service's 1992 Highlands Regional Study also encouraged regional action (Michaels et al. 1992). A federally funded work group created at the conclusion of the study, chaired by former New Jersey Department of Environmental Protection (DEP) commissioner Chris Daggett and staffed by the Regional Plan Association, recommended creation of a regional entity to help coordinate federal, state, and local land-use decisions. In 1993 Governor James Florio signed Executive Order 82, which created the Highlands Trust Advisory Board to make recommendations on lands most suitable for preservation. In 1999 state assemblyman Paul DiGaetano sponsored Assembly Joint Resolution No. 76 requesting the president and Congress to establish a Highlands National Forest Preserve in New Jersey. In 2001 the Highlands Coalition, which was a project of the New Jersey Conservation Foundation at the time, petitioned the New Jersey State Planning Commission to provide recognition for the Highlands in the State Development and Redevelopment plan similar to that provided the Pinelands and the Meadowlands. In response, the New Jersey Highlands was designated as the first special resource area in the state plan, which recognized the region as having unique characteristics or resources of statewide importance and recommended several planning and implementation strategies in the Highlands (Phelps and Hoppe 2002).

Governor McGreevey's Highlands Task Force. In 2003 Governor James McGreevey continued state policy discussions on the Highlands by signing Executive Order #70 on September 19, 2003, which established a Highlands Task Force, recognized the region as "an essential source of drinking water, provided clean and plentiful drinking water for one-half of the State's population," and stated that "maintaining the quality of life and preserving the natural resources of the Highlands region while providing for smart growth opportunities can best be accomplished through the development of a process to encourage acquisition, regulation and regional planning" (State of New Jersey 2003). The executive order also commended the New Jersey congressional delegation for its leadership to protect the Highlands through introduction of the Highlands Stewardship Act.

The formation of the Highlands Task Force was announced by DEP commissioner Bradley M. Campbell on September 20 at the annual meeting of the Highlands Coalition, which had become a broader four-state coalition with the Appalachian Mountain Club as fiscal agent. The announcement was made in Ringwood State Park (New Jersey DEP 2003). In addition to Commissioner Campbell, the nineteen-member task force included four other cabinet members, six representatives of local elected officials, four representatives of environmental organizations, two representatives of the development/business community, one representative of the farming community, and one member of the general public. The task force was charged with holding public hearings and submitting recommendations to the governor within 180 days "to preserve the natural resources of and enhance the quality of life in the Highlands region, including an examination of legislation, regulations, model local ordinances or other government action necessary."

On March 13, 2004, the Highlands Task Force released its action plan at a news conference at the Wanaque Reservoir urging lawmakers to designate almost half of the eight-hundred-thousand-acre region as a "preservation area" and to permanently preserve more than one hundred thousand acres still open to development within that area. The report warned that unless development trends were altered and an effective regional approach to the Highlands adopted, further development would degrade drinking water supplies, with water treatment costing the state $30.3 billion by 2054 (State of New Jersey 2004).

New Jersey Highlands Water Protection and Planning Act

On March 15, 2004, Sen. Bob Smith and Assemblyman John F. McKeon, the chairs of the Senate and Assembly environment committees, announced the start of a legislative process to protect the Highlands on the heels of the governor's Highlands Task Force report. At the event, Senator Smith warned: "In the past 13 years, the Garden State has seen five droughts, and shortages tend to be cyclical. While our water supplies, reservoirs and aquifers might be fully charged at the moment, we must take steps during the good times to ensure that we are not caught off guard during the next water emergency" (New Jersey Democrats 2004).

The two legislators announced a series of six public hearings, including three in the Highlands, between March 22 and April 22, 2004. They pledged to consider a number of the proposals put forth in the Highlands Task Force report and during the public hearings to develop a legislative solution for the Highlands (New Jersey Democrats 2004).

On March 29, 2004, the Highlands Water Protection and Planning Act, S1, was introduced by Senator Smith and referred to the Senate Environment Committee. Assemblyman John F. McKeon introduced a companion bill, A2635, on May 3 that was referred to the Assembly Environment and Solid Waste Committee.[13]

Many of the hearings that took place between March 22 and April 22 drew large crowds with heated testimony from environmentalists and others calling for protection of the region's critical lands and water supplies, and from home builders, farmers, and others concerned about jobs and private-property rights. An intensive lobbying and grassroots campaign was mounted by the Highlands Coalition and its lead member groups in New Jersey, including the New Jersey Chapter of the Sierra Club, the New Jersey Environmental Federation, New Jersey Public Interest Research Group, the New Jersey Conservation Foundation, New Jersey Audubon, and the Environmental Defense Fund, among others. The New Jersey Homebuilders Association and the New Jersey Farm Bureau campaigned against the legislation.

The Assembly Environment and Solid Waste Committee favorably reported A2635 out of committee with amendments on May 17, 2004. The bill had four primary components. First, the New Jersey Highlands region was divided roughly equally into a Preservation Area, in which regional planning would be mandatory and development would be strictly regulated, and a Planning Area, in which additional regulations would not apply and regional planning would be voluntary (see plate 36). Second, the bill established the Highlands Water Protection and Planning Council, which was charged with preparing and implementing a regional master plan for the Highlands region. Third, the bill required that most major Highlands development in the Preservation Area receive a Highlands Preservation Area approval from the Department of Environmental Protection (DEP) to certify consistency with existing environmental regulations as well as additional, statutorily prescribed environmentally protective land-use and water-protection requirements. This permitting system would be in effect for nine months while more comprehensive regulations were developed for the Preservation Area. Fourth, the bill required the DEP to adopt, within nine months, effective rules and regulations for a permanent Highlands permitting review program, setting strict standards for reviewing major Highlands development in the Preservation Area (State of New Jersey Legislature 2004).

Some activities and types of development in the Preservation Area were exempted from complying with the regional master plan and enhanced DEP regulations. The bill also contained provisions for landowner equity and for state aid to offset decreases in property tax revenues in municipalities with land located in the Preservation Area. The Highlands Water Protection and Planning Council was also required to establish and implement a transfer of development rights program (New Jersey State Legislature 2004).

The Highlands Water Protection and Planning Act, S1, was favorably reported out of the Senate Environment Committee on June 7, 2004, with the same primary components as A2635. Just three days later, on June 10, it was approved by the Senate (34–2) and the Assembly (69–10). Governor McGreevey signed the Highlands Water Protection and Planning Act into law on August 10, 2004, at an event on the Wanaque Reservoir (New Jersey State Legislature 2004).

The act required the Highlands Water Protection and Planning Council to prepare and adopt a regional master plan within eighteen months after the date of its first meeting, and after holding at least six public hearings. The regional master plan was to be updated at least once every six years after public hearings (New Jersey Highlands Council 2008).

The regional master plan was released in draft form in November of 2006. After twelve public hearings and thirty-six hundred written comments from the public, the final master plan was adopted by a 9–5 vote on July 17, 2008. "This document is a dramatic step forward in regional land-use planning, not just for protection of New Jersey's Highland resources, but at a national level," Highlands Council chairman John Weingart said upon announcing the final vote. Governor Jon Corzine, amid much controversy, allowed the veto period (thirty days after the ordinance or minutes are available) to lapse, and on September 5, 2008, the plan was passively approved.

The plan defines four geographic zones: a protection zone, a conservation zone that includes agricultural areas, an existing community zone, and a lake community zone. Standards to protect the Highlands natural resources and the capacity of landscape for additional development are established. Local governments are encouraged to adopt these standards in the Planning Area (as defined in the original legislation) and are required to follow the standards in the Preservation Area. The plan also defines the variety of tools and enforcement powers that the council can employ to encourage or ensure conformance, a range of carrots and stick including a Transfer of Development Rights (TDR) program, grants, and local indemnity from legal action. The passage of the plan and its enactment marks the start of a new era in the Highlands not just in New Jersey but across the remainder of the four-state region and, indeed, the nation.

The Plan. The Highlands Regional Master Plan (RMP) is divided into six chapters (New Jersey Highlands Council 2008). Chapters 1 through 3 provide an introduction to the region and the basis for, and recognition of, the corresponding provisions of the act that each of the goals, policies, and objects are meant to fulfill. Each chapter contains an in-depth analysis of critical resources through a number of maps, images, and definitions too numerous to mention here. Given the complexity of the act as well as the resources of the region, numerous technical reports were prepared to detail the scientific data collected and analyzed during the planning process. These documents are intended to support the plan and land-use regulations contained therein. The plan also establishes a science and research agenda for further study and understanding of the region.

Chapter 4 contains the goals, policies, and objectives aimed at mitigating the effects of land use on the areas of concern mentioned in previous chapters. "Goals are defined as broad statements of intent, with Policies providing a more detailed statement of direction. Objectives, in turn, provide the specific, substantive requirements that will be used to measure implementation progress and plan conformance" (New Jersey Highlands Council 2008, 137). Chapter 4 identifies the basis for the programmatic and conformance standards outlined in chapters 5 and 6. Each of the programmatic components in chapter 5 contains a list of goals, policies, and objectives that are addressed through specific implementation strategies, both regulatory and voluntary, and the creation of guidance documents.

The primary purpose of the act and Regional Master Plan is to protect the state's water supply through land preservation and growth mitigation strategies. But, unlike the New Jersey Pinelands, the Highlands Act did not legislate specific areas designated for growth. Instead, the act relies on strong regulation, direct preservation, the purchase of development rights, and the establishment of a regional TDR program. This approach has put far greater responsibility on the council and its staff to implement the plan's goal for land preservation and appropriate development over time and through the ups and downs of the real estate market.

Because of the high cost of land preservation and fluctuating sources of public funding for land acquisition, the TDR program arguably holds the greatest opportunity for large-scale land preservation in the region. However, there is significant cost of implementing a TDR program. While the programmatic component of the plan establishes a mechanism for funding municipal planning for TDR and the establishment of a TDR Bank, the act and plan provide limited—if any—incentive to grow in areas appropriate for receiving credits. To further facilitate the transfer of credits, the New Jersey legislature recently expanded the program beyond the seven-county region to allow the transfer of credits throughout the state (A602 and S80). The plan conformance process in the Preservation Area is mandatory; although the act has faced challenges from a few disgruntled landowners, the Highlands Council has found little resistance by municipalities to conformance requirements thus far.

Notably, the New Jersey state appellate court, on September 4, 2009, upheld a decision by a lower court on the validity of the act and RMP in a landowner case challenging the constitutionality of the act and plan. Landowners charged that the act violated their constitutional rights because it did not provide a viable means of landowner equity return through the TDR program. Landowners further challenged the validity of the science behind the Planning and Preservation Area boundaries defined in the act. Historically, in New Jersey, similar challenges to regional planning have been made unsuccessfully against the Meadowlands and the Pinelands regions.

Many municipalities in the Highlands are in both the Planning and Preservation areas. Conformance in the Planning Area is not mandatory but is encouraged in large part by the "legal shield" offered to towns as protection against lawsuits that builders might file against them for failing to provide adequate provisions for affordable housing. Many municipalities with land in both areas have petitioned for conformance of the Preservation Area only; however, eighteen municipalities have submitted "Notice of Intent" to comply with the Highlands regulations in the Planning Area and complete the conformance process. Presently, the council enjoys a high level of success, with fifty-six of eighty-eight municipalities submitting conformance petitions covering 95 percent of the Preservation Area and 35 percent of the Planning Area, for a total of 549,602 acres of voluntary conformance (see plate 36) (New Jersey Highlands Council 2010).

Summary and Conclusions

Long-term stewardship of such a complex landscape as the Highlands requires the creation of legal and administrative structures that can meld the interests of the millions of individual property owners, the 315 towns, four states, and federal agencies responsible for the future of the entire region. Acquisition of land and easements by conservation-minded agencies and organizations is a critically important tool. The success of the Sterling Forest partnership and the creation of the federal Highlands Conservation Act are examples of the wonderful successes that will set aside critical tracts of land in perpetuity. Similarly the ad hoc, advisory, and even supervisory mechanisms described in this chapter, such as the Spruce Run Initiative, Delaware Valley Regional Planning Commission, and Hudson Greenway Communities Council, can and are playing an important role in conservation in the Highlands; their ability to bring private, local, and regional interests together in a comprehensive way is by definition limited.

The ultimate success of New Jersey's Highlands Council and its more authoritative planning approach remains to be seen. The plan's implementation is complicated and fraught with technical and legal challenges, from defining the carrying capacity of specific watersheds to enabling the transfer of development rights between properties. The political tensions between competing interests are both difficult and expected. But the plan's creation and the manner in which it resolves these challenges and tensions will serve as an important metric for conservation in the other three states in the Highlands. While there are bistate planning entities elsewhere (such as the Columbia River Gorge Commission in Oregon and Washington and the Tahoe Regional Planning Agency in California and Nevada), the legal and cultural differences between Pennsylvania, New Jersey, New York, and Connecticut certainly make it simpler to consider regional planning on an individual state-by-state basis. The one interstate organization in the Highlands region, the Palisades Interstate Park Commission, has traditionally steered clear of land-use regulations, focusing instead on acquiring and managing properties such as Sterling Forest State Park. As a result, politicians, planners, and advocates from throughout the Highlands will look to New Jersey's Highlands Council in considering how best to address regional planning in their respective states.

These lessons will reach beyond Connecticut, New York, and Pennsylvania. Metropolitan areas such as those surrounding Hartford, New York City, and Philadelphia are now home to more than 80 percent of Americans and their jobs (Katz 2007). These complex regions and their agglomeration of industry, services, and consumers are the muscle of the United States economy. Their vitality depends on the management of natural resources and ecosystem services, such as the provision of clean drinking water, which can be addressed only though conservation at broader watershed to regionwide scales. Their ability to attract and retain the residents and businesses that drive the economy depend on close-to-home recreation, often in the region-shaping landscapes and estuaries. Our successful conservation of places such as the Highlands is critical to building a sustainable nation for the twenty-first century.

Acknowledgments

The authors would like to acknowledge former Regional Plan Association staff Amy Decker and Cara Griffin for contributions of material used in this chapter.

Notes

1. The New York Metropolitan region as defined by the Regional Plan Association includes thirty-one counties: Fairfield, Litchfield, New Haven, Bergen, Essex, Hudson, Hunterdon, Mercer, Middlesex, Monmouth, Morris, Ocean, Passaic, Somerset, Sussex, Union, Warren, Bronx, Dutchess, Kings, Nassau, New York, Orange, Putnam, Queens, Richmond, Rockland, Suffolk, Sullivan, Ulster, Westchester. The Philadelphia Principal Metropolitan Statistical Area and Hartford Metropolitan Statistical Area are defined by the United States census.

2. Data from figures 12.3 and table 12.1 in chapter 12. Time periods vary by state. For Pennsylvania, this estimate assumes that urban land increase per additional person in 1990–2000 was comparable to that estimated for 1980–1990 (about 0.4 acres).

3. New Jersey Legislature, 40:56A-8. "Joint Environmental Commission; creation by ordinance; members; compensation"; and New Jersey Legislature, 40:12–14. "Joint Municipal Action," New Jersey Permanent Statutes Database 40:12–14. http://lis.njleg.state.nj.us/cgi-bin/om_isapi.dll?clientID=39924222&Depth=4&TD=WRAP&advquery=%2240%3a12–14%22&headingswithhits=on&infobase=statutes.nfo&rank=&record={EFF0}&softpage=Doc_Frame_Pg42&wordsaroundhits=2&x=0&y=0&zz=.

4. Original board members of the New Jersey Conservation Foundation–staffed coalition were the New Jersey Conservation Foundation, Environmental Defense Fund, Regional Plan Association, Appalachian Mountain Club, Housatonic Valley Association, Wildlands Conservancy, and Scenic Hudson. Members of the regional board of the Highlands Coalition in 2005 included the Palisades Interstate Park Commission, the Trust for Public Land, Environmental Defense Fund, New Jersey Conservation Foundation, Appalachian Mountain Club, Morris Land Conservancy, Wilderness Society, Natural Lands Trust, Housatonic Valley Association, Association of New Jersey Environmental Commissions, Heritage Conservancy, Nature Conservancy, Passaic River Coalition, Westchester Land Trust, New York–New Jersey Trail Conference, Lancaster County Conservancy, Wildlands Conservancy, Open Space Institute, Scenic Hudson, Garden Club of America–NJ Chapters, Regional Plan Association, Audubon Pennsylvania, New Jersey Audubon, Sierra Club New Jersey Chapter, Adirondack Mountain Club, and Kent Land Trust.

5. Congr. Rec. 107th Congress (2001–2002), E1280–1281 (daily ed. July 17, 2002) (statement of Representative Gilman). http://frwebgate.access.gpo.gov/cgi-bin/getpage.cgi?dbname=2002_record&page=E1280&position=all.

6. Congr. Rec. 107th Congress (2001–2002), S6957–6958. http://frwebgate.access. gpo.gov/cgi-bin/getpage.cgi?dbname=2002_record&page=S6957&position=all.

7. Congr. Rec. 108th Congress (2003–2004), H3682 (daily ed. May 6, 2003). http://frwebgate.access.gpo.gov/cgi-bin/getpage.cgi?position=all&page= H3682&dbname=2003_record.

8. Highlands Conservation Act, Pub. L. No. 108–421, 118 STAT. 2375 (November 30, 2004). http://www.google.com/url?sa=t&source=web&cd=5&sqi=2&ved=0C DgQFjAE&url=http%3A%2F%2Fftp.resource.org%2Fgpo.gov%2Flaws%2F108%2F publ421.108.pdf&rct=j&q=Highlands Conservation Act&ei=0EF0TKTAGsPflgeIh LXJCA&usg=AFQjCNGBwUP8oSd6RC4iMXjRBQRia5lDfw&sig2=ShnDzIvdEW D8ejyOC_QYEw&cad=rjt.

9. Committee on Resources, H.R. Rep. No. 108–373, Part I. http://www.glin .gov/download.action?fulltextId=121385&documentId=184074&glinID=184074.

10. Congr. Rec. H12118–H12121 at 12120 (Nov. 21, 2003) (remarks of Representative Pombo). http://www.gpo.gov/fdsys/pkg/CREC-2003–11-21/pdf/CREC-2003– 11-21-pt1-PgH12118.pdf.

11. "Bill Summary and Status, 108th Congress (2003–2004), H.R. 1964." Available at Library of Congress, THOMAS, http://thomas.loc.gov/home/LegislativeData .php?&n=BSS&c=108.

12. GPO. 2004. Public Law 108–421—Nov. 30, 2004, 118 STAT. 2375 http://www .gpo.gov/fdsys/pkg/PLAW-108publ421/pdf/PLAW-108publ421.pdf.

13. NJ Leg. Assy, No. 2635. 211th Legislature. "Highlands Water Protection and Planning Act." http://www.njleg.state.nj.us/2004/Bills/A3000/2635_I1.HTM.

References

Boniface, C. 1999. "Comparative Analysis of Local Land Use Authority: New York, New Jersey, and Connecticut." Working Paper Series. Bronx, NY: Wildlife Conservation Society.

Good, R., and N. Good. 1984. "The Pinelands National Preserve: An Ecosystem Approach to Management." *Bioscience* 34, no. 3: 169–173.

Hitchings, B. G. 1998. "A Typology of Regional Growth Management Systems." *The Regionalist* 3, no. 1–2 (Fall): 1–14.

Katz, Bruce. 2007. "Metro Nation: How Ohio's Cities and Metro Areas Can Drive Prosperity in the 21st Century." Washington, DC: Brookings Institute.

Michaels, J. A., L. R. Neville, D. Edelman, T. Sullivan, and L. A. Dicola. 1992. "New York–New Jersey Highlands Regional Study." Radnor, PA: USDA Forest Service, Northeastern Area State and Private Forestry.

New Jersey Democrats. 2004. "Smith, McKeon to Begin Legislative Process to Protect Highlands." Press release, March 15. http://www.senatorbobsmith. org/files/3_2005–03-15_SMITH,_McKEON_TO_BEGIN_LEGISLATIVE _PROCESS_TO_PROTECT_HIGHLANDS.pdf.

New Jersey Department of Environmental Protection (DEP). 2003. "Governor McGreevey Forms Task Force to Protect Highlands." Press release, September 20. http://www.state.nj.us/dep//newsrel/releases/03_0130.htm.

New Jersey Future. 2005. *Success in the Highlands: Smart Growth Recommendations from New Jersey Future.* Issue 10, May. http://njedl.rutgers.edu/ftp/PDFs/3970.pdf.

New Jersey Highlands Council. 2008. "Highlands Regional Master Plan." http://
www.highlands.state.nj.us/njhighlands/master/rmp/final/highlands_rmp_
112008.pdf.

———. 2010. "Executive Director's Report." March 4. http://www.highlands.state.
nj.us/njhighlands/about/calend/2010_meetings/030410_presentation.pdf. Nolon, J. R. 1999. "Grassroots Regionalism under New York Law Encouraging Inter-
municipal Land Use Compacts." *New York Law Journal*, February 17. http://digital
commons.pace.edu/cgi/viewcontent.cgi?article=1177&context=lawfaculty.

Phelps, M. G., and M. C. Hoppe. 2002. "New York–New Jersey Highlands Regional
Study: 2002 update." Newtown Sqaure, PA: USDA Forest Service, Northeastern Area State and Private Forestry. http://www.na.fs.fed.us/highlands/maps_
pubs/regional_study/highlands.html.

Regional Plan Association and Environmental Defense. 2006. "The Economics of
Transferring Development in the New Jersey Highlands." October. http://www
.rpa.org/pdf/HighlandsTDR-Full_FinalOct2006.pdf.

San Diego Association of Governments. 2004. "Regional Comprehensive Plan for
the San Diego Region." San Diego, CA. http://www.sandag.org/programs/
land_use_and_regional_growth/comprehensive_land_use_and_regional
_growth_projects/RCP/rcp_final_complete.pdf.

Santa Ana Watershed Project Authority. 1974. "Joint Exercises of Powers Agreement
Creating Santa Ana Watershed Project Authority." December 6. http://www
.sawpa.org/documents/misc/JPA1975+ammends1-4.pdf (accessed June 25,
2010).

Skylands Greenway Task Force. 1992. *Skylands Greenway: A Plan for Action*. Trenton,
NJ: Governor's Skylands Greenway Task Force.

Somerset County Planning Division. 2007. "The Inter-Municipal Policy Agreement
between the Somerset County Planning Board and Governing Bodies within
Somerset County: Memorandum of Understanding; Projects of Regional Significance." http://www.co.somerset.nj.us/planweb/mppg/intermuni.htm.

State of New Jersey. 2003. Governor James E. McGreevey Executive Order 70. June 5.
http://www.state.nj.us/infobank/circular/eom70.htm.

———. 2004. "Highlands Task Force Presents Action Plan for Preservation of NJ's
Highlands Region." Press release, March 13. http://www.state.nj.us/cgi-bin/
governor/njnewsline/view_article_archives.pl?id=1802.

State of New Jersey Legislature. 2004. S1, 211th Legislature, "Highlands Water Protection and
Planning Act": Section 34. http://www.njstatelib.org/NJLH/lh2004/ch120.htm.

Stinson, J. 1996. "Utilizing Intermunicipal Agreements in Land-Use Decision Making." White Plains, NY: Pace Land Use Law Center. http://landuse.law.pace
.edu/landuse/documents/StudentArticle/Reg2/IntermunicipalAgrmnts.doc.

United States Environmental Protection Agency. (US EPA). 2003. New York: US
EPA Region 2. News releases. http://yosemite.epa.gov/opa/admpress.nsf/
d10ed0d99d826b068525735900400c2a/46fe7f835c25ba5e85257163005e1c7d!
OpenDocument.

Watershed Partnership for New Jersey. 2010. "Rockaway Watershed Partnership."
http://www.wpnj.org/Directory/PArtner.asp?pk=51.

15

Future Vision of the Highlands

Richard G. Lathrop Jr., Mary L. Tyrrell, and Myrna Hall

How does one describe the landscape of the Highlands? It depends on what time period you are considering: A mid-eighteenth-century frontier of largely unbroken forest. A mid-nineteenth-century industrial landscape dotted with miners' villages and ironworks belching smoke 24/7 amidst a scrubby cutover forest littered with the mine tailings. An early-twentieth-century landscape of second-growth forests on the uplands, the valleys a quilted patchwork of farmland and water resources just beginning to be tapped. Or fast-forward to the late twentieth and early twenty-first centuries, when the rural landscape is undergoing a radical transformation as forestland is fragmented and farmland abandoned to sprawling suburban/exurban development. And what about fifty years into the future?

Examination of the implications of future land-use change helps to inform the local and regional land-use planning process before ill-advised and irreversible land-use decisions occur. In the Highlands, the main pattern of land-use change is the conversion of forest and farmland to residential land composed mainly of owner-occupied, single-family detached houses (Lathrop, Hatfield, and Tulloch 2003; and Tyrrell et al. 2010). Land-use-change scenarios and models provide a valuable tool to investigate the process of change as well as potential future landscape configurations (Botequilha and Ahern 2002; Conway and Lathrop 2005).

Land-Use-Change Modeling in the Highlands

Two main approaches have been adopted in modeling future land-use change in the Highlands as part of the U.S. Forest Service–sponsored Highlands Regional Study: (1) a statistically based approach that determines the rate and spatial pattern of historical land-use conversion and extrapolates that rate into the future to map areas that have the highest likelihood for future development within a set time frame; and (2) a deterministic "build-out model" to map the form of the fully developed landscape while avoiding the complexity of predicting when the changes will occur. Both approaches are spatially explicit in that they use an extensive database of digital maps to model the constraints and influences posed by the biophysical, social, political, and regulatory environment to determine the location and scope of future development.

Although slightly different in details, the statistically based modeling approaches used by the Connecticut–Pennsylvania studies versus the New York–New Jersey regional studies are broadly comparable in overall form. The Connecticut–Pennsylvania study (Tyrrell et al. 2010) employed the land-use change GEOMOD model (Hall et al. 1995a, b; Pontius et al. 2001), while the New York–New Jersey study employed an econometric logistic probability modeling technique (Lathrop, Hatfield, and Tulloch 2003). This empirical modeling approach is based on the assumption that spatially explicit factors that correlated with development in the past are good predictors of where development is likely to occur in the future. The model includes physical factors that may increase the cost of building or may make a site more or less desirable, such as slope, soil stability, sunlight, and scenic view. The factors may relate to the economics of site selection or to the regional infrastructure, such as distance from towns, roads, or rail stations. Breaking the landscape up into small grid cells, the model ranks each grid cell as to its suitability (i.e., likelihood) for development. The models can be further stratified to include administrative jurisdictions such as town, county, or region.

Spatial location variables were found to be strongly related to the probability of development. As might be expected, close proximity to land that was already developed or to existing roads increased the probability of development in all four state models (Lathrop, Hatfield, and Tulloch 2003; and Tyrrell et al. 2010). Amenity values such as proximity to water or lakes were found to be important in New Jersey and Connecticut. Other physical factors such as farmland or low slopes or locational factors such as distance to train stations were also important. Where the models removed jurisdictional stratification and adopted a more regional approach, demographic factors tended to explain more of the variation in development patterns across the region than did physicoeconomic variables (Tyrrell et al. 2010). Demographic variables vary across the region and appear to attract or constrain new development accordingly. These demographic factors have less explanatory power at the town level—that is, when the analysis is stratified—because most of the demographic factors do not vary much within an individual town. Within a town, there is significantly higher correlation between hot spots for new development and areas of existing development or infrastructure such as roads. The land-use-change models predict that Morris, Sussex, and eastern Hunterdon counties in New Jersey; western Orange County in New York; Berks, Lancaster, Lehigh, and Montgomery counties in Pennsylvania; and the towns of Danbury, Torrington, and New Milford in Connecticut will be hot spots of future development. In Connecticut, New Jersey, and New York, development is projected to occur mostly on forested land, whereas it is projected to occur almost entirely on agricultural land in Pennsylvania.

The first step of a build-out model is to map "vacant" land, that is, land not presently developed and available for future development (deeded conservation lands or easements are removed from consideration). The second step is to further exclude land based on various regulatory constraints such as restrictions on filling and building on wetlands or wetland buffers or on steep slopes. The impact of alternative regulations can be examined by changing the footprint of these regulatory constraints, for example, by increasing setbacks from lakes, streams and wetlands to better protect water quality. The land that is deemed vacant in step one and not excluded based on step two is considered "available" for development. The final step is to incorporate zoning maps to determine the type and density of future development and to estimate the number of additional housing units that might potentially be built.

The low constraint (aka "business as usual" scenario) build-out modeling conducted as part of the New York–New Jersey Highlands Regional Study (Lathrop, Hatfield, and Tulloch 2003) suggested that approximately 32 percent of the study area (or 458,431 acres) were available for development, resulting in more than 230,000 additional housing units (133,266 in New Jersey and 98,314 in New York) and a population increase of approximately 47 percent (fig. 15.1). Similar analyses in Connecticut and Pennsylvania (Tyrrell et al. 2010) calculated that approximately 34 percent and 43 percent, respectively, of the state's Highlands area (230,148 acres in Connecticut and 596,207 acres in Pennsylvania) were available for development, resulting in more than 148,000 new housing units and a population increase of more than 130 percent in Connecticut and nearly 500,000 new housing units and a population increase of 115 percent in Pennsylvania (fig. 15.1). The build-out analysis projects that Connecticut and Pennsylvania Highlands could see more than double the growth (on a percentage basis) than expected in New Jersey and New York.

The conversion of rural land to urban and other built-up uses is a nationwide phenomenon that has sparked great concern on how development pressure may negatively affect the output and management of the nation's farms and forests (Alig, Kline, and Lichenstein 2004; Stein et al. 2005). In addition to outright conversion of farm- and forestland, fragmentation of the remaining lands is equally of concern (Adelaja and Schilling 1999; Heilman et al. 2002; Riitters et al. 2002). Nationwide projections suggest continued urban expansion over the next twenty-five years with the developed area to increase by 79 percent (Alig, Kline, and Lichenstein 2004), although available modeling studies do not address potential effects of the recent recession. While the Highlands Study does not project urban expansion in the Highlands region to increase as much as some areas of the country (Stein et al. 2005), the land-use change and build-out modeling does suggest that the projected land-use

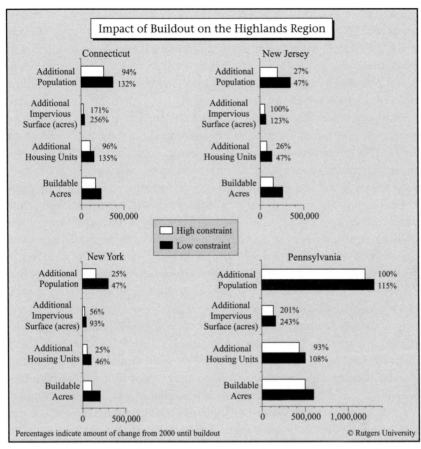

Figure 15.1. Impact of build-out on additional population, impervious surface, housing units, and buildable acres in the Highlands region by state under both a low- and high-constraint scenario. Note: Percentages indicate amount of change from 2000 until build-out. © Rutgers University.

change could have significant implications for the ecosystem services currently provided by the region.

Implications of Land-Use Change on Watershed and Forest Integrity

To make land-use-change models and future projections more relevant to the planning process, there has been a significant effort to link measurable changes in land cover with the expected environmental consequences of the projected land-use change. Within the Highlands region, a number of environmental indicators have been employed to assess the influence of urbanization on watershed and forest integrity, including area of human land-use alteration, amount of forest land, impacts on riparian zones, and the increase in impervious surface cover (Lathrop, Hatfield, and Tulloch 2003; Lathrop, Tulloch, and Hatfield 2007; Tyrrell et al. 2010). By coupling the land-use-change model predictions and the landscape environmental indicator analysis, one can assess the potential impacts on forest and watershed integrity based on several different scenarios of future development.

Because the quality and quantity of water are one of the key natural resources of the Highlands, the amount of impervious surface in a watershed serves as a key indicator of real and potential degradation (Schueler 1994). In nature, water is continually moving between the atmosphere, groundwater aquifers, lakes, and rivers. When land becomes developed, a portion of the parcel is necessarily covered with impervious surface such as asphalt and concrete. The creation of impervious surface changes the natural hydrologic cycle by impeding precipitation infiltration to groundwater while increasing the amount of surface runoff. Peak runoffs during storms are amplified in velocity and magnitude, which changes the load-carrying and erosion characteristics of stream channels. These changes have significant environmental consequences including impacts on groundwater recharge, frequency and magnitude of flooding, elevated nonpoint-source pollutant levels, and degraded biological activity (Kennen 1998; Brabec, Schulte, and Richards 2002). Research has shown that the water quality and environmental condition of a watershed are demonstrably related to the amount of impervious surface within the watershed. A landmark paper by Arnold and Gibbons (1996) described the relationship. Watersheds with less than 10 percent impervious surface cover are generally considered unimpacted, although recent work has shown degradation with percent impervious surface cover as low as 2.5 to 5 percent (Conway 2007; Schiff and Benoit 2007; Dietz and Clausen 2008). At levels greater than 10 percent impervious surface, all watersheds show signs of impact. As impervious surface reaches 30 percent and beyond, water quality typically becomes seriously degraded. As demonstrated in chapter 4 of this volume, increasing watershed impervious surface has documented impacts on a number of Highlands streamflow characteristics, from decreasing baseflow to increasing runoff.

Under both high- and low-constraint build-out scenarios, a significant amount of impervious surface is forecast to be generated with increases of 50 to 250 percent over current levels (fig. 15.1). Lathrop, Tulloch, and Hatfield (2007) examined the impact of the predicted increase in impervious surface at the HUC 11 watershed scale for the New York–New Jersey Highlands. Under the low-constraint scenario, the number of HUC 11 watersheds that would exceed the 10 percent impervious surface impact threshold would go from nine to forty-one. These increases in impervious cover will potentially degrade water quality and streamflow conditions in the watersheds of several major drinking water supply reservoirs such as the Croton Watershed, which supplies drinking water to New York City.

As identified in chapter 4, forests and wetlands play an important role in purifying, protecting, and storing large quantities of water (see also Millennium Ecosystem Assessment 2005a, 2005b). Of special concern are the riparian zones, that is, those areas immediately adjacent to headwater streams and other watercourses, as well as areas that may be more physically distant but are connected hydrologically through groundwater flow. Maintaining riparian zones composed of natural vegetation (i.e., forest or wetland) where human development or agriculture is excluded or minimized is a "best management practice" that helps protect downstream water quality by trapping sediment, immobilizing nutrients, and shading streams (NRC 2002). The land-use and land cover change studies undertaken as part of the U.S. Forest Service–sponsored Highlands Study document that a significant percentage of the region's riparian zones have been cleared of natural vegetation or otherwise altered by agriculture or development (Lathrop, Hatfield, and Tulloch 2003; Tyrrell et al. 2010). Connecticut showed the least impact with approximately 27–29 percent of the riparian buffer in altered land use versus Pennsylvania, which had the highest with more than 50 percent altered; New Jersey and New York fell somewhere in between. While the other states showed gradually increasing amounts of riparian zone alteration, Pennsylvania exhibited a reversing trend, which suggests that there has been some recent revegetation of riparian buffers in this agriculturally dominated landscape. Future land-use-change modeling forecasts that this alteration of riparian zones will increase across all four states.

In addition to their role in protecting the integrity of water resources, Highlands forests also serve as habitat for a range of plant and animal species (see chapters 9 and 10 in this volume). The Highlands are noteworthy for containing large expanses of contiguous, unfragmented forest that qualify as high-quality "interior" habitat—that is, far from the disturbances associated with the forest edge (Whitcomb 1977; Forman 1995). The amount of interior forest cover, as well as other measures of forest fragmentation, were used as indicators of forest integrity. During the past several decades, the amount of interior forest has declined in Connecticut, New Jersey, and New York and is forecast to continue to decline regionwide under projected future development (Lathrop, Hatfield, and Tulloch 2003; Tyrrell et al. 2010). This increase in altered riparian zones and declining interior forest cover does not bode well for the integrity of Highlands watersheds and forest habitats.

In summary, the coupled land-use-change modeling and landscape indicator analyses conducted as part of the U.S. Forest Service–sponsored Highlands Regional Study forecast that forest cover in general will continue to decrease and the remaining forests will become ncreasingly fragmented across the four-state region. Likewise, impervious surfaces and the alteration of riparian zone buffers are forecast to increase. These landscape indicators suggest that watershed and forest integrity will be significantly compromised under future development if that development continues under similar "business as usual" conditions. The models, however, allow assessment of the potential impacts to forest and watershed integrity based on other "what if" scenarios. For example, while the high-constraint build-out scenario affords greater environmental protection and lowers future urban growth, it is only a limited solution, in time forcing more rather than less sprawl.

Past as Prologue?

The land-use-change modeling analyses are not an absolute prediction of future conditions but rather a forecast of what might be expected to happen based on existing patterns and trends. While the land-use-change models suggest (if not assume) that prevailing patterns of urbanization of the Highlands will continue into the foreseeable future, are there any countervailing forces to suggest an alternative future for the Highlands—a future where the "highest and best use" may not be sprawling suburban / exurban development?

One alternative is the preservation of the remaining open-space areas in the Highlands through their purchase as publicly owned conservation parks, forests, or watershed management lands. As discussed in chapter 14, this option has been aggressively pursued in the past half century by a number of both governmental and nongovernmental organizations. Over the past twenty years, nearly 100,000 acres have been purchased in the New Jersey Highlands alone (New Jersey Green Acres 2008). Even with nearly 700,000 acres of the Highlands as publicly owned conservation lands, this still leaves more than 1.25 million acres of undeveloped open space in private ownership (Lathrop, Hatfield, and Tulloch 2003; Tyrrell et al. 2010). Using an estimate of $10,000 per acre in today's market, a back-of-the-envelope calculation suggests that more than $12.5 billion would be required to purchase it all—a vast sum and not a likely, or desired, possibility. Instead, a number of groups have targeted core conservation areas and connecting corridors. The U.S. Forest Service Regional Study identified nearly 180,000 acres in the Highlands deemed to have the highest conservation value as well as the highest likelihood of being developed in the near term (Phelps and Hoppe 2002; Tyrrell et al. 2010). While a broad spectrum of the public has actively supported "green acres"–type funding in the past, the continued availability of public funds to purchase open space is increasingly being called into question in the light of hard economic times and big state budget deficits.

Rather than turning the Highlands into a big park, another option is to preserve the open-space character of the Highlands by sustaining a "working" rural landscape—that is, maintaining the economic return from rural land through the pursuit of agriculture, forestry, outdoor recreation, and agro/ecotourism. The concept of a "working" landscape was central to the initial 1992 U.S. Forest Service–sponsored study of the New York–New Jersey Highlands (Michaels et al. 1992) and remains a component of the 2004 Highlands Conservation Act. The underlying premise is that is if landowners can receive sufficient economic return from their land, there will be a greater incentive to keep the land as farm- and forestland and a reduced incentive to "sell out" to development. A variety of federal and state policies have been implemented since the 1980s and 1990s in this regard: farmland preservation to maintain productive agriculture; conservation reserve programs to pay farmers to convert cropland to grasslands and other wildlife habitat; forest stewardship to promote private nonindustrial forestlands; and a variety of conservation easement programs to maintain open space. This amalgam of policies has been promoted as an alternative to the outright purchase of open-space lands as publicly owned parklands, wildlife management/game lands, and forestlands. The working landscape policies are predicated on the notion that there is not enough public money to buy up all the open space nor is this a desired outcome.

Whether these policies to maintain open space and a vital rural economy can succeed is still an open question. Part of the challenge has been an uphill fight against a booming housing market and rising real estate values during the later 1990s and into the 2000s that set a very high bar on the economic returns needed to make farm- or forestland sufficiently profitable (Adelaja and Schilling 1999). With the national economic recession that began in 2009, the housing market radically cooled, and new building starts slowed. Likewise, recent spikes in gasoline prices have reset the decision-making equation that many families have followed concerning the trade-off between longer daily commuting times versus lower real estate/housing prices. Finally, household size is decreasing and the population is aging, which may reduce market demand for exurban large homes. Are these temporary blips in the long-term trends of the past thirty years, or precursors of a new reality? Even before this recent downturn, some economists have suggested that urban sprawl might be ending in the New York City metropolitan region (Hughes and Seneca 2004) based on the relative shift of building permits from the suburbs to the urban core between 1994 and 2002. If these trends continue, the development pressure may ease, thus reducing the financial incentives for Highlands farmers and forest owners to cash out.

Other trends may also help boost the income side of the farmer's or forest owner's balance sheet. The push for locally grown and organic foods may promote the value of farmland and small-scale farming operations in close proximity to the large metropolitan regions of New York, Philadelphia, and Hartford (Brown 2009). The Highlands valleys could become a source for locally grown organic vegetables, artisanal cheeses, and range-fed livestock. In some locales within the Highlands, abandoned dairy farms are being replaced by horse estates with pastures converted to paddocks and milking barns to stables and equestrian rings. Aided by the lower property taxes assessed on farmland and farmland preservation policies as well as by the desire of wealthy urban dwellers for country estate living, horse farms are expected to continue to gain ground. Though the timber market is depressed at present, the large stock of hardwoods in the Highlands is reaching maturity and increasing in value as veneer and finishing lumber. Rising petroleum and natural gas prices have stimulated the development of alternative fuels. One that has found increasing popularity is wood pellets, a processed wood product that can be burned in woodstoves and heating systems (Consumer Reports 2007). These trends may provide a greater market for locally grown forest products. Likewise, the concern over the increasing concentration of carbon dioxide in the atmosphere and its role in climate change has focused greater attention on the role of forests in removing carbon from the atmosphere and sequestering it long term in wood and as organic matter in soils. Whereas traditionally forestland owners received an economic return only when they harvested timber, new cap and trade initiatives may provide an additional economic incentive for landowners to keep their lands in forest.

The availability of plentiful clean water supplies is reaching a crisis state in many portions of the globe. As discussed in chapter 5, New York City and other neighboring cities first looked to the Highlands as a source of clean drinking water in the late 1800s as local sources became increasingly polluted and disease prone. While major waterborne diseases have been largely eliminated by modern water treatment procedures here in the United States, new concerns have been expressed about the low levels of pesticides, herbicides, pharmaceuticals, and other anthropogenic chemicals that may still be found in treated drinking water, although generally below accepted safe standards. What is finding greater appreciation from a wider array of both government decision makers and the wider public is the critical role that watershed protection at the front end, rather than expensive filtration and purification technologies at the back end, plays in ensuring high-quality, clean drinking water. Undeveloped forested watersheds still provide one of best water purification methods yet devised. Proactive watershed protection strategies have taken center stage in the management of New York City's water supply in the Catskills as well as in the Croton system in the New York Highlands. As a result of the New York City Watershed Memorandum of Agreement, New York avoided filtering its Catskill/Delaware drinking water supplies provided that it embarked on an ambitious land acquisition and conservation easement program to keep its watershed lands in an undeveloped state (U.S. EPA 1997).

In New Jersey, there has been active discussion of the institution of a water tax to fund watershed protection. Some in the New Jersey legislature have advocated that such a tax could raise $150 million annually.[1] Were such a source of funding to become available, it could be used to put many watershed lands off limits to development and other inappropriate land uses either through fee simple purchase or conservation easements (where a property owner would be reimbursed for conservation-oriented management of the land). Additionally, storm and flood hazard mitigation assistance that provides for property acquisition and relocation assistance (e.g., the federal Robert T. Stafford Disaster Relief and Emergency Assistance Act[2]), sometimes referred to as "Blue Acres" programs (e.g., the New Jersey State Green Acres, Farmland and Historic Preservation, and the Blue Acres Bond Act of 1995[3]), could potentially be expanded to include inappropriate development or land uses such as in floodplains and riparian buffers or on erosion-prone steep slopes that impair water quality as well as exacerbate flooding damage. These lands could then be managed to restore their proper hydrological function.

As stated earlier, the build-out and land-use-change models assume that the present land-use policy and regulatory environment continues without major alteration into the foreseeable future. Build-out analysis relies heavily on the currency of the zoning data; as zoning adjustments are made, the build-out analysis fades in its ability to reflect the zoning of the region. For example, in New Jersey a master planning effort was conducted subsequent to the passage of the New Jersey Highlands Water Protection and Planning Act in 2004. Although the master plan adopted many of the constraints imposed as part of the high environmental constraints build-out scenario, it also resulted in major zoning changes that are not reflected in the earlier analysis conducted as part of the Forest Service–sponsored study. The master plan subdivided the New Jersey Highlands into planning and preservation areas. Zoning for future development has been significantly reduced in the preservation area, which has resulted in an estimated reduction in future housing units and population of approximately 75 percent (New Jersey Highlands . . . Council 2008a, b). If the other three Highlands states follow suit and adopt comprehensive planning efforts backed up by substantive regulatory authority, then the development scenarios forecast by the land-use-change models may likewise be substantially different for those states as well, with the amount of future urban growth dramatically reduced or relocated to less sensitive areas.

Conclusions

The build-out analysis suggests that approximately one-third of the Highlands constitutes "vacant" open lands available for development. If built to capacity under model projections, these areas will be inundated with more than 875,000 new housing units and population increases of more than 2 million new residents. The build-out analysis projects that Connecticut and Pennsylvania Highlands could see more than double the growth (on a percentage basis) than is expected in New Jersey and New York. The land-use change and build-out modeling suggests that the implications of the projected land-use change are quite profound, forecasting significant increases in impervious surface, altered riparian zones, and declining interior forest cover—all of which does not bode well for the future integrity of Highlands watersheds and forest habitats without substantive changes in either the amount of future development or the pattern of that development.

As outlined in chapter 14, the federal Highlands Conservation Act of 2004 adopts an advisory approach in pushing for an alternative future for the four-state Highlands region different from that forecast by the land-use-change models. In its lead role among federal agencies, the USDA Forest Service has served largely as a facilitator, funding studies, coordinating open-space preservation, promoting forest stewardship programs, and advocating best-management conservation and planning practices. Its ultimate goal is to maintain a working landscape of farms and forests that does not necessarily exclude but is not overwhelmed by exurban/suburban development. The ultimate success of this cross-state planning effort is uncertain, and there are few, if any, similar multistate bioregional models with which to compare. Alternatively, the more authoritative approach embodied by the New Jersey Highlands Council will serve as an illuminating case study on the efficacy of regional land-use planning in shaping the pace and pattern of development and in conserving the watersheds, farms, and forests on the New Jersey portions of the Highlands and may well serve as a model for the other three Highlands states.

Most of the effort in land-use planning in the United States revolves around decisions related to the development of otherwise vacant land. In most cases, this vacant land is farm- or forestland (green fields) although, increasingly, previously developed and abandoned urban lands (i.e., brown fields) are being redeveloped. Similarly, open-space conservation efforts presently focus on protecting extant "green fields" under the basic paradigm that, once developed, a property is forever spoiled. This paradigm is beginning to change, as reflected in the growing interest in restoration ecology (Palmer, Falk, and Zedler 2006) and the burgeoning efforts to restore the ecological integrity of degraded wetlands, river corridors, landfills, and industrial sites within major metropolitan regions across the country.

One of the more enduring lessons that the intertwined human and natural history of the Highlands demonstrates is the incredible resiliency that this temperate forest ecosystem possesses. One has only to visit the Edison Iron Works (as highlighted in this book's preface) or any of the hundreds of other abandoned iron-mining sites scattered throughout the Highlands to see firsthand how natural ecological succession can convert an industrial wasteland into a functioning forest within the space of one hundred years. Rather than simply engage in rearguard-action fighting over the remaining pieces of open space, the conservation community in the Highlands can apply these lessons to think more proactively. Are there other abusive land-use practices or abused sites that should be retired and actively or passively restored? Can a forest fragmented by development be reconnected by restoring a few key tracts? Can a watershed degraded by overdevelopment be restored by the removal of inappropriate development along with the revegetation of riparian forest buffers or erosion-prone slopes? Obviously, such a vision must be reconciled with the United States' strong tradition of respect for individual private property rights, but there is a model in the promotion of Blue Acres programs, where lands that are storm or flood damaged, prone to damage, or that buffer or protect other lands from damage can be acquired for conservation purposes. In the case of the Highlands, society's goal should be not solely to maintain the status quo but also to improve the region's high-quality water resources where they exist as well as restore those areas where they have been degraded. The bottom line: we are not necessarily bound to the Highlands as they are now but can envision an alternative future in which we completely rethink the existing pattern of development and how we manage the land with an eye toward enhancing the region's water resources as well as the overall quality of life for its residents. This might require retrofitting large swaths of existing developed areas with storm-water management strategies, redesigning and redeveloping older urban and suburban areas, clustering new development in appropriate locations, and in selected areas completely removing nonconforming development and restoring the landscape to forest. It is hoped that fifty to one hundred years from now humans will still be able to climb atop a Highlands summit and look out over a pastoral valley mosaic of farms, woodlots, and clustered urban centers rimmed by rugged uplands cloaked in green forest and dotted with sky blue lakes.

Acknowledgments

We would like to acknowledge Seth Myers, Jennifer Cox, and the rest of the Pennsylvania–Connecticut Highlands Study team for their assistance in developing the land-use models and build-out simulations for Pennsylvania and Connecticut. Likewise, we express our appreciation to David Tulloch and Colleen Hatfield and the rest of the New York–New Jersey Highlands Study team for their contributions. Finally, many thanks to Martina Barnes (formerly Hoppe) of the U.S. Forest Service for her shepherding of the various Highlands Study updates.

Notes

1. Sen. Conc. Res. 88, NJ 213th Leg., March 6, 2008. http://www.njleg.state.nj.us/2008/Bills/SCR/88_I1.PDF.

2. Robert T. Stafford Disaster Relief and Emergency Assistance Act, Pub. L.

No. 93–288, as amended, 42 U.S.C. 5121–5207. http://www.fema.gov/pdf/about/stafford_act.pdf.

3. "Coastal Blue Acres." http://www.state.nj.us/dep/greenacres/blue.htm.

References

Adelaja, A. O., and B. J. Schilling. 1999. "Innovative Approaches to Farmland Preservation." In *Contested Countryside: The Rural Urban Fringe in North America*, ed. O. Furuseth and M. Lapping. New Brunswick, NJ: Rutgers University Press.

Alig, R. J., J. D. Kline, and M. Lichenstein. 2004. "Urbanization on the U.S. Landscape: Looking ahead in the 21st Century." *Landscape and Urban Planning* 69:219–234.

Arnold, C. L., Jr., and J. C. Gibbons. 1996. "Impervious Surface Coverage—the Emergence of a Key Environmental Indicator." *Journal of the American Planning Association* 62, no. 2: 243–258.

Botequilha, L. A., and J. Ahern. 2002. "Applying Landscape Ecological Concepts and Metrics in Sustainable Landscape Planning." *Landscape and Urban Planning* 59, no. 2: 65–73.

Brabec, E., S. Schulte, and P. L. Richards. 2002. "Impervious Surface and Water Quality: A Review of Current Literature and Its Implications for Watershed Planning." *Journal of Planning Literature* 16, no. 4: 499–514.

Brown, L. R. 2009. *Plan B 4.0: Mobilizing to Save Civilization*. Washington, DC: Earth Policy Institute.

Consumer Reports. 2007. "Buyer's Guide to Pellet- and Wood-Burning Stoves: The Pros, Cons, and Costs versus Natural Gas, Oil, and Coal." January. http://www.consumerreports.org/cro/appliances/heating-cooling-and-air/wood-stoves/buyers-guide-to-pellet-and-wood-burning-stoves-1-07/overview/0701_pellet-stove.htm.

Conway, T. M. 2007. "Impervious Surface as an Indicator of pH and Specific Conductance in the Urbanizing Coastal Zone of New Jersey, USA." *Journal of Environmental Management* 85:308–316.

Conway, T., and R. G. Lathrop. 2005. "Alternative Land Use Regulation and Environmental Impacts: Assessing Future Pathways for a Suburbanizing Coastal Watershed." *Landscape and Urban Planning* 71, no. 1: 1–15.

Dietz, M. E., and J. C. Clausen. 2008. "Stormwater Runoff and Export Changes with Development in a Traditional and Low Impact Subdivision." *Journal of Environmental Management* 87:560–566.

Forman, R.T.T. 1995. *Land Mosaics: The Ecology of Landscapes and Regions*. Cambridge: Cambridge University Press.

Hall, C.A.S., H. Tian, Y. Qi, G. Pontius, J. Cornell, and J. Uhlig. 1995a. "Spatially Explicit Models of Land Use Change and Their Application to the Tropics." DOE Research Summary, no. 31 (ed. by CDIAC, Oak Ridge National Lab).

Hall, C.A.S., H. Tian, Y. Qi, G. Pontius, J. Cornell, and J. Uhlig. 1995b. "Modeling Spatial and Temporal Patterns of Tropical Land Use Change." *Journal of Biogeography* 22:753–757.

Heilman G. E., Jr., J. R, Strittholt, N. C. Slosser, and D. A. Dellasala. 2002. "Forest Fragmentation of the Conterminous United States: Assessing Forest Intactness through Road Density and Spatial Characteristics." *BioScience* 52:411–422.

Hughes, J. W., and J. J. Seneca. 2004. "The Beginning of the End of Sprawl?" Rutgers Regional Report, Issues Paper Number 21, May. New Brunswick, NJ: Edward J. Bloustein School of Planning and Public Policy. http://policy.rutgers.edu/reports/rrr/rrrmay04.pdf.

Kennen, J. G. 1998. "Relation of Benthic Macroinvertebrate Community Impairment to Basin Characteristics in New Jersey Streams." Fact Sheet FS-057-98. West Trenton, NJ: U.S. Geological Survey.

Lathrop, R., C. Hatfield, and D. Tulloch. 2003. "Section 2: Land Resources." In *New York–New Jersey Highlands Regional Study Technical Report*, NA-TP-04-03, ed. M. Hoppe, 45–219. Newtown Square, PA: USDA Forest Service.

Lathrop, R. G., D. Tulloch, and C. Hatfield. 2007. "Consequences of Land Use Change in the New York–New Jersey Highlands, USA: Landscape Indicators of Forest and Watershed Integrity." *Landscape and Urban Planning* 79, no. 2: 150–159.

Michaels, J. A., L. R. Neville, D. Edelman, T. Sullivan, and L. A. diCola. 1992. *New York–New Jersey Highlands Regional Study*. Radnor, PA: USDA Forest Service, Northeastern Area State and Private Forestry.

Millennium Ecosystem Assessment. 2005a. *Ecosystems and Human Well-being: Synthesis*. Washington, DC: Island Press. http://www.millenniumassessment.org/en/index.aspx.

Millennium Ecosystem Assessment. 2005b. *Ecosystems and Human Well-being: Wetlands and Water Synthesis*. Washington, DC: World Resources Institute. http://www.millenniumassessment.org/documents/document.358.aspx.pdf.

National Research Council (NRC). 2002. *Riparian Areas: Functions and Strategies for Management*. Committee on Riparian Zone Functioning and Strategies for Management. Washington, DC: National Academy Press.

New Jersey Green Acres. 2008. "2008–2012 New Jersey Statewide Comprehensive Outdoor Recreation Plan." Trenton: New Jersey Department of Environmental Protection, Green Acres Program. http://www.nj.gov/dep/greenacres/pdf/scorp.pdf.

New Jersey Highlands Water Protection and Planning Council. 2008a. "Highlands Regional Build Out Technical Report." Chester, NJ, June. http://www.highlands.state.nj.us/njhighlands/master/rmp/draft/draft_rbo.pdf.

———. 2008b. "Highlands Regional Master Plan." Chester, NJ, August.

Palmer, M. A., D. A. Falk, and J. B. Zedler. 2006. *Foundations of Restoration Ecology*. Washington, DC: Island Press.

Phelps, M. G., and M. C. Hoppe. 2002. *New York–New Jersey Highlands Regional Study: 2002 Update*. NA-TP-02-03. Newtown Square, PA: USDA Forest Service, Northeastern Area State and Private Forestry.

Pontius, R. G. Jr., J. Cornell, and C. Hall. 2001. "Modeling the Spatial Pattern of Land-Use Change with GEOMOD2: Application and Validation for Costa Rica." *Agriculture, Ecosystems and Environment* 85, no. 1–3: 191–203.

Riitters, K. H., J. D. Wickham, R. V. O'Neill, K. B. Jones, E. R. Smith, J. W. Coulston, T. G. Wade, and J. H. Smith. 2002. "Fragmentation of Continental United States Forest." *Ecosystems* 5:815–822.

Schiff, R., and G. Benoit. 2007. "Effects of Impervious Cover at Multiple Spatial

Scales on Coastal Watershed Streams." *Journal of American Water Resources Association* 43, no. 3: 712–730.

Schueler, T. 1994. "The Importance of Imperviousness." *Watershed Protection Techniques* 1:100–111.

Stein, S. M., R. E. McRoberts, R. J. Alig, M. D. Nelson, D. M. Theobald, M. Eley, M. Dechter, and M. Carr. 2005. "Forests on the Edge: Housing Development on America's Private Forests." General Technical Report PNW-GTR-636. Portland, OR: USDA Forest Service.

Tyrrell, M. L., M. H. Hall, S. Myers, J. Cox, E. Hawes, L. Yocom, S. Price, T. Worthley, and J. Stocker. 2010. "Section 2, Part 4 and Section 3, Part 4. Growth and Impact Analysis." In *Highlands Regional Study: Connecticut and Pennsylvania 2010 Update*, NA-TP-01–11, ed. M. Barnes, 62–87, 146–166. Newtown Square, PA: USDA Forest Service. http://na.fs.fed.us/pubs/stewardship/highlands_regional_study_ct_pa_10_print.pdf.

U.S. Environmental Protection Agency (EPA). 1997. "New York City Watershed Memorandum of Agreement." January 21. http://www.epa.gov/region2/water/nycshed/nycmoa.htm.

Whitcomb, R. F. 1977. "Island Biogeography and Habitat Islands of Eastern Forest. I. Introduction." *American Birds* 31:3–5.

Glossary

anadromous fish: Fish that spawn in freshwater but spend most of their lives in salt water.

analogue: Sets of conditions that management seeks to create or maintain.

aquifer: An underground layer of water-bearing bedrock or sediments.

basal area: The cross-sectional area of a tree measured at chest height.

bedrock: All solid rock of the earth's crust that lies beneath the soil and unconsolidated sediments.

braidplains: Networks of shallow channels in which glacial river-plain deposits are laid down.

calc-silicates: Metamorphic rocks related to marble but with varying amounts of additional minerals.

catadromous fish: Fish that spend most of their lives in freshwater and return to salt water to spawn.

chert: Microcrystalline quartz that is deposited in a marine environment under certain chemical conditions.

clastic rock: Rocks of sedimentary origin such as sandstone, siltstone, and shale.

colluvium: The eroded debris collected at the foot of hillslopes in aprons of rocky sediment.

consumptive water uses: Water uses that return some of the used water to the same watershed, with the remainder lost to evaporative or transpiration processes, such as irrigation.

crystalline rock: Tough, coarse rock that is generally resistant to weathering. As the rocks formed, individual minerals grew into large crystals that were tightly knitted together.

cyanobacteria: Blue-green algae.

depletive water uses: Water uses that remove the water entirely from the watershed through the transfer of raw, treated, or used water to another watershed or to coastal waters.

downcutting: Erosion by rivers that leads to deepening of valleys.

downwarping: The crust of the earth can locally subside to great depths by loading of sediments or plate tectonic interactions.

drumlins: A teardrop-shaped elongate hill of glacial sediment formed beneath a glacier.

ductile faults: A fault in which the rock deformed plastically without fracturing.

ecoregion: An ecologically and geographically defined area that contains a characteristic assemblage of natural communities, sometimes called a bioregion.

ecotone: A transition area between two adjacent ecological communities.

eutrophication: Excessive growth of aquatic plant life such as algae and floating plants due to overenrichment of nutrients; often leads to low dissolved oxygen levels as plants decay.

evapotranspiration: The loss of water to the atmosphere through a combination of water that evaporates from land and water surfaces, and the water taken up by plant roots and transpired through leaves.

fragipan: A dense, firm, water- and root-restrictive horizon formed in the lower subsoil.

glaciofluvial: Pertaining to streams fed by melting glaciers, or to the deposits and landforms produced by such meltwater.

glaciolacustrine: Features pertaining to glacially formed lakes.

gneiss: Banded crystalline metamorphic rock that is highly resistant to weathering and erosion.

headwater seeps: Wetland areas where groundwater flows to the surface to become the beginning of streams.

hematite: Rock composed of an iron oxide mineral (FeO_3) similar to magnetite but red or brown in color and more oxidized.

hydric soil: A soil that meets certain technical criteria that demonstrate prolonged periods of anaerobic (low oxygen) conditions.

hydrograph: A graph showing changes in water level or discharge over a period of time.

hydrologic cycle: The constant movement of water through a watershed.

hydrology: The source, flow patterns, depth, and chemistry of water.

integrated pest management (IPM): A holistic approach to pest control with the goal of reducing pesticide use by emphasizing alternative means of reducing pest populations.

lacustrine fans: Sand and gravel deposits laid down on lake bottoms at the mouths of subglacial tunnel channels.

mafic: Dark-colored rock that is rich in iron and magnesium.

magnetite: An iron-rich oxide (FeO_4) usually found among granitic rocks.

metamorphism: The change of a preexisting rock in its minerals and texture as a result of changes in temperature and pressure.

metasedimentary gneiss: A gneiss that was a sedimentary rock before undergoing metamorphism.

Mesozoic age: Geological age between 245 and 65 million years before the present.

migmatites: Mixed rock composed of both igneous and metamorphic rock.

molten iron: Liquid iron that can run into a series of molds to produce various iron products, such as tools and munitions.

moraine: Mixed sediment that piled at the end of a glacier as it melted.

mylonites: Fault rock that has recrystallized into a fine-grained texture and is oriented in linear patterns.

nappes: Rocks that were sheared to such an extent that they folded back over themselves, piling up to form flat-lying sheets and thickening the crust.

neotropical migrants: Birds that migrate south each fall to spend the winter months in warmer climates, returning north the following spring to breed.

Newark Supergroup: Includes continental sedimentary rocks and interbedded basaltic flow rocks of Triassic and Jurassic age that crop out in discrete elongate basins that lie parallel to the Appalachians in eastern North America.

ombrotrophic: A type of wetland that receives only precipitation as its source of water.

orogeny: A mountain-building event that involves the collision of two tectonic plates.

Paleozoic age: Geological age between 543 and 245 million years before the present.

palustrine: A type of wetland in which groundwater, overland surface flows, and precipitation are the major sources of water.

Pangean cycle: All plate tectonic events related to the formation and breakup of the supercontinent Pangea.

passive margin phase: A part of the tectonic development (geologic history) of an area characterized by a passive margin with sedimentary deposition and no earthquakes or volcanoes (not a plate margin).

passive margin sediments: Beds of shale, sands, and limestone deposited in an ocean basin margin with no volcanoes or major earthquakes.

pegmatite: A very coarse-grained igneous rock.

peneplains: A widespread plain developed through long-term erosion of an area.

periglacial climate: Severe freezing in areas bordering glaciers.

permafrost: Permanently frozen ground.

permeability: The degree to which aquifers have the ability to transmit water.

plucking: Erosion of bedrock by glacial cracking, prying, and block removal. See *quarrying*.

pluton: Igneous underground bodies of crystallized magma.

potable: suitable as drinking water.

Precambrian age: A geological age between the formation of Earth 4.6 billion years ago and the beginning of the Cambrian period 543 million years ago. Consists of the later Proterozoic and the earlier Archean periods. See *Proterozoic age*.

Proterozoic age: A geological age between 2.5 billion years ago and 543 million years ago. See *Precambrian age*.

quarrying: Erosion of bedrock by glacial cracking, prying, and block removal. See *plucking*.

quartzofeldspathic gneiss: Light-colored gneiss formed from volcaniclastic (see *volcaniclastic*) or similar materials and composed of medium- to coarse-size grains of the minerals quartz and feldspar.

radiometric dating: Measurement of the age of a material using the relative proportion of certain chemical isotopes such as carbon-14 that are lost through time by radioactive decay.

Reading Prong: A subprovince of the New England Uplands section of the Appalachian Highlands physiographic region; stretches from Pennsylvania to Connecticut.

Rodinian cycle: All plate tectonic events related to the formation and breakup of the supercontinent Rodinia.

riparian areas: Areas adjacent to and hydrologically connected with rivers and streams.

slag: Fused and vitrified impurities that separate from molten iron through the process of smelting.

soil series: A group of soils with a similar sequence of horizons formed in the same parent material under comparable climate and vegetation.

stratigraphy: Large-scale distribution and interrelations of the rock units.

stream baseflow: That part of a stream's discharge that is attributable to groundwater rather than surface runoff.

stromatolite mounds: Mounds of cyanobacteria that were common during the Proterozoic age and that occur as fossils in Proterozoic marble.

subglacial tunnel channels: Pipe-like conduits that drain meltwater from the base of a glacier.

supercontinent: When essentially all continents combine to make a single master continent.

talus: Bouldery deposits at the bottom of a cliff, formed by rockfall.

tectonic plates: Fragments of lithosphere (crust plus uppermost mantle) that cover and move around the surface of the earth and interact with each other.

till: A mixture of sand, silt, clay, gravel, and boulders laid down directly from glacial ice.

volcaniclastics: Sediments derived from volcanic lava flows interlayered with fragments of volcanic material.

Wisconsin (or Wisconsinan) age: The most recent period of continental glaciation in North America, from 80,000 to 10,000 years ago.

xenolith: A fragment of one kind of rock (for example, gneiss bedrock) incorporated into an igneous rock (for example, granitic matrix).

Notes on Contributors

Daniel D. Chazin is a life member of the New York–New Jersey Trail Conference and currently serves as a board member and as secretary, as well as chair of the Publications Committee. He has edited a number of publications on hiking in the New York–New Jersey area, including the *New York Walk Book*, *New Jersey Walk Book*, *Appalachian Trail Guide to New York and New Jersey*, and *Harriman Trails: A Guide and History*. Mr. Chazin is an attorney in private practice. Mr. Chazin received a BA from Yeshiva College in 1972 and a JD from New York University in 1975.

Vincent T. dePaul is a hydrologist with the U.S. Geological Survey, New Jersey Water Science Center. Mr. dePaul earned baccalaureate degrees in geography and geosciences from the College of New Jersey and has also studied water resources at Drexel University in Philadelphia. His professional experience includes a variety of water-resources studies; most recently, he has investigated the occurrence and mobility of radium in groundwater, salt-water intrusion into aquifers of the Atlantic Coastal Plain, and eutrophication in riverine environments. Over the past decade he has participated in several studies that have helped characterize the water resources in the Highlands region.

Joan G. Ehrenfeld is professor of ecology at Rutgers University, where she researches and teaches about plant and ecosystem ecology of both upland and wetland systems. She teaches courses on introductory ecology, wetland ecology, ecosystems ecology, and field methods in ecology. She currently serves on several state and federal advisory and regulatory committees, including the New Jersey Wetland Mitigation Council and the New Jersey Invasive Species Council, and, at the federal level, the Committee on Independent Scientific Review of the Everglades and the Ecological Processes and Effects Committee of the EPA Science Advisory Board. She is a Fellow of the Society of Wetland Scientists. Current research includes studies of nitrogen cycling and carbon sequestration in wetlands and forests, wetland diversity as a control on West Nile virus, plant-soil interactions resulting from exotic plant invasions, root dynamics as a component of invasion ecology, and urban ecosystem analysis.

Alexander E. Gates is a professor at Rutgers University–Newark and the chair of the Department of Earth and Environmental Sciences. He earned his PhD in geological sciences from Virginia Tech with specialization in structural geology and tectonics. His research has focused on processes of strike-slip faults, geochemistry of fault zones, and regional geologic mapping. Dr. Gates has written or edited nine books and been an author on more than seventy-five professional papers. He has appeared in several documentaries, including two on the Discovery Channel, and is commonly seen on television news, in newspapers, and in magazines for his research on local earthquakes. Dr. Gates served as president of both the Geological Association of New Jersey and the National Association of Geoscience Teachers, Eastern Section, and he is a Fellow of the Geological Society of America.

Thomas A. Gilbert joined the Trust for Public Land in January of 2008 to direct state and local conservation finance initiatives in the mid-Atlantic region. As chair of the New Jersey "Keep It Green" campaign, a coalition of more than 140 organizations working to renew and strengthen the Garden State Preservation Trust, he led a successful statewide campaign to pass a $400 million bond measure on the November 2009 ballot to continue open-space preservation efforts in New Jersey. Prior to joining TPL, Tom served as director of Eastern Forest Conservation for the Wilderness Society and executive director of the regional Highlands Coalition, where he led successful efforts to pass federal and New Jersey state legislation to protect the Highlands. He earned his MS in natural resources planning from the University of Vermont.

Steven Glenn has been a researcher in the Department of Science at Brooklyn Botanic Garden since 1994; currently he is the manager of the New York Metropolitan Flora Project. He received his BS from Purdue University in 1992. His research interests concentrate on the floristics of vascular plants in the New York metropolitan region, with particular emphasis on monitoring nonnative species and the historical decline of native species.

Myrna Hall, MS SUNY College of Environmental Science and Forestry (SUNY ESF) Forest and Natural Resources Management, is director of the SUNY ESF Center for the Urban Environment. Her research focuses on spatial modeling of land cover and land-use change and its ecological consequences, including water-quality impacts in the New York City, Catskill-Delaware, Onondaga Creek, and Wappinger Creek (New York) watersheds; glacier and vegetation change as a function of climate change in Glacier National Park, Montana;

carbon impacts of deforestation in South and Central America; urban heat island effects of sprawling development in San Juan, Puerto Rico; and urban socioecological metabolism under two recent NSF Urban Long Term Research Area Exploratory Awards (ULTRA-EX) in Syracuse, New York, and San Juan, Puerto Rico.

Elizabeth A. Johnson is currently manager of the Metropolitan Biodiversity Program at the American Museum of Natural History's Center for Biodiversity and Conservation. At the center, she initiates and directs state and regional biodiversity conservation programs, integrating information from the museum's scientific departments and regional collections directly into conservation-related research, education, planning, and management initiatives. Previously, she was director of science and stewardship for The Nature Conservancy in New Jersey. Johnson received a BS in wildlife biology and geology and an MS in ecology from Rutgers University.

Theodore W. Kury, PhD, is professor emeritus of geography at Buffalo State College, Buffalo, New York. He has spent more than forty years delving into aspects of the cultural-historical geography of the New York–New Jersey region and has authored numerous papers based upon primary materials found in archival collections throughout the mid-Atlantic region.

Richard G. Lathrop Jr. is a professor in the Department of Ecology, Evolution and Natural Resources and is director of the Grant F. Walton Center for Remote Sensing & Spatial Analysis at Rutgers University. He received his BA degree in biology from Dartmouth College in 1981, and an MS in forestry and PhD in environmental monitoring from the University of Wisconsin–Madison in 1986 and 1988, respectively. While wide-ranging in interest, his work is largely focused on the mapping and modeling of land use / land cover change (including natural habitat loss and alteration) and quantifying the potential consequences for ecological and natural resources systems at landscape and regional scales. Lathrop has had a long interest in the Highlands region and worked extensively with the U.S. Forest Service on the Highlands Regional Study.

Gerry Moore has been a researcher at Brooklyn Botanic Garden (BBG) since 2000, eventually becoming the director of the Department of Science. He received his PhD from Vanderbilt University in 1997 and was a postdoctoral researcher at Duke University. His research interests focus on the taxonomy and floristics of vascular plants, especially those in the New York metropolitan region. At the BBG, Dr. Moore's interests have focused on how the flora of the New York metropolitan region is changing. Dr. Moore has recently taken a new position as team leader of the National

Plant Data Team of the Natural Resources Conservation Service, Greensboro, North Carolina.

Corey Piasecki has a degree in environmental planning from Plymouth State University and is currently an associate planner with Regional Plan Association (RPA). Prior to joining RPA he was a planner with the New Jersey Office of Smart Growth and the office liaison to the New Jersey Highlands Council. During his tenure with the Office of Smart Growth, he was responsible for overseeing the cross-acceptance process for Morris, Passaic, Sussex, and Warren counties as well as providing in-depth comments on the New Jersey Highlands Regional Master Plan.

Robert Pirani is the Regional Plan Association's vice president for environmental programs and executive director of the Governors Island Alliance. His responsibilities include developing and directing programs in parks and open-space advocacy, land-use management, water-quality protection, and recycling and waste prevention. Publications include contributions to the *New York–New Jersey Highlands Regional Study* and *Regional Study Update*. Mr. Pirani holds a master's degree in regional planning from Cornell University and a bachelor's degree in environmental studies from Hampshire College.

Donald E. Rice is a hydrologist with the U.S. Geological Survey, New Jersey Water Science Center, where he has investigated water resources and water availability for more than twenty years. He is a graduate of Western Kentucky University and has significant professional experience in geographic information systems, groundwater flow, and water availability. He has worked on numerous studies that have characterized Highlands water resources.

William S. F. Schuster is an ecologist and has served as executive director of the Black Rock Forest Consortium in Cornwall, New York, since 1992 with adjunct appointments at Columbia University. He received his BA in biology at Columbia in 1978, his MS in forest ecology at Pennsylvania State University in 1983, and his PhD in ecology from the University of Colorado in 1989, and he served as a postdoctoral research fellow at the University of Utah prior to taking his position at the Black Rock Forest. His primary research interests are in ecology, ecosystem management, and environmental change. He has authored or coauthored more than fifty research publications and teaches and lectures in forest ecology and environmental science.

Richard K. Shaw is a soil scientist and the project leader at the New York City Soil Survey USDA–Natural Resources Conservation Service, where he is responsible for the mapping and characterization of urban soils across the metropolitan region. He earned a BS from the University of Maine, Orono, and an MS and PhD from Rutgers University, New Brunswick, New Jersey.

Michael Siegel is staff cartographer in the Rutgers Geography Department. He has been running the Cartography Laboratory and teaching undergraduate cartography courses in the Geography Department since 1988. He enjoys exploring the changing landscape of New Jersey, and maintains a website of historical New Jersey maps, which can be found at mapmaker.rutgers.edu.

Emily W. B. (Russell) Southgate, BS Denison University, has master's degrees in both botany and history (Duke University and Rutgers University, respectively) and a PhD in botany from Rutgers University. Her research has been in historical ecology, with numerous publications focusing mainly on the forest history of the northeastern United States. Her book *People and the Land through Time: Linking Ecology and History* (Yale University Press, 1997) is a handbook of methods, examples, and discussion of the importance of studying past human activities as part of understanding current ecosystems and of predicting future changes. She currently teaches historical ecology at Hood College and is pursuing research on eighteenth-century land-cover patterns in northern Virginia.

Scott D. Stanford received an MS in geology from the University of Wisconsin and a PhD in geology from Rutgers University. He has studied glacial and other surficial deposits in New Jersey as a research scientist with the New Jersey Geological Survey since 1983. His research includes geologic mapping of surficial deposits and Coastal Plain formations, geologic framework studies of glacial and other surficial aquifers, geologic aspects of earthquake-hazard assessment in New Jersey, and the geomorphology and Quaternary history of New Jersey and adjacent areas.

John C. F. Tedrow, PhD, is professor emeritus of soil science at Rutgers University at New Brunswick, New Jersey. He has worked for more than fifty years studying and mapping soils across the New Jersey and the mid-Atlantic region, culminating in the classic work *Soils of New Jersey.* He has also conducted numerous investigations of soils of the polar regions.

Mary L. Tyrrell is the executive director of the Global Institute of Sustainable Forestry at the Yale School of Forestry & Environmental Studies. She received a BA in mathematics from the University of New Hampshire, an MBA from Boston University, and an MS in forest science from Yale University. Her work focuses on land-use change, forest fragmentation, sustainable forest management, and U.S. private lands, with a particular emphasis on review and synthesis of scientific research, and on making scientific information available to forest managers and conservationists. She was the project manager for the *Highlands Regional Study: Connecticut and Pennsylvania Updates—Forest & Agricultural Resources Analysis and Growth and Impact Analysis* and senior editor of *Forests and Carbon: A Synthesis of Science, Management, and Policy for Carbon Sequestration in Forests.*

David W. Valentino is professor of geology at the State University of New York at Oswego in the Department of Earth Sciences, where he also serves as director of field studies and the geology program coordinator. He completed BA and MA degrees in geology at Temple University (1986, 1988), and a PhD in geology with specialization in tectonics at Virginia Polytechnic Institute and State University (1993). Dr. Valentino is a member of Sigma Xi and the American Geophysical Union, a Fellow with the Geological Society of America, an honorary member of Alpha Sigma Lambda, and has served as president of the New York State Geological Association (2005). His research focus is in the fields of structural and metamorphic geology, geochronology, and field studies with experience in the mid-Atlantic Piedmont, Hudson Highlands, and Adirondacks of New York.

Daniel J. Van Abs is senior director for planning and science with the New Jersey Highlands Council, where he manages staff efforts regarding implementation of the Highlands Regional Master Plan. (Material provided for this publication does not necessarily represent the views of the Highlands Council.) He previously held management positions with the New Jersey Water Supply Authority, the New Jersey Department of Environmental Protection, and the Passaic River Coalition. He holds a PhD in environmental science from SUNY–College of Environmental Science and Forestry and is lead author and project director of the 1996 New Jersey Statewide Water Supply Plan, the Raritan Basin Watershed Management Plan, and numerous other water-related plans, policy documents, and regulations. He is a licensed professional planner in New Jersey and a member of the New Jersey Clean Water Council.

Peter O. Wacker is professor emeritus of geography at Rutgers University. He is a cultural geographer who has used New Jersey as a "laboratory" for study. His books include *The Musconetcong Valley of New Jersey, Land and People: a Cultural Geography of Preindustrial New Jersey,* and *Land Use in Early New Jersey* (with Paul Clemens). He also coedited an atlas, *Mapping New Jersey,* with Maxine Lurie.

Otto S. Zapecza is a hydrologist with the U.S. Geological Survey, New Jersey Water Science Center, where he has performed water-resources investigations for more than thirty years. He is a graduate of Kean University and a professional geologist. Mr. Zapecza's career focus is in the design and application of hydrogeologic studies that support statewide and national water-resource management needs. Over the past decade he has led numerous studies that have helped characterize the quantity and quality of water resources in the Highlands region.

Index

The letter *f* following a page number denotes a figure and the letter *t* denotes a table.